APPLIED COMMUNICATION AND PRACTICE

FIRST EDITION

Bassim Hamadeh, CEO and Publisher

John Remington, Senior Field Acquisitions Editor

Gem Rabanera, Project Editor

Abbey Hastings, Associate Production Editor

Emely Villavicencio, Senior Graphic Designer

Trey Soto, Licensing Coordinator

Jennifer Redding, Interior Designer

Natalie Piccotti, Director of Marketing

Kassie Graves, Vice President of Editorial

Jamie Giganti, Director of Academic Publishing

ISBN: 978-1-5165-2226-2 (pbk) / 978-1-5165-2227-9 (br) / 978-1-5165-4711-1 (al)

APPLIED COMMUNICATION AND PRACTICE

FIRST EDITION

Written and edited by Matt Crick and Kelli Jean K. Smith
William Paterson University

cognella® ACADEMIC PUBLISHING

CONTENTS

Preface   X

CHAPTER 1: PROFESSIONAL COMMUNICATION PRACTICES
            AND CONNECTING IDEAS   1

Reading 1.1: Digital Natives and Digital Media in the College Classroom:
            Assignment Design and Impacts
            on Student Learning
            by Joseph A. Watson and Loretta L. Pecchioni   3

Reading 1.2: Documentary Storytelling: Making
            Stronger and More Nonfiction Films
            by Sheila Curran Bernard   19

Interview with a Professional   36

Conclusion   38

Classroom Activity   39

Key Terms   39

References   43

PART ONE   45

CHAPTER 2: TELEVISION PRODUCTION—TOOLS AND PRACTICE   46

Reading 2.1: An Introduction to Television Style: Modes of Production
            by Jeremy G. Butler   49

Reading 2.2: And Now No Word from Our Sponsor:
            How HBO Puts the Risk Back Into Television
            by Tony Kelso   61

Interview with a Professional   68

Conclusion   71

Classroom Activity   72

Key Terms   73

References   75

CHAPTER 3: FILM PRODUCTION—FILM AESTHETIC AND CRAFT   76

Reading 3.1: Digital Cinematography: Evolution of Craft
              or Revolution in Production?
              by John Mateer   78

Reading 3.2: Basic Lighting for Film and DV
              by Mick Hurbis-Cherrier   90

Reading 3.3: The Golden Age of Comic Book Filmmaking
              by Liam Burke   97

Interview with a Professional   104

Conclusion   105

Classroom Activity   105

Key Terms   106

References   106

CHAPTER 4: RADIO AND SOUND PRODUCTION—
              THEATRE OF THE MIND   108

Reading 4.1: Sound and Stories
              by Johnathan Kern   110

Reading 4.2: Multimedia Foundations: Core Concepts
              for Digital Design
              by Vic Costello, Susan Youngblood,
              and Norman E. Youngblood   115

Reading 4.3: Production Ethics
by Johnathan Kern   121

Interview with a Professional   131

Conclusion   133

Classroom Activity   134

Key Terms   134

References   136

CHAPTER 5: CITIZEN JOURNALISM   137

Reading 5.1: We the People: Part 1: Citizen Journalism
by Brian Carroll   139

Reading 5.2: Copyright and Trademark
by Michael G. Parkinson and L. Marie Parkinson   144

Reading 5.3: Investigative Journalism and Blogs
by Paul Bradshaw   153

Interview with a Professional   159

Conclusion   160

Classroom Activity   161

Key Terms   162

References   163

CHAPTER 6: BROADCAST JOURNALISM: WRITING, SPEAKING,
AND PRESENTING THE NEWS   164

Reading 6.1: Writing Broadcast News Scripts
by Rick Thompson   167

Reading 6.2: Conducting an Interview
by Jerry Lazar   173

Reading 6.3: Career as a News Reporter: Journalist   186

Interview with a Professional   191

Conclusion   192

Classroom Activity   193

Key Terms   193

References   194

PART TWO   197

CHAPTER 7: COMMUNICATION STUDIES   198

Reading 7.1: Emotional Intelligence:
            The New Science of Success
            by Jeff Feldman and Karl Mulle   200

Reading 7.2: Listening Pays Off
            by Chris Battell   206

Classroom Activity   210

Key Terms   211

References   211

CHAPTER 8: MEDIA STUDIES   212

Reading 8.1: The Multitasking Myth
            by Devora Zack   214

Conclusion   221

Classroom Activity   221

Key Terms   222

References   222

CHAPTER 9: JOURNALISM   223

Reading 9.1: Storytelling in the Age of Social News
    Consumption *by Steve Rubel*   226

Reading 9.2: SPJ Code of Ethics   228

Interview with a Professional   230

Conclusion   232

Classroom Activity   233

Key Terms   233

References   234

CHAPTER 10: PUBLIC RELATIONS   235

Reading 10.1: The Role of Storytelling in a Digital Age
    by Barbara Bates   237

Reading 10.2: Public Relations Society of America (PSRA)
    Member Code of Ethics   239

Interview with a Professional   242

Conclusion   243

Classroom Activity   244

Key Terms   245

References   245

CHAPTER 11: THEATRE AND COMEDY   246

Reading 11.1: Writing the Simpsons: A Case Study of Comic Theory
    by Edward J. Fink   249

Reading 11.2: The Science of Comedy:
    Can Humor Make the World a Better Place?
    by Stuart Jeffries   262

Interview with a Professional   265

Conclusion   266

Classroom Activity   267

Key Terms   267

References   268

CHAPTER 12: USING THE APPLIED MODEL IN YOUR
        ACADEMIC AND PROFESSIONAL CAREER   269

Interview with a Professional   276

Conclusion   278

Classroom Activity   278

Key Terms   279

References   279

PREFACE

Welcome to *Applied Communication and Practice*!

This book provides a comprehensive and detailed exploration of the key communication disciplines college and university students would find in academic departments. We've carefully written *Applied Communication and Practice* so that it clearly frames each communication discipline within a core structure of **story, skill, audience,** and **ethics**. We include a unique selection of current communication industry observations, selected readings, and classroom exercises, interconnected along thematic lines for various professional fields within the Communication discipline. Written in a professional, personal, and friendly style, *Applied Communication and Practice* is an excellent anchor and teaching guide in a media-rich and constantly changing communication environment.

Written for college and university students who are interested in careers in Public Relations, Radio and Audio Production, Television, Film, Theatre, Comedy, Media Studies, Broadcast and Digital Journalism, and Communication Studies, *Applied Communication and Practice* serves as an important resource in three main ways.

First, the book clearly sets forth, for the first time in a scholarly way, precisely how major fields within the communication discipline operate and connect to one another conceptually and also how they function practically, often simultaneously, in the professional world of communication. Second, this knowledge is then reinforced through discussion and suggested classroom exercises. As a result, students gain a solid scholarly understanding of communication careers that expands and informs their professional choices, expectations, and practices.

Third, scholars and professionals have contributed to this book, and they provide professional, academic, and life-skills advice. Author Dr. Matt Crick is a practicing documentary filmmaker and published educator. He has worked in several broadcast television and production environments and has over 25 years of professional storytelling experience. He has also distributed a feature-length documentary. Dr. Kelli Jean K. Smith, coauthor, is a published Communication Studies scholar.

Last, several short interviews with professional communicators from each of the allied fields—network television, public relations, and film sound design to name a few—provide a strong sense of what happens daily in professional communication environments, and this makes the book a very useful, accessible, and practical tool that can be used throughout a student's academic career.

Several faculty and students at William Paterson University helped us with this book. In particular, we'd like to thank COMM 1190 adjunct instructor Catherine Bertani and Department of Communication faculty members Dr. Diana Peck, Dr. Liz Stropple, Dr. Joanne Lee, Professor Liz Birge, Professor Lorra Brown, and Television Studio Manager Al Clarke.

We're glad you've come along this journey with us.
Matt Crick
Kelli Jean K. Smith

CHAPTER 1

Professional Communication Practices and Connecting Ideas

WHAT'S THIS BOOK ABOUT?

First, the book clearly sets forth, for the first time in a scholarly way, precisely how the communication disciplines work and relate to one another conceptually and also how they function practically, often simultaneously, in the professional world. This knowledge is then reinforced through discussion and suggested classroom exercises. As a result, students gain a strong scholarly understanding of communication careers that expands and informs their academic and professional choices, expectations, and practices.

Second, scholars and professionals have contributed to this book, and they provide professional, academic, and life-skills advice.

Last, several short interviews with professional communicators from each of the allied communication fields provide an authentic view of what happens daily in professional communication environments.

A Brief Word on the Readings

Readings were selected using a broad set of measures. We're aware that each discipline has its own unique set of criteria, and this fact serves as an important guideline for us. The reading selections in *Applied Communication and Practice* are college and university reading level difficulty, challenging in some ways, depending, of course, on the student, but useful as mini-anchors and guideposts for faculty. While we attempted to find readings that discuss each of the main concepts in the **Applied Communication Model**—story, skill, audience, and ethics—this wasn't always possible. For instance, Media Studies is a discipline that has many competing and sometimes contradictory theories and perspectives. There are readings throughout the book from noted writers and scholars that strengthen the book's conceptual framework. The readings also shed light on how certain technical aspects in each communication discipline function in practice (i.e., how to edit, how to write a press release) as well as conceptually (i.e., what is the communication message meant to convey?) The readings will guide students and instructors in their understanding of each communication topic and inspire reflection and discussion in the classroom.

Finally, as mentioned, this book offers a clear explanation of the various communication disciplines and explores the connections between them. Many colleges and universities offer Communication as a broad field of study in what are often called "umbrella" departments or programs. Think of this book as an anchor for understanding how each communication discipline works, in a basic way; how those disciplines connect; what professionals and educators have written about them; and how the disciplines can be discussed and debated in an academic and professional way.

WHO IS THIS BOOK'S AUDIENCE?

This book is intended for college and university students interested in careers in communication, and we believe this audience is very special.

A Millennial Tale—Your Story

Many scholars believe your generation, commonly called the Millennial Generation, is very different than any other generation that came before it. Author Jean M. Twenge, in her book *Generation Me*, observed some important things about the Millennial Generation with whom you might share some key characteristics. Dr. Twenge looked at the results of "more than 30 studies on generational differences, based on data from 11 million young Americans" (4), and her research showed that if you were born as of January 1, 1982, you might not be much of a follower. In fact, like Twenge's own university students, you're probably more "open-minded" and "independent" (29). *Generation Me* can be found at http://www.generationme.org/ and offers an interesting perspective on the millennial generation and that perspective is strengthened by social science research statistics from large groups and from across generations.

Let's assume that you are a millennial and that you're independent and open minded. To some degree, you probably value personal expression, as well; in fact, advertisers and marketers have research that shows you do. For instance, wearable technologies like mobile phones and colorful headphones provide an excellent way for you to self-identify and share your best self with the world.

Technology and Other Distractions

Communication Studies scholars argue that there are many types of distractions, such as psychological, physical, and emotional, and a professor wouldn't necessarily always see these kinds of distractions during a classroom lecture. These days, people also believe that the millennial generation is obsessed with technology, and those technological obsessions are highly disconnected from academic pursuits; scholars believe these obsessions contribute to poor academic performance. In some high schools, students are forced to put mobile phones in locked metal boxes with a special number on the front or individual numbered pouches hanging on the classroom wall.

Few people would argue that learning is *potentially* hampered by overuse of technology; however, researchers have also demonstrated how technology in the classroom aids learning if used in specific ways. Watson and Pecchioni point this out vis-a-vis Hedberg, who argued that "a 'disruptive pedagogy' shifts from using technology to teach the same content, to using technology to help students become active participants not just in their own learning but in creating knowledge" (Watson and Pecchioni, 2011, p. 308). Think of it this way, it's not whether professors should allow texting in class that's the important issue but whether students are using texting in ways that help them create new knowledge and become more active learners.

We recognize and appreciate that you are different than we were at your age and that an effective and useful textbook needs to be planned, designed, and created with you in mind. Simply put, like your professor, we want you to succeed, and this sincere desire frames this book. Understanding content that appears unconnected, like the type of content in *Applied Communication and Practice*, is an especially difficult challenge for someone completely new to the communication disciplines. The content that follows presents a variety of perspectives—theories and practical applications included—so your learning approach and success using this textbook might require some independent and open-minded thinking.

READING 1.1

DIGITAL NATIVES AND DIGITAL MEDIA IN THE COLLEGE CLASSROOM: ASSIGNMENT DESIGN AND IMPACTS ON STUDENT LEARNING

by Joseph A. Watson and Loretta L. Pecchioni

The use of multimodal learning techniques is becoming more widespread, however, the pedagogical discourse surrounding its implementation into classroom and course design is complicated as these technologies are either demonized or viewed as the panacea for curriculum ills. Educators are faced with unique challenges when investigating how to experiment with the best ways to produce classroom experiences that use digital media. This case study examines the implementation challenges and learning outcomes related to such an experiment by reviewing and assessing the use of digital media in a health communication course, specifically through the development of documentaries. Creating an effective assignment requires addressing the development of technical skills along with course content and providing guidance and feedback throughout a semester-long project. Creating an effective assignment is pointless without sufficient learning outcomes. Because this assignment engaged students with both the course content and digital media, their learning experiences were enhanced and improved their group collaboration, critical thinking and media literacy skills.

Keywords: digital media; college classrooms; student learning; critical thinking skills; media literacy; group collaboration

INTRODUCTION

The use of multimodal learning techniques is becoming more widespread within academia as the new media become a greater influence in everyday life and as digital technologies become more readily accessible. Typically, pedagogical discourse surrounding the implementation of technology into classroom and course design is complicated.

Joseph A. Watson and Loretta L. Pecchioni, "Digital Natives and Digital Media in the College Classroom: Assignment Design and Impacts on Student Learning," *Educational Media International*, vol. 48, no. 4, pp. 307-320. Copyright © 2011 by Taylor & Francis Group. Reprinted with permission.

Often new media and digital technologies are either demonized or viewed as the panacea for curriculum ills. Despite questions about how to effectively incorporate new and digital media into the classroom, little doubt remains that the ability of teachers and students to use these technologies effectively is of the highest importance. Video now dominates web-content and opens up new opportunities for global collaboration (Anderson, 2010).

Educators are faced with unique challenges when investigating how to experiment with the best ways to produce classroom experiences that utilize digital media while producing positive learning outcomes (Hedberg, 2011). These challenges are sometimes rooted in the assumption that the technology inherently creates a richer learning environment. Other times, these challenges are rooted in a knowledge gap between instructor and student about the intricacies of digital media technologies. Perhaps more problematic is the dangerous assumption that students living in new media environments automatically comprehend how to use the technologies or produce their own work. Because instructors cannot and should not assume technical knowledge among their students, balancing course content with learning to effectively use the technology is also a challenge. The key pedagogical question becomes how to effectively incorporate these technologies into the classroom environment so that student learning is enhanced through greater engagement with the course content.

These questions about student engagement were evident in the course that serves as the case study for this analysis: a senior-level college course in health communication. Although video clips, still photos, and other artifacts have long been incorporated in communication courses to illustrate concepts and generate class discussion and analysis, the creation of new materials by the students has generally been limited to course assignments such as oral presentations and written exercises. In this particular course, these standard assignments

had included a group oral presentation analyzing a health campaign and an individual research paper examining a topic of interest to the student. The group assignment was problematic in that students displayed the ability to *describe* the rhetoric behind a campaign but were often lacking a critical aspect to their descriptions. In addition, students did not demonstrate genuine group collaboration as each one was able to handle his or her portion of the presentation and avoid working in complex or creative ways with other members. Their papers also lacked a level of critical analysis of the health-related information that they examined. The desire to enhance their learning experiences led to experimentation with having the students create documentaries about a health-related issue of relevance to them.

The driving force behind the documentary assignment described and analyzed in this case study was not technology-centered. The instructors were not interested in, for example, whether students learn more from an online lecture than a live one. Rather, we wanted to adopt a more learner-centered approach to the course. Instead of forcing students to adapt to the demands of the latest technologies, we wanted to implement the available technologies within a structure that could meet the needs of this generation of digital natives (Prensky, 2001). A key factor in assessing this need is for students of the digital era to *produce* new media as well as consume it. Mayer (2005) suggested that asking the question "what can we do with multimedia?" is adopting a technology-centered approach that is doomed to fail. Adopting a student-centered approach leads us to ask the question: "how can we adapt multimedia designs to help students learn more?" In essence, the question of "what can we do?" remains, but the motivation is different (Mayer, 2005). The goal is not merely to test new technologies but to use them in order to test human cognition. As Hedberg (2011) argued, a "disruptive pedagogy" shifts from using technology to teach the same content to using technology to help students become active participants not just in their own learning, but in creating knowledge.

Experimentation in adapting traditional course assignments with digital media technologies is an obvious way to add to institutional and educational discourses about how to create better learning and literacy amongst students. With the documentary assignment, students were asked to produce as well as consume one another's digital media content. The goal of such an assignment is the creation of meaningful learning, where knowledge is organized and integrated for higher retention. Enhancing their critical thinking and media literacy skills and their abilities to function within complex group dynamics are ways to engender meaningful learning. It is in this spirit that we began our project in the hopes of being able to: (1) describe and analyze the development and refinement of the documentary assignment over the course of three years in order to offer advice and guidance to others interested in these issues; and (2) assess the impact of the assignment on student learning.

RESEARCH DESIGN

Before we discuss the assignment and our findings in detail, a note on the design of our study seems appropriate. One of the greatest challenges of educational research is addressing the range of design issues that arise. As Slavin (2007) discussed, standard quantitative designs typically require control and treatment groups with random assignment. In an educational setting, however, treatment and teacher effects can be difficult to disentangle. The ultimate design would be to have random assignment of students, teachers, schools, and treatments. When trying to understand the impact of an innovation such as a new instructional strategy, this level of control requires a commitment of resources that seems unwarranted until the innovation has undergone the equivalent of pilot testing.

Case studies provide an opportunity to examine in depth the process as well as the outcome of innovations (Fraenkel & Wallen, 2009; Slavin, 2007). The goal is to provide detailed descriptions of what happened in a particular situation, attending to a myriad of contextual factors using a wide range of data sources, including the perspectives of students and teachers. Because of our interest in understanding how students engage with digital media during the learning process, we designed a series of opportunities to learn from them as we were making our own observations related to their activities and learning. This case study, then, focuses first on the process of the assignment as well as its apparent successes and failures. Each year, based on what we learned the previous year, we made adjustments. Therefore, we begin by describing what we did, highlighting adjustments that have been made along the way, and then move to an assessment of the documentary assignment and its impact on student learning. Our interpretation of the data will reveal how we believe that students' experience and knowledge were enhanced through meaningful and complex group collaboration and demonstrated increases in critical thinking and media literacy skills. We conclude by offering recommendations for adapting the assignment for other's use.

THE DATA AVAILABLE

In describing and assessing the assignment of making a documentary in the health communication course, we had available several different sources of information although three forms provide the bulk of our supporting evidence. With regards to the development and refinement of the structure and elements of the assignment, we relied on both our own observations and feedback from the students. With regards to assessing the impacts on student learning, the documentaries themselves demonstrate the application of their knowledge, skills, and abilities although we also draw on student comments and our own observations.

FIELD NOTES AND OBSERVATIONS

Throughout each semester over the three years to date, the authors took notes about our observations of the students' in-class and studio[1] behavior, the questions they asked about the assignment, as well as email exchanges and office visits. We met regularly to discuss the process, address questions as they arose, develop additional materials and consider adaptations for the future.

THE FOCUS GROUPS

We wanted to get feedback from the students on their experiences of making a documentary. We chose to conduct focus groups at the end of the first two years to hear their perspectives and help them focus on evaluating the process rather than feeling they were being personally evaluated as might have occurred in individual interviews (Fraenkel & Wallen, 2009). A set of questions was developed and divided into two major sections: process and student learning. The process section focused on such topics as feedback and guidance. The student learning section focused on topics such as how working on their documentaries engaged them with course content. Each session ended with asking them if the assignment should be made in the future and, if so, what changes should be made.

For our purposes here, the specific statements made by students during the focus groups are of less importance than is the impact their comments had on refining the assignments and assessing their perceptions of their own learning. Therefore, detailed quotations are not used, but rather summary statements derived from the comments of the groups as a whole.[2]

The Documentaries

Each group (24 in 3 years) produced a 10–15 minute documentary. Because our focus was on student engagement with course content more than technological skills, we developed an evaluation rubric reflecting this focus. Elements of the evaluation included: content, organization, and production elements that were not equally weighted.[3] Evidence of their learning was gleaned from examining the strengths and weaknesses of the individual documentaries, comments made by the students during the focus group sessions as well as the instructor of record's global impressions comparing their performance to more standard assignments.

CLASS STRUCTURE AND ASSIGNMENTS

As mentioned, concerns about student learning drove the desire to develop an alternative course assignment in hopes of finding an approach that would enhance their learning experience. Design considerations included such issues as how to balance technical training with the course content, but also what set of checkpoints and assessments would effectively monitor student progress and help them make steady progress on this semester-long project.

BEGINNING THE GROUP PROCESS

The process of the health-related documentary assignment began with dividing the students into groups. In the first two years, the instructor assigned the class members to their groups based on a survey that gauged their interests, skills and comfort levels with working in groups, being sensitive to narrative conventions, and working with technology. Based on comments from students, in the third year the class members organized themselves into groups. Because they know each other from other classes, they believe that they are more likely to select a cohesive working group. Although the number and types of group dynamic issues were similar to those when the instructor assigned group members, when they selected their own groups they attributed problems that arose to their own decision making and not to the instructor.

After being assigned to their groups early in the second week of the semester, their first meeting was devoted to establishing expectations and producing a written contract for working together. They were also given class time to meet and begin brainstorming about particular topics that interested them. The next week, the groups received approval for potential ideas and were given feedback and guidance on how to refine their ideas.

PROVIDING STUDENTS WITH TECHNICAL VOCABULARY

One of the first undertakings for this assignment was to surround the students with a critical framework for making films. Only a handful of students had any prior experience in using digital video technologies and even fewer had familiarity with cinematic vocabulary or technique. In addition, since their projects would be documentary films, the students needed to be conscious of the genre's conventions. An initial challenge was to devise an activity that would engage their critical and creative energies as well as introduce them to the potentialities of the documentary process. Although media literacy was a pedagogical goal, we were cautious not to place too much emphasis on the technical components lest the students felt they were enrolled in a film production or criticism course. The central focus of the course needed to remain rooted in health communication.

In order to provide them with some ideas about how to go about asking and answering relevant questions, introducing them to documentary film seemed necessary. The first year, one week of class was devoted to a whole-class screening of Michael Moore's health documentary, *Sicko* (2007). The decision to use *Sicko* was based on many factors, but primarily we wanted to generate argumentation and analysis and engage them in ways of thinking about how to build an argument visually. For the screening, a discussion guide was provided to direct their viewing to take note of particular aesthetic qualities and content of the documentary and they

wrote a group response using these questions. A class session was devoted to discussing this documentary on both content and aesthetic elements.

While screening *Sicko* did generate discussion about Moore's cinematic choices and his biases, it also generated considerable concern about being able to emulate that level of work. In the second and third years, a list of shorter (typically one-hour or less) health-related documentaries was posted and each group selected one of interest to screen and analyze outside of class. Again, a discussion guide was provided and a discussion about content and aesthetic elements was held in class. Somewhat surprisingly, their written responses and in-class discussion about the documentaries was more in-depth and nuanced than when we screened *Sicko* together. Using shared class time for other course content rather than screening the documentaries was not only efficient, but led to the groups working together to produce a written analysis and they began to establish their joint work ethic.

PROVIDING STUDENTS WITH TECHNICAL SKILLS

One on-going concern was how to introduce the students to camera work and the editing software while maintaining focus on course content. Because most students did not have any meaningful background in movie production, we felt compelled to at least offer basic instruction. One class session was devoted to the basics of camera work. Examples of different camera angles were shown and their purposes briefly discussed. The groups then checked out cameras and shot examples from a short list. They returned to the studio to view their footage. This brief training established a familiarity with the equipment and how images appeared differently on the camera screen and on the computer screen.

A greater challenge existed in introducing the students to the editing software, Final Cut Pro®. During the first two years, we held short training sessions during class and encouraged them to sign up for additional training workshops. This approach, however, did not seem to prove effective in that students reported growing frustration across the semester with using the software. Trouble learning the technology overshadowed exploration and creativity. For the third year, an individual assignment was added which required each student to go to the studio (outside of class time) to view selected training components from www.lynda.com and produce a two–minute minute video with basic audio and visual transitions. Nearly every student (94%) successfully completed this assignment. They reported that the assignment took them on average four hours. Throughout the semester, the instructor of record heard very little with regard to frustrations about learning the software. The students reported that the exercise gave them a better idea about how long it takes to do editing work and they planned accordingly. Although they continued to feel that the documentary assignment is extremely time consuming, they spent more time moving forward on their projects and less time struggling with managing the technology itself.

PROVIDING STUDENTS WITH STRUCTURE

Once the students had basic technical training and each group had decided on a topic, a number of checkpoints were put in place to help them stay on track and to provide opportunities for them to receive feedback from the instructor and/or from their peers. For example, each group was required to shoot at least two minutes of raw footage to encourage them to become familiar with the cameras and transferring footage to the lab's computers. Two weeks later they were required to turn in at least four minutes of edited footage which required them to not only be shooting footage, but to begin the editing process. Each group turned in a narrative for their documentary, essentially an extended outline of the arguments they would present and how they would be presented. Groups were given feedback to refine their approaches. During the

third year, a group work plan was added which required the group to schedule activities such as interviews, searching for resources, and editing along with assigning individual responsibilities for each activity. The addition of the work plan helped group members communicate more effectively as they planned, delegated responsibilities, and renegotiated with each other when someone did not fulfill a task as laid out on the written document.

During the first two years, at the end of Week 11 (out of a 16-week semester), the groups posted a rough cut of their documentaries to a private class blog. For the third year, the rough cuts were viewed on computers in the studio during a class period. Members of one group were required to view and critique another group's first cut. Each group then responded to those critiques by listing the comments that were made on the rough cut and deciding whether or not to accept those suggestions and why. Holding the screening during class time increased the number of individuals who provided feedback while also generating more specific and creative feedback that could be implemented into the final product. Following this exercise, in the third year, each group provided a revised work plan that reflected the schedule for completing their projects. Weeks 15 and 16 were devoted to in-class presentations of the documentaries. Groups made copies of the documentaries on DVDs. Audience members, including the instructors and class members, filled out evaluations of the final cuts.

ASSESSING THE IMPACTS ON STUDENT LEARNING

While one goal of this case study is to describe the process of developing and refining this assignment, of greater importance is the examination of how incorporating technology into the classroom impacted student learning. After all, if student learning is not enhanced, then the effort of incorporating a complex technological assignment is not worth the energy. Based on the evidence we have, when compared to more standard assignments, student learning was enhanced through their creation of a documentary. In particular, group collaboration, critical thinking and media literacy skills were positively impacted.

DEMONSTRATION OF COMPLEX GROUP DYNAMICS AND COLLABORATION

One of the initial issues driving the creation of this assignment was that the group assignment of an oral presentation critiquing a health campaign reflected low levels of group collaboration. Because the range of requisite skills in that assignment was relatively narrow, it was too easy for groups to divide up the sections of the presentation or for strong students to do most of the work and then hand other group members a script for the day of their presentation. Creating their own documentaries was believed to require a broader range of skills that would increase meaningful collaboration. The first question to be addressed then was whether they collaborated with each other on this project. The answer is a resounding yes. Based on their responses during the focus groups and our observations throughout each semester, the students felt that this project required that everyone participate in meaningful ways. No one person had all the skills or time available to complete the project. While some students were better at researching background information, others were better at conducting interviews and yet others at editing the different elements together into a coherent storyline. Their interdependence was evident in the level and types of conflict experienced within groups, the need for using collaborative problem-solving skills and the amount of learning from each other that occurred as they developed their documentaries.

The need to collaborate and thus rely on each other to produce a product brought about more stress and conflict in the groups' dynamics. Although the second author has assigned semester long group projects for over ten years, the documentary assignment generated the first time that groups directly asked the instructor to participate in a meeting to work through issues regarding group dynamics. Typically, a group would experience personality conflicts or a lack of commitment on the part of one member. Some groups more successfully negotiated these challenges, but all found solutions to their conflicts that allowed them to complete their projects.

The experiences of conflict, however, also played into their need to develop and enhance their collaborative problem solving skills. They often found communicating with each other in an effective manner challenging. Many of the difficulties they experienced reflected the fact that they were reluctant to challenge each other. During the focus groups, the students generally agreed that their group dynamics were an important element of their learning in the class. They discussed specific communication issues such as negotiating deadlines and responsibilities, the lack of open communication, and communicating in a timely fashion. Because of the range of skills needed, an important element of the group dynamics was the distribution of responsibilities among the group members. Problems did arise when some members shirked their responsibilities by being unavailable or demonstrated a lack of initiative. Although attempts were made to help the students figure out how to distribute the workload relatively evenly, groups that experienced conflict also reported feeling that the amount of work was unevenly distributed because some people did not fulfil their role obligations. While we initially expected them to use various forms of social media to interact outside of the classroom, based on their comments and complaints, it appears that a few students continued to be unavailable to their group in spite of efforts to reach out to them through these avenues. Naively, perhaps, we expected them to be more willing to challenge each other when using mediated forms of communication. Mediated communication, however, did not appear to make it easier to ask questions or challenge positions.

In spite of the problems reported, students also discussed what they learned from each other through this process. While they reflected on their own strengths and thought about what they had to contribute to their group (and potential future employers), they appreciated that others in the group had other qualities. Students who had difficulty getting and staying organized appreciated other group members who took the lead in this area. Students who felt they did not have a great appreciation for aesthetics enjoyed it when other group members helped them to think in new ways about how to frame an argument, especially with regard to supporting visual elements. Members of groups that functioned effectively, not surprisingly, reported the most enjoyment from the collaborative learning environment.

DEMONSTRATION OF CRITICAL THINKING

Consistent with Mayer's (2005) argument that technology should be incorporated into the classroom in ways that enhance student-learning, the second goal of the documentary assignment was to enhance critical thinking skills. Starting with the assumption that critical thinking is rooted in problems that result in active engagement on the part of the students, we adapted Bean's (2001) process of designing a written assignment that helps students to: identify problems and pose interesting questions; explore, imagine, analyze, and evaluate information relevant to their questions; and, allow time for ideas to incubate to encourage reformulation and editing of relevant information. Details regarding each of these elements are provided below.

Identifying Problems and Posing Interesting Questions

The first group assignment for the documentary was to select a topic and develop a question that would drive their documentary. Our role during this part of the process was to provide each group with feedback and encourage them to consider alternatives. As a result, each group had a question to answer or a set of positions to explore, although some groups asked what we considered to be more interesting questions. For example, with the swine flu in the news during the spring of 2009, one group was surprised to learn that people use hand sanitizers incorrectly. Their documentary reported on the correct use of hand sanitizers in a factual manner which was informative, but not a critical analysis. On the other hand, each year one group has addressed obesity and its related health consequences by focusing on regional cultural norms that make changing life styles more complicated. One group examined playing video games by first addressing the negative stereotypes of gamers and then exploring the health benefits of playing these games. Not surprisingly, binge drinking among college students has been a popular topic each year. While four groups addressed the relatively standard issues of drinking and driving or the consequences of alcohol poisoning, one group moved beyond these basics by examining the consequences of alcohol in social interactions, such as "drunk texting".

Assessing Information Relevant to their Questions

Two elements regarding relevant information emerged: the range of sources used to develop and support their arguments and issues of objectivity and subjectivity in presenting these arguments. When compared with the health campaign analysis, the creation of a documentary did seem to encourage them to seek out information from more sources and to consider how those different sources fit together or argued against each other.

During the health campaign analysis presentations, the groups had Power Point® slides, played public service announcements created by the campaign and displayed parts of the campaign's website (e.g., children's games to learn about brushing their teeth). In the documentaries, the students drew upon information from websites, popular press and research journals, interviews with individuals who had expertise with their topic either through professional training or personal experience, and what they called the layperson, such as students on campus, plus they incorporated footage from movies, television shows, public service announcements, news coverage and music to further incorporate popular culture sources into their analysis.

Engaging their audience, especially class peers, had not been a serious consideration in the oral presentations on health campaigns. In making their documentaries, the groups considered ways in which to relate to their audience. For example, interviews with students on campus not only provided the student perspective, but helped the audience to relate to the topic by examining their level of knowledge about the issue. By shooting footage in recognizable locations on campus, they were able to place the interviews into a familiar context and create identification with their audience. When groups selected topics that they thought might be of less interest to the typical college student, they made efforts to find ways to generate interest. For example, one group addressed issues of heart disease in women and what young women should be doing to protect their heart health. They opened with short clips of students answering the questions: "what is the most common killer of women?" and "what is heart disease?" These efforts to connect with their audience indicated thought about how best to get their attention, especially for issues that might not typically be considered of high concern to them.

When we began discussing documentaries as a film genre, the majority of the students assumed that these forms project an objective picture of reality. As we discussed the documentaries that were screened, we began the process of asking them to consider the nature of objectivity and subjectivity in more complex ways. Placing the students in the position of filmmaker forced them to be aware of their own biases. Thinking through not only what material would be included in their projects, but also how that material would be presented encouraged them to develop a richer understanding of their own biases and how they wanted to influence their audience members about that material.

An additional benefit of working on the documentaries was that it heightened their awareness of the ways in which mediated health messages are constructed. Their critical thinking skills were particularly evident in a class activity in which they brought a health-related advertisement to class. In groups, they discussed issues regarding target audiences, message choices, combining textual and visual elements of arguments, source credibility and voice of the advertisement. The level of engagement during the discussions was very high. Of particular note, they seemed more attuned to visual images and their rhetorical messages than in the past.

Incubation Time for Reformulating and Editing Information

The most critical element in creating time for reformulating and editing information was having frequent checkpoints early on so that a more complete rough cut was screened, thus producing more meaningful feedback. Groups that procrastinated and were shooting footage the week before the assignment was due to be screened did not produce strong projects. For the groups that met the time deadlines, they did indeed have time to reconsider some of their choices and to further elaborate on their arguments. The refinement of the timing and types of checkpoint and feedback assignments has improved this process. In the third year, we more successfully encouraged steady progress that gave each group time to produce a quality product. Overall, the documentaries were much stronger than they had been in the past and this seemed to be primarily due to them learning more about the technical aspects of the software early on so they could focus on the creative elements and having earlier deadlines that resulted in them having more time to edit and refine in the last two weeks.

DEMONSTRATION OF MEDIA LITERACY

Media literacy is focused on providing students with the skills necessary to question the accuracy and authenticity of information in all its forms. They need to have the ability to make reflective, critical responses to this information. The screening and subsequent discussions of the health-related documentaries allowed students to engage with such responses. But media literacy is about more than just consuming information. A media literate individual is able to produce, create, and successfully communicate information in all its forms (Alvermann, Moon, & Hagood, 1999). With the documentary assignment, the students were asked to engage with and produce from digital media tools. Their comments about artistic freedom, production frustrations, and technological understanding demonstrate evidence of a strong, creative learning experience.

The Process of Producing a Movie: the Headaches and Joys of Digital Media

At the most basic level of knowledge and skills, the students had to develop a sufficient understanding about the rudiments and conventions of "making a movie". Providing them with these basic skills and knowledge then allows them to move into more creative aspects of the project and, hopefully, more engaged learning. On the basic technical level, some groups did experience glitches, such as shooting footage in more than one format or shooting interviews with poor lighting or distracting background noise. Their initial responses to these

problems, was "isn't there a way to just *fix that*?" These groups soon learned that not all problems could be easily solved without reshooting footage. Having a better understanding of the challenges to "getting it right" helped them to appreciate the work of the documentarians screened at the beginning of the semester by questioning what kinds of challenges they may have encountered in their projects. In addition, they reported having a much greater appreciation for the amount of time and energy required to shoot, edit, and polish even a few minutes of footage. Getting the students into the studio to work on the introductory editing exercise early in the semester seemed to lay a strong foundation for this basic knowledge and helped the students to move forward on their projects with more confidence and more realistic planning.

Although each year the groups were required to develop the equivalent of an outline for their projects, having them write a narrative that addressed visual as well as textual elements along with a work plan seemed to provide them with the most effective structure. These assignments helped the group members consider the visual threads that would create narrative sequencing as well as how the project would be shot and composed/edited. Attention to the ways in which the different layers of the medium interact was particularly evident in their revised narratives and work plans as they identified changes to their original plans, offering more nuanced understanding of how their arguments could be supported.

For those groups that made steady progress and met the established deadlines, they found the creative freedom refreshing. These groups had time to polish their projects. For example, one group had a member who designed visual effects for the opening sequence. Since their topic was smoking, he wanted to generate digital smoke around the text of their opening credits. Another group included a text box in which key points were added as the medical professional listed them during her interview. Several groups worked to refine their interview footage so that it would be more appealing to the audience by incorporating smoother transitions and interweaving the interviews of several individuals to more effectively demonstrate how these multiple perspectives were in agreement or contradicted each other. The groups who were more organized also had time to incorporate more apt musical interludes or include appropriate sound effects to reinforce their messages.

Learning about Fair Use Practices

Although we had briefly addressed issues of fair use the first two years, we felt the need to more clearly address these issues in the third year because one second year group had basically produced a "mash-up" with more than 50% of their video consisting of news coverage and movie clips which were presented without attribution for the works used. One full class period was used during which the first author offered several examples to illustrate the issues surrounding intellectual property and directed the students to relevant websites for their further investigation. As the legal concerns of intellectual property are fluid in today's media environment, we wanted to reinforce these issues for our students. As a result, the groups were more explicit about acknowledging others' work as well as thinking more critically about how they were appropriating that work. They also demonstrated a greater appreciation for their own intellectual property as noted in the next section.

Engagement with the Technology and Learning

An unexpected outcome of the documentary assignment has been the level of engagement on the part of students because of the different nature of screening their documentaries when compared to other types of assignments, even oral presentations. Students tend to write papers with their instructor as the primary audience.

They rarely share their written work with each other or anyone outside the class. Oral presentations are more public in that the other class members are part of their audience. Although such presentations may be anxiety-provoking for some students, their impermanence means that no one outside of the class is likely to see their performance. All three years of the documentary assignment, at least some of the students have been excited to share their work with others outside the classroom setting. Some of this excitement is the novelty of such a project. Some is due to the pride they feel in having produced an interesting product. Some of the excitement, however, seems to be due to the medium itself. Whatever the motivation, for many students the possibility of sharing their work with others generates greater engagement in all elements related to the production of their work. Engaging in an assignment that moves them from consumers to producers of digital media arouses their curiosity and awareness in ways that seems difficult to achieve through any other means.

RECOMMENDATIONS FOR IMPLEMENTATION

While we highly recommend having students make a documentary and will continue using this assignment, designing the assignment to be learner-centered rather than technology-centered requires considerable thought. As an instructor, you need to consider how this kind of assignment connects to your course content and the specific learning objectives you want the assignment to meet. Starting with a documentary or movie lays a foundation of shared information, but do appropriate cinematic documents exist that are relevant to your content area? Whatever types of examples you choose, holding an in-class discussion about the nature of moving media and how arguments might be made as well as identifying the course-related topics of each one provides students with a basic vocabulary as they approach their own projects. Courses other than health communication may not have as many dramatic portrayals as examples. This structure, however, can easily be used to engage students in asking questions about a topic and collecting the perspectives of individuals who have been impacted by or are informed about the topic. Other types of assignments may also be beneficial. For example, a colleague in engineering had students develop a two-three minute video addressing an ethical issue. Adapting this kind of assignment for younger students might require a less demanding project. The second author knows a colleague at another university who sponsors a contest for students in eighth through twelfth grade in which they do video reports of science books, relaying what they found exciting and/or perplexing about the content.

Once you have decided that this could be an effective learning tool for your students you have to determine if you have the resources available on your campus for students to be successful. The necessary resources include not only hardware (e.g., cameras and tripods) and software (e.g., Final Cut Pro®, although you might choose to have them use whatever they already have available, such as iMovie®), but also knowledgeable people who have time dedicated to enhancing student knowledge regarding the use of the soft- and hardware. We had the luxury of having a studio that was dedicated to working with students on these kinds of projects. Not all campuses will have these kinds of facilities. So how might you go about doing this kind of assignment? One solution could be the use of the learning community model in which two courses are taught in conjunction with each other, but focus on different content. Therefore, you could combine a production course with a content course. Students from each course would have different responsibilities for joint final projects in which the production class students would provide the technical expertise and the students

in the content course would provide the content expertise.

Whatever you decide on for the product portion of the assignment, the process portion is the most critical. Establish a number of checkpoints and deadlines to allow for feedback throughout the process. Early deadlines representing incremental progress provide structure and develop confidence. Learning the basic technical elements early leaves time for more creative aspects to emerge later in the project. Having time to re-evaluate their work and to incorporate meaningful feedback into their projects not only produces better quality projects, but enhances their learning.

CONCLUSION

Concerns with student-learning drove the generation of the assignment addressed in this case study. In our opinion, the assignment was a success, but not without challenges. Students reported that they could not successfully produce a documentary on an individual basis. Because the assignment required a range of skills, they had to work together to accomplish their goals. In the process, they developed their interpersonal skills as they organized themselves, made decisions, negotiated responsibilities and managed conflict. They learned the benefits of having group members with a range of skills upon which to draw so that they could successfully achieve their mutual goal. They demonstrated critical thinking skills as they researched their chosen topics and developed their arguments for the documentary. As producers of digital media, they learned to question the nature of the multitude of health-related messages to which we are exposed through the production of their own messages and gained a greater respect for the complexities of the technology itself. As a result, we believe that student learning was enhanced through the process of developing their own documentaries.

NOTES

1 The university provides studio space with equipment and personnel available to assist students in a range of communication-based projects.

2 Details of the process, however, are important to note. Time slots were selected across times of the day and days of the week and individuals signed up for convenient times. Each year, a graduate student from the department who had experience with focus groups conducted these sessions. Before the topic guide questions were engaged, the students were informed that the instructor of record would not review their comments until after grades were posted as was the case. All of the sessions were digitally recorded in audio format only to help ensure student anonymity. After the focus groups were completed, the individuals conducting the sessions transcribed the materials. Because our focus was on their comments, they were transcribed to capture the conversation at that level rather than to capture linguistic features (Macnaughten & Myers, 2004). Because of our interest in assessing the students' experience of the process, the transcripts were not content analyzed in the sense that categories were identified and counts made (Keyton, 2006). Each of the authors individually reviewed the transcripts and identified key passages that captured the students' perspectives regarding what was positive and negative about the process and their learning.

3 All materials are available from the second author.

REFERENCES

Alvermann, D.E., Moon, J.S., & Hagood, M.C. (1999). *Popular culture in the classroom: Teaching and researching critical media literacy.* Mahwah, NJ: Lawrence Erlbaum.

Anderson, C. (2010, July). How web video powers global innovation. TEDGlobal 2010. Retrieved August 26, 2011, from http://www.ted.com/talks/chris_anderson_how_web_video_powers_global_innovation.htmlAndersAAndersonl.

Bean, J.C. (2001). *Engaging ideas: The professor's guide to integrating writing, critical thinking, and active learning in the classroom.* San Francisco, CA: Jossey-Bass.

Fraenkel, J.R., & Wallen, N.E. (2009). *How to design and evaluate research in education.* Boston: McGraw-Hill.

Hedberg, J.G. (2011). Towards a disruptive pedagogy: Changing classroom practice with technologies and digital content. *Educational Media International, 48,* 1–16.

Keyton, J. (2006). *Communication research: Asking questions, finding answers.* Boston: McGraw Hill.

Macnaughten, P., & Myers, G. (2004). Focus groups. In C. Seale, G. Gobo, J.F. Gubrium, & D. Silverman (Eds.), *Qualitative research practice* (pp. 65–79). London: Sage.

Mayer, R. (2005). *The Cambridge handbook of multimedia learning.* New York: Cambridge University Press.

Moore, M. Producer & Director (2007). *Sicko.* USA: Dog Eat Dog Films.

Prensky, M. (2001). Digital natives, digital immigrants. *On the Horizon, 9*(5), 1–6.

Richardson, W. (2006). *Blogs, wikis, podcasts, and other powerful web tools for classrooms.* Thousand Oaks, CA: Corwin Press.

Slavin, R.E. (2007). *Educational research in an age of accountability.* Boston: Pearson.

WHAT SHOULD YOU GET OUT OF THIS BOOK?

There are many things you should get out of this book. But here are the five most important. First, you should remember and understand what the terms used within each communication discipline mean, including the name of the discipline, such as Communication
Studies. Second, when you're exposed to particular media messages, you should be able
to apply the new knowledge you have learned, understand how that knowledge is used in
creating media messages, and make an educated assessment about where that message
comes from and how communication professionals created the message in the first place.
For instance, you should be able to describe the format and design of the particular media
message. Once you've read the book, you should also understand how all the communication disciplines connect and relate to one another using the Applied Communication
Model—story, skill, ethics, and audience—and how you as a communicator connect with
a specific communication discipline. Third, you should be able to **analyze** and **evaluate**
the knowledge you've gained about a particular communication discipline in light of rapidly evolving and ubiquitous media content.

Fourth, once you've read *Applied Communication and Practice*, you should be able to
create effective media messages yourself using the Applied Communication Model as your
conceptual framework. For example, through class exercises and discussion, you should be
able to demonstrate in written, oral, or some other form how the Applied Communication
Model can be used as a "lens" when looking at the Public Relations profession even if
you're not a PR major.

Finally, and this is the most complicated and difficult "take away" from reading *Applied
Communication and Practice*, you should be much closer to deciding on the major you'd
like to pursue and, perhaps, the communication career in which you'd like to work. Life
balance, parental influence, financial realities, and personal relationships are just a few of
the challenges when it comes to selecting a major and your career choice.

HOW DO I NAVIGATE THIS BOOK?

This book is structured like many academic books with some exceptions. Of course, the
content is divided into chapters, but those chapters correlate to professional communication disciplines. So, inside the chapter is content about a particular communication
discipline, like Theatre or Comedy. Keep in mind, we often write about how a particular
discipline, like television production, for instance, shares things in common with other
communication disciplines. For instance, there is no television without audible sound like
music, sound effects **(SFX)**, or voices; otherwise, it's called radio. You'll also notice that
portions of the book are devoted to short interviews with professionals. These interviews
are especially important. We've done the work of approaching a professional communicator, talked with her/him, and asked questions we think someone new to the industry might
want to know—someone like you.

The book provides some foundational exercises customized to each specific discipline.
We hope that if you participate in the classroom discussions and do the exercises, the

information will become cemented in your mind, and decisions about your career will be less difficult. What follows are some other suggestions for how to further maximize this book's value for you and spark a good classroom experience.

ACADEMIC AND APPLIED COMMUNICATION

As we've mentioned, this textbook introduces university and college students to the broad discipline of Communication and the important skills professional communicators' practice in their allied fields. *Applied Communication and Practice* presents a first, comprehensive analysis and details useful practical tools for one of the most popular academic majors—*Communication* with a capital "C." According to a recent article in the *Princeton Review*:

> Communication majors tend to be great storytellers with quick wits and fiery personalities. You'll spend a significant amount of time scrutinizing different kinds of presentations—such as speeches and scripts—and the strategies behind the messages that speakers and writers use to make their points. You'll learn about verbal and nonverbal messages, audience reaction, and the varied effects of different communication environments (Franek 2016).

It's useful to think about Communication in two ways: as an **academic** pursuit and as an **applied** pursuit. Communication could also be understood in another way: a discipline that can be researched and written about as a combination of both applied and academic knowledge. But, for the purposes of this chapter, let's stick to what's sometimes called **binary thinking** and discuss Communication as only applied and academic.

For *Applied Communication and Practice,* we make a distinction between the two types of academic experience students most often encounter at the college and university levels. The typical discipline-specific experience for Communication students is often academic and applied. Although the terms *academic* and *applied* look and sound different, they are related, and, in fact, a professor teaching in one of the communication disciplines might employ teaching and learning goals based in both knowledge areas.

When thinking about university and college level coursework, the word *academic* encompasses the most important concepts of a particular discipline. A strictly *academically* focused course would also include sub concepts related to the particular discipline's foundational concepts or **theories**. When using the word *academic,* the theory or theories that frame a particular discipline are often emphasized rather than practical skills. For instance, in television production, the concept of **depth of field** is critical to understanding how to make a well-composed shot. In Media Studies, the concept of **political power**, as represented in film and television, helps us understand which groups of people are underrepresented in popular media.

The word *applied* is the **concrete** expression of media centered work in the professional world of Communication, like a television camera operator or a Media Studies professor and what each of them do on a daily basis. The word *applied* can also represent the dominant theories and ideas in a discipline. For instance, a professor might teach an applied course emphasizing skills but also discuss an academic theory or idea during an in-class demonstration. An applied teaching style is more concrete and utilizes very practical examples to highlight concepts but is also somewhat theoretical.

Each chapter in *Applied Communication and Practice* includes commentary from experts in the most common areas of the communication discipline, and those experts work in the broader allied fields of Communication, namely Public Relations, commonly called "PR," Television production, Film production, Radio and Sound production, Communication Studies, Broadcast Journalism, Media Studies, Citizen Journalism, and Theatre and Comedy. Four principles connect each discipline and create the Applied Communication Model.

The Applied Communication Model's core principles—story, audience, ethics, and skill—connect you with important ideas and common practices in the world of professional communication and academic study. Figure 1.1 provides an illustration of the Applied Communication Model.

THE APPLIED COMMUNICATION MODEL

Figure 1.1 As you'll see in the model, everything is connected to you.

Story

Sheila Curran Bernard points out, "At its most basic, a story has a beginning, middle, and end" (Bernard 2007, 15). There are several other important storytelling components Bernard points out in *Story Basics* as it specifically relates to documentary storytelling.

DOCUMENTARY STORYTELLING: MAKING STRONGER AND MORE NONFICTION FILMS

by Sheila Curran Bernard

STORY BASICS

A *story* is the narrative, or telling, of an event or series of events, crafted in a way to interest the audience, whether they are readers, listeners, or viewers. At its most basic, a story has a beginning, middle, and end. It has compelling characters, rising tension, and conflict that reaches some sort of resolution. It engages the audience on an emotional and intellectual level, motivating viewers to want to know what happens next.

Strategies for good storytelling are not new. The Greek philosopher Aristotle first set out guidelines for what he called a "well-constructed plot" in 350 BCE, and those basics have been applied to storytelling—on stage, on the page, and on screen—ever since. Expectations about how story telling works seem hardwired in audiences, and meeting, confounding, and challenging those expectations is no less important to the documentarian than it is to the dramatist.

Don't be confused by the fact that festivals and film schools commonly use the term *narrative* to describe only works of dramatic fiction. Most documentaries are also narrative, which simply means that they tell stories (whether or not those stories are also *narrated* is an entirely different issue). How they tell those stories and what stories they tell separates the films into subcategories of genre or style, from cinéma vérité to film noir.

A few storytelling terms:

EXPOSITION

Exposition is the information that grounds you in a story: who, what, where, when, and why. It gives audience members the tools they need to follow the story that's unfolding and, more importantly, it allows them inside the story. It doesn't mean giving away everything, just giving away what the audience needs, when the audience needs it. Exposition is occasionally discussed as something to be avoided, but it's necessary to an audience's understanding of the film, and its presentation, usually in the first act, doesn't have to be heavy-handed.

Exposition in theater used to be handled by the maid who bustled onstage at the start of a play and said, to no one in particular, or perhaps to a nearby butler, "Oh, me, I'm so very worried about the mistress, now that the master has gone off hunting with that ne'er-do-well brother of his, and without even telling her that his father, the Lord of Pembrokeshire, has arranged to sell this very house and all of its belongings before a fortnight is up!" In documentary films, the corollary might be those programs that are entirely front-loaded with narration that tells you information you're unprepared for or don't really need to know—and when you do need the information, you generally can't remember it. Front-loading also frequently occurs when filmmakers decide to put the entire backstory—all of the history leading up to the point of their story's attack—at the beginning of the film.

Exposition can be woven into a film in many ways. Sometimes expository information comes out when the people you're filming argue: "Yeah? Well, we wouldn't even be in this mess if you hadn't decided to take your paycheck to Vegas!" Sometimes it's revealed through headlines or other printed material, as some exposition is conveyed in *The Thin Blue Line*. Good narration can deftly weave exposition into a story, offering viewers just enough information to know where they are. (Voice-over material drawn from interviews can sometimes do the same thing.) Exposition can also be handled through visuals: an establishing shot of a place or sign; footage of a sheriff nailing an eviction notice on a door (*Roger & Me*); the opening moments of an auction (*Troublesome Creek*). Toys littered on a suburban lawn say "Children live here." Black bunting and a homemade shrine of flowers and cards outside a fire station say "Tragedy has occurred." A long shot of an elegantly dressed woman in a large, spare office high up in a modern building says "This woman is powerful." A man on a subway car reading an issue of *The Boston Globe* tells us where we are, as would a highway sign or a famous landmark—the Eiffel Tower, for example. Time-lapse photography, title cards, and animation can all be used to convey exposition, sometimes with the added element of humor or surprise—think of the cartoons in *Super Size Me*.

THE NARRATIVE SPINE, OR *TRAIN*

Films move forward in time, taking audiences with them. You want the storytelling to move forward, too, and to motivate the presentation of exposition. In other words, you want the audience to be curious about the information you're giving them. When exposition involves backstory—how we got to where we are now—it's often a good idea to get a present-day story moving forward (even if the story is in the past) before looking back. This overall story—your film's narrative spine—has been described by producers Ronald Blumer and Muffie Meyer of Middlemarch Films (*Benjamin Franklin, Liberty! The American Revolution*) as the film's *train*.

The train is the element of story that drives your film forward, from the beginning to the end. Get a good train going, and you can make detours as needed for exposition, complex theory, additional characters—whatever you need. Sometimes, these detours let you seed in information that will pay off later in the film; sometimes, the detours are motivated by the train, and the audience *wants*

to take a side track to learn more. Look […], and you'll see how much of a documentary can be "off track" and, if the train is powerful enough, never feel like it's doing anything but moving steadily forward. The trick is to get the train going and to remember to get back on "on track" in a reasonable period of time. If you don't have a train going, those detours will seem unfocused and, more than likely, dull. Your train will be derailed.

Here's an example: You're thinking of telling a story in chronological order about this guy named Jim Jones who becomes a Pentecostal minister in Indiana and has an interracial church and it's the 1950s and—it's not very interesting. But if you pick up this same story much later in time, as a congressman goes to Guyana to rescue some Americans from what their relatives fear is a dangerous cult, and the congressman is killed while members of this cult line up to drink cyanide-spiked juice, chances are the audience will stay with you as you break away from this train to explore the decades of social, political, cultural, and even personal change that created Jim Jones and the tragedy of Jonestown. The drama is already there; it's a matter of finding the "creative arrangement," the strongest way to tell it.

In considering the train, it helps to think about drawing in an audience that doesn't know or care one way or another about the topic you're following. Some people are deeply curious about space exploration, for example, but many people aren't. If you're creating a film that you hope will reach a general audience, whether at a museum, on television, or in theaters, you need to think about how to get a story under way that will grab that audience. Then—and this is what makes you a good documentary filmmaker, not a mediocre one—you want to see how much information that story will allow you to convey even to the disinterested, because you're going to *get* them interested.

In other words, rather than pandering to the lowest common denominator—creating a breathless film about space exploration that's filled with platitudes and exciting music, but little else—your goal is to create a film that's driven by a story, one that will motivate even general viewers to *want* to know more of those details that thrill you. They'll grow to care because those details will matter to the story unfolding on screen. The train of *Super Size Me* is a 30-day McDiet, for example, but look at how much information the film conveys about nutrition and obesity. The train in *Daughter from Danang* is a reunion between an Amerasian woman and the Vietnamese mother who gave her up for adoption 22 years earlier, but in the telling you learn about social and political history during the last years of the Vietnam War.

An interesting example of a film with a less apparent train is *An Inconvenient Truth*. The film is reportedly built around a PowerPoint presentation developed by former Vice President Al Gore and presented by him to a range of audiences. We see him on a lecture tour, and these speeches (and voice-overs) are intercut with sync and voice-over from a more introspective conversation Gore had with filmmaker Davis Guggenheim about his life, career, and family. The train of this film doesn't come from the subject of global climate change, nor did the filmmakers build a train around any particular lecture tour itinerary. The train builds from Gore's first words, "I used to be the next president of the United States." The personal, introspective essay about Gore drives this film, although in terms of screen time and import, it takes a backseat to the warnings about global warming.

A good exercise is to watch a number of successful documentaries that are very different in subject and style and see if you can identify the train. You also might want to see if, given the same subject and story, you could find another train. How might it change the film's look? Length? Effectiveness?

THEME

In literary terms, *theme* is the general underlying subject of a specific story, a recurring idea that often illuminates an aspect of the human condition.

Eyes on the Prize, in 14 hours, tells an over-arching story of America's civil rights struggle. The underlying themes include race, poverty, and the power of ordinary people to accomplish extraordinary change. Themes in *The Day after Trinity*, the story of J. Robert Oppenheimer's development of the atomic bomb, include scientific ambition, the quest for power, and efforts to ensure peace and disarmament when both may be too late.

The best documentary stories, like memorable literary novels or thought-provoking dramatic features, not only engage the audience with an immediate story—one grounded in plot and character—but with themes that resonate beyond the particulars of the event being told. *Sound and Fury*, for example, is not only about a little girl and her family trying to decide if she should have an operation that might enable her to hear, it's also about universal issues of identity, belonging, and family.

"Theme is the most basic lifeblood of a film," says filmmaker Ric Burns. "Theme tells you the tenor of your story. *This* is what this thing is about." Burns chose to tell the story of the ill-fated Donner Party and their attempt to take a shortcut to California in 1846, not because the cannibalism they resorted to would appeal to prurient viewers but because their story illuminated themes and vulnerabilities in the American character. These themes are foreshadowed in the film's opening quote from Alexis de Tocqueville, a French author who toured the United States in 1831. He wrote of the "feverish ardor" with which Americans pursue prosperity, the "shadowy suspicion that they may not have chosen the shortest route to get it," and the way in which they "cleave to the things of this world," even though death steps in, in the end. These words presage the fate of the Donner Party, whose ambitious pursuit of a new life in California will have tragic consequences.

Themes may emerge from the questions that initially drove the filmmaking. On one level, *My Architect* is about a middle-aged filmmaker's quest to know the father he lost at the age of 11, some

30 years before. But among the film's themes are impermanence and legacy. "You sort of wonder, 'After we're gone, what's left?'" Kahn says in bonus material on the film's DVD. "How much would I really find of my father out there? ... I know there are buildings. But how much emotion, how much is really left? And I think what really kind of shocked me is how many people are still actively engaged in a relationship with him. They talk to him as if he's still here. They think of him every day. In a way I find that very heartening."

ARC

The *arc* refers to the way or ways in which the events of the story transform your characters. An overworked executive learns that his family should come first; a mousy secretary stands up for himself and takes over the company; a rag-tag group of kids that nobody ever notices wins the national chess tournament. In pursuing a goal, the protagonists learn something about themselves and their place in the world, and those lessons change them—and may, in fact, change their desire for the goal.

In documentary films, story arcs can be hard to find. Never, simply in the interest of a good story, presume to know what a character is thinking or feeling. Only present evidence of an arc if it can be substantiated by factual evidence. For example, in *The Day after Trinity*, physicist J. Robert Oppenheimer, a left-leaning intellectual, successfully develops the world's first nuclear weapons and is then horrified by the destructive powers he's helped to unleash. He spends the rest of his life trying to stop the spread of nuclear weapons and in the process falls victim to the Cold War he helped to launch; once hailed as an American hero, he is accused of being a Soviet spy.

In *The Thin Blue Line*, we hear and see multiple versions of a story that begins when Randall Adams's car breaks down on a Saturday night and a teenager named David Harris offers him a ride. Later that night, a police officer is shot and killed by someone driving Harris's car,

and Adams is charged with the murder. The deeper we become immersed in the case, the more clearly we see that Adams's imprisonment and subsequent conviction are about politics, not justice. He is transformed from a free man to a convicted felon, and that transformation challenges the viewer's assumptions about justice and the basic notion that individuals are innocent until proven guilty.

In *Murderball*, a documentary about quadriplegic athletes who compete internationally in wheelchair rugby, a few characters undergo transformations that together complement the overall film. There's Joe Soares, a hard-driving American champion now coaching for Canada, whose relationship with his son changes noticeably after he suffers a heart attack. Player Mark Zupan comes to terms with the friend who was at the wheel during the accident in which he was injured. And Keith Cavill, recently injured, adjusts to his new life and even explores wheelchair rugby. All of these transformations occurred over the course of filming, and the filmmakers made sure they had the visual material they needed to *show* them in a way that felt organic and unforced.

PLOT AND CHARACTER

Films are often described as either plot or character driven. A *character-driven* film is one in which the action of the film emerges from the wants and needs of the characters. In a *plot-driven* film, the characters are secondary to the events that make up the plot. (Many thrillers and action movies are plot driven.) In documentary, both types of films exist, and there is much gray area between them. Errol Morris's *The Thin Blue Line* imitates a plot-driven *noir* thriller in its exploration of the casual encounter that leaves Randall Adams facing the death penalty. Circumstances act *upon* Adams; he doesn't set the plot in motion except inadvertently, when his car breaks down and he accepts a ride from David Harris. In fact, part of the film's power comes from Adams's inability to alter events, even as it becomes apparent that Harris, not Adams, is likely to be the killer.

In contrast, *Daughter from Danang* is driven by the wants of its main character, Heidi Bub, who was born in Vietnam and given up for adoption. Raised in Tennessee and taught to deny her Asian heritage, Bub is now estranged from her adoptive mother. She sets the events of the film in motion when she decides to reunite with her birth mother.

As in these two examples, the difference between plot- and character-driven films can be subtle, and one often has strong elements of the other. The characters in *The Thin Blue Line* are distinct and memorable; the plot in *Daughter from Danang* is strong and takes unexpected turns. It's also true that plenty of memorable documentaries are not "driven" at all in the Hollywood sense. *When the Levees Broke*, a four-hour documentary about New Orleans during and after Hurricane Katrina, generally follows the chronology of events that devastated a city and its people. As described by supervising editor and coproducer Sam Pollard, there is a narrative arc to each hour and to the series. But the complexity of the four-hour film and its interweaving of dozens of individual stories, rather than a select few, differentiate it from a more traditional form of narrative.

Some films present a "slice of life" portrait of people or places. With shorter films, this may be enough, particularly if there is humor involved. *Where Did You Get That Woman?*, for example, offers a portrait of a Chicago washroom attendant, and in the light-hearted *Gefilte Fish*, three generations of women explain how they prepare a traditional holiday dish. (The third generation, the filmmaker, unscrews a jar.) With longer films of this type, there still needs to be some overarching structure. Frederick Wiseman's documentaries are elegantly structured but not "plotted" in the sense that each sequence makes the next one inevitable, but there is usually an organizing principle behind his work,

such as a "year in the life" of an institution. Still other films are driven not by characters or plot but by questions, following an essay-like structure (employed, for example, by Michael Moore in *Fahrenheit 9/11*). Some films merge styles: *Super Size Me* is built around the filmmaker's 30-day McDonald's diet, but to a large extent the film is actually driven by a series of questions, making it an essay. This combination of journey and essay can also be found in Nathaniel Kahn's *My Architect* and Per Saari's *Why He Skied*.

DRAMATIC STORYTELLING

Because *dramatic* storytelling often refers more specifically to character-driven stories, it's worth looking at some of the basic elements that make these stories work. As set out by authors David Howard and Edward Mabley in their book, *The Tools of Screenwriting*, these are:

- The story is about *somebody* with whom we have some empathy.
- This somebody wants *something* very badly.
- This something is difficult—but possible—to do, get, or achieve.
- The story is told for maximum *emotional impact* and *audience participation* in the proceedings.
- The story must come to a *satisfactory ending* (which does not necessarily mean a happy ending).

Although Howard and Mabley's book is directed at dramatic screenwriters, the list is useful for documentary storytellers as well. Your particular film subject or situation might not fit neatly within these parameters, so further explanation follows.

WHO (OR WHAT) THE STORY IS ABOUT

The *somebody* is your protagonist, your hero, the entity whose story is being told. Note that your hero can, in fact, be very "unheroic," and the audience might struggle to empathize with him or her. But the character and/or character's mission should be compelling enough that the audience cares about the outcome. In *The Execution of Wanda Jean*, for example, Liz Garbus offers a sympathetic but unsparing portrait of a woman on death row for murder.

The central character doesn't need to be a person. In Ric Burns's *New York*, a seven-episode history, for example, the city itself is the protagonist, whose fortunes rise and fall and rise over the course of the series. But often, finding a central character through which to tell your story can make an otherwise complex topic more manageable and accessible to viewers. We see this strategy used in *I'll Make Me a World*, a six-hour history of African-American arts in the 20th century. For example, producer Denise Green explores the Black Arts Movement of the 1960s by viewing it through the eyes and experience of Pulitzer Prize–winning poet Gwendolyn Brooks, an established, middle-aged author whose life and work were transformed by her interactions with younger artists who'd been influenced by the call for Black Power.

WHAT THE PROTAGONIST WANTS

The something that somebody wants is also referred to as a goal or an objective. In *Blue Vinyl*, filmmaker Judith Helfand sets out, on camera, to convince her parents to remove the new siding from their home. Note that a filmmaker's on-screen presence doesn't necessarily make him or her the protagonist. In Steven Ascher and Jeanne Jordan's *Troublesome Creek: A Midwestern*, the filmmakers travel to Iowa, where Jeanne's family is working to save their farm from foreclosure. Jeanne is the film's narrator, but the protagonists are her parents, Russel and Mary Jane Jordan. It's their goal—to pay off their debt by auctioning off their belongings—that drives the film's story.

Active versus Passive

Storytellers speak of active versus passive goals and active versus passive heroes. In general, you want a story's goals and heroes to be active, which means that you want your story's protagonist to be in charge of his or her own life: To set a goal and then to go about doing what needs to be done to achieve it. A passive goal is something like this: A secretary wants a raise in order to pay for breast enhancement surgery. She is passively waiting for the raise, hoping someone will notice that her work merits reward. To be active, she would have to do something to ensure that she gets that raise, or she would have to wage a campaign to raise the extra money she needs for the surgery, such as taking a second job. Not all passivity is bad: Randall Adams, locked up on death row, is a passive protagonist because he can't do anything, which is part of what makes the story so compelling. In general, though, you want your protagonist to be active, and you want him or her to have a goal that's worthy. In the example of the secretary, will an audience really care whether or not she gets larger breasts? Probably not. If we had a reason to be sympathetic—she had been disfigured in an accident, for example—maybe we would care, but it's not a very strong goal. Worthy does not mean a goal has to be noble—it doesn't all have to be about ending world hunger or ensuring world peace. It does have to matter enough to be worth committing significant time and resources to. If you only care a little about your protagonists and what they want, your financiers and audience are likely to care not at all.

Difficulty and Tangibility

The something that is wanted—the goal—must be *difficult* to do or achieve. If something is easy, there's no tension, and without tension, there's little incentive for an audience to keep watching. Tension is the feeling we get when issues or events are unresolved, especially when we want them to be resolved. It's what motivates us to demand, "And then what happens? And what happens after *that*?" We need to know, because it makes us uncomfortable *not to* know. Think of a movie thriller in which you're aware, but the heroine is not, that danger lurks in the cellar. As she heads toward the steps, you feel escalating tension because she is walking *toward* danger. If you didn't know that the bad guy was in the basement, she would just be a girl heading down some stairs. Without tension, a story feels flat; you don't care one way or the other about the outcome.

So where do you find the tension? One solution is through conflict, defined as a struggle between opposing forces. In other words, your protagonist is up against someone (often referred to as the *antagonist* or *opponent*) or something (the *opposition*). In Barbara Kopple's *Harlan County, U.S.A.*, for example, striking miners are in conflict with mine owners. In Heidi Ewing and Rachel Grady's *The Boys of Baraka*, the tension comes from knowing that the odds of an education, or even a future that doesn't involve prison or death, are stacked against a group of African-American boys from inner-city Baltimore. When a small group of boys is given an opportunity to attend school in Kenya as a means of getting fast-tracked to better high schools in Baltimore, we want them to succeed and are devastated when things seem to fall apart.

Note that conflict can mean a direct argument between two sides, pro and con (or "he said, she said"). But such an argument can also weaken tension, especially if each side is talking past the other or if individuals in conflict have not been properly established. If the audience goes into an argument caring about the individuals involved, though, it can lead to powerful emotional storytelling. Near the end of *Daughter from Danang*, the joyful reunion between the American adoptee and her Vietnamese family gives way to feelings of anger and betrayal brought on by the family's request for money. The palpable tension the audience feels stems not from taking one side or another in the argument, but from empathy for both sides.

Weather, illness, war, self-doubt, inexperience, hubris—all of these can pose obstacles as your protagonist strives to achieve his or her goal. And just as it can be useful to find an individual (or individuals) through whom to tell a complex story, it can be useful to personify the opposition. Television viewers in the 1960s, for example, at times seemed better able to understand the injustices of southern segregation when reporters focused on the actions of individuals like Birmingham (Alabama) Police Chief Bull Connor, who turned police dogs and fire hoses on young African Americans as they engaged in peaceful protest.

Worthy Opponent

Just as you want your protagonist to have a worthy goal, you want him or her to have a worthy opponent. A common problem for many filmmakers is that they portray opponents as one-dimensional; if their hero is good, the opponent must be bad. In fact, the most memorable opponent is often not the opposite of the hero, but a complement to him or her. In the film *Sound and Fury*, young Heather's parents oppose her wishes for a cochlear implant not out of malice but out of their deep love for her and their strong commitment to the Deaf culture into which they and their daughter were born. Chicago Mayor Richard Daley was a challenging opponent for Dr. Martin Luther King, Jr., in *Eyes on the Prize* specifically because he *wasn't* Bull Connor; Daley was a savvy northern politician with close ties to the national Democratic Party and a supporter of the southern-based civil rights movement. The story of his efforts to impede Dr. King's campaign for open housing in Chicago in 1966 proved effective at underscoring the significant differences between using nonviolence as a strategy against *de jure* segregation in the South and using it against *de facto* segregation in the North.

Note here, and throughout, that you are not in any way *fictionalizing* characters who are real human beings. You are evaluating a situation from the perspective of a storyteller, and working with what is there. If there is no opponent, you can't manufacture one. Mayor Daley, historically speaking, *was* an effective opponent. Had he welcomed

King with open arms and been little more than an inconvenience to the movement, it would have been dishonest to portray him as a significant obstacle.

Remember that the opposition does not have to have a human face. In *The Boys of Baraka*, the goals of the boys, their families, and their supporters are threatened by societal pressures in Baltimore and by political instability in Kenya, which ultimately puts the Baraka program in jeopardy. In *Born into Brothels*, similarly, efforts to save a handful of children are threatened by societal pressures (including not only economic hardship but also the wishes of family members who don't share the filmmakers' commitment to removing children from their unstable homes), and by the fact that the ultimate decision makers, in a few cases, are the children themselves. The audience experiences frustration—and perhaps recognition—as some of these children make choices that in the long run are likely to have significant consequences.

Tangible Goal

Although difficult, the goal should be *possible* to do or achieve, which means that it's best if it's both concrete and realistic. "Fighting racism" or "curing cancer" or "raising awareness of a disease" may all be worthwhile, but none is specific enough to serve as a story objective. Follow your interests, but seek out a specific story that will illuminate it. *The Boys of Baraka* is clearly an indictment of racism and inequality, but it is more specifically the story of a handful of boys and their enrollment in a two-year program at a tiny school in Kenya. *Born into Brothels* illuminates the difficult circumstances facing the children of impoverished sex workers in Calcutta, but the story's goals are more tangible. Initially, we learn that filmmaker Zana Briski, in Calcutta to photograph sex workers, has been drawn to their children. "They wanted to learn how to use the camera," she says in voice-over. "That's when I thought it would be really great to teach them, and to see this world through their eyes." Several

minutes later, a larger but still tangible goal emerges: "They have absolutely no opportunity without education," she says. "The question is, can I find a school—a good school—that will take kids that are children of prostitutes?" This, then, becomes the real goal of the film, one enriched by the children's photography and exposure to broader horizons.

Note also that the goal is not necessarily the most "dramatic" or obvious one. In Kate Davis's *Southern Comfort*, a film about a transgendered male dying of ovarian cancer, Robert Eads's goal is not to find a cure; it's to survive long enough to attend the Southern Comfort Conference in Atlanta, a national gathering of transgendered people, with his girlfriend, Lola, who is also transgendered.

EMOTIONAL IMPACT AND AUDIENCE PARTICIPATION

The concept of telling a story for greatest *emotional impact* and *audience participation* is perhaps the most difficult. It's often described as "show, don't tell," which means that you want to present the evidence or information that allows viewers to experience the story for themselves, anticipating twists and turns and following the story line in a way that's active rather than passive. Too often, films tell us what we're supposed to think through the use of heavy-handed narration, loaded graphics, or a stacked deck of interviews.

Think about the experience of being completely held by a film. You aren't *watching* characters on screen; you're right there with them, bringing the clues you've seen so far to the story as it unfolds. You lose track of time as you try to anticipate what happens next, who will do what, and what will be learned. It's human nature to try to make sense of the events we're confronted with, and it's human nature to enjoy being stumped or surprised. In *Enron: The Smartest Guys in the Room*, you think Enron's hit bottom, that all of the price manipulation has finally caught up with them and they'll be buried in debt—until someone at Enron realizes that there's gold in California's power grid.

Telling a story for emotional impact means that the filmmaker is structuring the story so that the moments of conflict, climax, and resolution—moments of achievement, loss, reversal, etc.—adhere as well as possible to the internal rhythms of storytelling. Audiences expect that the tension in a story will escalate as the story moves toward its conclusion; scenes tend to get shorter, action tighter, the stakes higher. As we get to know the characters and understand their wants and needs, we care more about what happens to them; we become invested in their stories. Much of this structuring takes place in the editing room. But to some extent, it also takes place as you film, and planning for it can make a difference. Knowing that as Heidi Bub got off the airplane in Danang she'd be greeted by a birth mother she hadn't seen in 20 years, what preparations did the filmmakers need to make to be sure they got that moment on film? What might they shoot if they wanted to build up to that moment, either before or after it actually occurred? (They shot an interview with Heidi and filmed her, a "fish out of water," as she spent a bit of time in Vietnam before meeting with her mother.) In the edited film, by the time Heidi sees her mother, we realize (before she does) how fully Americanized she's become and how foreign her family will seem. We also know that the expectations both she and her birth mother have for this meeting are very high.

You want to avoid creating unnecessary drama—turning a perfectly good story into a soap opera. There's no reason to pull in additional details, however sad or frightening, when they aren't relevant. If you're telling the story of a scientist unlocking the genetic code to a certain mental illness, for example, it's not necessarily important that she's also engaged in a custody battle with her former husband, even if this detail seems to spice up the drama or, you hope, make the character more "sympathetic." If the custody battle is influenced by her husband's mental illness and her concerns that the children may have inherited the disease, there is a link that could serve the film well. Otherwise, you risk adding a layer of detail that detracts, rather than adds.

False emotion—hyped-up music and sound effects and narration that warns of danger around every corner—is a common problem, especially on television. As in the story of the boy who cried wolf, at some point it all washes over the viewer like so much noise. If the danger is real, it will have the greatest storytelling impact if it emerges organically from the material.

Story refers generally to what we tell other people using the tools and skills learned in a particular **Major**. Whatever the story, the goal is to motivate the person or people experiencing the story to think, feel, or do something. The story can be written, verbal, aural, visual, tactile, or a combination of all of these. Many people believe that the story, also sometimes known as the script, press release, or news rundown, is the most important part of the message. An argument can be made that if your story is weak, it doesn't matter if you have the best tools, most skilled people, and the biggest budget because the communication message will be lost.

Audience

Generally, the term *Audience* refers to the person or people who experience your story. The audience can be very specific and a group you deliberately try to reach with your particular story. For example, in the Public Relations major, the audience reads a written story in the form of a press release. The press release is sent to traditional news organizations and other outlets. In Broadcast Journalism, audience refers to the people who watch a newscast. In Theatre and Comedy, it's the people who have paid for theatre tickets. In the early days of mass entertainment, for example, in Shakespeare's time, the townspeople watched as his plays were performed. The general concept of an audience hasn't changed much since then, i.e., audiences are still groups of people or even a single person if you're interviewing for a job; but, today, most media content and programming is designed to attract so-called **niche** audiences. A niche audience can still be a large group of people, but these groups might be particularly desirable because of income level, buying habits, race, gender, or ethnicity, for example.

There are other ways to think about an audience. For instance, many Media Studies scholars are interested in what's known as **audience commodification**. This is a fancy way of imagining an audience as a group whose consumption (television viewing, downloading, sharing) of media content serves primarily an economic function. This idea suggests that audiences have monetary value, i.e., the more people who watch the Super Bowl, the more money an advertiser can potentially make on a new shampoo. But if the Super Bowl is a blow-out at half time, and 50 percent less people watch the game after the half-time show, the **television network** has to provide what's called a **make good,** and the advertiser will get its money back or more advertising space on that network at a similar broadcast time. If getting as many people to watch as possible is the main goal of the story, what happens to the media message? A Media Studies scholar would suggest that programming quality suffers, and unique populations like people of color, people in poverty, and children are then stereotyped or not represented at all in mass entertainment. These groups don't have as much money to spend. Programming choices become limited, too. For instance, if you're a transgendered 13-year-old and watch narrow representations of what a 13-year-old should be, let's say as only male or female, then the commercial, music video, TV show, or blog doesn't really represent you at all.

Skill

A well-told story encourages the viewer/audience to think, feel, or do something. In order to tell a good story, the story's creator must have strong **skills**. Skills can take the form of video editing or camera and writing skills, for example. In Communication Studies, skills can take the form of clear, verbal communication of goals or effective use of **rhetoric** and strong public speaking, which often lead to high audience engagement as evidenced in the most recent presidential election. In Public Relations, good skills can take the form of effectively managing a communication crisis within an organization.

Radio and Sound production skills are not just technical, as in knowing how to operate a professional mixing board. DJ's and producers become adept at learning the difference between how loud sounds should be and what sounds go together well. This might seem basic to you, but remember that you aren't born with these skills, they must be taught, learned, remembered, and applied in new situations in which new and exciting media content can be created.

Ethics

The last principle, **ethics**, is, perhaps, the hardest for university students to understand. In the context of this book, ethics refers to how each communication major organizes around unique guiding professional principles and moral choices, often outlined in the form of company rules and regulations and the expected and socially acceptable behaviors from company workers, vendors, artists, and human resource directors. For example, in documentary filmmaking, there are ethical challenges, such as whether you should use someone's on-camera interview if she/he has suddenly decided she/he really doesn't want you to use it but has already signed a **personal release** authorizing you to use the interview.

Below, you'll see how one organization defines ethics in the area of business. This example demonstrates how ethics are defined by using concrete examples that are linked to personal behavior. According to Edward Lowe Foundation:

- Treat your employees well. Pay fair wages, and keep your promises. Act quickly to put an end to any kind of harassment, and show the same high level of respect for all your employees. Payoff: Low turnover, high employee motivation and productivity. Commitment to growing your company.

- Be honest in all business dealings. Pay suppliers the amount agreed upon, and on time. Be fair with customers, not over-charging and not inflating the quality or potential of your products or services. Payoff: A sterling reputation that will help sustain your company even when times are tough.

- Be socially responsible. Don't pollute the environment; recycle when possible. Heed protests of company policy or actions. Give back to the community through charity fund-raising or other worthy causes. Payoff: Goodwill that enhances your reputation as a positive force in the community (Conroy 2016).

Now that you have an understanding of the main foundational principles of the Applied Communication Model, let's review five important learning techniques in *Applied Communication and Practice*. No one can guarantee the final grade you'll earn in your courses, but if you adhere to the following practices religiously, it's a safe bet you'll avoid unnecessary confusion, frustration, and fear about what's expected of you in the classroom and, perhaps, in your future job.

BOOK TIPS AND TRICKS

Tip #1—Read this Book

You'll see in many academic textbooks that an important tip is to read the chapters in the book. The "job" of any academic book is to present you with a set of ideas in each chapter. Many of those ideas will be new and, perhaps, complex, and, most likely, at the end of reading the book and taking notes, attending lectures, and doing the assignments, you'll recognize and understand the important themes that connect all of the book's chapters. Our hope is that you will understand and accept the overall purpose of this book and its personal value to your academic and future professional life.

Ideally, your new knowledge and understanding will lead to improved grades and help you make more informed decisions about what type of communication career you might be interested in pursuing and what type of communication discipline will help you get a leg up. Reading this book is practice for how to approach new information and challenges in communication jobs. You should become familiar with all communication messages whether the message is in the form of a press release, instruction manual, or television script, and you should, *at the very least*, understand the words used to describe the main ideas or arguments in every chapter.

> *The Trick*—Be open minded. Your professor wants you to succeed. Can you imagine a reason why a normal, hard-working person would want you to fail and then be blamed as contributing, at least in part, to your failure? Professional educators don't think like that, so be open minded and trust that the book you've purchased (a) is designed to help you succeed, (b) provides lots of information you don't already know written with the purpose of getting you and your brain excited about learning new things, and (c) if you read the book your chances of being academically successful in the class, especially if you ask questions about topics or information you don't understand, significantly increase. Also, your chances of finding the major best suited for you improve as well.

Tip #2—Attendance is Key

As you've most likely learned, attendance in university and college classes is expected but is not always required. Professors know from good research that class attendance strongly connects with academic success across various disciplines. Attending class and using all the tools available to you, including good note-taking and study skills, is the best recipe. Also, in college and university classrooms, there are many distractions, not just the psychological or emotional distractions you might be experiencing *at the moment*. Certainly, technology— more so than good subject matter or enthusiastic and engaging professors—can strongly influence your desire to study and learn. For instance, some professors argue that it's not a good idea to put lectures online because students don't go to class although there's no research that shows a strong **cause and effect**. Still, academic research does establish that technologies like YouTube, PowerPoint, and online resources might contribute to *lower* attendance in college classes along with other factors (Twenge 2006, 28). Most likely, no one will force you to go to class, but unless you have a photographic memory it will be difficult to succeed, especially in your first year, if you don't attend class and take notes.

> *The Trick*—Memorize this recipe for academic success: **Class Attendance and Study Hard.** That's right, we spelled C.A.S.H. to help you remember. Are we obsessed with money? Of course not, but attending class and studying hard saves *you* money. For example, you won't repeat as many courses because of a failing grade, and you can graduate sooner, thus, saving you (or your parents) even more money! C.A.S.H. also keeps you on track academically, so you don't need to take out more student loans. Finally, C.A.S.H. gets you into the workforce more quickly. More years working mean more time for you to plan and interview for better jobs, move up in the world, and save more for

retirement. Most experts believe Social Security won't provide much income for you upon retirement, so it's best to start planning now.

Tip #3—Time Management and Skills

Right now, it's likely you're in a college or university communication course that's more applied than strictly academic. Remember that an applied communication course is often designed to give you an excellent overview of a particular discipline or, as in the case of this book, an overview of many types of disciplines and how they relate to each other. How can you be academically successful with your work and personal commitments and the demanding requirements in technically challenging courses? Good study skills, note-taking skills, and careful attention to details will help. Managing your time is crucial, and designing a structured plan for your day helps. If you do well in an applied course, it's likely you'll be well prepared for your preferred major classes down the road. You'll also understand your chosen **field** better and how other content areas relate to that field. A side benefit for you, but an important one, is that after reading this book, you'll be better trained to manage and organize lots of information; this is also important when writing a book, making a film, or launching a public relations campaign.

> *The Trick*—Schedule your time so you can easily eliminate distractions and embrace the present moment. As university professors, we're amazed that more students don't have a calendar or write things down. The benefit of having a calendar isn't just that it keeps your appointments and plans straight—a calendar also gives you a reason to say "no" when the unplanned and really awesome distractions come along. When Dr. Crick—one of the authors of this book—was first in college, he claims he wasted inordinate amounts of time. Crick says, "I just listened to music, hung out with friends, and generally sought out every possible distraction even if that distraction wasn't looking for me in the first place. My first year at University, I was put on academic probation, but I knew how to juggle. I didn't manage my time too well."

You also need to have space in your schedule for unplanned and exciting professional and academic opportunities. This means scheduling a certain amount of elasticity in your daily routine. Put another way, you can't have everything scheduled to the very minute; life doesn't work that way. Traffic, arguments with your partner, job and family responsibilities involve *people*. You can't control people. Have a clear weekly plan with built in flexibility and you'll stay on track.

Tip #4—Understanding Course Content

If professional educators knew exactly how to *guarantee* learning every time for every student, there wouldn't be students who fail classes, and everyone would be academically successful. Does that sound like a world we live in? We've had many conversations with colleagues and also people working in the private sector about what students should know when they graduate from a college or university. Everyone agrees there's no single answer or method that will ensure that you understand the material in a specific course, can apply new knowledge and skills effectively or that you'll be great at your job and get promoted. However, concrete things like being on time, being organized, and good communication skills will always rate high in friends, family, and employers' minds. Some parents would like university professors and administrators to certify that their daughter or son will get a job upon graduation. Unfortunately, we can't do that. However, there are some things we can do in the classroom that lead us all in the right direction.

For instance, professors test your knowledge on content they think is important to your professional preparation and academic growth. You're asked to write essays and research papers so that you'll learn how to synthesize different kinds of information and express your ideas in a clear, creative, and convincing argument. Most educators agree that a student who effectively answers an essay question or writes a strong research paper has demonstrated a measurable level of learning. Finally, there is a reliable and proven model upon which many professional educators use to design assignments and **curriculum**. University students, especially those new to college life like you might be benefit from learning about it.

A famous educator, Dr. Benjamin Bloom, developed a hierarchy of learning. When this hierarchy of learning is carefully integrated with course material and assignments, the hierarchy provides a good way to determine whether and what a student has learned. It's called **Bloom's Revised Taxonomy**, and it will help you see what you want to learn, have some sense of whether you've learned it, and also how you learned it. Taxonomy is just a fancy way of saying *a method or system of organizing and labeling concepts*. Figure 1.2 below shows the essential components of Bloom's Revised Taxonomy. Bloom's Revised Taxonomy, as scholars have suggested, isn't an inflexible way of understanding and learning new things, and as you'll see, "the requirement of a strict hierarchy has been relaxed to allow the categories to overlap one another" (Krathwhol 2002, 215). For example, you can *remember* and *understand* new knowledge simultaneously.

The New Version of Bloom's Taxonomy

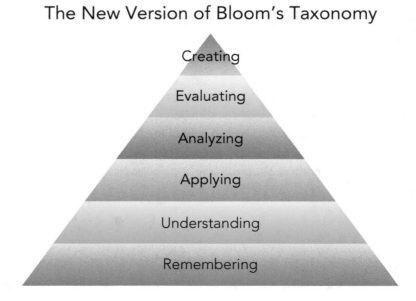

Figure 1.2

Let's take the example of video editing and use Bloom's Revised Taxonomy to understand how a student might learn about video editing. In the *remembering* phase, a student is taught the steps of how to select two points in time on a digital "piece" of video footage and taught how this portion of video is edited. Later, perhaps minutes, hours, or days later, the student should be able to recall the training she/he received.

The *understanding* phase could be achieved and learning would occur if a student could then *apply* the skills of selecting two points in time on a *different* "piece" of video footage based on having been taught those skills days or weeks before. A student and professor would recognize the *analyzing* phase when the student is able to select any point in time on a piece of footage and consider what effect her/his choices might have on the overall meaning of the project's story once those edits are made.

The *evaluating* phase is evident when the student is able to look at **someone else's editing** and make judgments about the effectiveness or how good the pacing is in the edit based on a set of criteria the student has been taught. An example of the *creating* phase using our video editing scenario is when a student is shown the final edited version of a professionally produced commercial and is then given all of the footage that was used in the commercial to create a completely new commercial with a totally different meaning than the original.

You might notice in the previous example that the highest and most complex level of information processing—*creating*—is often the most valued in the communication disciplines and the professional world. Put another way, just knowing the correct steps when using editing software isn't the same thing as being a professional editor charged with telling stories set in the Marvel Universe.

> *The Trick*—Focus on learning well the most common and expected skills in your chosen discipline. This book will help you identify what your professor and your future employers might expect regarding the most desirable skills. Practice those skills and master them because if you don't practice the skills, you won't remember them. If you don't remember the skills, how will you apply them? If you can't apply what you've learned, how will you be able to analyze? Evaluating and creating are impossible without reaching the other levels in Bloom's Revised Taxonomy. Lastly, people who *only* know and understand the skills but haven't mastered them for a specific discipline are often limited financially in the long run and cannot remain competitive in the job market.

Tip #5—Take Care of Yourself

Every student is a unique and special person, but taken as a group in an academic environment we see some commonalities. One theme that comes up each time we teach is the struggle most students experience when trying to balance school, work, and life. Since each student is different, there's no "one size fits all" fix. But when we look at the possible reasons a student might struggle with balance, some reasonable assumptions can be made.

First, when you attend college the first time, everything is new, exciting, maybe frightening, and essentially you're on your own to figure things out. Advisers and professors are available for help, but the assumption is that you'll ask for help when you need it and won't choose to suffer in silence. Also, you have many identities in college: student, friend, lover, child of your parents, etc. Many times, these identities are in conflict, and this causes stress. Poor stress management negatively affects overall balance. As a student, you must make time to relax and take a breather … but not too much. Remember Class Attendance and Study Hard—C.A.S.H.

A second reason for an *out of balance* life while attending a university or college is financial. Weak financial skills and procrastination when dealing with financial realities contribute to poor balance. As a student, a good way to get a handle on your finances is to contact the college or university you're considering attending to speak with the Financial Aid Office. The staff can give you a good idea of how much a semester will cost in terms of classes, books, lodging, and transportation. Then, you should add about 10–15% onto the top of that number! Unless you've lived in a place for at least a year or two, how could you possibly know how much it *actually* costs to live there? The last challenge to college-life balance is philosophical and requires some self-reflection.

In your first year as a university or college student, write down the reasons you're taking classes. Is it because you don't want to disappoint your parents? If so, you're a good son or daughter, but aren't you supposed to be getting something out of the experience as well? Are you in school because there aren't any jobs in your preferred field? Before you claim this common complaint for yourself and shout, "Yes! There aren't jobs!" Ask yourself, "How can talking and thinking like this help me?"

Be honest: why are you in school? No one else can truly answer this question but you. If you're not sure, ask for help from someone you trust. The sooner you figure out what's brought you to higher learning, the sooner you'll find positive life balance and start building your future.

> *The Trick*—Raise the panic flag right away. You, your parents, the state and the federal government, are all paying substantial sums of money for you to attend a university or college. Also, along with your tuition, room, and meal costs, educational institutions spend millions on support services and staff to help you. We've been teaching at the college and university levels for a combined total of over 25 years, and we've spoken, counseled, and helped thousands of students. But there are many more students who ignored what we and other professionals had to say.

We'd like to suggest that you contact the people who can help you immediately when you recognize you've got an issue that needs to be resolved. For example, if you see that you're headed toward a grade lower than a "C" in a class, speak with your professor, your adviser, or a professional counselor in Student Health Services right away. You can't graduate from any accredited educational institution in the United

States with a G.P.A below a 2.0, which is often considered a "C-" by most academic institutions.

Another time to seek help is when you feel overwhelmed or depressed. At times, people get overwhelmed and depressed, and that's expected. However, there is no reason whatsoever for suffering when there are good people to help you through the tough times. An education professional will know how to advise you in this situation and where to send you for the best source of help.

Last, take time out of your daily schedule to relax and reflect on your college life. Ask yourself important questions like "How am I really doing here?" and "What do I really want out of this place?" Take your emotional temperature frequently. Different techniques work for each person. The important thing is to ask for help in the first place.

The rest of this Introduction chapter describes how subsequent book chapters are organized.

HOW IS THIS BOOK ORGANIZED?

Part One and Part Two

Applied Communication and Practice is divided into two sections: Part One and Part Two. Part One contains chapters on Television Production, Film Production, Radio and Sound Production, Citizen Journalism (Digital Journalism), and Broadcast Journalism. Part Two contains chapters on Communication Studies, Public Relations, Journalism, Theatre and Comedy, Media Studies, and the book's conclusion.

Part One of this book, written by Matt Crick, covers valuable technical, aesthetic, and theoretical information useful when creating audio and video messages in a variety of mass media. You'll learn about using specialized equipment and software programs along with the theories and perspectives that guide the creative process. Part Two, written by Kelli Smith, focuses on areas of study that include fewer technical skills and more academic applications. These areas help you understand human behavior in a way that lets you explain, predict, and control the outcomes of your interactions. You will also gain strong communication skills that are useful in all the communication professions.

Chapters

Just like book chapters, other forms of media like videos, blogs, and websites require you to learn and practice specialized ways of organizing information, but all those mediums use different terminology. For example, in long-form television, the organizing term is **episode;** for film and plays, the common term is an **act** as part of a **script;** and in television news, the term is **block or news block.** What's essential here is that you understand that in order to create and fully understand almost every type of media product in the communication disciplines you are required to learn new terms at the levels of story, skills, ethics, and audience. Dr. Crick describes this type of knowledge as "knowing how the sausage is made." And, like how sausage is *really* made, you might not want to know exactly what's involved in the process at this moment, but when you become enlightened, many opportunities you can't imagine will become available.

A couple of unique characteristics that make up the DNA of *Applied Communication and Practice* is that each chapter contains a classroom activity for you and your professor that ties together the chapter's main ideas but can also be easily customized based on classroom demographics, dynamics, and personal taste. Also, throughout the book, we have short interviews with experts in the field called *Interview with a Professional*, designed to give you special insight about how a professional communicator practices her/his particular communication discipline in the world outside your college or university.

Discussion of Each Communication Discipline

Each chapter contains a discussion of how a specific communication discipline–like Communication Studies, Media Production (Television, Film, Radio, and Audio), Media Studies, Theatre, Comedy, Broadcast and Citizen Journalism, and Public Relations–might look in an academic and an applied context. In the Discussion section, we've included first-hand observations and ideas and tried to clarify exactly what is meant when a person uses specific communication terms like "communication studies." Most importantly, we have attempted to connect the core concepts of story, skill, audience, and ethics with the specific communication discipline in each chapter.

The term **discipline**, when used in an academic setting, means a specific kind of knowledge as in "the media studies discipline." Discipline can also refer to special training or skills, and in a college or university, a discipline might also take the form of a major. This term is probably most familiar to you. In the communication field, we have a unique challenge: the word communication in an academic institution can mean talking with someone, writing a script or press release, shooting and editing a video, giving a speech, shaking hands, sending an email, and on and on. As a result, learning about the communication disciplines in this book is complicated. Communication—the broad concept which frames all other types of knowledge and careers we discuss in this book—is itself very broad and incorporates practices and perspectives from fields like Psychology and Anthropology.

Interview with a Professional

Applied Communication and Practice incorporates short interviews with professionals who work in a particular profession currently, in the recent past, or who have been paid for the professional work they've done. The *Interview with a Professional* sections are invaluable for students interested in employment or advanced academic opportunities. As you might guess, there are countless careers available in all of the communication disciplines, and it would be impossible to interview professionals who represent every possible career. Still, each candid interview provides an excellent window into the world of the communication professional.

Below is an interview with a social media professional.
Interviewed by Matt Crick, Spring, 2017.

Sam DeMuro, M.A., is an educator interested in social change through storytelling. She has worked as a communications professional, educator, counselor, and LGBTQ youth advocate in higher education, nonprofit, and public health settings for the past 10+ years. Her academic background and research have focused on LGBTQ youth and women in film/TV and identity politics, including the use of social media as community building. She holds an M.A. in Gender/ Cultural Studies and a B.A. in Women's Studies and Psychology and currently manages social media and digital communication for educators in California's public schools and colleges.

Why are good communication skills important in your field?

I like to tell people, we cannot forget about the "social" part of social media. While much of a social media manager's work can be done from behind a phone or computer, face-to-face conversations and connections are still incredibly important to be effective. Many of my strongest connections on social media have come from communicating with someone in person and then extending our relationship online.

It is also very important to be able to identify your audience and then shape your communication strategy based on it. Being able to communicate a message clearly and succinctly (sometimes in 140 characters!) is not only important to ensure the social media platform is used correctly but to also get your message across to a targeted audience.

What specific skills do you use the most?

The skill I use the most, and probably the most underrated skill, is curation. While social media managers do create a lot of their own unique content, much of our job is taking something that is already created and then repurposing, shaping, and adding context or perspective to a piece of content. Editing a great video, retweeting, adding text to a photo, or figuring out a way to tweet out something again but from another angle are all examples of how I might curate content daily.

Writing, of course, is incredibly important. Social media allows for creative writing as well as journalistic styles.

In terms of PR and Marketing, what skills do you find lacking in others?

Humor. While humor can be tricky and relative, when it's done well, it's what makes social media so special. If a social media manager can capture something that is happening in pop culture and then connect it to her/his brand/product/ service, it relates to people on a human level. Pop culture can be looked down upon in some intellectual circles, but for a social media manager, it's important to have a pulse on what's happening in the world around us to be relevant.

How have the knowledge or skills you gained at a college or university been useful to you in terms of your career?

College taught me how to critically think about the world around me. I was lucky to have excellent professors and writers who pushed me to examine myself and question everything. As I learned about social justice issues, it helped me find myself, gain language to talk about identity, and helped me have more compassion and interest in others.

What advice would you give to Communication majors? Pitfalls to avoid, that sort of thing.

Take some time in college to get to know yourself. Communication, at times, can feel like this broad thing that can be applied to many fields. Learn about what your passions and interests are. I truly feel that anyone can learn social media skills, but it's important to spend time learning about a particular field or interest. For instance, even though I could do social media at many different companies or organizations, I know I would have a really hard time managing social media for a bank or a pharmaceutical company because I am not interested in those fields. For me, realizing I was passionate about social justice issues first, helped me decide the kind of places I wanted to work and put my skills to use. Never stop asking questions!

Thinking back on your career choices, what decision are you most proud of?

I'm most proud of the work I've done with young people and college students. Students are changing the world, and I'm learning so much from them every day. I try to give back to my students I've worked with over the years. They've taught me so much, and the least I can do is write a letter of recommendation, give job advice, check in, and be a mentor.

Conclusion

At the end of each chapter, a *conclusion* section offers a recap of that chapter's content and sums up the chapter's main ideas points.

In this Introduction chapter, we've tried to give you an overview of the book's content, purpose, value, and practical use. We've also provided a foundational model known as the Applied Communication Model, which links all the main communication disciplines and also explains how professional communication careers and their related academic twins connect.

We've also provided some practical tips for you that relate to overall success in a college or university and explained the landscape of this book in conceptual and practical ways. Finally, we've told you stories about our own experiences, experiences with our students, and most importantly tried to imagine the best way to communicate with you so that you will think, feel, and do something after reading a chapter.

KEY TERMS

Throughout each chapter, you'll find a set of key words and terms that are useful in understanding the content of a specific chapter. Key words and terms will be in **bold type**. At the end of each chapter, there will be a list of definitions called Key Terms. You can also find the words and terms in the book's **Index** and corresponding page numbers in which they're used.

Classroom Activities

Each chapter includes a classroom activity for you and your professor that relates to the content of a specific chapter. Below you'll find this chapter's classroom activity.

CLASSROOM ACTIVITY

Imagine a time before you started college or university. What were the activities and experiences you enjoyed the most? Did you need training or special knowledge to participate in the activity or experience?

1   Pick three activities or experiences you enjoyed before you came to college or university.
    Write down those activities in as much detail as you like.

2   For no more than 20 minutes, in groups of no more than three, each person then shares her/his three activities and experiences.

3   Each person writes down one question for someone else in the group which relates to what was shared.

4   After 20 minutes, the entire group decides which communication discipline(s) most easily could be a career based on the group members' activities and experiences.

5   The group elects one person to present the group's decision to the entire class.

KEY TERMS

Academic—a general term that is meant to include all coursework having to do with intellectual study at a college or university. This word is also used to describe a person who creates and shares information in a particular discipline, like a communication professor. Academic knowledge is often formalized in ways specific to a discipline and realized using formal methods of evaluating and critiquing.

Act—part of a written script that has traditional functions like establishing the characters and the tension between them. A well-written act advances the overall story and engages the reader. In Western cultures, a typical script has three main acts.

Analyze—an intellectual skill that privileges heavy use of logic, constructive criticism, and careful questioning in order to solve a problem or understand phenomena.

Applied Communication Model—a set of concepts that when practiced in personal and professional communication contexts establish strong connections between the communicator and the message being created and subsequently how effectively the intended message is interpreted.

Applied—this term refers to coursework and information typically offered at a college or university that has practical use outside of an academic environment. Applied communication often takes the form of a set of specific skills rather than a theory. Professional communicators use applied skills in the creation of particular communication messages typical in their field.

Audience—a concept in the Applied Communication Model. Audience refers to a group of people experiencing a particular communication message. There is a specific audience for every message professional communicators create.

Audience Commodification—describes an audience as a group that should be treated as consumers that have monetary value. This strict view of an audience presupposes that content should be created to attract the greatest audience and, therefore, make the most money for the media creator.

Binary Thinking—a system of thought that encourages imagining and talking about an idea, a person, a communication message, or an audience in terms of "either/or," "good/bad," "right/wrong." This system of thought ignores all other possibilities and solutions for communication problems and is typically considered an inefficient, simplistic, and exclusionary form of thought, especially at a college or university.

Block—refers to content created for broadcast television shows. A block is written content that contains a variety of information including information about prerecorded content, commercials, and script content. There are different types of blocks, depending on the show genre.

Bloom's Revised Taxonomy—a learning hierarchy developed by Dr. Benjamin Bloom widely used by professional educators.

Cause and Effect—also known as *causation*. *Cause and effect* is a way of thinking and is used to explain why people behave in certain ways. For example, some people believe the fact that you have a mobile phone causes you to text during class even when listening to an exciting lecture; the effect of texting is lower levels of student engagement during lectures leading to lower academic performance. In scholarly research, a cause and effect relationship requires high-levels of statistical analysis, scientific evidence, and multiple experimental testing.

Class Attendance Study Hard (C.A.S.H.)—an acronym for college and university students that describes key elements of academic success.

Communication—when written as *Communication* with a capital "C," this word refers to the broad, academic study of the various disciplines associated with it and describes entire scholarly programs of study in colleges and universities.

Concrete—when used comparatively, this word denotes something that exists in the physical world rather than an idea in someone's mind. For instance, a *kiss* is, often times, the concrete expression of the abstract concept of *love*.

Cultural Studies—a theory-based academic field of study that emphasizes how cultural products, especially media, influence audiences and serve to reinforce stereotypes and negative representations of those groups with less political and economic power. At the same time, cultural studies propose that cultural products are designed specifically to keep certain privileged groups in power.

Curriculum—the structure of academic courses in a particular degree program. A good curriculum evolves with the culture and sets forth an achievable academic plan and path to graduation for college and university students.

Depth of Field—describes the distance *between* the foreground and background of a camera's image where the image is in *sharp focus*.

Discipline—used to describe specific academic and professional branches of knowledge and practice in Communication.

Ethics—a concept in the Applied Communication Model. Ethics are a set of principles and practices used in a variety of communication contexts designed to encourage decisions which lead to desirable communication outcomes. Relates to the guiding principles that govern communication professions. For example, ethics often take the form of company rules and regulations whose purpose is to ensure fairness, honest business dealings, and social responsibility.

Evaluate—evaluating occurs when you experience a communication message and determine the meaning of the message for yourself using a variety of skills and your five senses.

Episode—a clearly defined story that can be created in a variety of forms and uses various technologies. An episode is part of a longer series and typically follows characters as they solve problems, experience life, and create relationships. Since the widespread development, use, and distribution of streaming content through services like Netflix and Amazon Video, there is no limit to the length of a single episode. This is not the case in broadcast television because there are commercials throughout the episode.

Field—another term for a communication discipline.

Index—contains page numbers where relevant words, phrases, and terms in a book appear. The Index is in the back of the book.

Major—the common term for a specific academic discipline as in *Public Relations major*. However, at many colleges and universities, Communication is considered a broad discipline in which students work toward a general communication major with specialization in media production, communication studies, broadcast journalism, etc.

Make Good—occurs when a television, film, print, or other content distributor makes an error in the design, delivery, or timing of an advertiser's commercial and must rerun the commercial or compensate the advertiser due to the error.

News Block—a specific type of written content in block form used only in television news.

Niche—refers to a narrow audience that has an interest in specific types of programs. As of 2018, we are in an age of niche programming rather than strictly a mass programming broadcast model.

Personal Release—a legally binding and written document that on and off-camera participants sign for producers and production companies. The personal release shields media content creators from potential lawsuits and represents formal approval to use a person's voice and image for the stated purpose.

Political Power—in the context of this book, political power refers to how specific cultural groups are portrayed in the media and whether the audience perception of that portrayal empowers that cultural group or strips power from them. Many scholars believe television in the 1970s was responsible for some of the most stereotyped representations of people of color, particularly in crime dramas, and that some of these stereotypes still exist today and are perpetuated by the mainstream media.

ProTools—professional audio production software used for editing the sound portion of a media message.

Rhetoric—the art and craft of effective public speaking which employs specific oratorical techniques in order to achieve high audience engagement.

Script—the formal, guiding written document from which a complete film, series, presentation, plays, and performance is created.

(SFX)—common initials used to describe *special effects* used when writing a script.

Skill—a concept in the Applied Communication Model. Skill refers to specific abilities and techniques that accomplish certain communication goals. In the communication disciplines, skill often manifests as technical in nature but not always. Sometimes, skill appears as *natural*, like being a good public speaker when, in fact, it's the result of years of specific training.

Story—a concept in the Applied Communication Model. Story also refers to the traditional way of constructing a narrative and has at the basic level, a beginning, middle, and an end, like in a feature film. Story can also be your way of conveying your history, i.e., the events you've witnessed, the people you've met, and the lessons you've learned. Generally speaking, *story* refers to a logical, organized method of communicating information that will often have creative elements.

Television Network—this phrase refers to a connected group of television broadcast stations across the United States. A television network is designated by three letters (i.e., ABC, FOX, NBC, CBS) and are typically headquartered in large cities like New York, Chicago, and Los Angeles, where programming decisions, content creation, and administrative decisions are made that affect all of the television stations that are part of network. Typically, the network provides programs to its affiliate television stations, and those stations broadcast the content.

Theories—are systems of thought designed to explain cultural phenomena and influences. Theories are often structured using observations that somehow relate to the phenomena. For example, building a theory around the observation that music videos often represent men and women stereotypically, despite more balanced gender representations in everyday culture, would require the examination of music videos themselves. Theories are abstract rather than concrete.

REFERENCES

Alexander, Victoria, and Richard Edward Hicks. 2014. *Does Class Attendance Predict Academic Performance in First Year Psychology Tutorials?* School of Psychology, Bond University, Gold Coast, Queensland, Australia.

Bernard, S. C. 2007. *Story Basics.* Documentary storytelling: making stronger and more dramatic nonfiction films. Waltham: Focal Press.

Conroy, K. 2016. Why You Need Good Business Ethics. Retrieved on February 13, 2016. from http://edwardlowe.org/why-you-need-good-business-ethics/.

Franek, Rob. 2016. Top 10 College Majors. Retrieved on March 1, 2017, from https://www.princetonreview.com/college-advice/top-ten-college-majors.

Krathwohl, D. R. 2002. "A revision of Bloom's taxonomy: An overview." *Theory into practice*, 41 (4): 212–218.

Twenge, J. M. 2006. Generation me: Why today's young Americans are more confident, assertive, entitled—and more miserable than ever before. New York: Free Press.

Watson, J. A., and L. L. Pecchioni. 2011. "Digital natives and digital media in the college classroom: assignment design and impacts on student learning." Educational Media International 48 (4): 307–320. doi:10.1080/09523987.2011.632278.

PART
ONE

INTRODUCTION
BY MATTHEW CRICK

pplied Communication and Practice is an effort to connect several communication disciplines with the Applied Communication Model's core principles—story, ethics, skills, and audience. However, the book is also a combination of different sets of teaching, research, and writing styles. This approach isn't a completely new way to write a book, but it does require brief explanation.

For Part One, my goal was to provide information that reflects my experience with a wide variety of professional media and communication environments. My hope is that I've written Part One in a way that gives you a unique insight into how the communication industries function and the types of jobs available. That said, I chose to include and write about specific areas of each communication discipline and left other areas out. I selected content that would be easily understood, applicable in the communication industries, most interesting and timely, and areas with which I have personal and professional experience.

I selected what I believe are accessible readings, but they aren't necessarily easy readings. Part One's discussion questions provide overall context for the chapter and are linked to the readings. Finally, I tried to create interesting classroom activities that reflect the chapter content and encourage practical application of core communication concepts. The chapter activities come from my own teaching experiences, but a few of my colleagues were kind enough to let me adapt some of their own ideas in the spirit of collaboration.

CHAPTER 2

Television Production—Tools and Practice

INTRODUCTION

It's important to keep in mind that the word **television** has multiple uses and meanings. The word *television* most often refers to a distribution technology, which is connected through access points called **television stations.** TV stations are located all around the country, and stations broadcast programming—transmitted electronically—to your home through **cable, satellite,** or **over the air** (OTA). For the purposes of this chapter, the word television is used to describe the distribution network over which content is delivered and also to describe a set of specific creative tools and technologies, like studio cameras and television control rooms. Television distribution and television programming are deeply integrated into our everyday lives and not only reflect what's happening currently but also the history of television itself.

Key Components of Television

Between 1948 and 1950, television set ownership increased from one percent to 50 percent (Campbell, Martin, and Fabos 2014) and, today, televisions are in over 90 percent of the households, making it a very powerful medium. There are many reasons why television is considered a **mass medium** but two major reasons are (1) specialized and ubiquitous technology is used to distribute television and (2) the programming that airs on television is equally widespread. If we take a look at television distribution and television programming, arguably barely scratching the surface, we get a glimpse into the television's structure and purpose.

Distribution

You'll recall that television can be distributed in a variety of ways—cable, OTA, streaming, etc. Regardless of how the television broadcast enters a household, the number of households that a television program can reach is *economically* important. The numbers of households watching a TV show is critical because networks use that number to determine how much advertisers who place ads during the show should be charged.

Television networks use the **Nielsen** company's audience data—collected from millions of paper television diaries and **people meters** to aggregate and measure viewing habits (Nielsen 2017)—and this helps networks determine market value for the programs you watch. Distribution has always been a key component of television broadcasts from the early days of television sets, which viewers actually "tuned" to a specific TV channel by getting up off the couch and turning the knob on the front of the TV. Life improved dramatically, at least in some ways, when the TV remote channel changer was introduced.

Regarding TV distribution, cable television provider Time Warner, now Spectrum, recently introduced technology that will measure viewer choices by inserting advertisements during *live* television broadcasts and measuring viewer habits when they use the TWC TV app (Poggi 2016). This deliberate integration of a traditional form of content delivery (cable) and new user driven technology (mobile phone apps) demonstrates how influential and technologically advanced mobile and wireless technology have become. However, it wasn't always this way.

In the early 2000s, several wireless industry titans, like Sprint and Verizon, made clips from television shows available to subscribers (Dawson 2012) in an effort to create new revenue streams and sell more advertising. Most agree this experiment didn't work too well early on and created confusion, what scholar Rick Altman called a "crisis of identity" between mobile and television (Altman 2007). Consumers, advertisers, and TV network sales people were confused, too. But that changed, and over a decade later, streamed content from ABC, CBS, NBC, FOX is common and **monetized**. We now have many more programs, a lot of it from decades past, available to view anywhere and at anytime, using a variety of technologies and distribution methods.

TV Programming

Television programming is constantly changing based on cultural influences, economic demands, new technology, and regulatory concerns. Broadcast television has a rich history of creating programming content. The 1970's were a particularly unique time for TV dramas; for instance, shows like *Roots* and *Little House on the Prairie* reflected a strong interest in depicting American history and a desire to recapture the "truth" of what America was really like (Rymsza-Pawlowska 2014). Of course, television is only presenting us with one version of what life is like. Still, production values, writing, and acting were regarded as exceptional in *Roots* and *Little House*; these two shows attracted millions of viewers at a time when there were only three television networks: ABC, NBC, and CBS.

Another popular television programming format is the **sitcom**, or the situation comedy. A common storyline for sitcoms is family life, and this is true today with the show *The Middle* and was true in the 1980s and late 1990s when *Roseanne* was popular. While these two shows are family sitcoms, they're structure is very different and reflects unique economic and cultural realities that are historically situated. ABC's original *Roseanne* (not the recently canceled 2018 version) was about a working class family struggling together, relatively happy but not rich. The lead character, Roseanne Barr, was the center of the show's storyline, the show was named after her, and she was seeking to balance her work and life. On the other hand, ABC's *The Middle*, currently programmed on Tuesday nights, focuses on geographic location, material wealth, and a resignation from the lead character "Frankie" that things might get better but probably not (Grabowski 2014). *The Middle* is, for better or worse, a reflection of current anxieties, trends, and struggles in American life.

TELEVISION PRODUCTION AND THE APPLIED COMMUNICATION MODEL

Television has changed dramatically since the first broadcast transmission, especially in terms of audience viewing habits. For instance, as a millennial, it's likely you don't watch much traditional broadcast television, i.e., programming that appears on a specific day and time on a broadcast **network** like ABC, CBS, Fox, or NBC. Seventy-eight percent of so-called "On Their Own" millennials—those people who live on their own with no children—access an online streaming service like Netflix or Hulu (Nielsen 2015, Q4). Millennials comprise a coveted **demographic** of 18–34-year-olds. Typically, this group spends more money on products like deodorant, beer, and snacks. Broadcast television networks rely on advertising as a main source of revenue, and in the past, 18–34-year-olds watched lots of television commercials. However, current research shows that many 18–34-year-olds don't watch regular broadcast television, thus, TV advertising revenue has diminished. Advertisers spend less money for television ads because the prize audience just isn't there every night watching television commercials.

Television Tools

Audience viewing habits have significantly influenced how content for television is created and the tools that are used. For instance, more than ever, television networks rely on so-called *event* television like sporting events or entertainment programs which draw large audiences for advertisers and more money for the network. Programs like the Super Bowl and the Oscars are designed and created using television production tools including several cameras and control rooms. Author Jeremy Butler describes utilizing many cameras as a "mode of production" called **multiple-camera production**. In the following reading, Butler sets forth the common tools and practices used when telling stories for broadcast on television, explains the primary stages of production, and highlights the two main forms of television production: single and multicamera production.

AN INTRODUCTION TO TELEVISION STYLE: MODES OF PRODUCTION

by Jeremy G. Butler

In order to investigate why television programs look and sound the way they do, we must understand the process by which they are made. Throughout this [reading], we emphasize the close analysis of the television text. We use detailed descriptions of plot points, camera angles, dialogue, lighting, set design, and so on to argue for certain interpretations of that text. And when talking about elements of visual and sound style we must often, one might say, *reverse engineer* the text.[1] We must make assumptions about how a text was assembled in order to better disassemble it. You may notice that we don't often guess at the intentions of the people who made a television text while we do this disassembly. We avoid those guesses on purpose, because it is extremely difficult to know with any certainty, for example, what director Pamela Fryman was thinking on the set on the day she decided to zoom out to capture some action instead of cutting to a wider shot.[2] And yet, we must know some fundamental things about the production practices of the television industry in order to know that camera zooming is even possible. (It wasn't possible when television first began to flourish in the 1940s.) If we see objects within the camera frame begin to shrink in size, we "reverse engineer" what we see on the screen and identify it as the camera zooming out.

Fundamental to understanding the TV industry's production practices is the concept of **mode of production**. A mode of television production is an *aesthetic* style of shooting that often relies upon a particular *technology* and is governed by certain *economic* systems. Television production forever blends aesthetics, technology, and economics—resulting in conventionalized practices for the actual making of

TV. Television's mode of production is influenced by standards of "good" television (aesthetics), by the available camera, sound and editing equipment (technology), and by budgets (economics)—along with other factors such as governmental policies and laws and network standards.

In the US, television programs are created according to the "rules" of two predominant modes of production: **single-camera** and **multiple-camera** (also known as **multi-camera**). In its purest form, a single-camera production is filmed with just one camera operating at a time. The shots are not recorded in the order in which they will appear in the final product, but instead are shot in the sequence that will most efficiently get the production done on time and under budget. Consider, for example, a scene composed of shots alternating between two characters named Eugene and Lydia. Shots 1, 3, 5, 7, and 9 are of Eugene and shots 2, 4, 6, 8, and 10 are of Lydia. The single-camera approach to this scene would be to set up the lighting on Eugene, get the camera positioned, and then shoot the odd-numbered shots one after another. Then Lydia's lighting would be set up and the camera would shoot all the even-numbered shots of her. Later, the shots would be edited into their proper order.

Multiple-camera productions have two or more cameras trained on the set while the scene is acted out. In our hypothetical 10-shot scene, one camera would be pointed at Eugene, while the other would simultaneously be pointed at Lydia. The scene could be edited while it transpires or it could be cut later, depending on time constraints. Sequences in daily soap operas, talk shows, and game shows may be edited while they are shot, but weekly sitcoms tend to be edited after shooting.

These modes of production are more than just a matter of how many cameras the videographer/cinematographer brings to the set. They define two distinct approaches, whose differences cut through

- **pre-production**: the written planning for the shoot;
- **production**: the shoot itself;
- **post-production** (often simply called "post"): everything afterward, including editing and sound design.

In this [reading], we will briefly cover these three phases and detail significant aspects of pre-production.

Historically, the single-camera mode of production came first. It developed initially in the cinema and has remained the preeminent way of making theatrical motion pictures. On television, it is the main mode used to create prime-time dramas, music videos, and nationally telecast commercials. As it is also the site for the development of most production practices, we will begin our discussion there. Subsequently we will consider the multiple-camera mode of production, which dominated television production when it first evolved as a mass medium in the 1940s. Sitcoms, soap operas, game shows, sports programs, and newscasts are shot using several cameras at once. Although multiple-camera shooting has developed its own conventions, its underlying premises are still rooted in certain single-camera concepts.

Before discussing the particulars of these modes of production, it should be noted that the choice of single-camera or multiple-camera mode is separate from that of the recording medium (film or video). Up until the 2000s, most single-camera productions were shot on film and not on video, but high-definition, digital video (DV) has since come to replace film on many single-camera productions. An early, notable convert to DV was George Lucas, who shot *Star Wars: Episode II—Attack of the Clones* (2002) in that format while most of Hollywood was still committed to shooting on film. Multiple-camera productions are also not tied to one specific format. They have a long history of being shot on both film and video. Regardless of whether single-camera or multiple-camera productions originate on film or video, virtually all post-production editing is now done on a computer, in a digital format. As we shall see, these modes of production are not determined by their technological underpinning—although that is certainly a consideration. Rather, they depend as much on certain economic and aesthetic principles as they do on technology.

SINGLE-CAMERA MODE OF PRODUCTION

Initially it might seem that single-camera production is a cumbersome, lengthy, and expensive way to create television images, and that television producers would shy away from it for those reasons. But television is not a machine driven solely by the profit motive. When analyzing television, we must be wary of slipping into an economic determinism. We must avoid the mistaken belief that television producers' aesthetic decisions and technological choices will always be determined by economic imperatives, that it's always "all about the money." In a study of how and why the Hollywood film industry adopted the single-camera mode of production, David Bordwell, Janet Staiger, and Kristin Thompson contend that technological change has three basic explanations:

1 Production efficiency: does this innovation allow films to be made more quickly or more cheaply?

2 Product differentiation: does this innovation help distinguish this film from other, similar films, and thus make it more attractive to the consumer?

3 Standards of quality: does this innovation fit a conventionalized aesthetic sense of how the medium should "evolve"? Does it adhere to a specific sense of "progress" or improvement?[3]

Although single-camera production is more expensive and less efficient than multiple-camera, it compensates for its inefficiency by providing greater product differentiation and adhering to conventionalized aesthetic standards. Because single-camera mode offers more control over the image and the editing, it allows the **director**, the person in charge on the set, to maximize the impact of every single image. Consequently, it is the mode of choice for short television pieces such as commercials and music videos, which rely upon their visuals to communicate as powerfully as possible. Commercials in particular need a distinctive style to distinguish them from surrounding messages that compete for our attention.

STAGES OF PRODUCTION
Pre-production

To make single-camera production economically feasible, there must be extensive pre-production planning. Chance events and improvisation would be expensive distractions. The organization of any single-camera production—whether an NBC sitcom episode or a Pepsi commercial—begins with a **script** or **screenplay**. Preparation of single-camera television typically evolves through four revisions or drafts of the script: the writer's draft, table draft, network draft, and production draft. Examining each stage of the revision process illuminates how much of the work done in pre-production determines what happens during shooting and post-production. In other words, *pre-production* scripting is where the *production* work and the *post-production* editing of scenes are originally conceptualized. If writers, directors, and producers don't plan to shoot a specific shot, there will be nothing for the camera operator to shoot or the editor to cut! Moreover, a consideration of script revision also shows the fundamentally collaborative nature of television production.

The writer's draft is the initial version of the script, prepared by a scriptwriter, or, as is the case in many comedy shows, assembled by a team of scriptwriters. This rough draft is worked over by the director and producers in order to prepare the table draft. In comedies, a "table reading" is conducted where the cast and key creative members of the crew, along with network executives, literally sit around a table and read through the table draft. (Dramas often skip this step.) From this quasi-performance, the creative personnel get a sense of what will get laughs and what won't. And the network executives are introduced to the material so that they can then give their "notes" to the writers and director. The notes are incorporated by the writers into a network draft, which the executives approve. Finally, the writers and director do yet another tweak of the script to prepare it for actual shooting—resulting in the production draft or **shooting script**. Further revisions might yet be made during shooting, with additional pages (in different colors) inserted into the production draft. In order to ensure consistency through all these drafts, each step of the revision process is overseen by the **showrunner**, the producer responsible for the actual creation of individual episodes. In television, showrunning producers wield much more clout than directors. In fact, many showrunners come to producing through writing and not directing—although they may wind up directing eventually. Some examples of showrunners who established themselves as scriptwriters first include Shonda Rhimes (*Grey's Anatomy*), David Chase (*The Sopranos*), Amy Sherman-Palladino (*Gilmore Girls*), Matthew Weiner (*Mad Men*), and Joss Whedon (*Buffy the Vampire Slayer*).

```
EXT. SUBURBAN STREET - DAY

We're DRIVING down a tree-lined suburban street. We finally
stop at a well-kept UPPER MIDDLE CLASS house complete with
white picket fence.

                    MARY ALICE (V.O.)
          My name is Mary Alice Scott. When you
          read this morning's paper you may
          come across an article about the
          unusual day I had last week.

CLOSE-UP - MARY ALICE SCOTT

The camera pulls back to reveal an ATTRACTIVE WOMAN IN HER
EARLY 30'S wearing gardening gloves, emerging from the house.
She crosses to the flower bed and begins pruning.
```

Figure 2.1 Marc Cherry's script for the *Desperate Housewives* pilot indicates setting and dialogue in a strict format.

Each episode goes through this four-script process, with the significant exception of a series' debut episode or **pilot**. In today's television industry, broadcast and cable networks do not develop pilots with their own production personnel. It's not like the old days in the Hollywood movie industry where writers were on staff to a studio like Warner Brothers and cranked out movie ideas all day long. Instead, independent writers and producers—freelancers, one might say—verbally present or **pitch** their series ideas to networks. If a network is sold on a pitch, it will request a **treatment** from the writer who pitched it. If this four- to five-page overview of an episode is approved by a network, then it will commission a pilot script. Such a script is used to persuade network executives to actually record a pilot episode. And then, finally, if the pilot episode is deemed a success by the network, it will commit to an order of several episodes, but not necessarily an entire season of shows. For example, NBC initially ordered only five episodes of *The Office*. Figure 2.1 shows an excerpt of the pilot script that Marc Cherry wrote for *Desperate Housewives* (aired on October 3, 2004), which led to ABC shooting the pilot and ordering episodes from his production company. Thus, pitches, treatments, and pilot scripts are part of what one might call the *pre*-pre-production phase of a television program's life.

Commercials, animation, music videos, and other visually complicated, single-camera television productions will take the pre-production planning one step further and create **storyboards**, which consist of drawings of images for each shot or of several images for complicated shots (Figure 2.2). Storyboards indicate the precision with which some directors conceptualize their visual design ahead of time. Alfred Hitchcock, for example, was well known for devising elaborate storyboards. For him, the filmmaking process itself was simply a matter of creating those images on film. Similarly, when director Ken Kwapis was preparing to shoot *ER* (1994–2009) episodes, he created shot lists to account for each shot in every scene:

1   EXTREME LOW ANGLE/WIDE on Benton & Carter (in wheelchair). CAMERA LEADS them down the hall. O.S. wheel gets stuck in door.

2   REVERSE CLOSE on Carter/OTS Benton. Conversation about Benton's dating m.o.

3   INSERT Wheel jammed in door.

4   WIDE on Carter & Benton, from inside Recovery Room. Carter snaps. Benton frees the wheelchair, pulls him into the room and sits on the bed. ARC to MEDIUM WIDE 50/50 Carter & Benton.

1. Car speeds recklessly down a tree-lined road.

2. Woman and man in front seat. He drives.

3. The road; his point of view.

4. Front seat, same scene as in #2.

5. Woman looks toward man.

6. Her hand reaches for wheel.

Figure 2.2 During the planning of a television program, a storyboard may indicate the framing and composition of individual shots.

Storyboards and shot lists show how single-camera productions are, in a sense, pre-edited during the pre-production stage. Even before a single shot is captured, the basic editing of the episode has been conceived.

Production

In this mode of production, a single camera is typically used on the set and the shots are done out of order (although there are exceptions to this). Actors typically rehearse their scenes in entirety, but the filming is disjointed and filled with stops and starts. Because the final product is assembled from all these fragments, a **continuity person** must keep track of all the details from one shot to the next—for example, in which hand the actor was holding a cigarette and how far down the cigarette had burned. Nonetheless, small errors do sneak through, illustrating just how disjointed the whole process is. For instance, in Figure 2.3, a frame enlargement from a *Northern Exposure* (1990–95) scene, there is a dishrag is on actor Janine Turner's shoulder. At the very beginning of the next shot, Figures 2.4 and 2.5, the dishrag has disappeared.

Figure 2.3 *Northern Exposure*: A match cut starts with Maggie beginning to sit down ...

Figure 2.4 ... and then continuing to sit (due to a continuity error, she has lost the dishrag that was on her shoulder) ...

Figure 2.5 ... settling into a medium closeup. The change in camera angle helps to make the continuity error less noticeable to the viewer.

The "production" stage of making television is under the immediate control of directors. They approve the lighting and set design, coach the actors, and choose the camera angles. Most television directors do not create the scripts they direct (which is done in pre-production), and most do not have total control over the editing (post-production). However, the actual recording process (the production phase) is their direct responsibility.

Post-production

The task of the technicians in post-production is to form the disjointed fragments into a unified whole. Ideally the parts will fit together so well that we will not even notice the seams joining them. The editor consults with the director and producers to cut the shots together. Once the editing of the image has been finalized or "locked" in narrative production, the **sound editor** and **musical director** are called upon to further smooth over the cuts between shots with music, dubbed-in dialogue, and sound effects. Of course, in music videos and many commercials the music provides the piece's main unifying force and is developed well before the visuals. Indeed, the music determines the visuals in those cases, not vice versa, and becomes part of the pre-production planning.

MULTIPLE-CAMERA MODE OF PRODUCTION

Although a good deal of what we see on television has been produced using single-camera production, it would be wrong to assume that this mode dominates TV in the same way that it dominates theatrical film. The opposite is true. Although prime-time is currently divided equally between single-camera and multiple-camera, programs outside of prime-time—daytime soap operas, syndicated game shows, weekend sports coverage, and late-night talk shows—are almost all multiple-camera productions. Obviously, multiple-camera production is the norm on broadcast television, as it has been since the days of television's live broadcasts—virtually all of which were also multiple-camera productions (Table 2.1).

Table 2.1: Top Ten Prime-Time Shows: 1950–51

Of the following, all but the Westerns (*The Lone Ranger* and *Hopalong Cassidy*) and *Fireside Theatre* were telecast live using multiple camera technology. (1950–51 was the first season during which the A.C. Nielsen Company [which became Nielsen Media Research] rated programs.)

1.	*Texaco Star Theater*	6.	*Gillette Cavalcade of Sports*
2.	*Fireside Theatre*	7.	*The Lone Ranger*
3.	*Philco TV Playhouse*	8.	*Arthur Godfrey's Talent Scouts*
4.	*Your Show of Shows*	9.	*Hopalong Cassidy*
5.	*The Colgate Comedy Hour*	10.	*Mama*

It is tempting to assume that since multiple-camera shooting is less expensive and faster to produce than single-camera, it must therefore be a cheap, slipshod imitation of single-camera shooting. This is the aesthetic hierarchy of style that television producers, critics, and even some viewers themselves presume. In this view, multiple-camera is an inferior mode, a necessary evil. However, ranking modes of production is essentially a futile exercise. One mode is not so much better or worse than another as it is just different. Clearly, there have been outstanding, even "artistic," achievements in both modes. Instead of getting snarled in aesthetic snobbery, it is more important to discuss the differences between the two and understand how those differences may affect television's production of meaning. In short, how do the different modes of production influence the meanings that TV conveys to the viewer? And what aesthetic principles do they share?

STAGES OF PRODUCTION

Pre-production

Narrative programs such as soap operas and sitcoms that utilize multiple-camera production start from scripts much as single-camera productions do, but these scripts are less image-oriented and initially indicate no camera directions at all. Sitcom and soap-opera scripts consist almost entirely of dialogue, with wide margins so that the director may write in camera directions. The sort of detailed description of action we see in Cherry's script for the *Desperate Housewives* pilot (Figure 2.1) would seldom appear in a soap-opera script. Storyboards are seldom, if ever, created for these programs. Multiple-camera scripting is emblematic of the emphasis on dialogue in such programs. The words come first; the images are tailored to fit them.

Non-narrative programs (game shows, talk shows, reality TV, and so on) have even less written preparation. Instead, they rely upon a specific structure and a formalized opening and closing. Although the hosts may have lists of questions or other prepared materials, they and the participants are presumed to be speaking in their own voices, rather than the voice of a scriptwriter. This adds to the program's impression of improvisation.

Production

A multiple-camera production is not dependent on a specific technological medium. That is, it may be shot on film or videotape (analog or digital), recorded **direct to disk** (i.e. the video is stored digitally on a hard disk), or even broadcast live. The sitcom *Two and a Half Men* (2003–) is filmed, but the soap opera *Days of Our Lives* (1965–) is captured on high-definition, Digital Betacam videotape. Non-narrative talk shows and game shows are recorded in various video formats. Some local news programs and *Saturday Night Live* are telecast live—as daytime soap operas used to be in the 1950s and 1960s.

If a program is shot on film, the editing and the addition of music and sound effects must necessarily come later, during post-production. If a program originates on video, however, there are the options of editing in post-production or while it is being recorded. (Obviously, a live program must be edited while it is telecast.) Time constraints play a factor here. Programs that are broadcast daily, such as soap operas and game shows, seldom have the time for extensive editing in post. Typically, the director will edit a version of the show during the production stage, while the feeds from all the cameras are being recorded. This **line cut**, as it is known, is created by the director switching among the three or more cameras while the show is going on. Later, the line cut is used by the show's editors as a rough guide while they cut the recorded camera feeds.

The choice of film or video is, once again, dependent in part on technology, economics, and aesthetics. Since the technology of videotape was not made available until 1956, there were originally only two technological choices for recording a multiple-camera program: either film live broadcasts on **kinescope** by pointing a motion-picture camera at a TV screen; or originally shoot the program on film (and then broadcast the edited film later). Early-1950s programs such as *Your Show of Shows* (1950–54) and *The Jack Benny Show* (1950–65, 1977) were recorded as kinescopes. In 1951, the producers of *I Love Lucy* (1951–59, 1961) made the technological choice to shoot on film instead of broadcasting live. Although this involved more expense up front than kinescopes did, it made economic sense when it came time to syndicate the program. A filmed original has several benefits over kinescope in the syndication process. It looks appreciably better than a kinescope and is easier and quicker to prepare since all the shooting, processing, and editing of the film have already been done for the first broadcast. [An] early 1950s kinescope of *The George Burns and Gracie Allen Show*, exemplify the inferior image quality of that process. An *I Love Lucy* episode from the same era would have looked much better, due to its relatively high resolution. Since producers make much more money from syndication than they do from a program's original run, it made good economic sense for *I Love Lucy* to choose film over live broadcasting and kinescope. Moreover, its enormous success

in syndication encouraged other sitcoms in the 1950s to record on film.

After the introduction of videotape, the economic incentive for multiple-camera productions to shoot on film no longer held true. A videotape record of a live broadcast may be made and that videotape may be used in syndication. This videotape—unlike kinescopes—looks just as good as the original broadcast. Until recently, producers who shot film in a multiple-camera setup did so primarily for aesthetic reasons, because film used to hold a slight edge over video in terms of visual quality. However, the introduction of high-definition digital video in the early 2000s spelled the end for film's visual superiority. Today it is nearly impossible to distinguish HD video from film when viewed on all but the largest, highest-definition television screen. Consequently, many "prestige" multiple-camera productions that would have been shot on film ten years ago are now being shot in HD.

Multiple-camera narrative programs that are filmed and those videotaped narrative programs that are edited in post-production follow a similar production procedure. The actors rehearse individual scenes off the set, then continue rehearsing on the set, with the cameras. The director maps out the positions for the actors and the two to four cameras that will record a scene. The camera operators are often given lists of their positions relative to the scene's dialogue. Finally, an audience (if any) is brought into the studio.

A multiple-camera episode is performed one scene at a time, with 15- to 20-minute breaks between the scenes—during which, at sitcom recording sessions, a comedian keeps the audience amused. One major difference between single-camera and multiple-camera shooting is that in multiple-camera the actors always perform the scenes straight through, without interruption, unless a mistake is made. Their performance is not fragmented, as it is in single-camera production. Each scene is recorded at least twice, and if one or two lines or camera positions are missed, individual shots may be shot in isolation afterwards.

Further, in multiple-camera sitcoms, the scenes are normally recorded in the order in which they will appear in the finished program—in contrast, once again, to single-camera productions, which are frequently shot out of story order. This is done largely to help the studio audience follow the story and respond to it appropriately. The audience's laughter and applause are recorded by placing microphones above them. Their applause is manipulated through flashing "applause" signs that channel their response, which is recorded for the program's **laugh track**. The laugh track is augmented in post-production with additional recorded laughter and applause, a process known as **sweetening** in the industry.

The entire process of recording one episode of a half-hour sitcom takes about three to four hours—if all goes as planned.

Live-on-tape productions—such as game and talk shows—are similar in their preparation to those edited in post-production, but the recording process differs in a few ways. Once the videotape starts rolling on a live-on-tape production, it seldom stops. Directors use a **switcher** to change between cameras as the scene is performed—creating their line cut. The shots are all planned in advance, but the practice of switching shots is a bit loose. The cuts don't always occur at the conventionally appropriate moment. In addition to the switching/cutting executed concurrently with the actors' performance, the scene's music and sound effects are often laid on at the same time, though they may be fine-tuned later. Sound technicians prepare the appropriate door bells and phone rings and thunderclaps and then insert them when called for by the director. All of this heightens the impression that the scene presented is occurring "live" before the cameras, that the cameras just happened to be there to capture this event—hence the term live-on-tape.

The resulting performance is quite similar to that in live theater.

In soap operas, individual scenes are not shot like sitcoms, in the order of appearance in the final program. Since soap operas have no studio audience to consider, their scenes are shot in the fashion most efficient for the production. Normally this means that the order is determined by which sets are being used on a particular day. First, all the scenes that appear on one set will be shot—regardless of where they appear in the final program. Next, all the scenes on another set will be done, and so on. This allows the technicians to light and prepare one set at a time, which is faster and cheaper than going back and forth between sets.

As we have seen, narrative programs made with multiple cameras may be either filmed or videotaped and, if taped, may either be switched during the production or edited afterward, in post-production. Non-narrative programs, however, have fewer production options. Studio news programs, game shows, and talk shows are always broadcast live or shot live-on-tape, and never shot on film. This is because of their need for immediacy (in the news) and/or economic efficiency (in game and talk shows). Participants in the latter do not speak from scripts, they extemporize. And, since these "actors" in non-narrative programs are improvising, the director must also improvise, editing on the fly. This further heightens the illusion of being broadcast live, even though most, if not all, such programs are on videotape.

Post-production

In multiple-camera programs, post-production varies from the minimal touch-ups to full-scale assembly. Live-on-tape productions are virtually completed before they get to the post-production stage. Their final cuts are often quite close to their line cuts and most of their music and sound effects have already been added. But similar programs that have been recorded live but *not* switched at the time of recording must be compiled shot by shot. For instance, sitcoms often record whatever the three or four cameras are aimed at without editing it during the actual shoot. The editor of these programs, like the editor of single-camera productions, must create a continuity out of various discontinuous fragments.

HYBRID MODES OF PRODUCTION

Single-camera and multiple-camera modes of production have become less and less distinct over the years. Or, to put it another way, they have become more and more like one another. We have emphasized their differences here to help the reader understand the particulars of each approach, but the day-to-day practices of television production in the US blur the distinction between them. There are "single-camera" shows that sometimes use more than one camera on the set and there are "multiple-camera" shows that sometimes use just one. We'll conclude our consideration of modes of production, then, by recognizing their increasingly hybrid nature.

First, there are several instances when single-camera productions bring a second (or third or fourth) camera onto the set. The most common is for scenes using explosions, car crashes, or other practical effects on the set. If a building can only be set on fire once, then the director is sure to use numerous cameras to capture it from a variety of angles (and as a backup in case one camera has a technical issue). But another, somewhat surprising use of two cameras on single-camera productions is for simple conversation scenes. Some directors on single-camera productions prefer to bring in a second camera to capture additional angles during the simplest of scenes and to allow actors to play through a scene with fewer interruptions.

The hybridity of single- and multiple-camera modes of production is not a one-way street. Just as some single-camera productions make use of multiple cameras, so some multiple-camera productions incorporate single-camera techniques.

This is most evident in sitcoms. When Tom Cherones directed episodes of the multiple-camera show *Seinfeld*, he often filmed shots after the studio audience departed, where he brought a single camera into the set, moved walls around, and captured images from angles not possible during the multiple-camera shooting process. And *How I Met Your Mother* (2005–) has developed its own, virtually unique, hybrid mode of production. It mostly looks like a conventional, multiple-camera, laughtrack-accompanied production recorded on a studio set with a live audience, but it's actually shot without an audience. Its directors do use three (or more) cameras while shooting, but the lack of an audience and a longer-than-usual shooting schedule (three days instead of one) allow them to move the cameras into the set in order to create shots that would normally be impossible in a multiple-camera shoot.

Thus, we can find single-camera programs borrowing techniques from the multiple-camera mode of production and vice versa. Does this crossover negate the division we have made between the two modes? No, but it does mean that the number of cameras on a set is not the ultimate determinant of which mode a program employs. Instead, the principal difference between the two modes stems from their underlying aesthetic. Multiple-camera mode of production borrows its aesthetic from the theater. It is *as if* the actors were up on a vaudeville stage and the cameras were in the audience recording their performance as it occurs live, without retakes. It is *as if* the cameras do not control their movements and speech, but just capture them as they happen. We viewers know some of this is untrue, but liveness and this sense of live performance are central to the illusion of multiple-camera productions. In fact, the multiple-camera show *Cheers* (1982–93) asserted its liveness each week by proclaiming that "*Cheers* was filmed before a live studio audience." In contrast, single-camera mode of production borrows its aesthetic from the cinema, from films made for release to theaters. In this case, it is *as if* the actors' performances had been broken into small pieces. It is *as if* the camera controlled their every movement and speech. It is *as if* these fragments were then assembled in an editing room, which is where the performance is finally constructed. The performance does not exist in the real world in order to be recorded. Instead, the performance is fabricated out of these fragments.

In the everyday world of television production, these aesthetics seldom exist in pure form, but the choice of one approach over another has a major effect on a television program's technological needs (types of cameras, editing equipment, etc.) and economic requirements (single-camera is more expensive than multiple-camera). Moreover, it determines many elements of the program's pre-production, production, and post-production phases.

SUMMARY

To analyze television style, we must have a fundamental understanding of its two principal modes of production: single-camera and multiple-camera. Single-camera mode of production came first, originating in the cinema; but multiple-camera has been central to television since the 1940s. The single-camera mode typically uses one camera on the set to record fragments of a scene, which must be assembled later. The multiple-camera mode aims several cameras at the actors and the set in order to simultaneously capture their performances as they occur.

These modes of production influence the three principal stages of TV making: pre-production, production, and post-production. In this chapter, we comment on several aspects of these stages, but we will return to them in more detail in the other chapters in this part of the book. In anticipation of the discussion of production and post-production work, we do here specify the scripting that goes on during pre-production: the writer's draft, table draft, network draft, and production draft. A program's showrunner oversees all stages

of pre-production scripting and may request detailed storyboards to augment the script if visual design is particularly important.

Pure forms of these modes of production seldom exist in the contemporary television industry. Rather, hybrid modes of production are becoming more and more common. "Single-camera" productions will bring extra cameras on set to capture explosions or additional camera angles of a conversation scene, and "multiple-camera" productions will rely on single-camera techniques to shoot on the set after the audience has left. The hybrid nature of the modes of production illustrates that economics, the bottom line, does not entirely determine how a television program will be shot. As always, the creation of television blends economic concerns with aesthetic principles and technological resources.

FURTHER READINGS

The current state of modes of U.S. television production and the culture surrounding them are assayed in John Thornton Caldwell, *Production Culture: Industrial Reflexivity in Film and Television* (Durham, NC: Duke University Press, 2008). Production studies is also advocated in Jennifer Holt and Alisa Perren, eds., *Media Industries: History, Theory and Method* (Malden, MA: Blackwell, 2009); and Vicki Mayer, Miranda J. Banks, and John T. Caldwell, eds., *Production Studies: Cultural Studies of Media Industries* (New York: Routledge, 2009). For readers curious about the early days of American television, Edward Stasheff and Rudy Bretz, *The Television Program: Its Writing, Direction and Production* (New York: Hill and Wang, 1956) offers an interesting perspective on how TV was made in the mid-1950s.

The specific evolution of single-camera production is comprehensively described in David Bordwell, Janet Staiger, and Kristin Thompson, *The Classical Hollywood Cinema: Film Style and Mode of Production to 1960* (New York: Columbia

University Press, 1985). John Ellis, *Visible Fictions: Cinema: Television: Video* (Boston: Routledge, 1992) is not as exhaustive, but it does begin the work of analyzing the multiple-camera mode of production.

The scripting process is the subject of many books—many of which are "how to" books providing advice on breaking into the television business. Although such books can be revealing in their presumptions about how the TV industry works, they often are written like advice columns and thus are little help to the analyst who wants to reverse engineer television style. A few books that are useful to the TV critic are: Pamela Douglas, *Writing the TV Drama Series: How to Succeed as a Professional Writer in TV* (Studio City, CA: Michael Wiese Productions, 2005); Jean Rouverol, *Writing for Daytime Drama* (Boston: Focal Press, 1992); Alan Schroeder, *Writing and Producing Television News: From Newsroom to Air* (New York: Oxford University Press, 2009); and Evan S. Smith, *Writing Television Sitcoms* (New York: Perigee Books, 1999). If you are interested in experimenting with scriptwriting yourself, but are confused about the format required, you should try some of the free scriptwriting software available online. Clive Young provides an overview of "5 Free Online Screenwriting Programs," *Fan Cinema Today*, June 3, 2009, tvcrit. com/find/screenwriting.

Handbooks for television production provide many insights into the conventions of television's visual and sound style. Two foundational texts are Gerald Millerson, *Television Production*, 14th ed. (Boston: Focal Press, 2009) and Herbert Zettl, *Television Production Handbook*, 10th ed. (Belmont, CA: Wadsworth, 2008). A more ambitiously theoretical approach is taken in Gorham Kindem, *The Moving Image: Production Principles and Practices* (Glenview, IL: Scott, Foresman, 1987). Kindem endeavors not just to describe television's common practices, but also to articulate the aesthetic rationales of those practices. Kindem's book is currently out of print, but Gorham Kindham and Robert B. Musburger, *Introduction to Media Production: The Path to Digital Media Production*, 4th ed. (Boston: Focal, 2009) covers many of the same aesthetic concerns in addition to offering practical instruction in video production.

The sole attempt to create an entire stylistics of television production is Herbert Zettl, *Sight Sound Motion: Applied Media Aesthetics*, 6th ed. (Belmont, CA: Wadsworth, 2010). Zettl's ambitious undertaking is occasionally idiosyncratic and quirky—and also quite provocative. The most thorough guide to interpreting television's visual style, however, is not a TV book at all: David Bordwell and Kristin Thompson, *Film Art: An Introduction*, 9th ed. (New York: McGraw-Hill, 2010). Although Bordwell and Thompson have nothing to offer on some crucial aspects of television (e.g. multiple-camera editing), they provide an extensive introduction to understanding cinema production.

NOTES

1   Film theorist and historian David Bordwell uses this specific phrase in *Figures Traced in Light: On Cinematic Staging* (Berkeley: University of California Press, 2005), 250.

2   Bordwell responds to the intentional fallacy issue: "This framework does not claim access to intentions as mental episodes, only to intentions as posited sources of patterns of action. Again, we reverse-engineer" (Bordwell, 257).

3   David Bordwell, Janet Staiger, and Kristin Thompson, *The Classical Hollywood Cinema: Film Style and Mode of Production to 1960* (New York: Columbia University Press, 1985), 243–44.

Multicamera and single-camera production help **producers** create appropriate programs for the intended audience and distribution channels. Tools like cameras, lighting, and editing equipment are critical, and without them, we would see only blackness coming from our monitors and **second-screens**. In fact, it's been said that without light, there would be no TV.

Episodic Television

As mentioned, the way audiences watch programs has changed dramatically, but audience tastes have also changed, giving a significant rise in popularity to what's known as **episodic television.** On-demand viewing and online-streaming-only content creators have added new and exciting programs to the viewing experience.

Scholars suggest that with the television show *The Sopranos* in the early 2000s, pay television giant HBO established itself in an ever-growing and popular television genre called episodic television. This type of storytelling can be experienced via traditional television distribution, cable, or streamed over the Internet. Episodic television is not a new story format, and there have been dramatic episodic programs on TV for decades. What's unusual, as our next author points out, is that the episodic programs distributed through pay television and relatively new streaming services such as Netflix take creative risks that traditional broadcast networks don't typically take. NBC, for instance, has **Federal Communication Commission (FCC) regulations** and advertisers to worry about and wouldn't be able to air a program like *Game of Thrones* without significant editing.

READING 2.2

AND NOW NO WORD FROM OUR SPONSOR: HOW HBO PUTS THE RISK BACK INTO TELEVISION

by Tony Kelso

HBO: RISK AS EMBEDDED IN THE CORPORATE CULTURE

Judging from its list of accomplishments and accolades, HBO indeed appears to occupy a different space than commercial network television. In 2004, for instance, according to *USA Today* (September 28, 2004: D1), it collected more Emmys than the four major broadcast networks combined. Praise from the critics has bordered on redundancy. In a comment that epitomizes this tendency and takes the discourse to a hyperbolic level, *The New York Times* once hailed *The Sopranos* as "the greatest achievement in American pop culture in the last quarter-century." Not only has HBO evoked acclaim for its quality programming, however, it has also stirred considerable analysis from scholars.

David Lavery (2002) writes, for instance, that *The Sopranos* is "heavy" with significance, even to the extent that it has spawned the sub-field of *"Soprano studies"* (Lavery, 2006: 6). In a book on feminism in popular culture, Joanne Hollows and Rachel Moseley (2006) offer a summary of the debates surrounding feminism in the "post-feminist" *Sex and the City*. This program, too, has triggered lively scholarship (see Akass & McCabe, 2004, for one notable example of an entire book devoted to academic work on *Sex and the City*). Nor is the "buzz" associated with HBO confined to the halls of academia and offices of journalists. *The Sopranos* and *Sex and the City*, for example, have signified full-fledged cultural phenomena. Maurice Yacowar (2002) notes that on Sundays, when a new episode of *The Sopranos* was telecast, restaurant business in some areas declined because people stayed home to view the characters' latest ventures. Lavery (2002: xii) describes a lexicographer predicting that the next edition of the *Oxford English Dictionary* will include *Sopranos* citations. Meanwhile, *Sex and the City* was "discussed around countless water-coolers across America" and appeared on the cover of *Time*, a rare happening for a sitcom (McCabe & Akass, 2004: 2). Aside from all this buzz, HBO translates into economic success—in 2001 it generated more profit than any other network (Peterson, 2002). What can account for such symbolic and monetary triumph? Part of the answer, as this selection suggests, lies in HBO's political economic structure and business model.

The traditional argument on how HBO stands apart from the rest goes like the following: Based on the evidence, as demonstrated above, there is a quality divide between pay TV in general (and HBO in particular) and commercial television. Because HBO is dependent on subscribers rather than advertisers for its main source of revenue, it can take risks without fear of upsetting sponsors (C. Anderson, 2005; K. Anderson, 2005; Auster, 2005; Weinman, 2006). Not only does HBO not have to worry about offending corporate

backers, it can also produce plots that develop slowly instead of building toward mini-climaxes before commercial interruptions. Furthermore, as a pay service, HBO does not have to contend with government censorship violations or the public service requirements that other networks, at least in theory, must fulfill (Auster, 2005; Rogers et al., 2002; Weinman, 2006). Nudity, utterly profane language, and especially violent representations are fair game for HBO. But there is still more to it than freedom from advertisers and censors. The network, in a sense, is *forced* to take risks. If it relies on millions of everyday viewers to relinquish a few extra dollars each month for the opportunity to view programming they cannot get on commercial TV, then HBO simply must continuously distinguish itself from broadcast and basic cable stations if it hopes to remain viable. Consequently, HBO, through both marketing efforts—including its slogan, of course—and program creation, has attempted to focus on "counter-programming" and resisting the commercial networks' formulaic approach as illustrated earlier (Auster, 2005; *Broadcasting & Cable* [Supplement], November 2002: 6; Friend, 2001; McCabe & Akass, 2004). Because it is guided by "first-order commodity relations" (Rogers et al., 2002), that is, in direct transaction with audiences rather than in a relationship centered on selling their attention spans to advertisers, HBO has not generally obsessed over ratings (K. Anderson, 2005; Peyser, 2006; Rogers et al., 2002). "We don't care how many people watch our shows," one HBO insider once declared in *The Economist* (November 21, 1998: 95). "We just want people to decide at the end of the month that it's worth renewing their sub-scription." HBO can ignore individual ratings because all it needs to ensure is that it delivers to each subscriber *something* worth paying for. This means, therefore, that the network must explic-itly attend to audience satisfaction based not on quantitative data, but qualitative measures, and evaluate its *total* programming schedule. No wonder, then, HBO has been remarkably recognized for producing some of the most novel television programming of the past two decades. In addition, as already implied, the premium station is not timid about tackling socially demanding subjects, such as third-wave feminism (*Sex and the City*), drug addiction (*The Corner*), and (egad!) death (*Six Feet Under*). Despite taking such chances (or perhaps *because* of them), each of these programs resonated with large audiences. Again, unlike the commercial networks, which appear to be steered by the notion that TV viewing is not something one seeks out but a habitual activity, HBO is able to furnish programming that people really want to see rather than simply settle for (Magder, 2004).

The buzz that HBO must incite to mark itself from commercial networks, however, does not simply happen through programming choices and "organic" means. The pay channel, as mentioned earlier, also engages in intense promotional and branding efforts designed to buttress the perception that it is somehow unique. Apprehending its need to convince people to increase the size of their cable bills, HBO began spending heavily on promotion from the start (Albiniak, 2003); building a brand identity has been essential (McCabe & Akass, 2004; Rogers et al., 2002). Moreover, unlike commercial outlets that come aggregated through standard cable packages, HBO is a brand that can actually be *bought* (Ross, 1999). Similar to the manner in which a manufacturer of an everyday consumable uses branding to symbolically connote that its bottled water, deodorant, or lip balm is different from the rest (even though the dissimilarities are in fact negligible), HBO adopts the same tactic (although in this case, HBO, in general, has seemingly been able to live up to its claim of distinction). The network's challenge is particularly fierce because brand loyalty is tough to achieve. "Churn," or the tendency for a portion of subscribers to forego HBO each month, is

endemic. Building a strong brand identity is one method for minimizing churn, which is intended to not only create the impression that HBO is truly one-of-a-kind and therefore worth paying for, but also that those who opt into HBO's lineup belong to a special set of viewers who thereby acquire "consumer capital". In this sense, direct marketing endeavors and programming go hand in hand— the shows function, in part, as devices or product placements that augment HBO's brand (Epstein et al., 2006; McCabe & Akass, 2004; Rogers et al., 2002). The premium service's promotional energies have appeared to pay off, at least until recently (more about this later). One qualitative study published in 2000 noted that HBO was one of the four most recognized and remembered cable networks, an especially remarkable finding given that it serves far fewer homes than the other three, each of which resides in the realm of basic cable (Bellamy & Traudt, 2000).

In a word, as alluded to on previous occasions, it boils down to "quality." Instilling its programs with contradictions and complexity generally unseen on commercial networks, HBO can disseminate "real adult drama" (Lavery, 2002; Willis, 2002; Yacowar, 2002). Accordingly, partially due to its political economic structure, HBO can also emphasize creative freedom, which, ostensibly, only a first-order commodity station can offer (Rogers et al., 2002: 53). Moreover, the network appears to have internalized this ethic into its very corporate culture (Auster, 2005; Friend, 2001; McCabe & Akass, 2004). It comes as no shock, then, that so many artists known for their considerable creative talents are attracted to the prospect of working for HBO (Auster, 2005: 227). A number of industry insiders have revealed the relief that follows from escaping the inhibiting commercial networks to bask in the relative liberty that comes with a stint at the network. When David Chase, quoted above, originally sought a taker to his *The Sopranos*, he was turned down by several commercial outlets (although FOX showed initial interest it eventually pulled out; Lavery, 2006; Lavery & Thompson, 2002; Peyser & Gordon, 2001). Discussing his move from the commercial networks to HBO, he states: "I had just had it up to here with all the niceties of network television. … I don't mean language and I don't mean violence. I just mean storytelling, inventiveness, something that really could entertain and surprise people" (Fresh Air, 2004). Alan Ball, writer for Six *Feet Under*, echoes the theme that commercial networks do not appreciate the audience enough to believe it can comprehend sophisticated plots. "The difference between working for a network and for HBO is night and day," he says. At ABC, Ball was admonished to "articulate the subtext" and "spoon feed" information (Weinraub, 2000). The creator of HBO's provocative prison drama *Oz*, Tom Fontana, complains about how commercial television tends to resort to copycat formulas. "The networks go with the prevailing wind. If a show works on one network, they want one just like it" (Peyser & Gordon, 2001).

DELVING DEEPER INTO INSTITUTIONAL ADVANTAGES

Much has already been stated about the traditional reasons given for why HBO has the capacity to enact a more innovative stance toward programming. In this section, additional institutional advantages will be highlighted, and then tendencies that *contradict* the idea that the pay service is free from customary economic constraints will be elucidated.

Without doubt, in striving to ensure quality programming, HBO frequently establishes considerably larger production budgets than its commercial counterparts. It can devote such enormous resources, in part, because it neither produces many original shows (far more of its schedule is still devoted to second-run Hollywood films), nor, most of the time, creates as many programs per season for its series as the big broadcast corporations develop. "The reality is," states Nick Davatzes, former President and CEO of A&E Television Networks, that HBO functions less as a network

than as "a movie studio almost" (Chunovic, 2002). Further, because it depends on subscribers rather than ratings, HBO can allow its series to slowly accumulate a large audience (Auster, 2005; Friend, 2001; McConville, 1999; Rogers et al., 2002). A commercial show, under the surveillance of advertisers, must immediately post strong results in Nielsen's charts or likely wind up on the chopping block before viewers even have a chance to find the new program in their television listings. HBO, conversely, handling its content as fine wine, has the luxury of waiting for buzz to kick in as more and more people discover its distinctive offerings. Neither *The Sopranos* or *Sex and the City*, for example, had they been accepted by commercial networks to begin with, might have had the opportunity to reach the status of cultural phenomena because their ratings performances during their respective first seasons were not particularly sparkling. Having fewer scheduling restraints, which enables it to target certain evenings for maximum buzz (for instance, Sunday nights were used to premiere new *Sex and the City* and *The Sopranos* episodes) and repeat shows throughout the week, also contributes to HBO's advantage in cultivating an audience over time.

Despite the fact that HBO does not follow a commercial sponsor business model, it must be clearly grasped that the pay station is not utterly free of advertising. It may not place 30-second spots between segments of programming, but HBO indeed engages in product placement transactions. *Sex and the City*, for instance, is notorious for drawing attention toward designer labels, especially for shoes. In fairness, however, the implicit plugs often appear to work within the spirit of the show and add to its feeling of authenticity—*Sex and the City's* main characters, after all, love to shop. Moreover, HBO, as a rule, does not accept direct payment for its placements (Atkinson, 2003; Edwards, 2004). On the other hand, by inserting freely provided products into the texture of its programs, the network benefits by lowering its sizeable production costs. Consequently, its placements are not always particularly subtle. In one episode of *The Sopranos*, for example, Tony asks the character Johnny Sack about his Maserati: "Kinda draws attention, no?" The conversation continues:

TONY: Absolutely. And in a Guinea gray, looks fantastic.
JOHNNY: Tops out at 176 miles per hour. Standing quarter, 13 and change.

This is hardly the stuff of "seamless" integration. Obviously, HBO is not above overtly plugging a brand to offset costs. A larger issue to consider, then, is to what extent the premium service challenges the consumer ideology that commercial networks relentlessly circulate. The tendency to promote a worldview centered on buying things, though, is probably not as pronounced in the case of HBO—arguably, even more so than its commercial rivals, it disseminates polysemic messages that both affirm and undermine dominant capitalist ideology. This theme will be touched on again later in the selection. Ultimately, though, HBO is still located within a commercial structure. As noted above, marketing is a fundamental component of its enterprise. HBO might be different, but not *so* different. Though, of course, "It's sort of not TV. It's HBO" would not resonate as a tagline.

At the same time, HBO is not immune from corporate influence. It is, for sure, part of the Time Warner empire. If its business model were to yield diminished returns, it is hardly likely that its parent company would simply endorse the cause of producing quality programming for quality's sake and that HBO would not hear from the suits at headquarters. In addition, as a member of the extended family, HBO's programs serve as commodities for other Time Warner enterprises (Bignell, 2004). Yet overall, in spite of its economic constraints, when placed side-by-side with the commercial networks, HBO's structure and philosophy seem to promote an environment in which creative individuals can collectively express their talent and inventiveness can flourish.

HBO'S DISTINCTION FROM ITS PAY-TV RIVALS

Until now, a number of factors have been cited to demonstrate why HBO has earned a reputation of offering more quality fare than its commercial competitors. Yet HBO is not alone in the pay-TV universe. If other premium services adhere to a similar political economic structure, then why have they not achieved the same cachet as HBO? To answer the question would require a case-by-case examination beyond the scope of this selection. Yet one comparison will be attempted: HBO vs. Showtime. The choice deserves special attention because the latter represents the former's most long-standing rivalry.

Over the course of its run, Showtime has indeed enjoyed moderate success. By 1999, the boom in direct-satellite subscriptions had given a boost to the channel (Kafka, 1999). As of this writing, *the L word* is in its third season and signifies Showtime, too, places a premium on risk—the program is the first one in American television history to concentrate its action on the lives of a group of mostly lesbian women (Sedgwick, 2006). Robert Greenblatt, Showtime's president of programming, admitted he was committed to "making some noise" with the series. His wish appeared to be materializing, as the drama, early on, generated a 300 percent larger audience in primetime than other Showtime originals (Anderson-Minshall, 2006: 13). *The L word* followed on the heels of another show based on explicitly homosexual themes, *Queer as Folk*, which was modeled after a UK series of the same name. Together, these two programs have helped gay programming more fully enter "mainstream" commercial distribution. Furthermore, in 2005, Showtime drew its own share of critical acclaim, garnering an uncharacteristically significant number of Emmy nominations (Hill, 2005). Historically somewhat content to reside in the shadows of

HBO, so it seems, Showtime has lately shifted course and implemented an increasingly vigorous effort to directly compete with its nemesis (Frutkin, 2004; Rutenberg & Carter, 2003; Weinraub, 2000). The network, in fact, had hired Greenblatt in 2003 to revamp its corporate climate and take a more aggressive stance toward HBO.

Despite the similarities between HBO and Showtime—the focus on risk and quality, "edgy" programming; and the production of content that sparks lively debate among journalists and academics alike—there are differences as well. These points of distinction illuminate why, in part, HBO has secured far greater profits and significantly more critical commendation than Showtime. For starters, HBO has a much larger financial base on which to operate. But how did such fortune transpire to begin with? HBO's head start accounts for one reason. As Greenblatt mentions, "they [HBO] got into the series business way before we did, so they've had a long time to gain momentum and try shows that didn't work and ultimately find their way into shows like *The Sopranos*" (Lafayette, 2005a). "They became a generic for cable TV," Matthew C. Blank, Showtime's chairman, adds (Frutkin, 1999). Showtime, consequently, has been playing catch-up ever since its beginnings. Accordingly, HBO has the resources to dedicate to expansive marketing campaigns and, not surprisingly, has been considerably more adept at the process (Frutkin, 1999). Moreover, HBO has an advantage in procuring inclusion in cable packages, given that its owner, Time Warner, owns a huge stable of cable systems (Frutkin, 1999; Kafka, 1999).

Still, HBO's economic structural factors cannot entirely account for why it has towered over Showtime. Corporate agency probably provides much of the answer as well. Put simply, HBO is plainly better at executing the same recipe than its competitor. As Greenblatt concedes, the gap between the two networks is a result of HBO "being at the top of their game … and doing it as well or better than anybody else does it" (Frutkin, 2004).

Showtime, for years, utilized a niche programming strategy (Frutkin, 2004). But this tactic appears to be changing as the network seeks to expand its reach. *Weeds*, a suburban comedy ("dramady"? [Goodman, 2006]) *a la Desperate Housewives*, yet one in which marijuana plays a key role (ah, there's the risk!), has been generating the ever-elusive buzz. Besides receiving critical attention, it has also captured the fascination of audiences—after one season it became the most highly rated program on Showtime (Pope, 2006). With *The Sopranos* nearing completion and HBO's *Deadwood* and *Big Love* serving as poor substitutes in cultivating a large following, Showtime could finally be mounting a serious threat to HBO's preeminence. Yet with only about half the number of subscribers as HBO (Pope, 2006), Showtime faces an uphill climb. In the post-television age, circumstances change quickly. Stay tuned.

NOTE

1   Brown notes, "The views in this paper are my own and do not represent the views of the Federal Communications Commission, its Commissioners, or its staff" (Brown & Cavazos, 2005: 17).

REFERENCES

Akass, K. & McCabe, J. (eds) (2004) *Reading Sex and the City*. London: I.B. Tauris.

Albiniak, P. (2003, June 23) "Sex And Marketing: HBO Has Long Been Known For Heavy Promo Spending", *Broadcasting & Cable*. 18.

Anderson, C. (2005) "Television Networks and the Uses of Drama", in G.R. Edgerton & B.G. Rose (eds) *Thinking Outside the Box: A Contemporary Television Genre Reader*. Lexington: University Press of Kentucky.

Anderson, K. (2005, August 1) "I Want My HBO", *New York*. 18.

Anderson-Minshall, D. (2006) "Sex and the Clittie", in K. Akass & J. McCabe (eds) *Reading The L Word: Outing Contemporary Television*. London: I.B. Tauris.

Atkinson, C. (2003, August 4) "Absolut Nabs Sexy HBO Role: 'Sex and the City' Features Fake Ad", *Advertising Age*. 6.

Atkinson, C. (2005, February 28) "HBO's Playbook: Playing Hard to Get", *Advertising Age*. 3.

Auster, A. (2005) "HBO's Approach to Generic Transformation", in G.R. Edgerton & B.G. Rose (eds) *Thinking Outside the Box: A Contemporary Television Genre Reader*. Lexington: University Press of Kentucky.

Barnouw, E. (1990) *Tube of Plenty: The Evolution of American Television, 2nd edition*. Oxford: Oxford University Press.

Bellamy, R.V., Jr. & Traudt, P.J. (2000) "Television Branding as Promotion", in S. Eastman (ed.) *Research in Media Promotion*. Mahwah, NJ: Lawrence Erlbaum.

Berman, M. (2004, February 23) "A Pity About City", *MediaWeek*. 38.

Berman, M. (2006, June 12) "HBO's Midlife Crisis", *MediaWeek*. 38.

Bignell, J. (2004) "Sex, Confession and Witness", in K. Akass & J. McCabe (eds) *Reading Sex and the City*. London: I.B. Tauris.

Brown, K. & Cavazos, R. (2005) "Why is this Show So Dumb? Advertising Revenue and Program Content of Network Television", *Review of Industrial Organization* 27: 17–34.

Butsch, R. (2003) "Ralph, Fred, Archie, and Homer: Why Television Keeps Recreating the White Male Working-class Buffoon", in G. Dines & J.M. Humez (eds) *Gender, Race, and Class in Media, 2nd edition*. Thousand Oaks: Sage.

Chunovic, L. (2002, October 28) "Broadcast Feels HBO's Influence: 'Kingpin' Drama is NBC's Answer to 'The Sopranos' ", *Electronic Media*. 15.

Edwards, J. (2004, January 23) "HBO's 'No Ads' Attitude Keeps Top Programmes Out of Reach", *Campaign*. 17.

Elliott, S. (2003, October 10) "Stuart Elliott in America", *Campaign*. 14.

Elliott, S. (2005, January 11) "Would a Cleaned-Up Version of 'The Sopranos' Still Be Too Naughty for Most Sponsors?", *The New York Times*, http://select.nytimes.com/search/restricted/article?res=F30A14F934SD-0C728DDDA80894DD404482. Retrieved August 3, 2006.

Epstein, M.M., Reeves, J.L. & Rogers, M.C. (2006) "Surviving 'The Hit': Will *The Sopranos* Still Sing for HBO?", pp 15–25 in D. Lavery (ed.) *Reading The Sopranos: Hit TV from HBO*. London: I.B. Tauris.

Flint, J. (2000, April 7) "With Eyes on Cable, Networks Permit Racier Plots, Unprintable Dialogue—Success of HBO's 'Sopranos' is Impetus, as is a Nation Inured to Sex Scandals", *The Wall Street Journal*, Eastern Edition. B1.

Flint, J. (2004, January 5) "HBO's Next Business Model; Theatrical Films, Syndication and DVDs Supply Revenue, Supplementing Subscriber Fees", *The Wall Street Journal*, Eastern Edition. B1.

Flint, J. (2005, June 8) "As Critics Carp, HBO Confronts Ratings Decline", *The Wall Street Journal*, Eastern Edition. B1.

"Fresh Air: 'The Sopranos' Writer and Director David Chase" (2004, March 2) Radio Program, National Public Radio, Washington DC.

Friend, T. (2001, May 14) "The Next Big Bet: Is a Family of Depressed Morticians HBO's Best Hope for Life After 'The Sopranos'?" *The New Yorker*. 80.

Frutkin, A.J. (1999, November) "Searching for Buzz: Despite a Renewed Commitment to Original Programming, Showtime Remains in the Shadow of HBO", *MediaWeek*. 38.

Frutkin, A.J. (2004, October 18) "Analyze This: Robert Greenblatt is Helping Showtime Find its Inner Self by Enlisting A-level Hollywood Talent", *MediaWeek*. 18.

Gitlin, T. (1985) *Inside Prime Time*. New York: Pantheon Books.

Goetzl, D. & Halliday, J. (2002, March 18) "Taking Cue from Cable, Gingerly", *Advertising Age*. 63.

Goldstein, D. (2005, September 19) "FX Aims for HBO's Cachet: Higher-Brow Original Programming is Grabbing Audiences and Advertisers", *Business Week*. 90.

Goodman, T. (2006, August 11) "Greatness of 'Weeds' Could Make Showtime Must-Pay-for-Television", *The San Francisco Chronicle*, Final Edition. E1.

Haley, K. & Knight, B. (2002, November) "Rocking the Industry: HBO has Redefined Excellence in TV Entertainment. What's Next?", *Broadcasting &.Cable*. 3.

Hermes, J. (2006) "'Ally McBeal,' 'Sex and the City' and the Tragic Success of Feminism", in J. Hollows & R.J. Moseley (eds) *Feminism in Popular Culture*. Oxford: Berg.

Heuton, C. (1994, May 30) "Is There Life After Pay Cable?" *MediaWeek*. 14.

Hill, L.A. (200S, August 15) "Broadcast Brings Back the Buzz: Newcomers, Network Resurgence Provide Compelling Plot for this Year's Contest", *Television Week*. 29.

Hollows, J. & Moseley, R. (2006) "Popularity Contests: The Meanings of Popular Feminism", in J. Hollows & R. Moseley (eds) *Feminism in Popular Culture*. Oxford: Berg.

Hughes, M. (2004, August 24) "Highly Anticipated 'Joey' May Be Best Comedy on TV This Fall", *Gannett News Service*, http://web.lexis-nexis.com/universe/document?_m=5c3c2f44b5a2269b8b79670c0c8e7e68&_docnum=1&wchp=dGLbVlbzSkVb&_md5=3a0f8ffc5b37d8c-9bc4 cc2a3c7557a2f. Retrieved August 8, 2006.

Kafka, P. (1999, August 9) "Win, Place, Showtime", *Forbes*. 52.

Lafayette, J. (2005a, January 3) "It's Showtime for 'Hate' Pilot: One Pay Cable Drama Project's Journey from Development to Delivery", *Television Week*. 1.

Lafayette, J. (2005b, August 22) "Sony to Solo on 'Nip' Preem; FX's Single-Sponsor 'Launch Nights' Enable Advertisers to Stand Out", *Television Week*. 1.

Lavery, D. (2002) " 'Coming Heavy': The Significance of *The Sopranos*", pp xi–xviii in D. Lavery (ed.) *This Thing of Ours: Investigating The Sopranos*. New York: Columbia University Press.

Lavery, D. (2006) "Introduction: Can this Be the End of Tony Soprano?" pp 1–14 in D. Lavery (ed.) *Reading The Sopranos: Hit TV from HBO*. London: I.B. Tauris.

Lavery, D. & Thompson, R.J. (2002) "David Chase, *The Sopranos*, and Television Creativity, pp 18–25 in D. Lavery (ed.) *This Thing of Ours: Investigating The Sopranos*. New York: Columbia University Press.

Levinson, P. (2002) "Naked Bodies, Three Showings a Week, and No Commercials: The Sopranos as a Nuts-and-Bolts Triumph of Non-Network TV", pp 26–31 in D. Lavery (ed.) *This Thing of Ours: Investigating The Sopranos*. New York: Columbia University Press.

Magder, T. (2004) "The End of TV 101: Reality Programs, Formats, and the New Business of Television", in S. Murray & L. Ouellette (eds) *Reality TV: Remaking Television Culture*. New York: New York University Press.

McCabe, J. with Akass, K. (2004) "Introduction: Welcome to the Age of Un-Innocence", in K. Akass & J. McCabe (eds) *Reading Sex and the City*. London: I.B. Tauris.

McConville, J. (1999, October 25) "Competition Driving HBO: Merges Film Units to Maintain Momentum", *Electronic Media*. 1.

Peterson, T. (2002, August 20) "The Secrets of HBO's Success", *Business Week Online*, http://web.ebsco-host.com/ehost/detail?vid=4&hid=9&sid=d9dfcl3e-1cf7-4e0c-8e22-09e127661341%40SRCSMl. Retrieved August 2, 2006.

Peyser, M. (2006, May 1) " 'Sopranos' Takes a Hit", *Newsweek*. 15.

Peyser, M. & Gordon, D. (2001, April 2) "Why the Sopranos Sing: Nothing Else on TV Can Touch HBO's Mob Hit—That's Got the Network Suits Watching Their Backs. Will 'The Sopranos' Change the Face of Television?" *Newsweek*. 48.

Poniewozik, J. (2004, June 21) "S_x and the Scissors", *Time*. 22.

Pope, K. (2006, August 6) "For Showtime, Suburban Angst is Fast Becoming a Ratings Delight", *The New York Times*, Final Edition. B26.

Rogers, M.C., Epstein, M., & Reeves, J.L. (2002) "*The Sopranos* as HBO Brand Equity: The Art of Commerce in the Age of Digital Reproduction", pp 42–57 in D. Lavery (ed.) *This Thing of Ours: Investigating The Sopranos*. New York: Columbia University Press.

Ross, C. (1999, December 6) "Funny About HBO … It Works", *Advertising Age*. 20.

Rutenberg, J. & Carter, B. (2003, June 30) "Sex and Death Just Like HBO, but Showtime Gets No Love", *The New York Times*, Late East Coast Edition. Cl.

Sedgwick, E.K. (2006) "Foreword: The Letter L", in K. Akass & J. McCabe (eds) *Reading The L Word: Outing Contemporary Television*. London: LB. Tauris.

Stanley, T.L. (2004, October 11) "Cutting-Edge FX Hailed as Next HBO", *Advertising Age*. 3.

Weinman, J.J. (2006, April 3) "Is it Time to Declare HBOver? It Used to Be the Only Place to Go for Daring Unconventional Shows. Not Anymore", *Maclean's*. 54.

Weinraub, B. (2000, November 20) "Cable TV Shatters Another Taboo; A New Showtime Series Will Focus on Gay Sexuality", *The New York Times*, http://select.nytimes.com/search/restricted/article?res=F10F14F9355F0C73 8ED-DA80994D8404482. Retrieved August 3, 2006.

Willis, E. (2002) "Our Mobsters, Ourselves," pp 2–9 in D. Lavery (ed.) *This Thing of Ours: Investigating The Sopranos*. New York: Columbia University Press.

Worrell, N. (2002, October 28) "Quick Takes: What Can Commercial Television Do to Compete with the Crop of Popular Shows on HBO?" *Electronic Media*. 8.

Yacowar, M. (2002) *The Sopranos on the Couch: Analyzing Television's Greatest Series*. New York: Continuum.

Each article in this chapter presents observations about two distinct but related parts of storytelling for a mass audience. Butler's article described the basic tools and technology in studio- and location-based storytelling, as well as how you might begin the process of creating a story for television. You've also read about the rise of episodic television in a subscriber-based television **ecosystem** like HBO, how this form of programming is tailored to specific audiences, and what those audiences truly want to see. Also, subscriber-based television lacks the advertising commonly found in broadcast television. Author Tony Kelso also pointed out HBO's role as a network of "proactive programming."

Interview with a Professional

Franz Joachim is General Manager and CEO at New Mexico PBS.
Interviewed by Matt Crick, Spring, 2017.

Why are good communication skills important in your field?

Communicating is what we do. Good communication is our job. Anytime you have more than one person working together you need communication. The better the communication, the more likely the outcome will be what is desired. If we are not communicating effectively with each other, we cannot expect to effectively communicate anything to our viewers. The complexity of the system we use to distribute five television channels, twenty-four hours a day requires a lot of coordination and, therefore, communication. Deciding what to air, finding the programming, scheduling it, recording the programs, promoting the programs, and finally actually playing the programs out requires coordination of thousands of actions by dozens of employees.

What specific skills do you use the most?

Listening and picking the right medium, the right venue, are the two communication skills I value most and try hardest to practice. Empathy and open-mindedness are up there as well, but I think they are subsets of effective listening. I'm not as concerned with nonverbal communication. I find that it is very subjective, often misinterpreted with too much weight being placed on it. And I think it's too often used as an excuse for not really listening to what is being said.

I like to manage by walking around. I make a circuit of the station's fifty or so employees at least once a day when I'm in town. This gives me the opportunity to check in, listen to what they are dealing with, and provide context to what they are involved in. That context is important to both sides, allowing me to appropriately guide, helping the employees understand why they are doing what they are doing. But just as important, that context provides me with an intimate view of station's operations.

The one-on-one relationship extends to our viewers, as well. We have a portal that allows any viewer to reach out to us with a comment or question. Our policy is every communication received is responded to. With a few exceptions, we adhere very closely to this policy. There are a few who abuse the access, and we are more circumspect in our responses to them. But, the vast majority of emails or phone calls into the station are responded to by the station employee with knowledge of the circumstances under discussion.

We recently had a catastrophic failure of our on-air server, losing hundreds of hours of programming. We had to change up our program schedule completely for a few days. We put out communications online and over the air but still needed to field hundreds of calls and emails. Placing a high value on one-on-one communication, I spent the better part of three days listening and responding in person to each and every call and email that came in. The value of the relationships we built with viewers through this process was demonstrable both in maintaining their trust but also their financial and emotional support.

What skills do you find lacking in others?

The communication skill I find most lacking is empathy. As often as not, during my walkabout, my conversations provide context to a challenge an employee has with another. Letting the employee know why this other employee is doing what they are doing the way they are doing it often clears the path for progress.

Email contributes to the appearance of a lack of empathy. Because email is so impersonal and casual, communications can appear to lack empathy when that wasn't the intention. Email is rife with misunderstanding. I have coached more than a few employees to start with a face-to-face-conversation or phone call, if necessary, and follow up with an email for clarity and review.

In terms of your career trajectory, what benefits and/or value did your college/university education provide?

I may be a terrible person to ask. I was a horrible student in college. I skated through high school with excellent grades without having to learn any real study skills, so college came as a real surprise. I ended up skipping a lot of classes to work more at the university-owned public television station, driving my GPA into the basement. So, initially the real value in my college education was the access it provided to on-the-job training in what became my field.

After I tanked and got kicked out of school for poor performance, I spent a few years in the private sector. I wasn't interested in a management track, so a degree just didn't seem important. I soon figured out that the lack of a degree was going to be an impediment to any real success regardless of my preferred track. I was destined for a series of low-paying, dead-end jobs. So, following some of the rare advice my father gave me, I headed back to school, finishing my degree over the course of eight or nine years, working a full time job, and taking classes at night. I can't say that the course content itself played much of a role in the short term. But, the discipline of sticking it out did. And later in my career specific classes, such as Broadcast Law and the programming class taught by one of my bosses at the station, laid an important base.

So, to provide a short answer, the discipline and rigors of a college academic experience, the access to student jobs and internships through the college, and the open doors the degree itself offered were the greatest value I derived.

In your field, how best can universities and colleges aid in a student's career plans?

Based on my long experience hiring and working with students, as much as my own experience as a student, providing real world opportunities is one of the best things a university and college can do to aid in a student's career plans. Help them find internships and student jobs that actually expose them to workplace expectations.

What advice would you give to Communication majors?

Pick your minor carefully, and chose something that will challenge you. I picked engineering. I was a terrible engineer. But the rigors of the math and science, the requirement for critical thinking, and the necessity for looking beyond the obvious are crucial to my own success. And it doesn't hurt that I actually grasp some of what my engineering team is talking about. Some the colleagues I rely on most came in with Anthropology or History as minors or even majors.

Be humble. Assume you don't know and be fearless in asking questions. It goes to listening. Ask a question but be humble enough to listen to the answer and think about the answer after the fact. Think about why you got the answer you did and whether it aligns with your own experiences.

And never let someone pass you off with the "it's just common sense" answer. There is no such thing. "Common sense" is used to hide ignorance or malfeasance. More often than not, the phrase is used to justify a preconceived notion that cannot be supported with fact. Do not use it and do not accept it as an answer.

Thinking back on your career choices, what decision are you most proud of?

Two career choices of which I'm most proud come to mind, and they are related by the same underlying motivation: to grab every opportunity even when they seem to conflict.

When the Berlin Wall fell in 1990, I had the means and opportunity to go Germany to witness this seminal moment first hand, and I chose not to. It is one few great regrets in my life. But that regret drove me to focus on how and why I make the choices I do.

The choice to go back to school and get my degree made everything else that followed possible, including my marriage, my son, and, of course, my career, the three greatest joys in my life. They all followed directly or indirectly from the choice to return to school and get my degree. But when it was presented to me as a choice between continuing in my career or going to school, I found a way to choose both.

The other choice was to pursue the position of General Manager of New Mexico PBS, the position I currently hold. I did not think I would like the job, and I did not feel that I was prepared for it. I felt I needed a few more years in the number two role. In fact, during the exit interview with my predecessor as she was leaving the job, we both agreed that I would be a much better General Manager if I had a couple of more years [of experience]. However, she did encourage me to apply [the observation] that one does not get to choose the timing, you just get to choose whether to pursue an opportunity or not. The job was open, and I had to choose to go for it or risk never having the opportunity again. As it turns out, I love the job; I am good at it, and those lessons I needed to learn, I learned on the job much as I always have.

Conclusion

Good television, whether it's for broadcast, streaming, download, or some other future format begins with a good story that's written down in a **script** and/or **storyboard** format. Following the preproduction, production, and postproduction process, you'll be able to more easily create outstanding content suitable for any distribution mode.

The *economics* of electronic storytelling—equipment rental, legal and distribution costs, and budgeting all the aspects of your project—can significantly influence how the story is made, especially if any of the project phases are incomplete or managed poorly. Fortunately, costs of production and barriers of entry into television production are lower than ever. Start your story on paper, in a word processing program, or even as an idea scrawled on a bar napkin. Then, determine which television production tools can make your vision come to life and where you'll distribute your story.

CLASSROOM ACTIVITY

Using your knowledge from the articles in this chapter, complete the following classroom activity within 45 minutes, not including "pitch" time.

Activity Specifics

You'll be randomly placed in teams of three. Your Creative Team (CT) will be responsible for creating the next great Netflix original program and will be pitching your idea to a well-known Netflix executive (your professor) at the end of your 45-minute time limit. You will have two minutes to pitch your idea, you will be timed, and your pitch must be written down.

Questions you might answer to build a good pitch:

1   How will you determine what kind of show you'd like to produce?

2   What type of television production technology will you use?

3   Do you intend your show to be sold to broadcast television?

4   What's the story, and who's your audience?

Other considerations when structuring your pitch:

1   What are some ways TV shows are distributed and how is Netflix different?

2   How might you divide up your Creative Team in order to achieve the goal of being able to pitch a show in a minute?

3   What advantages/limitations does a company like Netflix present for a new show

DISCUSSION

In the Jeremy Butler article, he discussed modes of production.

1   Name some examples of what he meant?

2   What does Butler mean by preproduction, production, and postproduction?

3   Describe author Tony Kelso's opinion of broadcast television content.

4   Provide evidence from the article for your answer.

5   Why, according to Kelso, is broadcast television risk adverse?

6   What does Kelso mean by this?

KEY TERMS

Cable—a relatively new technology, when compared with traditional broadcast television, that delivers audio and video signals through a thick wire buried underground or often fastened to existing telephone poles. Cable companies offer a variety of program types in a package form and charges consumers monthly while traditional commercial television is no charge to the consumer. Cable offers premium services like HBO and Showtime, and cable content is produced using different governmental guidelines than broadcast television.

Demographic—refers to specific characteristics in a particular population. The financial success of a broadcast television network is closely tied to an understanding of the audience for a particular television program, and this informs the types of commercial advertising that is sold for placement in television shows.

Ecosystem—a relatively new term in the communication industries. Ecosystem refers to the production technologies and processes that encompass the creation and delivery of television programs. For instance, 4K television programs require a different ecosystem, which is different than the ecosystem for high-definition programs.

Episodic Television—a type of electronic storytelling that includes several episodes, often six initially, that vary in length and contain important and detailed plot points, characters, and events. Through subsequent viewing of each episode, the program's entire story is revealed to the audience. In broadcast television, this type of program can have as much as 15 minutes of commercials; cable television typically has even more.

Federal Communication Commission (FCC) regulations—the governmental body in the United States responsible for setting policy, enforcing rules, and licensing television stations.

Mass Medium—technology that reaches a large audience delivering a variety of programming.

Monetized—a term that refers to the process of creating and receiving economic benefit. Common ways of monetizing include advertisements that automatically appear on most YouTube videos.

Multiple-Camera Production—refers to electronic storytelling using more than one video camera. Typically, multiple camera productions—multicam productions for short—are created in a television studio or similar space and require additional technology to match the technical specifications between each camera, edit together the image from each camera, and create a feeling of transparency in the story for the audience that feels like real life.

Network—a group of television stations, often called *affiliates that* are linked through a central organization like ABC, NBC, or CBS via technology, television programs, and economics. Affiliates can buy programs produced by the network, create new programs to sell to other affiliates, or refuse to air certain types of programs based on the community standards at their affiliate television station.

Nielsen—the premiere ratings and audience measurement company for mass media.

Over the Air (OTA)—refers to distribution technology that uses the electromagnetic spectrum to deliver television, radio, and other forms of content to a variety of technologies including mobile phones, televisions, car radios, etc.

People Meters—an electronic device in the shape of a box that connects to a television and records programs when the television is on. Data is collected daily and sent back to Nielsen.

Producers—the person or persons responsible for making sure a television program is completed on time and on budget. A producer has "front-line" authority and responsibility for the overall quality of the program.

Satellite—refers to technology that orbits the Earth. Satellites are responsible for relaying television station signals, which carry television programs through the air.

Second-screens—a relatively new term in television, which refers to other devices that can deliver programs to a user whenever she/he would like. Second screens provide access to traditional broadcast content for viewers who do not have cable or large monitors in their homes through "apps" housed in mobile technologies like phones, laptop computers, and tablets.

Script—the written document that describes in detail the story planned for production.

Sitcom—short for situation comedy.

Storyboard—illustrated frames of action and dialog, based on a script that portray the story planned for production.

Television—a word that has multiple meanings. Refers to an actual piece of equipment, a television, that receives programming and displays that programming for you in the form of sound and picture. *Television* also refers to a specific type of programing that is broadcast using a variety of technologies around the world, often in a live as-it's-happening presentation. Broadcast television programs usually contain commercial advertisements broken into specific time segments; commercials distinguish television from other forms of electronic storytelling like film. Finally, television is also a *system* that transmits images and sound that's linked by technology and physical buildings.

Television Stations—groups of technologically linked organizations which produce television content, broadcast that content within a certain geographical limitation, and purchase television programs from other sources for broadcast. Television stations are considered local entities and operate within established governmental broadcasting guidelines. Television stations broadcast digital signals through the air for home or office viewing.

REFERENCES

Altman, R. 2007. *Silent film sound*. Columbia University Press.

Butler, J. G. 2011. An Introduction to Television Style: Modes of Production, *Television: Critical Methods and Applications*. Routledge.

Campbell, R., C. Martin, and B. Fabos. 2014. *Media & culture: Mass communication in a digital age*. Bedford/St. Martin's, NY, NY 480–481.

Dawson, M. 2012. "Defining Mobile Television: The Social Construction and Deconstruction of New and Old Media." *Popular Communication* 10 (4): 253–268.

Grabowski, M. 2014. "Resignation and Positive Thinking in the Working-Class Family Sitcom." *Atlantic Journal of Communication* 22 (2), 124–137.

Kelso, T. 2008, And Now No Word From Our Sponsor: How HBO Puts the Risk Back Into Television, *It's Not TV: Watching HBO in the Post-Television Era*. Taylor & Francis: UK.

Lynch, Jason. 2016. "How Millennials Consume TV Depends on Which Stage of Life They're In: Nielsen report examines the demo's viewing habits." *Adweek* Retrieved on March 24. from http://www.adweek.com/tv-video/how-millennials-consume-tv-depends-which-stage-life-theyre-170393/.

"TV Ratings: How We Do It." 2017. Retrieved on March 13, 2017, from. http://www.nielsen.com/us/en/solutions/measurement/television.html.

Poggi, J. 2016. Time Warner Cable Moves Into Adressable TV Advertising, *Advertising Age*. Retrieved on March 13, 2017, from http://adage.com/article/media/time-warner-cables-moves-addressable-tv-advertising/303015/.

Rymsza-Pawlowska, M. J. 2014. "Broadcasting the Past: History Television, 'Nostalgia Culture,' and the Emergence of the Miniseries in the 1970s United States." *Journal of Popular Film and Television* 42 (2), 81–90.

CHAPTER 3

Film Production—Film Aesthetic and Craft

INTRODUCTION

The word *film* can mean a variety of things, depending on the people you're talking with and the college or university you're attending. For instance, *film* can mean telling visually driven stories using particular tools associated with feature films. Large film cameras that require multiple crews to manage, big sets and lighting, expensive camera lenses, and exotic locations are often part of what it takes to create a feature film. However, shooting *film* doesn't necessarily mean you're working with all of the above and it's not likely, these days, you're capturing images on a **celluloid medium**. In fact, you probably won't ever see, touch, or learn about how celluloid film is recorded *in-camera*, edited, or projected. Except, perhaps, in a film history course.

In this chapter, when the word *film* is used, we're not referring to celluloid film, a recording format that requires exposure in-camera and special equipment to see what's been recorded. The film must then be sent to the film lab for processing, returned, edited for image and sound, and then "printed" and duplicated. When *film* is used in this chapter, we're referring to a special production process that employs a variety of storytelling techniques, tools, and aesthetics that differ from television, especially multi-camera live-switched television production, although that gap has significantly narrowed in the last 20 years.

Motion Pictures

Often called *motion pictures*, film has a long technological history. For example, in the late 1800s, Eadweard Muybridge, a British photographer, captured still photographs of a horse running on a racetrack. When viewed in rapid succession, his photos proved that a horse's four hooves were off the ground simultaneously, at different points in time, showing the horse briefly floating in mid-air. (Visit *Freeze Frame: Eadweard Muybridge's Photography of Motion* exhibit at the National Museum of American History's website at http://americanhistory.si.edu/muybridge/.) This discovery may not seem very important to us today, but Muybridge's photos took advantage of a phenomenon known as **persistence of vision**, an optical illusion created in the human mind that explains why we believe we see smooth motion in films and animation. We don't see each an individual image or a frame of video "frozen" in time like a Selfie or an Instagram photo because persistence of vision creates the *illusion* of motion (Dirks 2017). Before Muybridge and his discoveries, few people even knew about persistence of vision, and no one demonstrated it so famously with still photographs. Persistence of vision applies in the world of television and video technology. However, television and video rely on electronic processes rather than film projection—which displays an image using light.

Traditional filmmaking sometimes relies on an analog process rather than a digital one, at least for the **acquisition** or production phase, and emphasizes cameras and lenses, lighting, camera framing to create a mood or tone, etc. If you're interested in learning more about how film is different than other forms of storytelling, several websites like http://nofilmschool.com/ and https://www.lynda.com/Filmmaking-training-tutorials/1314-0.html provide good overviews and specific training techniques. Of course, pursuing a degree in film production IRL (in real life) is a good idea, as well. You will be exposed to a variety of filmmaking approaches, and people, learn clever workflows from experts in the discipline and face creative challenges you won't experience when just learning online.

FILM PRODUCTION AND THE APPLIED COMMUNICATION MODEL

At this point, you know when film is used to tell stories and that the process is technologically different than television in several ways. Film also employs particular conventions and non-technological techniques to shape stories, like how an image is framed and use of light to create mood and tone in a dramatic scene. Along these lines, a key production position in filmmaking is known as the **cinematographer**, and John Mateer's article on Digital Cinematography provides an overview of this crucial and complicated job.

DIGITAL CINEMATOGRAPHY: EVOLUTION OF CRAFT OR REVOLUTION IN PRODUCTION?

by John Mateer

The debate concerning the impact of the introduction of digital technologies into the filmmaking process and the emergence of digital cinema has been raging for well over a decade. "Evolutionists," as exemplified by John Belton's 2002 article "Digital Cinema: A False Revolution," view new technology and associated methodologies as a natural progression consistent with other technical advancements in cinema (100). "Revolutionists," including Ganz and Khatib, argue that these technologies have not only irrevocably altered filmmaking practice but have fundamentally changed the nature of cinematic storytelling (and thus the viewer experience) as well (Ganz and Khatib 21). What is interesting to note in both Belton's article and Ganz and Khatib's article is that there is a presupposition that the relevant technological evolution had plateaued at the time of writing such that the question of the impact of digital technologies on cinema could effectively be answered. Yet it can be argued that the most significant advancements in filmmaking technology have occurred since these articles were written. Recently released camera systems such as the Red One and Arri Alexa are claimed to have created a brave new world of data-centric production. A recent interview in *Variety* with Michael Cioni, owner of Light Iron Digital, a postproduction facility catering specifically to data-centric production, sums this up: "You can't

make film smaller. You can't make 35mm be 8K resolution no matter what you do. You can't have a [film] camera be four pounds. You can't fit a 400-foot magazine in a smaller space. It can't improve at the rate Moore's Law says we can predict technical improvements [in digital systems]" (qtd. in Cohen).

No longer does a camera department require light-tight temperature-controlled spaces to load camera magazines or store reels of film. Workstations with multiple RAID arrays and linear tape backup systems have taken their place. Dailies, so called because of the time it took to develop the film and create one-light prints to check the quality and aesthetics of a day's shoot, now take mere minutes to create, no longer requiring the specialist skills of a photochemical lab. But for all of this change, has the process of filmmaking been fundamentally altered? Is this truly a new era in which the cinematographer has become more of a data-capture specialist than a visual artist? Or do these advances in camera systems simply represent the latest chapter in the evolution of filmmaking as Belton originally argued? This article sets out to explore these questions by looking at the craft of cinematography for current mainstream production and how it has been affected by technological innovation.[1]

WHAT IS A CINEMATOGRAPHER?

Cinematography is an art-form but at the same time it's a craft, and it is definitely a combination of the two … You have to light, you have to compose and you have to create movement. Those are the three elements of cinematography.
　　　　　—Owen Roizman (qtd. in Fauer 1: 234)

John Mateer is a senior lecturer in film and television production at the University of York in England. He has worked as a producer and director in both the United Kingdom and the United States for more than twenty years, most recently as the visual effects producer for the feature film *The Knife That Killed Me* for Universal Pictures (UK).

Roizman's definition arguably represents the most common view of cinematography. Cinematographers work with a director to develop a visual means of interpreting the story. In narrative film, this process typically includes the breaking down of scripts first by acts, then by scenes, and finally by dramatic beats. At each stage, primary and secondary themes are interpreted in terms of tone and desired audience response. From this, details of setting and basic production design begin to emerge, leading to a definition of a visual style. For the director, this serves as the backbone of the production bible, providing a framework for more detailed dramatic analysis. For the cinematographer, it represents the beginning of a blueprint to enable physical production to realize the look of the piece. As the process continues, some form of visualization usually takes place. Working methodologies can differ significantly from project to project and director to director, with the cinematographer's control over visuals ranging anywhere from being a slave to dictated camera positions (such as Hitchcock's reputedly definitive storyboarding or the tight requirements of visual effects–based work) to holding nearly free reign over position, composition, and even blocking (as in Woody Allen projects). Irrespective of the amount of creative freedom granted, the cinematographer will ultimately determine the position of lighting sources and the quality of that light (e.g., color, hardness of shadows, and opacity) to achieve the desired dramatic objectives.

The lesser-known side of the cinematographer's role is more mundane but no less important. Commercial film and television productions are expensive, so it is imperative that principal photography be successful. For the cinematographer, this means that light levels need to be calculated precisely to ensure proper reproduction and exposure within the latitude of the recording medium. Film stocks and electronic image sensors vary in their sensitivity to light and ability to reproduce certain visual spectra, so understanding the technical attributes of these is vital not only for production but for also ensuring that image quality is suitable for the postproduction process and mastering. Related to this, the cinematographer must be certain that the recording medium has sufficient robustness to cope with shooting conditions—be they dust, moisture, or vibration—which can affect recording. These conditions also dictate which specific camera systems and accessories are needed to enable shooting, which in turn can affect the cameras' mobility and the viability of complex shots. All of these logistical considerations must be considered with respect to the time it will take to prepare and shoot and, most importantly to producers, with respect to the overall cost. The modern professional cinematographer is part artist, part scientist, and part businessperson, and technology has always been a key tool in supporting his or her ability to fulfill all three roles.

THE ROLE OF FILM

Film stock has been revered as the gold standard for feature film and narrative broadcast-television projects for decades. Modern-day stocks are very sensitive and can handle a significant range of brightness within one frame (known as "latitude" measured in f-stops). Film is also remarkably durable, which is a prime consideration for cinematographers, studio executives, and archivists alike. But for all of its strengths, film is far from a perfect recording medium. Because it is a physical system, the duration of shots is directly linked to the length of the strip of film itself. Film relies on photochemical reaction to capture light, so a chemical process is required to render images in a finished form. This means that specialist equipment must be used to process the negative and print the footage. As a light-sensitive material, stock must be kept in controlled conditions prior to exposure and development (Kodak). Because of their mechanical nature, film cameras must be continually checked for light-tightness and cleanliness as well as calibrated for physical registration to ensure the film is accurately and securely stopped for each frame of exposure. Professional film cameras are expensive, and this, coupled with the cost of the film stock itself and secondary processing, means that shooting with film can be costly, particularly in comparison to other types of image recording.

THE EVOLUTION OF DIGITAL MOTION PICTURES

Although digital recording of moving images first began to appear in the 1970s, it was not seen as viable for any type of commercial work until the mid-1980s ("Grass Valley"). The television industry began to embrace these technologies once it was shown that digital cameras could outperform their tube-based predecessors and that savings could be made with a digital workflow.[2] However, from a cinematographic perspective, even the newest systems of that time were woefully lacking in their technical capabilities. Standard-definition digital video has too low a resolution (about 0.4 megapixels), too little latitude (about six to eight f-stops compared with film's thirteen to fourteen), and insufficient color depth, making it unsuitable for anything beyond stylized low-budget cinema work. Although initial digital systems did provide freedom for small independent filmmakers, the technology was not yet developed enough to support mainstream film-making. Studios have long had strict requirements with regard to image quality and thus a conservative approach to new technologies.

In the late 1990s, Sony and Panavision engaged in a formal collaboration to explore how digital video technology might be utilized for film-style production. The first system emerging from this collaboration was the Sony HDW-F900 24p camera, which recorded to a new type of tape deck known as HDCAM (Kalley). Both components evolved from Sony's broadcast television systems, with the camera utilizing charge-coupled device (CCD) sensors to record images. For the first time, a digital camera could offer resolution approaching 16mm film stocks, with improved latitude and color fidelity. Likewise, the adaptation of traditional cinema lenses

from Panavision allowed optical characteristics such as depth of field to be controllable in a way similar to the control granted by film cameras. Despite the advances, take-up of this new system was initially limited. This changed when George Lucas decided that he wanted a completely digital workflow for *Star Wars Episode II: Attack of the Clones* ("Sony and Panavision about to Deliver"). For that picture, Sony and Panavision refined their systems, ultimately leading to the commercial introduction of HDCAM SR in 2003, which represented a significant enhancement to HDCAM. The success of the film showed the industry that digital high-definition (HD) recording technologies were approaching the color fidelity and latitude of film.

At the same time, the digital intermediate (DI) process—where film negatives are scanned into digital form for editing, compositing, and picture finishing—was becoming standard practice in Hollywood. By the time HDCAM came onto the market, the notion of working in a completely digital postproduction environment, though not universally embraced, was becoming understood and accepted. The ability to copy or alter digital data an infinite number of times without any degradation or loss in quality demonstrated the advantages that digital systems could provide. HD digital video systems have a resolution of 1,920 × 1,080, which is not appreciably less than 2K (2048 × 1556), which is common for DI. This meant that workflows established through the evolution of the DI process could be adapted to HD material. As a result, the introduction of these new HD systems into the production pipeline represented a logical evolution in the application of digital technologies to the filmmaking process.

From an "on set" perspective, working with HD systems does not differ radically from standard film or television production methodologies and represents a hybrid of the two. The "look" of the project is effectively burned in to the tape recording—that is to say it cannot be fundamentally altered—in the same way it would be in film. Exposure is still determined based on the dramatic requirements of the scene, with limitations in latitude and other recording characteristics of the HD system taken into account, as would be the case for film. Unlike film, recorded output of HD systems can be played back on set. Aside from confirmation that recording has been successful, there is little difference between this and video assist systems. From a camera assistant's perspective, focus pulls and other during-shot activities are completely unchanged. Off set, cans and reels of film are replaced with magnetic tape cassettes, but the rules of storing and cataloguing footage are similar, again borrowing from TV workflows. The only significant handling difference is that tape is reusable, so it is vital that camera assistants ensure that recording tabs are switched off, so that tapes are not accidentally recorded over. From a practice perspective, it is evident that shooting with HD, though somewhat different from film, does not represent a new paradigm but the amalgamation of existing technique, albeit with additional considerations related to the technology. According to Victor Nelli Jr., "[m]ost of the procedure is the same. The equipment is much harder to troubleshoot. It no longer is a piece of film passing by a hole. There are so many things to the HD format. [Crew] do need to be up to date" (qtd. in Rogers).

Sony was by no means the only manufacturer to develop digital camera systems targeted at high-end production during this period. Panasonic and Thomson (the latter drawing on expertise from its acquisition of Technicolor in 2000) also created systems based on CCD imaging sensors; the VariCam and Viper are still used for television and feature film work, though neither is viewed by the industry as definitive. From a financial perspective, the costs associated with these systems—both the costs of procuring the equipment for production and the associated postproduction costs—are not appreciably lower than those of film. Despite straightforward workflows and advances in digital imaging technologies, many veteran cinematographers remained (and some still remain) skeptical as to whether these digital systems could ever truly supplant film. In large part this is due to CCD technology, which has a different look from film. The following remark by Oscar-winning cinematographer Wally Pfister typifies the view: "The range of colors that you can record with the best digital cameras is also a joke when put head-to-head with 35mm negative … Why anybody would replace a proven image capture system with vastly inferior technology is beyond my comprehension" (qtd. in Fisher).

Film processes light in a fundamentally different way from CCDs. It records more information in shadow and highlight areas, with less in midtones. This nonlinear approach means that it is better able to capture and reproduce detail at extreme areas of brightness. On the other hand, CCDs and other digital systems are designed such that light is processed linearly, giving equal weighting to dark, mid, and bright tones. (A useful discussion of the nature of film log versus the linear processing of video can be found in Wright's *Digital Compositing for Film and Video*.) In order for footage shot with a CCD-based system to look like film, a data transformation process is required to simulate the nonlinear distribution of luminance. Because this effectively means redistributing data and introducing information that was not originally present, artifacts are generated that would not be present in film. Likewise, once light levels reach a certain threshold, all data is capped at that point. If the brightness is greater than the CCD can handle, the signal is "clipped," that portion of the image goes pure white, and all detail is lost. The opposite is true with dark areas going to pure black ("crushed"). Negative film is much more forgiving at extreme ranges of brightness. It too can clip whites or crush blacks, but the change is usually much less pronounced. Other differences, such as the look of visual noise (e.g., chrominance or luminance artifacts compared to film grain) and the grid-based nature of CCD sensors, mean that a true film look can only ever be approximated through this type of technology.

THE ADVENT OF DIGITAL CINEMA

The emergence of digital cinema is arguably linked to technological advancements in image reproduction systems in parallel with significant increases in performance and decreases in costs for computer systems. The two are related in that high-quality image data requires significant storage space as well as computer processing capability to render finished footage. Cinematographically, advances in CMOS (complementary metal-oxide semiconductor) imaging technology have enabled a more efficient path to an all-digital workflow. CMOS sensors can respond more rapidly to light than CCDs, and they also have the benefit of requiring less external processing of the raw digital data. Although both of these imaging sensors started development at roughly the same time (the late 1960s), it was not until comparatively recently that CMOS technology matured to a point where its image reproduction capability reached that of CCD ("CCD vs. CMOS"). Three CCD chips are typically used—one each to capture red, green, and blue picture data—but only one CMOS chip is required to capture full-color information. This means that CMOS sensors work in a manner that more closely resembles film. Indeed, one of the major early shortcomings of CMOS technology when used in cameras was its slow shuttering, such that fast-moving vertical objects in a frame could appear distorted—the dreaded "rolling shutter" effect that also plagued early film-camera systems (as exemplified by Lartigue's classic 1913 photo, *Car Trip*). Wheeler gives a good overview of the technical aspects of digital cinema systems in his book *High Definition Cinematography* (43).

In 2005, seeing the emerging take-up of HD systems to replace film for television projects, Arri was the first of the traditional film camera manufacturers to utilize a CMOS chip for a "digital film" camera. The D20 represented a middle ground between film and HD video systems. The active recording area of its CMOS sensor was equivalent to super 35mm film, so it had similar optical characteristics to film systems (in areas such as depth of field, for example). It also featured a resolution of 2,880 × 2,160 pixels, which is approximately the same as 2K film scans for digital intermediate. Operationally, the D20 had an adjustable mechanical shutter just as Arri film cameras do, and many of the accessories and basic components of Arri's cameras were directly compatible with the D20. In Filmstream mode, the recorded data was captured in logarithmic form, mimicking the way film responds to light. This data output would be transferred either to tape (using HDCAM SR) or to proprietary data cartridges. The data itself was handled using methods not unlike those for scanned film in DI workflows. However, production and post with the D20 was cumbersome. Given that there were comparatively few D20s in the field, no clear consensus emerged regarding work-flows. This led to a view among cinematographers (and producers) that the D20 was best utilized only in specific situations that lent themselves to digital production, such as stylized looks (as in Guy Ritchie's *RocknRolla*, shot by David Higgs) or visual effects work (as in the ferryboat fire sequence shot by Sam Nicholson for ABC's *Grey's Anatomy*). Indeed, at the time Arri itself conceded this point in its publicity, looking at digital not as a replacement for film but as simply another supporting tool. Bill Lovell, digital camera project manager for Arri, stated, "Film will continue to be the preferred acquisition format when its benefits are paramount, but if digital is the tool for the job, then we have a camera here for you to do it" (qtd. in "ASC Technology").

At roughly the same time, a start-up company also launched, proclaiming that they would "[change] the face of the motion picture industry" ("Red History"). Red Digital Cinema was founded by businessman Jim Jannard, a keen amateur photographer and film buff who was dismayed by the high cost and technical conservatism of industry film and HD camera systems and thought he could do better. Rather than develop cameras from a classical cinematography perspective, Jannard drew inspiration from the data-centric design of the then-emerging DSLR systems. He assembled a team of electronics experts to develop a CMOS chip that could effectively duplicate how film reacts to light but could be packaged in such a way that postproduction could be accomplished using commonly available computer desktop tools such as Apple's Final Cut Pro. From the start, Jannard and his followers proclaimed this to be a revolution, and the company structure reflects this. Red Digital Cinema's Ted Schilowitz, known as the "Leader of the Rebellion," explains:

> The company does not work in a normal hierarchy ... There are some really brilliant people that work on the team that don't fit into the normal convention of who you might think would build a camera ... [We envisioned] a 4K future that would be affordable, logical and accessible for a lot of people, and a lot of people were highly sceptical ... ("HD Expo")

The first commercial Red system, Red One, was released in 2007. Although technologically it was not radically different from the Arri D20, a number of key differences did represent a shift from conventional film and HD systems. The CMOS chip developed by Red, Mysterium, had a full resolution of over 4K, which was significantly larger than Arri's and was the largest commonly available imager format made (similar to Super 35mm film). Likewise, the chip had extended latitude and sensitivity similar to mid-level film stocks. Rather than using tape recorders or bespoke data cartridges, the Red One could record to commonly available CompactFlash cards and portable hard drives. This reliance on established data technologies ensured that production and postproduction support could be accomplished through time-tested IT methods. A very low price point for the camera body itself ($17,500 on release) meant that the overall cost for a Red system was significantly less than HD systems and a fraction of the cost of a film system.

To give an example, the following table details the costs of a one-week shoot in Los Angeles for a total of ten hours of footage (including videotape-based dailies) shot using different systems (prices are from a survey of Los Angeles suppliers conducted in August 2011).[3]

Chart 3.1: Cost Comparison for One-Week Shoot in Los Angeles for Ten Hours of Footage

	Arri 435 ES (35mm film)	Sony SRW-9000 (HD video)	Arri Alexa (digital cinema)	Red One (digital cinema)
Package Rental Cost (based on three-day charge)	$8,145	$9,360	$8,610	$6,360
Recording Media	$24,920 (Kodak 5260)	$900 (HDCAM SR tape)	$0 included	$0 (included)
Processing	$4,800 (0.12/ft)	$0	$0	$0
Duplication/Backup	$0	$1,900 ($100/hr + tape)	$300 ($100/hr)	$300 ($100/hr)
Telecine/DataCine (supervised, for dailies)	$6,750 ($225/hr)	$6,750 ($225/hr)	$6,750 ($225/hr)	$6,750 ($225/hr)
Total	**$44,615**	**$18,910**	**$15,660**	**$13,410**

At first the industry was highly skeptical. Wild claims of increased performance and low cost ran rife at trade shows, but Jannard was canny in promoting his new systems to filmmakers he knew to be tech-savvy. Peter Jackson became the first "name" director to shoot with a Red. A self-proclaimed early adopter of new filmmaking technologies, he heard about the development of the Red One and expressed his interest in the company. In preparation for NAB 2007, the annual trade show of the National Association of Broadcasters, Jannard asked Jackson if he would be interested in making a short film as a demonstration (reportedly on an unpaid basis). Intrigued by the system, Jackson agreed and created

Crossing the Line, a twelve-minute period World War I drama, in only two weeks ("Ready for Takeoff"). The film was well received at NAB, and the industry took notice, with other established directors, including Steven Soderbergh, soon looking to try the new camera. Given such directors' clout within the business, the system gained legitimacy, and industry take-up began. Producers became particularly enamored of Red because they could see the financial advantages of the system.

By 2010, more than 9,000 Red One systems had been sold. To put this in perspective, Sony produced approximately 2,500 CineAlta F900s (and variants) between 2002 and 2010, so Red's market penetration was truly remarkable for a specialist professional system. Mainstream feature films, including *Ché* (parts 1 and 2, both shot by Soderbergh), *The Book of Eli* (Don Burgess), and *The Social Network* (Jeff Cronenweth), as well as US network television series such as *Southland* (NBC), *Leverage* (TNT), and *Sanctuary* (Syfy), demonstrated the viability of Red to the Hollywood studios.

This did not go unnoticed by Arri, which launched Alexa in 2010 in response. Alexa has a very similar architecture and workflow to the Red One but a more filmic image quality. Not to be outdone, Red introduced a new 5K camera, the Epic, in 2011. Which camera is the more effective tool is a matter of debate—Reds are more affordable; Alexa has greater image reproduction capability—but there is no disputing that Arri, with its rich and comparatively conservative history in the development of film cameras, has recognized and embraced the notion that digital cinema represents the future of acquisition. As noted by Michael Cioni, digital has now surpassed film as the recording medium of choice for mainstream film and television production (Cohen).

NEW DIGITAL CINEMA TECHNOLOGIES AND THE CINEMATOGRAPHIC PROCESS

Even with the significant technological advances that Red and Alexa represent, the core tasks of cinematography have remained unchanged. Lens choice, shot composition, and means of facilitating camera movement are still the same. The relationship between the exposure index of the recording medium, the aperture setting, the exposure time, and the required level of illumination is also unaltered. Lighting design still needs to consider the latitude of medium as well as the dramatic requirements of the scene. That is not to say that there are not operational differences.

By definition, digital cinema production systems are data-centric. Recorded images are nothing more than computer files, so they must be handled using IT procedures, similar to other digital data. This has led to the creation of new roles for on-set production such as the digital imaging technician (DIT). The DIT's chief responsibility is to ensure the integrity of the data (i.e., to confirm that the recordings are correct) as well as to archive it to ensure that there are reliable backups in case of loss or corruption of the original recording media. In the film realm, these would have been the duties of the clapper/loader. He or she would have been responsible for loading film magazines, storing and cataloguing exposed reels, and maintaining the camera components. Now the focus of this role is centered on shooting tasks—marking actor positions, recording camera notes, and so on—allowing the DIT to handle most technical camera matters.

Changes in the cinematographic process lie in the nature of exposure and recording. Unlike film or tape, exposure for Red or Alexa is not "burned in" to the medium. As a result, so long as brightness falls within the recording range of the image sensor, the captured data can be altered without any loss in quality. In other words, if a shot appears to be overexposed to the naked eye, but distinct data is present for all areas in the shot (i.e., the brightest parts are not just one shade of white but actually consist of a subtle range of tonalities), the brightness can be changed in postproduction to provide correct exposure. Setting exposure for these systems is about capturing as much data as possible rather than creating the exact look per se. That is not to say that differences in contrast between areas within a shot are ignored, but rather, in order to give the maximum amount of control over the image in grading, the cinematographer purposefully exposes the image using as much of the exposure range as possible without clipping white highlights even if the "look" of the shot is intended to be moody and dark. By creating a rich data set—akin to a "thick negative" in film—the cinematographer is able to utilize the entire dynamic range of the camera. However, this approach means that control over the final look of the image now rests with the grader of the project. It has always been the case that color timers could alter color balance and brightness of film footage, but the nature of data-centric image capture is such that much more extreme and fundamental changes can be made.

Photo 3.1: Red One footage pre-grade.

Following is an example of a properly exposed shot from a Red One using the "thick negative" model. Shadow areas are purposefully overexposed to preserve detail: the histogram at the bottom represents the amount of data captured at different brightness levels. Left represents pure black and right pure white, with the height representing the amount of picture with that level of brightness per color channel. Note that none of the data goes to either extreme, so that as much of the image information is recorded as possible. In the finished, graded image, the exposure has been manipulated digitally such that it is now correct. The contrast has been increased and brightness extended to enhance the dynamic range of the image.

To many cinematographers, the notion that someone in postproduction has final control over the look of their work is untenable and threatens their art. Mark Sawicki's remarks typify this view:

> Unfortunately, after a century of cinema the art of cinematography is threatened by the rush of technological change and the ease of digital capture. … Highly sensitive sensor chips that can shoot by starlight have brought about the erroneous conclusion

by some producers that you don't need to light anymore as if the art of lighting amounts to merely obtaining an exposure. … Camerawork is so much more than so called "product acquisition."

Yet others, even those with traditional backgrounds, have recognized the imaging power that digital cinema systems can provide irrespective of protocol. Vilmos Zigmond says, for example, "After seeing *The Girl with the Dragon Tattoo* shot on the new Red Epic camera … the only thing I could think was that this looked like it was shot on 65mm film or with an IMAX camera. The latitude and detail was incredible. I was so impressed that I will be shooting my next feature on Epic" (qtd. in Jannard).

Photo 3.2: Red One footage post-grade.

It is clear that the cinematographer's role has evolved with the introduction of digital cinema systems but does this represent a fundamental change in the role?

CONCLUSION: REVOLUTION OR EVOLUTION?

Revolutionists, as described by Kirsner in his discussion of "innovators" (5), claim that the rise of digital technologies, including Red and Alexa, represents a fundamental change in feature film production. No longer are individual, discrete frames recorded to a frame of film or specific location on a magnetic tape. Now, image data generated by the camera is captured using traditional computer hardware. As mentioned earlier, this meant the establishment of a new DIT role and changed the responsibilities of the clapper/loader. Likewise, postproduction has seen the introduction of data wranglers, who take the raw data and convert it into the different formats required for different stages of postproduction—for example, small QuickTime files for off-line editing, DPX files for visual effects and grading work, and so on. The tremendous quantity of data means that new methods of asset management have had to be developed to catalogue and index footage to ensure easy access. Because the entire program is digital, editing and grading are no longer tied to specialist equipment or facilities. Shows can be edited, graded, and even finished on laptop computers, representing a freedom in working that has never been seen before. Likewise, digital content is easily repurposed from one platform to the next. Platform variants for DVDs, Blu-Ray, mobile phones, and other devices can be created directly and at low cost. The availability of professional-caliber equipment at a greatly reduced cost has meant that barriers to entry have been lifted.[4] Greater access to equipment has enabled independent filmmaking to flourish. The last argument put forth is simply that of commerce. All major equipment manufacturers—Arri, Panavision, Sony, Panasonic, and others—have modified or developed new designs based on technologies and methodologies used by a previously unknown start-up company. To many, Red has indeed fulfilled its promise of revolution.

Evolutionists counter that although there are new roles associated with production and post using new digital cinema systems, the fundamental aspects of cinematography—script interpretation, visualization, lighting design and planning, lens choice, camera movement, and so on—have remained virtually unchanged. Roles have adapted as technology has developed, but this has been an evolutionary process. Systems used in the creation of motion pictures have been emerging and changing for well over a century: hand-cranked cameras gave way to motorized systems; film stocks grew in gauge and sensitivity; color systems were introduced, developed, and refined, as was sound; wide-screen formats have come and gone in a wide range of aspect ratios; and the list goes on. It could be said that the only constant in feature film production is change. As such, digital cinema technologies simply represent the latest development, and there are bound to be others. The editing process is effectively unchanged as well, driven by the need to juxtapose shots as a story requires. New technologies and associated techniques make this easier and more efficient, but the editor's role is the same. Indeed, even the digital intermediate process evolved through the

application of new technologies to existing postproduction techniques (namely, the replacing of physical optical printers with a digital counterpart).

For viewers, it is impossible to distinguish between films that utilize a DI process and those that do not. As Bill Pope notes, "[t]he point is, [DI] looks great and it's indistinguishable from film" (qtd. in "*Spider-Man 2* Set to Deliver"). The all-digital nature of the DI process is directly analogous to the all-digital production pipeline involved with cameras such as Red and Alexa. If the viewer cannot see a difference between movies shot on film and those shot digitally, how can the use of a digital technology be considered revolutionary? Of course, film-based, HD video–based, and digital cinema–based programs have different looks because each process introduces a different type of artifact into the recording. But this is arguably no different from variations in the grain patterns or color characteristics of standard film stocks.

Throughout the history of cinema, there have often been alternative platforms for showcasing film content—from audio soundtracks adapted for radio to versions cut for TV broadcast to videotape for videocassette distribution. This is nothing new. To evolutionists, the bottom line is that the essence of the filmmaking and film-watching experiences is unchanged, and thus, digital cinematography is simply yet another landmark in the evolution of cinema.

Much of the innovation with regard to film production and delivery systems has historically been driven by commerce. Producers and studios have always sought to create products attractive to the market in such as way as to maximize profit. In this sense, the evolution and take-up of digital camera systems is similar to the arrival of sound. As Douglas Gomery describes it, the adoption of sound technology was driven by economic benefit to the studios (1). For a period, limitations in the emerging technologies and related production methods had a negative effect on the presentation of story, but these issues were resolved fairly quickly, resulting in a greater number of higher-profile (and higher-budget) projects moving to sound. The slow take-up of the first HD and digital camera systems for mainstream film-making, leading to the current reliance on digital camera systems for network television and big-budget features (e.g., *Pirates of the Caribbean: On Stranger Tides*, budgeted at roughly $250 million and shot solely on Red Epic), mimics this. The effect of the introduction of digital camera systems in production has been far less obvious to the viewer, but the impact on the business of film is arguably the same. Hollywood studios are conservative by nature to ensure profitability. Thus, production methods have evolved with new technologies rather than completely changing when new systems are available. The mainstream cinematographer's role may be slightly different with the advent of digital technologies, but the importance of cinematographers' work to Hollywood's bottom line means that the role has not been (nor could it be) radically altered.

Kirsner explores the development of feature film technologies from the silent era to the present day just prior to the take-up of digital cinema systems. He categorizes industry attitudes and perceptions into three camps—innovators, those who adopt new technology and push it to its limits; preservationists, those who cling doggedly to established tried-and-true systems; and sideline sitters, those who will wait for a consensus to form once a new technology stabilizes (5). He demonstrates how these camps reappear on a cyclical basis as new systems are developed. Digital cinema can be viewed in the same light. Underpinning Kirsner's thesis is the idea that movies themselves have not fundamentally changed; the nature of cinema, the relationship between the screen and the audience, has evolved but is essentially the same. The same arguably can be said about cinematography and the cinematographic process.

The tools of the cinematographer have changed, and methods have been adapted accordingly, but fundamentally, the role is still centered on the creation of images through the understanding of light, optics, and story. Gabriel Bernstein sums up the introduction of digital tools to the cinematographic process nicely:

I think cinematography will continue to be what it is. ... For us, it will remain a discussion about lighting ratios, controlling our contrast ratios, our faces, trying to get enough detail in the shadow areas and trying to get enough detail in the highlights. For us, the art and technique of cinematography will continue. Our palette will still be there. Maybe our colors will change, but the film look will continue. Cinematography has not essentially changed in 100 years and it's not going to change. It is the process of artistry that will evolve. (qtd. in Fauer 2: 25)

NOTES

1   This article was completed in August 2012.

2   "Workflow" refers to the step-by-step process of acquiring and manipulating picture and/or sound to create a motion picture (e.g., shooting, recording, editing, grading, mastering). In a digital context, this may require the use of specific file formats, software, and/or hardware systems at different stages. Not all systems are compatible, and thus, designing work-flows is an important component of the technical side of filmmaking.

3   Data for the cost-comparison table was gathered on a like-for-like basis of production packages from established Los Angeles vendors that have a history of supporting commercial projects. Quotes for the Arri camera package were obtained from Otto Nemenz, and quotes for the other three packages came from Abel Cine. Lab and consumable prices are an average based on quotes from Los Angeles suppliers. All data was compiled in August 2011.

4   It is common for Red camera packages to be rented at heavily discounted rates that are significantly lower than those given for other camera systems. This, plus the ability to conduct postproduction on personal computer systems with comparatively inexpensive software such as Final Cut Pro Studio, represents a landmark shift in the accessibility of true theatrical-grade production tools for low-budget independent filmmakers.

REFERENCES

"ASC Technology Committee Examines Arriflex D-20." *Arri Group*. ARRI, 11 Jan. 2005. Web. 14 Nov. 2011.

Belton, John. "Digital Cinema: A False Revolution." *October* 100 (Spring 2002): 98–114. Print.

"CCD vs. CMOS." *Teledyne Dalsa*. Teledyne DALSA, 2011. Web. 14 Nov. 2011.

Cohen, David. "Landmark Year for Digital." *Variety*. Reed Elsevier, 7 July 2011. Web. 14 Nov. 2011.

Fauer, Jon. *Cinematographer Style: The Complete Interviews*. 2 vols. Los Angeles: American Society of Cinematographers, 2008. Print.

Fisher, Bob. "Why 10 of the World's Top Cinematographers Have Still Not Bought into the Digital Revolution." *MovieMaker* 30 Nov. 2009. Web. 14 Nov. 2011.

Ganz, Adam, and Lina Khatib. "Digital Cinema: The Transformation of Film Practice and Aesthetics." *New Cinemas: Journal of Contemporary Film* 4.1 (2006): 21–36. Print.

Gomery, Douglas. *The Coming of Sound*. New York: Routledge, 2005. Print.

"Grass Valley: 50 Years of On-Air Innovation." *Grass Valley*. Grass Valley USA, 2011. Web. 14 Nov. 2011.

"HD Expo Presents Interviews with the Experts: Ted Schilowitz." *HD Expo*. Nielsen Business Media, 6 Mar. 2008. Web. 23 Sept. 2011.

Jannard, Jim. "Video: TED talks with Landmine Media at NAB 2011." *REDUser.net*. Landmine Media, 2011. Web. 7 July 2011.

Kalley, William. "Filmed in Panavision: An Interview with Sony Electronics' Larry Thorpe." *From Script to DVD*. N.p., 27 Sept. 2004. Web. 14 Nov. 2011.

Kirsner, Scott. *Inventing the Movies: Hollywood's Epic Battle between Innovation and the Status Quo, from Thomas Edison to Steve Jobs*. Seattle: CreateSpace, 2008. Print.

"Ready for Takeoff: Peter Jackson Takes the Time to Provide an Exclusive Update on *The Lovely Bones*, *The Dam Busters*, *Halo*, Wingnut Interactive, and a Great Deal More." *On Film*. Mediaweb, 1 May 2007. Web. 14 Nov. 2011.

"Red History." *Red Digital Cinema*. Red.com Inc., n.d. Web. 23 Sept. 2011.

Rogers, Pauline. "Cinematographers Discuss the Do's and Don'ts of Shooting in HD." *International Cinematographers Guild*. International Cinematographers Guild, Feb. 2005. Web. 14 Nov. 2011.

Sawicki, Mark. "A Plea to Preserving the Art of Cinematography." *MasteringFilm*. Focal Press, 2011. Web. 14 Nov. 2011.

"Sony and Panavision about to Deliver First Prototype 24 Frame Progressive High Definition Camera System to Lucasfilm." *All Business*. AllBusiness.com, 15 Nov. 1999. Web. 14 Nov. 2011.

"Spider-Man 2 Set to Deliver the Sharpest, Clearest Motion Picture Images Ever." *eFilm*. eFilm, 3 Sept. 2004. Web. 14 Nov. 2011.

"Technical Information Bulletin: Storage and Handling of Unprocessed Film." *Kodak*. Eastman Kodak, 2002. Web. 14 Nov. 2011.

Wheeler, Paul. *High Definition Cinematography*. 3rd ed. Oxford: Focal Press, 2009. Print.

Wright, Steve. *Digital Compositing for Film and Video*. 3rd ed. Oxford: Focal Press, 2010. Print.

A cinematographer is concerned with what happens in the camera frame and expertly uses a **film aesthetic**. For instance, a cinematographer is concerned about creative elements like lighting choices, how far or close shots appear to the audience, color scheme, the types of camera lenses used to convey specific meaning, how much action is happening in the frame, etc. Mateer argues that technology has always been a part of storytelling using film and the film aesthetic. From the late 1800s, when stories were merely photographs of daily life viewed through hand-cranked rudimentary equipment, continuing with the stories you tell each day using a mobile phone and the latest app, it's still technology capturing the story. However, if there's not enough good light to see the story even the best technology won't do the job.

You'll notice from Mateer's description of a cinematographer's job that lighting is a very important part of filmmaking. In fact, lighting is equally important for television and **digital video** storytelling. Lighting is a valuable skill, even if you're not an expert yet, and is often the difference between professional storytelling and the amateur stuff you see in the "epic fails" on YouTube.

In the next reading, Mick Hurbris-Cherrier provides an excellent overview of lighting basics, the essential properties of light, and the important concept of **color temperature**.

BASIC LIGHTING FOR FILM AND DV

by Mick Hurbis-Cherrier

Movie lighting is an art form in which the interplay of light, shadows, color, and movement serve as fundamental expressive elements in the telling of a story. Whether you are shooting on film or video, using only sunlight or using 20 movie lights, with lighting designed for a realistic style or a stylized look, it all comes down to finding a lighting scheme that is appropriate for this scene, at this moment, in this story. Like all art forms, there is really only one absolute rule to dramatic lighting—make it work. If you can justify the lighting design of a scene within the overall intentions of the project, then do it. However, as with all art forms, "making it work" also means having the skill and control to actually pull "it" off. With lighting, the more knowledge you acquire about the history, conventions, and approaches of dramatic lighting and the more control you develop over the materials, tools, and techniques of the craft, the more successfully you will achieve your vision. To gain this sort of control you must start with a solid foundation, which means knowing what tools you have at your disposal and how those tools work. It also means knowing some basic principles of light and lighting. Principles, unlike rules, can be applied creatively, used to improvise, and serve as the foundation for creative exploration and expression. As the great cinematographer Maryse Alberti tells us, "You have to master your tools and stay in the creative zone. It begins with knowing what you want your images to look like and why."

A thorough understanding of lighting principles is especially important to student and independent filmmakers, who are typically making films on a tight budget and time schedule. Lighting is the most time-consuming and labor-intensive process in making movies. It takes muscle and many hours to get lighting gear onto a set, into position for shooting, broken down afterward, and loaded back onto the truck. Hollywood films look like Hollywood films because they have all the time, money, and manpower they need for elaborate lighting schemes and setups. But just as with every other element of a filmmaker's art, money and size don't necessarily translate into a good or successful film. Ingenuity, imagination, and a practiced eye are your primary resources for using light to tell your story with visual eloquence and impact. If you really want to learn about lighting, stay away from the Hollywood blockbusters, which have an army of grips, gaffers, and electricians and several five-ton grip trucks filled to the brim with state-of-the-art lighting and grip equipment. Not only can these films make you feel that your resources are insufficient, but in fact, this surfeit of resources often proves to be an encumbrance that threatens to supersede the creative impulse with logistics and pure technical procedure for its own sake. Anyone who goes to the movies on a regular basis sees many films that were made with virtually limitless access to lighting gear and labor but that nonetheless feel lifeless. This feeling comes, in no small measure, from the lighting approach itself, which, for all of its professionalism, often is simply big, blunt, and overproduced rather than uniquely expressive.

Both film students and independent filmmakers should look instead at the filmmakers who have made great movies with very little—whether out of necessity or by choice—and who have conceived of simple, elegant, and expressive lighting designs. For example, look at the brilliantly innovative films from the French New Wave like *Masculin/Féminin*

Figure 3.1 Expressive and innovative lighting with modest resources. Top row: (*left*) Godard's *Masculin/ Feminin* (1966), (*middle*) Miller's *Personal Velocity* (2002), (*right*) Wong's *Chungking Express* (1994). Bottom row: (*left*) Figgis' *Leaving Las Vegas* (1995), (*middle*) Denis' *Nenette et Boni* (1996), (*right*) Fassbinder's *Ali: Fear Eats the Soul* (1974).

(Godard/Kurant); the New German Cinema movement like *Ali: Fear Eats the Soul* (Fassbinder/ Jürges); the more recent American Independent and European films like *Personal Velocity* (Miller/ Kuras), *Leaving Las Vegas* (Figgis/Quinn), and *Nanette et Boni* (Denis/Godard); and, of course, the fearless lighting of recent Asian films like *Chungking Express* (KarWai/Doyle) (Figure 3.1). These pictures all had relatively modest lighting resources but used them with a profound understanding of artistry and technique, which can teach us far more about lighting, camerawork, and storytelling than the latest $150 million Hollywood production.

The great cinematographer Néstor Almendros made a critically important point when talking about his work lighting and shooting Eric Rohmer's *La Collectionneuse* (1966). In his interview for the book *Masters of Light* (by Dennis Schaefer and Larry Salvato), Almendros talks about his naturalistic lighting approach, working with Rohmer, and how few lights and crew they discovered they actually needed to make the film: "[We] realized that most technicians had been bull***ing, you know, and inventing uses for enormous amounts of light to justify their importance, to justify their salaries and to make themselves look like someone who knows a secret, when there is technically very little to know."

THE FUNDAMENTAL OBJECTIVES OF LIGHTING

Whether we are lighting with a grip truck filled with movie lights, a small portable lighting kit, or just the sun, there are five fundamental objectives to lighting any scene: (1) exposure and visibility, (2) depth and dimension, (3) narrative emphasis (4) tone and mood (5) consistency. The most rudimentary and utilitarian function of movie lighting is *exposure and visibility*, ensuring a scene will register on our imaging medium and a viewer can see details. However, anyone can blast thousands of watts of light at a scene and guarantee that the viewer will see absolutely everything! Expressive lighting, on the other hand, involves lighting for the dramatic needs of the scene. This means manipulating light sources, shadows, and colors to create the visual look appropriate for your scene and story. [Lighting] angles and shadows are significant factors in creating or minimizing *depth and dimension* within a shot, and this contributes significantly to the composition of the frame. Additionally, we must consider how our lighting scheme works to compliment the *visual narrative emphasis* that may be required in a scene. For example, lighting to reveal some details clearly while perhaps concealing others; or to create areas of greater and lesser prominence within a shot; or lighting to create visual relationships between characters or maybe characters with their environment. These aspects of lighting function in tandem with shot composition and set design to give emphasis to visual information and to guide the viewer's attention. Very closely related to this is the fourth objective of lighting, to establish a particular (and appropriate) *emotional tone or mood* for a scene. The inclusion or elimination of shadows, the range of colors in a scene, the hardness or softness of the light, the direction from which lights come: all of these lighting choices, when conceived intelligently from the content of the script, can have a profound impact on the emotional tone that will be communicated to an audience. The way we use, control, and manipulate our sources of light to create narrative and emotional emphasis plays an enormous role in the overall visual style of the cinematography and therefore the film. That style can be naturalistic or stylized. Finally, with so many possible lighting variables available every time we set up a new scene, we need to be vigilant that our lighting schemes *remain consistent* from shot to shot and scene to scene so that the finished film has a unified visual style (even if specific lighting details change to reflect tonal shifts in the story). If we light each shot without considering the larger canvas we run the risk of creating shots that look fine on their own, but will not edit next to other shots (lighting continuity) or scenes which break the emotional tone of the film.

THE FUNDAMENTAL SOURCES OF LIGHT

Anything that gives off light, from the blazing midday sun to a candle, can be used as a lighting source in a scene. **Natural light** is a term meaning a light source coming from nature, a source that is not artificial. Usually we mean the sun when we talk about natural light, but the term also applies to light that comes from nonelectric sources, whether or not they are indeed naturally occurring, like campfires,

candles, and fireplaces. If your scene included flashes from lightning bolts, that, too, would be a natural light source. **Artificial light** is any light source that generates light though electricity. Artificial lights can be as big as a 50,000-watt movie light or as small as a flashlight (Figure 3.2).

The term **available light** refers to light sources that ordinarily exist in any given location. For example, if we walk into a grocery store with our camera and simply shoot by the light of the fluorescent fixtures overhead or if we shoot in a bedroom illuminated only by the sun streaming in from a window, we are shooting with available light. And, as you might suspect, **mixed lighting** refers to combining available sources and artificial lights to achieve the look we're after. It's very common to use the sun as one light source and artificial lights another (Figure 3.3).

Very often natural or available light sources are not powerful enough to create an exposure, but we nonetheless want the audience to feel like

Figure 3.2 An 18,000-watt HMI on location (*top*) and a flashlight in *The Blair Witch Project* (1999) (*bottom*). Usable artificial lights come in many sizes.

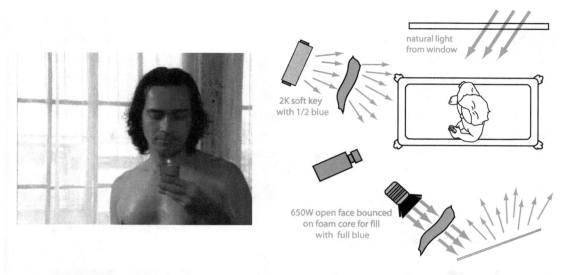

Figure 3.3 In this scene, from Katherine Hurbis-Cherrier's *Ode to a Bar of Soap* (1998), mixed lighting (artificial and sunlight) has been balanced for color temperature and quality. See the color insert.

that particular source is illuminating the scene. For example, a character is watching TV and we want the audience to believe that the glow from the screen is the only light illuminating her face, but the glow from a TV (or candle, or fireplace, or 25-watt reading lamp, etc.) is almost never strong enough to get a good exposure, especially if your character is some distance away. In this sort of situation we bring in an artificial light to duplicate the color, quality, and direction of the ostensible light source, but at a higher intensity (Figure 3.4). While this light obviously remains off screen, the ostensible source is often shown in the scene.

This strategy of using movie lights to duplicate where light would logically be emanating from is called **motivated lighting**. Motivated lighting is a central strategy for creating naturalistic lighting designs.

THREE ESSENTIAL PROPERTIES OF LIGHT

Light sources don't simply give off generic light: every light source emits a light that has specific characteristics that contribute to the look of your scene. Three of the basic properties of light that give any light source its distinctive character are **intensity, hard versus soft**, and **color temperature**.

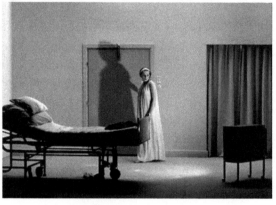

Figure 3.4 The real glow of a TV could not produce enough light for an exposure, so its output was amplified with the use of a movie light in Ingmar Bergman's *Persona* (1966).

INTENSITY

Light **intensity** is the strength of the light emitted by a source and, as we mentioned earlier, is measured by a light meter in footcandles. Direct sunlight is obviously a very intense source of light, although the actual intensity changes depending on its angle at various times of day. With artificial light, intensity depends on the **wattage of the lamp** used (500 watts, 1,000 watts, etc.) and on the **reflector system**. When we speak of lamp wattage we use the symbol "K" to stand in for "thousand." So a 1,000-watt light is called a 1K and a 2,000-watt light is called a 2K. (Do not get this K mixed up with the "K" symbol used for degrees Kelvin, when referring to color temperatures.) A very common movie light is a 1K Fresnel with a color temperature of 3,200°K.

Some lighting instruments have a **specular reflector system**. A specular reflector system uses a highly polished, mirror-like surface to reflect the light from the lamp and is very efficient in maintaining the intensity of the lamp wattage. Other instruments use a **diffuse reflector system** to soften the light, and this cuts down the intensity (Figure 3.5). In addition, some lighting units employ a lens in front of the lamp to help control the directionality of the beam, but this, too, cuts down the intensity of the light.

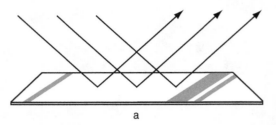 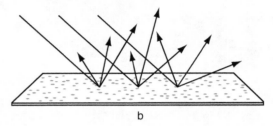

a   b

Figure 3.5 A specular surface, like a mirror or a polished reflector (a) maintains the directionality of the light rays it reflects. A diffused surface (b), like foam core or a matte reflector, scatters the light rays, changing the quality of the light from hard to soft.

The intensity of incident light on your scene is also greatly affected by the lighting unit-to-subject distance. The farther away an instrument is placed from the subject, the weaker the light is falling on the scene. This diminishing intensity as the unit is moved away follows the **inverse square law**, which says that the intensity of light falls off by the square of the distance from the subject (Figure 3.6).

Obviously the converse applies when you bring a light in closer, to increase its intensity on the subject. If the inverse square law seems like a lot of calculation to do on the set, you can simply apply this rule of thumb: if you double the distance between the lighting unit and your subject, say from 10 feet to 20 feet, the strength of the light will fall off four times and will be only one-fourth the intensity compared to the original position. If you halve the distance between the subject and the lighting unit, you will increase the light intensity four times from the original position.

HARD VERSUS SOFT

The lamps for the most commonly used film lights involve a wire filament, enclosed in a glass bulb, surrounded by a vacuum of inert gases, heated to the point where it glows white hot. That glowing filament becomes the **point source** of the lamp's illumination, creating a highly directional beam. Light that travels directly from a lamp to the subject is referred to as a **hard light** or **directional light**, because the light rays, which travel straight and parallel to each other, all fall on the subject from a single angle, causing sharp shadows and bright highlight areas. Lighting instruments with specular reflector systems preserve this hardness because a specular surface, like a mirror, redirects the light rays yet maintains their direct and parallel path. Units that do not illuminate directly from the lamp but instead reflect the light off an unpolished, white surface emit a **diffused** or **soft light**. The unpolished surface scatters the light rays in a variety of angles, disturbing their parallel paths (Figure 3.7).

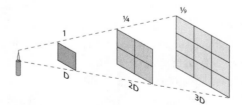

Figure 3.6 The inverse square law. Doubling the distance from the light source to our subject means that the illumination is spread over four times the area and is therefore only one fourth the intensity.

Figure 3.7 Hard light creates sharp shadows (*left*) because the light beams maintain their parallel direction. Soft light (*right*) creates diffused shadows because the scattered light beams reach the subject from many directions.

Figure 3.8 Hard light can be softened (diffused) by applying diffusion material in front of it (*left*) or by bouncing it off a white surface, like foam core (*right*).

Diffused light rays do not hit the subject from the same angle and therefore create softer shadows and smoother highlights. This sort of lighting instrument is called a soft light. It's important to note that the larger the area of the diffused bounce surface is, the softer the light will be.

Understanding this principle, you can see that it is not difficult to soften the light from a hard lighting instrument by simply bouncing it off any diffused surface, like a white wall or a white bounce board. You can also soften light from a hard lighting unit by placing **diffusion media** in front of the beam (Figure 3.8). Diffusion media scatters the light rays in a way similar to that achieved by bouncing light off a diffusing surface. Be aware, however, that diffusing light either way decreases its intensity. It's also important to understand that the terms "hard" and "soft" describe a characteristic of light and should not

be viewed as a value judgment. One is not better than the other. As with so many other things, the appropriate choice is based primarily on applying the appropriate aesthetic choice for the content of your story (Figure 3.9).

COLOR TEMPERATURE

Different sources of light favor different areas of the light spectrum, and the tonality that a light favors is called its **color temperature**. Color temperature is measured by the Kelvin scale. In discussing film color sensitivity, we already mentioned that average daylight is 5,600° K (quite blue), but the sun can change color temperature dramatically over the course of the day; the late afternoon sun can dip to around 4,000°K, and dawn and dusk can be as warm as 2,000°K.

The most common artificial lighting instruments for medium-scale film and DV production

Figure 3.9 The decision to use hard or soft light depends on the aesthetic needs of your film. Although both of these shots use a low-key lighting approach, S. Coppola's *Lost in Translation* (2003, *left*) uses soft light, while Boe's *Reconstruction* (2003, *right*) uses hard light, which explains their radically different look and feel.

are **tungsten lights** (tungsten-halogen) (also called **quartz lights**), which have a color temperature of 3,200°K (quite warm). Tungsten lights are efficient and powerful for their wattage, but they burn hot and so require ventilation and careful handling. Another kind of light commonly used in bigger budget productions is the **HMI** (hydrargyrum medium-arc iodide). HMIs are designed to emit a light that matches daylight color temperature, 5,600°K. HMIs are very efficient lights and burn cooler than tungsten lights, but they require a heavy power ballast in addition to the lighting unit itself. This additional encumbrance along with a higher

rental price make the HMI primarily a professional lighting unit (Figure 3-10).

Figure 3-10 Lighting units are designed in either Tungsten (*left*) or daylight color temperatures, also called HMI's (*right*) to make the balancing of mixed lighting easier.

FILM LITERACY

As Paul Messaris points out, film literacy has been traditionally rooted in the idea that the audience/viewer of the film must bring some sort of prior experience and understanding in order to understand what she/he is seeing—a sort of **cinematic** literacy (Messaris 2014). For example, when a person watches director Sam Raimi's 2002 *Spider Man* and sees mild-mannered, bookish, eyeglass-wearing Peter Parker on screen walking to school it's likely that person will assume that Peter Parker is (a) the main character, (b) probably has a secret, and (c) is also the hero. The person understands what she/he is watching precisely because she/he has seen and perhaps read *Spider Man* comics and is probably familiar with other superhero stories. This prior knowledge contributes to film literacy. As a result, the audience understands what the film's moving images mean and has expectations of what will and should happen in the film before they even pay for the movie ticket.

In the next reading, author Liam Burke highlights how audiences connect with comic book films released between 2000 and 2009. He describes three main reasons for this connection and the huge North American success of these films. First, many audience members were dealing with real-life trauma post-9/11 when films like *Spider Man* were released. Also, digital film techniques improved significantly during this time, making superhero stories more accessible and more believable. Last, comic books have a preexisting audience who are dedicated fans and easily connect with multiple comic book universes, and this translates easily into large audiences for movies based on comic book characters.

THE GOLDEN AGE OF COMIC BOOK FILMMAKING

by Liam Burke

YOU'LL BELIEVE A MAN CAN FLY

He began not as flesh and blood, but as a simple line drawing. His comic strip has thrilled millions around the world. The magic of radio gave to his name a breathless signature and sound. Then with television came a whole new generation who idolize his exploits. Today, at last, his evolution is complete. Brought to life by the awesome technology of film … . Until now his incredible adventures had been beyond the power of any known medium to realize, but now the greatest creative and technical minds of the motion picture world have gathered to meet the challenge of *Superman*. He has come of age, our age. This Christmas Superman brings you the gift of flight. *Superman* is now the movie.

—*Superman: The Movie* original trailer

From the earliest adaptations, filmmakers have emphasized the importance of the latest technology in bringing comics to the screen. For instance, the framing device for the appropriately titled *Winsor McCay, The Famous Cartoonist of the N.Y. Herald and his Moving Comics* (Blackton and McCay 1911), saw McCay (playing himself) proposing to a roomful of doubting colleagues that he will "make four thousand pen drawings that will move." Following one month of toil, the naysayers (and audience) are stunned when McCay brings his *Little Nemo in Slumberland*

characters to life by using animation techniques more sophisticated than anything previously seen. Over sixty years later, *Superman: The Movie* traded on its spectacular effects with the tagline, "You'll Believe A Man Can Fly."[1] More recently, chairman of 20th Century Fox, Tom Rothman, argued that a leaked workprint of *X-Men Origins: Wolverine* (Hood 2009), which included the full footage, was a "complete misrepresentation of the film" as "none of the effects shots were in any remotely final form" (Spines "Exclusive: Fox Chairman").

Thus, it is unsurprising that the most widely cited catalyst for the modern comic book adaptation trend is technical innovations, in particular digital technologies. For example, without exception, all of the comic creators and filmmakers interviewed for this study cited technology as one of the causal factors for the comic book adaptation trend, with *Green Hornet* screenwriter Evan Goldberg eschewing ritualistic necessity, ideological precepts, and a variety of other possibilities to confidently state, "I think it is only because of effects."[2] Many commentators echo the industry. For instance, zeitgeist skeptic Bordwell notes the "importance of special effects" in his assessment of the trend ("Superheroes for Sale"). Similarly, Bukatman comments, "It's no accident that this wave of superhero films followed the development of ever more convincing CGI [computer-generated imagery] technologies" ("Why I Hate

Superhero Movies" 122). How fans used digital technologies to increase their visibility, and the visibility of their objects of devotion, [...] should not be undervalued or ignored. However, taking its cue from the industry and commentators, this section will focus on the argument that digital filmmaking techniques were the catalyst for the unprecedented number of comic book film adaptations produced since 2000.

There are a number of persuasive arguments to support this technological determinist position. Firstly, many commentators believe that special effects attract audiences, with D. N. Rodowick contending that CGI allows for "market differentiation" and the chance to "bolster sagging audience numbers" (1398). The audience research for this study certainly supports this argument. For instance, fourteen of the eighty-two respondents who qualified their expectations of the surveyed films offered some variant of "special effects," with responses including: a 26–30-year-old male non-fan at *Thor* who expected a "good action movie with very good special effects (to be seen in the cinema)," a male fan (21–25) who anticipated that *Green Lantern* would be a "CGI heavy film with more action than story," and a 26–30-year-old female non-fan who hoped that *The Adventures of Tintin* would have "good 3D effects."

This argument is further supported by the unique events surrounding the leaking of the *X-Men Origins: Wolverine* workprint one month before its May 1, 2009, release. The print, which 20th Century Fox estimated was downloaded 4.5 million times, included all the footage that appeared in the theatrical version with the greatest difference being that some effects shots were unfinished. Rather than detract from the film's box office, *Entertainment Weekly* cited tracking figures that suggested the leak might have helped generate interest in the film (Spines "Tracking Data"). Despite the ready availability of the film for weeks prior to the official release, the attraction of the completed effects in a cinematic experience (i.e., surround sound, big screen, and a large audience)

was enough to ensure that the film still achieved blockbuster status ($373 million worldwide). Such examples suggest that special effects are important to the comic book adaptation and its audience, which makes a compelling case for filmmaking technology to be recognized as one of the chief causal factors in this modern filmmaking trend.

Another point raised by those who subscribe to the technology argument is that comics have been waiting on film technology to reach the point where their often-heightened images could be convincingly portrayed. In discussing the green screens used in his comic book adaptation *Sin City* (2005), director Robert Rodriguez states, "Technology helps push the artform and create new ideas" ("15 Minute Flick School"). Echoing Rodriguez, Bordwell suggests that the "fantastic powers of superheroes cried out for CGI (computer-generated imagery), and it may be that convincing movies in the genre weren't really ready until the software matured" ("Superheroes for Sale"). Similarly, comic book creator Grant Morrison writes in his book *Supergods*, "Technology had caught up with the comics and believing a man could fly was as easy as believing a giant could be a midget" (322).

Such arguments are not unique to comic book adaptations. Even a cursory view of film production history provides many examples in which filmmaking technology was seen to influence what sources were adapted and how they made their way to the screen. For instance, Naremore notes how the advent of sound "produced a great appetite for literature among Hollywood moguls" ("Introduction" 4), and Michele Pierson writes that "the real history of science-fiction film is the history of its production technology" (165).

Perhaps the connection between technology and adaptation is more forcibly made with comics because the source material, particularly in its mainstream American form, has often aspired to cinematic qualities. Comic books first gained popularity by featuring the power fantasies that no other medium could effectively convey.[3] Readers would see heroes perform feats that could only be described in novels and on radio or poorly presented in cinema. Despite the potential for comics to mitigate many of cinema's limitations, American comic books still often sought cinematic qualities. For instance, it has been noted that many comic book stories and characters were inspired by cinema (Feiffer 30), yet developed in directions the film form was still unable to travel. Thus, Batman was Douglas Fairbanks released from the confines of gravity and 1930s film production technology; the impossible beasts of 1950s Marvel comics, such as Droom, The Living Lizard!, confidently stomped across cities when the best that film could offer was a rubber-suited stuntman shuffling down a scale-model Tokyo; and *Sin City* achieved a true film noir aesthetic of startling whites and impenetrable blacks that traditional cinematography was unable to create. As Stan Lee summarized, "We had to wait until the special effects were developed to the point where they could do all those things" (Burke *Superhero Movies* 151–52).

Thus, the argument seems to be that many of the most popular comic book stories were merely in a seventy-year incubation waiting for a more appropriate medium—cinema—to develop the tools necessary to depict these power fantasies.[4] While such arguments further position technology as the chief causal factor in the development of today's comic book adaptation trend, they are open to charges of reductionism. At the very least, the suggestion that comics were a placeholder for these stories diminishes the form's status as its own vital art form with a unique means of expression. Furthermore, technology is not Batman—it does not appear from nowhere, exert its influence, and then retreat into the shadows. Its relationship to the social sphere demands a more nuanced understanding.

* * *

Murphie and Potts describe a technological determinist position as "one-sided" (17), and suggest Brian Winston's linguistics approach to modeling change as a possible corrective. In his historically based analysis Winston describes how "generalised forces coalesce to function as a transforming

agency" which he calls "supervening social necessities." It is these supervening social necessities that move a prototype "out of the laboratory and into the world at large" (6). Possible factors that might have compelled the development and wider diffusion of digital filmmaking technologies include: the audience's appetite for greater screen realism, the filmmaker's wish for absolute control, and the financier's need to reduce budgets. [...] This relay back-and-forth may be partly attributable to the representational overlap that these graphic narrative mediums enjoy. The desire to narrow this semiotic gap might also be considered one of the supervening social necessities that compelled the innovation of digital filmmaking techniques and influenced their wider diffusion.

While filmmakers adapting comics might have only enjoyed certain technical standards with the advent of digital cinema, prior to such innovations they did not confine themselves to the limits of their era, but expanded their range of tools to better match the source material. For instance, many critics have discussed how the oft-cited special effects have brought about changes that are "conceptual rather than fundamental" (Sutton 388).[5] Comparing an underwater sequence from *The Spirit* (Miller 2008) with one from the much earlier adaptation *Danger: Diabolik!* (Bava 1968), one can see an example of how many modern special effects are often little more than digitally upgraded smoke and mirrors. *The Spirit* producer Deborah Del Prete boasted that the use of digital backlot technology allowed the film's cast to appear as if underwater while maintaining their hair and makeup, much as they would in a comic (*The Spirit* DVD commentary). However, a similar effect was achieved four decades earlier by simply placing a water tank between the camera and actors for *Danger: Diabolik!* Similarly, Michael Cohen, in his essay "Dick Tracy: In Pursuit of a Comic Book Aesthetic," demonstrates how the 1990 film used pre-digital technology (e.g., makeup, costumes, and mattes) to match its source as effectively as more modern films. Thus, the desire to adapt comics, and adapt them faithfully, predates the recent advent of digital technologies.

Furthermore, many filmmakers, inspired by comics, went beyond such creative solutions to push forward the technologies of the time. Winsor McCay is arguably the father of the comic book film adaptation. In order to bring his *Little Nemo in Slumberland* characters to the screen in 1911, the innovative creator advanced the techniques developed by film pioneers Emile Cohl and J. Stuart Blackton (who would co-direct McCay's film) to create the first sophisticated animated film, *Winsor McCay, The Famous Cartoonist of the N.Y. Herald and his Moving Comics*. Similarly, as this section's epigraph points out, "the greatest creative and technical minds of the motion picture world … gathered to meet the challenge of *Superman*." One of those challenges was the application of motion-control photography, popularized by *Star Wars* (Lucas 1977), to live-action actors rather than model spaceships. Thus, even though the special effects breakthroughs of *Star Wars* might have provided filmmakers with the confidence to adapt

Superman in the late 1970s, the comic character's specificities compelled them to push the technology further. This cyclical relationship between comic book adaptations and technology continued into the digital age.

As the McCay example suggests, many filmmakers have gravitated towards animation as a way to replicate comics. Animation afforded filmmakers a mastery of mise-en-scène absent in pre-digital cinema, and through its application one can see filmmakers reaching for qualities that would later be realized in the digital age. For instance, in the first live-action *Superman* serial (1948), sequences in which the character would fly saw actor Kirk Alyn substituted with a cel animated hero.[6] While the application of this technique was dictated somewhat by budget, thirty years later animation was still being considered to make Superman fly for the blockbuster *Superman: The Movie*.[7] Today, a number of adaptations still incorporate basic animation with live action footage to approximate

Figure 3.10 In the 1948 *Superman* serial, actor Kirk Alyn was replaced by cel animation during the flying sequences.

the source material and demonstrate fidelity (e.g., *American Splendor, The Losers,* and *Scott Pilgrim*).[8]

Such examples tally with cartoonist Robert C. Harvey's celebration of the more malleable comic form in his 1996 book *The Art of the Comic Book.* Harvey begins his argument by stating that the "images in comics can be more readily tampered with and modified than the images in film, which must reproduce pretty much what the eye sees in nature," before conceding that animation allowed for some of the control comic creators enjoy and ultimately suggesting that "animated cartoons are a third medium" (175). However, in the years following Harvey's statement the wider proliferation of digital filmmaking techniques dramatically reshaped the ontology of the film image, with many suggesting that cinema had now joined the plastic arts.

Many scholars agree that the "in-your-face special effects of these films are red herrings" (Prince "Film Artifacts" 24), and that the most important consequence of digital film technologies is the degree of control it confers on the filmmaker. For instance, commenting during the early days of digital filmmaking, *Batman & Robin* (Schumacher 1997) visual effects supervisor John Dykstra said, "When the ability to create images in the digital environment a pixel at a time arrived [the visual effects supervisor role] got to be much less an engineer [role] and much more a designer [role]" ("Freeze Frame"). Citing Soviet montage theorist Lev Kuleshov, John A. Berton predicted this shift in a prescient 1990 essay, writing, "Kuleshov seems to call for exactly what digital cinema offers: complete control over every structural element in both the world space and screen space of the shot" (8).[9]

Echoing Harvey's earlier observation, new media scholar Lev Manovich believes that many of the antecedents of digital filmmaking can be found in animation, a viewpoint shared by several commentators and borne out by the history of the comic book adaptation.[10] Where once Kirk Alyn took to the skies as Superman through the use of a hand-drawn hero, today Henry Cavill allows a digitally constructed Man of Steel to carry out much of the high-altitude heroics—a more convincing, but no less constructed intermediate. Comic book adaptations are not simply at the vanguard of the transition to a more malleable film image. The desire to achieve the high aesthetic criterion set by the handcrafted comic book source was one of the supervening social necessities compelling development of these digital filmmaking techniques.

Bullet-time, the slow-motion technique in which the camera appears to move around a near-frozen object, was first popularized in the 1999 film *The Matrix.* The film's creators, the Wachowskis, have cited comics as the inspiration for the technique, with Lana (then Larry) explaining, "Comics are a graphic-type storytelling where you could freeze a moment and make an image that sustains. As a counterpart, you can't really do that in film. We tried to do that" ("Follow the White Rabbit"). Antecedents to bullet-time exist, including comic book adaptation *Blade* (Norrington 1998), but as the film's visual effects supervisor John Gaeta explained, "bullet-time is something that was conceived for *The Matrix* specifically, but I think it's the by-product of the directors observing the controls coming into place. And then they asked the right questions at the right time" ("What is Bullet-time?"). Thus, without their comic book inspiration, the Wachowskis might not have asked the "right questions," and bullet-time would not have been applied in *The Matrix* where its popularity led to the technique's wide diffusion. Thus, in much the same way that the *Little Nemo in Slumberland* comic provided the impetus to develop more sophisticated animation techniques, the desire to achieve comic-like images has propelled digital technology in directions unforeseen by its creators.

It is not only the heightened imagery of comics that has prompted this innovation, but also the creators themselves. Like McCay's foray into early animation, today's comic creators have proven to be among the artists best positioned to shape this more malleable film image. Prior to the success of *Sin City*, the only Hollywood film to use a digital backlot for the entirety of its production was *Sky Captain and the World of Tomorrow* (Conran 2004), which, despite a large budget and A-list cast, underperformed at the box office.[11] By contrast, the co-director of *Sin City*, comic book artist Frank Miller, was described as having "not only mastered the technology but ... used it with artistry" (LaSalle 1). Furthermore, the film's graphiation,[12] attributed to Miller, was cited by many as one of the reasons for the film's success.[13] Also released in 2005 was the low-budget, digital-backlot production *MirrorMask*, directed by *Sandman* artist Dave McKean and written by his comic book collaborator Neil Gaiman. Although this film garnered less attention than *Sin City,* critics uniformly cited comic book creator McKean's effective use of digital technology as the most successful aspect of the production.[14]

NOTES

1   Warner Bros. president of marketing at the time of the production of *Superman: The Movie,* Andrew Fogelson, remarked that the tagline, "You'll Believe A Man Can Fly," was "the single most important part of the whole marketing campaign. It was our way of saying to the ticket-buying world: 'We've learned how to do things in movies you've never seen before' and what better way to do it than to give you this spectacular version of Superman" ("Taking Flight: The Development of Superman").

2   Among the interview responses to the question of why so many comic book adaptations have been produced in the past two decades were: "The most obvious reason is the technology finally advanced to the point where you can do a movie about a superhero whether it's a Silver Surfer, Green Lantern, Thor or whoever"

(*Batman* executive producer Michael E. Uslan); and "one [catalyst] is simply the technology has gotten to the point where you can legitimately realize some of these characters on film in a way that you might not have been able to do twenty years previously" (Marvel Comics senior vice-president of publishing Tom Brevoort).

3   Writing in 1996, cartoonist and critic Robert C. Harvey noted, "Comic books were the ideal medium for portraying the exploits of super beings. They were nearly the only medium at the time ... only in comics could such antics be imbued with a sufficient illusion of reality to make the stories convincing" (35).

4   A number of commentators believe that cinema's recent annexation of the mainstream comic book industry's power fantasies will benefit the form (McCloud *Reinventing Comics* 212–13), with comics scholar Brad Brooks suggesting "that since now movies can use CGI, there is no need for comics to have superheroes in them" (Regalado 118).

5   Stephen Prince notes how Georges Méliès "used papier-mâché and stop-motion tricks where filmmakers today use computers" ("Filmic Artifacts" 26). Bukatman, also citing early cinema, points out that special effects are "only a more recent manifestation of optical, spectacular technologies" (*Matters of Gravity* 91), while Aylish Wood sees little distinction between the matte paintings of *Ben-Hur* and the digitally created Colosseum of *Gladiator* (378).

6   Other serials produced by Columbia at this time also employed cel animation to create "special effects," including *Captain Video: Master of the Stratosphere* (Gordon Bennet and Grissell 1951), in which "Captain Video and the Ranger left their hidden Earth headquarters and blasted off, via a crudely animated cartoon spacecraft" (Harmon and Glut 50). Other serials to employ this technique

were the comic strip adaptations *Bruce Gentry* (Gordon Bennet and Carr 1949) and *Blackhawk* (Gordon Bennet and Sears 1952).

7 Supervisor for optical effects Roy Field describes how animation was tested during the development of *Superman: The Movie*, "but alas, it wasn't photo-real enough" ("The Magic Behind the Cape").

8 Comic book adaptations were obviously not the only films to integrate live-action footage with animation during these pre-digital eras. As Paul Wells notes of Ray Harryhausens work in fantasy and adventure films, "Animation itself, however, is also often perceived as an 'effect' within live-action film-making, for example in the work of Ray Harryhausen in feature films from *The Beast from 20,000 Fathoms* (1953) to *Clash of the Titans* (1981) in which his stop-motion animated creatures and figures were the central aspect of the narrative and spectacle" (28).

9 As one of the innovators and early practitioners of digital technologies, George Lucas, remarked in a 1995 interview, "We've changed the medium in a way that is profound. It is no longer a photographic medium. It's now a painterly medium" *(A Personal Journey)*. A number of scholars have echoed Lucas's assessment that cinema is now closer to the plastic arts. John Belton notes of the increased malleability of the film image: "In the old days, filmmakers used to say they would 'fix it in post [-production].' Now with DI, they tend to say they'll 'make it in post'" (59). Similarly, Stam believes "filmmakers no longer need a pro-filmic model in the world; like novelists, they can give artistic form to abstract dreams" ("Introduction" 12).

10 In a 2007 report on the Irish film and television industry, it was noted that "many of the skills and techniques of animation are fundamental to feature film and television drama postproduction. Indeed, as special effects continue to build importance in feature film the crossover between animation and feature film has grown significantly" (*Creating a Sustainable Irish Film* 14). Similarly, Wells believes that animation techniques are fundamental to modern filmmaking: "Arguably, virtually all contemporary cinema is reliant on animation as the key source of its story-telling devices and effects" (28). These more recent assessments tally with Lev Manovich's contention that "digital cinema is a particular case of animation that uses live action footage as one of its many elements" (302).

11 *Sky Captain and the World of Tomorrow* had a production budget of $70 million, but only grossed $38 million at the North American box office. By contrast, *Sin City* had a production budget of $40 million, yet went on to gross $74 million at the North American box office.

12 Philippe Marion in *Traces en cases* terms "the graphic and narrative enunciation of the comics" as "graphiation" (Baetens 147).

13 Mick LaSalle of the *San Francisco Chronicle* cited Miller's influence on the film in his review of *Sin City:* "The film uses a combination of live action, performed by real actors, and computer graphics to transform Frank Miller's graphic novels into moving pictures" (1).

14 On its release, film reviewers identified the inventive use of digital technologies as one of the strongest elements of *MirrorMask*, with Roger Ebert writing in his largely negative review that "the movie is a triumph of visual invention," with Lisa Schwarzbaum summarizing, "CG effects and digital animation employed with avant-garde panache in a live-action adventure … an unusual collaboration between lord-of-the-cult multimedia artist Dave McKean and king-of-the-comics Neil Gaiman."

Interview with a Professional

David Gordon, Technical Engineering Manager at CRTV, LLC.
Interviewed by Matt Crick, Spring, 2017.

Why are good communication skills important in your field?

Good communication skills are important because they allow for a team to be flexible when problems (inevitably) arise. Poor communication means low productivity and slow reaction time.

What specific skills do you use the most?

Using language in a way that promotes inclusivity and a positive work environment, i.e., using "we" instead of "you." Everyone has different ways of understanding and learning things; by making the effort to understand that person's learning curve, you are empowering her/him and yourself as well.

In terms of filmmaking and production, what skills do you find lacking in others?

The ability to problem solve and budgeting.

How have the knowledge or skills you gained at a college or university been useful to you in terms of your career? How would you have prepared differently while you were in school?

They created a vague map of how the media industry is laid out. I learned just enough to know that this is the field I want to work in but not enough to understand how or what I want to do. While in school, I would have worked a lot more on personal creative projects and gotten involved on hands-on production work.

What advice would you give to Communication majors about to enter the workforce? Pitfalls to avoid, that sort of thing.

You will only learn what you like to do and what you are good at by trying everything once. Don't close doors because it's "not your thing." The more you know about how the bigger picture works, the better you will be at your specific profession.

Thinking back on your career preparation choices, what decision are you most proud of? What would you have done differently?

I am most proud of taking initiatives to learn equipment and talk to people who were outside of what was required during both of my internships. Because of those initial impulses to extend myself outside of the "norm," I made the connections to get to where I am now. In turn, I am now going through the same process of advancing in my career through connections I made the effort to create. What I would have done differently is start caring about my career choices sooner during my university years. I could have been three steps ahead of where I am now had I started making an effort earlier.

Conclusion

Just like in the early days of filmmaking, there will always be technological advances and different ways to distribute filmed content. However, the movie theatre experience for many has changed. For instance, today, audiences can see high-quality storytelling—from the writing to the lighting—in the comfort of their homes, on demand. *Variety*, Hollywood's online and in-print news source, reported in July of 2016 "the audience of 18- to 39-year-olds has declined over the past five years, according to the Motion Picture Association of America." But in television and online spaces like HBO, Showtime, Netflix, and Amazon "content continues to be compelling, with production values that rival those on the big screen" (Lang and Rainey 2016).

The art of film production—what's in the frame, the director's *vision* for a film, the mood or tone of a scene, or how effectively the story suspends our disbelief—is critical. For many people, these qualities define whether a film is excellent or horrible. Learning the art of film production takes years of practice and experience. The craft of film production, i.e., the tools, standards, industry protocols, and production process continues to evolve, and it's easier and cheaper than ever to access and tell new stories that will reach worldwide audiences. Mastering the craft of film production is subject to constant and unpredictable shifts from all sides: technology, culture, industry, and economics.

CLASSROOM ACTIVITY

You've been selected by a mobile phone manufacturer to participate in a competition to create a commercial for its new mobile phone. However, there are strict guidelines you must follow in creating your story. The title of the commercial campaign is: Max's Mobile.

1   Students will be placed into groups of three.

2   One person is designated as the commercial's cinematographer, one person is the actor, and one person is the producer/director.

3   Each group has a total of 45 minutes to write and shoot a 30-second commercial for the competition.

4   A basic script containing all the images and words must be created. Since there is no editing that can be done, the script must show the exact shot/image, exact length, and exact order of images and sound.

5   All images and sound must be recorded with only one mobile phone.

6   Once all the commercials are complete, each team will present its commercial, and one team will be judged the winner.

DISCUSSION

1   In Liam Burke's article on comic book films, he emphasizes how relatively new film technology has helped bring comic books to life on the big screen. What is Burke talking about, specifically?

2   In your own words, describe three-point lighting using the Hurbis-Cherrier reading.

3   Using the Internet as your resource, locate an interesting video no longer than five minutes that describes the concept of persistence of vision. Present this video to the class and teach your classmates about the concept.

KEY TERMS

Acquisition—refers to the production stage when content such as images and sound are recorded for editing into a visual story.

Celluloid Medium—this term refers to the original physical, plastic format used to record images when shooting a film mechanically. Celluloid is transparent and flammable.

Cinematic—a complex term that generally refers to high-quality, well-acted, well-written, and emotionally driven visual storytelling.

Cinematographer—sometimes called a Director of Photography, this person is responsible for the overall image capture and lighting on a film set. Cinematographers are experts in how lighting affects the quality of the image and are skilled at manipulating this phenomenon.

Color Temperature—a way to describe the color attributes of light. Color can be considered to be on a spectrum of warmer or cooler temperatures. The Kelvin scale is typically used to determine the color attributes of light in television and video production.

Digital Video—also known by the initials *DV*. Digital video describes the process of electronically recording images and sound using image sensors and circuits which process information as 1's and 0's inside a camera or camera and audio recorder system.

Film Aesthetic—the combination of the mechanical or digital process of film production and the illusion or illusions created in the mind of the audience.

Persistence of Vision—a term that is considered part of a larger psychological and physiological process that allows human beings to perceive continuous motion in film and television images.

REFERENCES

Burke, L. 2015. *The comic book film adaptation: exploring modern Hollywood's leading genre*. Univ. Press of Mississippi.

Dirks, Tim. 2017. Innovations Necessary for the Advent of Cinema. AMC filmsite. Article retrieved from http://www.filmsite.org/pre20sintro.html.

Freeze Frame: Eadweard Muybridge's Photography of Motion. National Museum of American History. Retrieved on February 24, 2017, from http://americanhistory.si.edu/muybridge/.

http://nofilmschool.com. Retrieved on February 26, 2017.

https://www.lynda.com/Filmmaking-training-tutorials/1314-0.html. Retrieved on February 26, 2017.

Hurbis-Cherrier, Mick. 2012. *Basic Lighting for Film and DV, Voice and Vision: A Creative Approach to a Narrative Film and DV Production*. Waltham: Focal Press, 269–274.

Lang, B., and J. Rainey. "2016. Box Office Meltdown: Hollywood Races to Win Back Summer Crowds." *Variety*. Retrieved on February 26, 2017, from http://variety.com/2016/film/features/box-office-decline-summer-blockbusters-the-bfg-1201822322/.

Mateer, John. 2014. "Digital Cinematography: Evolution of Craft or Revolution in Production?" *Journal of Film and Video*, 3–15.

Messaris, Paul. 2014. "Film: Visual Literacy." In *Encyclopedia of Aesthetics*, 2nd Ed, ed. Michael Kelly, 189–191. New York: Oxford University Press.

CHAPTER 4

Radio and Sound Production—
Theatre of the Mind

INTRODUCTION

Similar to television broadcasting, radio broadcasting has gone through significant changes in the last 25 years and has a rich history. First developed as a wired technology called the **telegraph** in the 1840s, within 20 years undersea cables connected the coasts, but the technology couldn't reproduce a voice (Campbell and Fabos 2014). While it might seem odd to you, reproducing the human voice wasn't possible until the 1880s when James Maxwell published the theory of **electromagnetic waves,** and then Heinrich Hertz's experiment with two steel balls and an electrical spark proved that electricity could travel between two points. Finally, Guglielmo Marconi discovered that by connecting the telegraph developed by Samuel Morse and Heinrich's **wave transmitter,** the human voice could travel through the air using wireless (Archer 1971).

Inventor Lee De Forest, interested in ways to make the human voice more easily understood, developed the **Audion**, or vacuum tube, which significantly amplified radio signals like **Morse Code** and, later, voices. It's no surprise that commercial broadcast radio became popular after De Forest's invention. Radio receivers ("radios") were mass-produced, and people could buy very large radio receivers for their homes. In the 1940s and 50s, modern radio takes the form of dramatic and music programs broadcast over the air into cars, regulated, like television would be years later—by the **Federal Communication Commission (FCC)**. Today, we hear what used to be called "radio" through premium, commercial-free and non-FCC regulated satellite providers like Sirius XM and via the Internet through apps.

Radio and How It's Made

Generally the term **radio** refers to the broadcast of content through the air as well as a specific type of entertainment and news genre. Similar to television stations, radio content is packaged, promoted, and distributed throughout the country transmitted via **radio stations** owned and managed by large media conglomerates or independents. But you can also find radio programs created by individuals and companies "broadcast" throughout the Internet; your favorite radio stations probably have a streaming version of the radio station broadcast. Whether it's music, commercials, interviews, or live concerts, sound-only (no picture) programs are created using sound production tools and techniques. Editing software like Pro Tools and expensive vocal microphones that use **pop filters** and highly sensitive **ribbons** to enhance a person's vocal quality are types of production tools. The result is that the audience hears voices more easily and thus understands when a story is told with emotion, authenticity, and honesty. **Podcasts** have also become an important and personal way to tell dramatic and captivating stories.

History and the Power of the Human Voice

Radio relies on the vocal quality and presence of the radio host/performer and her/his ability to tell a story that captures and holds the listener's attention. The majority of commercial radio programming owes its success to storytellers who have compelling voices and stories to share. A deep discussion of the intricate legal and cultural history of radio broadcasting in the United States is beyond the scope of this book, but the human voice has shaped a pervasive, powerful and relatively new programming segment of radio broadcasting: talk radio. Two important factors influenced the rise of talk radio: the difference between how the human voice sounds versus how music sounds and the repeal of what was called the Fairness Doctrine. Much of the programming American's listen to today is in the form of talk radio, delivered via radio waves or **podcast**.

Early radio stations broadcast their signals over an **AM** band. However, good reproduction of music or **stereo** cannot be done well in the AM broadcast band. For instance, the high and low music notes don't reproduce well. However, the human voice sounds just fine on AM, and in the 1980s, radio hosts became very popular partly because of the AM audiences who listened. AM stations also needed listeners because the newest broadcast stations—**FM** stations—played music, had popular music **DJ's**, and broadcast in stereo (Wallace 2005). Another historical event that bolstered the success of talk radio long into the future was the repeal of the **Fairness Doctrine**.

The Fairness Doctrine, a 1949 FCC rule, was designed to protect free speech by requiring broadcast stations to "devote reasonable attention to the coverage of controversial issues of public importance" and had to provide "reasonable, although not necessarily equal" chances to radio broadcasters and those from the public at large on opposing sides to share divergent opinions on the public airwaves (Jensen 2013). Essentially, the Fairness Doctrine required commercial (for profit) radio stations to ensure equal time for opposing viewpoints throughout the broadcast programming day. The Fairness Doctrine was revoked in 1987, and most experts believe this decision gave rise to conservative talk radio. The Fairness Doctrine was completely eliminated in 2011 (Matthews 2013).

The technological development of radio as a future broadcast medium and legal shifts influenced how programs were created and distributed to audiences. Today, the hardware and software used to create radio and audio programs and the special qualities of the human voice, like the ability to control articulation, pitch, and amplitude (Hanna 2017), combine to paint a unique picture in the mind of the listener. Finally, radio and sound production require specific skills, storytelling ability, and ethics—key principles illustrated in the Applied Communication Model.

RADIO AND SOUND PRODUCTION AND THE APPLIED COMMUNICATION MODEL

Stories that are reported using radio, sound technologies, and distribution differ from other mediums. For instance, there are fewer distractions when listening to a radio program; no visual information is available to us. Also, there is a feeling of intimacy listening to a radio broadcast or sound production, which is sometimes lacking in other forms of media, like television or film. In the following article, Jonathan Kern shares his views on what makes radio and audio production different in the world of news reporting.

READING 4.1

SOUND AND STORIES

by Johnathan Kern

Radio has proven to be quite a survivor as a news medium. After all, radio listening was a big fad of the 1920s (as was the Charleston), and historians of broadcasting will tell you that radio's "Golden Age" ended more than fifty years ago. Television could have put radio out of business in the 1950s and '60s, but it didn't, and the proliferation of cable news channels in the 1980s and '90s could have made radio news irrelevant—but that didn't happen either. In the last decade or so, the Internet has

emerged as a popular source of news, especially for younger people, accelerating the decline in newspaper subscriptions. But even as newspapers lost readers to the Internet, public radio's audience actually grew—from 14.6 million weekly listeners in 2000 to 23 million in 2006. These days, "radio" has less to do with a specific kind of receiver or a means of sending signals from a transmitter than with a way of communicating news and information through words and sound. A "radio show" may be broadcast, or streamed on a Web site, or downloaded in a podcast; soon it could be delivered to a mobile phone, or to another sort of handheld device that gets its data from a nearby wireless access point. But even as the technology is changing, the process of reporting and producing audio news and information today is much the same as it was when NPR began in the early 1970s; and "radio" continues to be a convenient way to describe all forms of mass communication relying primarily on the spoken word. So it's worth considering what it is about this aging medium that continues to be so attractive to people, especially when there are so many alternative ways to find out what is happening.

Radio is portable. People have been listening to the radio in their cars since the 1930s, and pocket-sized transistor radios have been around for half a century. Today you can buy headphones with built-in radios and MP3 players that also contain FM tuners. Water-resistant sets work in the shower, and satellite receivers make it possible to hear the same strong radio signal as you travel from one state to another. People can and do listen to the radio while they jog, cook, drive, work, or bathe—something that can't be claimed by either print or TV.

Radio is intimate. No matter how big the audience, a good radio host thinks of himself as talking to a single person—the one who's tuning in—rather than to listeners as a group. (For that reason, if you're on the air and asking people, say, to call in to your program with their recollections of Martin Luther King, it's always better to ask, "What do *you* remember about Martin Luther King?"—as opposed to "We'd like to invite listeners to tell us what they remember ...") Program directors and other executives sometimes underestimate how tight the bond is between the person who talks on the radio and the ones who are listening. The departure of a longtime host of a news magazine can prompt thousands of angry letters, phone calls, and even petitions. People feel that they've lost a friend.

Radio is nimble. Most of the time, a radio reporter can carry all of his equipment—a recorder, microphone, and a computer—in one bag. You don't need a camera crew or a satellite truck, as TV reporters do; and it certainly doesn't matter what you're wearing or whether you've had time to comb your hair. As a radio reporter, if you can get to the scene of a news event, you can report on it, even if your gear consists of little more than a cell phone. (In fact, on many breaking stories, TV *becomes* radio—networks just display a still photo of their correspondent or a map of the area where the event is taking place, and have their reporter phone in the story.)

Few things affect us more than the human voice. Certainly there are photographs that touch us, and TV often can tell a story with vividness and immediacy, and newspaper stories often have great quotes. But people convey what they feel both through their words and through the sound of their voices. During a radio interview, we often can hear for ourselves that a politician is dismissive, or that a protester is angry, or that a Nobel Prize winner is thrilled and exhausted; we don't need a reporter to characterize them for us. And public radio especially allows people to speak at some length; an interview in a news magazine might run as long as eight minutes. We don't force ourselves to reduce a person's insights and emotions to a single ten-second sound bite. Even in transcription, this exchange exposes the tremendous sadness and loss of a farmer in Wales as she describes how the Ministry of Agriculture shot all of her 228 dairy cows after some of them contracted foot-and-mouth disease:

HOST: Did you watch?
JONES: Oh, my God, no! Oh, no! I heard it.
That was enough. I heard it.

Watched? No, no. I said goodbye to them all. But they just shot them where they stood. Oh, no. Watched? No way. I watched them burn afterwards. Of course, I needed to be there for them. I had to watch that, and now I m living with the horror of it all. I think its the most harrowing experience I could ever, ever, ever imagine going through.

I say, my ten-year-old daughter knew every one of those cows by name. She didn't have to look at their numbers. She knew who they were by their faces. I could have gone in blindfolded and touched everybody's udder and I could have told you exactly which cow it was.

Sound tells a story. The art of public radio journalism entails most of the skills practiced by television or newspaper reporters—finding sources, conducting interviews, digging through documents, getting to the scene of the action, observing carefully—plus one that is unique to our medium: *listening*, or "reporting with your ears." The right sound—the whine of an air raid siren in wartime, the echoes in a building abandoned because of a chemical spill, the roar of a trading pit in Chicago—can substitute for dozens or hundreds of words, and can be as descriptive and evocative as a photograph.

Today, NPR distributes news reports in many different ways—through its member stations, via satellite, over the Internet, in podcasts, even to cell phones—and it often provides written versions of them on the Web. But radio's greatest strengths remain the power of sound to tell a story, the expressiveness of the human voice, and the intimacy of the medium.

There are also some big challenges to reporting news on the radio.

Just as newspapers and Web sites are laid out graphically—in space—radio programs are laid out in time; radio producers argue over *when* a story will be heard, not which page it will be on, and we measure story lengths in minutes and seconds, not in column inches or words. On the radio, you need to find ways to communicate information that a newspaper can easily convey with a headline, or a photo, or a graph. Think about how much you can learn just by scanning the front page of a daily paper. A banner headline—especially in a paper that rarely runs them—tells you there's momentous news. If there are two or three items related to the lead story on A1, you know that the big story of the day has eclipsed most other events—at least in the minds of the newspaper's editors. On the other hand, a more diverse selection of front page stories suggests an average news load. And a big picture of a pumpkin patch, or of children keeping cool in the water from a fire hydrant, or of couples lounging in the park on a spring day, sends the message there hasn't been much news at all. There may also be a front page index to tell you about developments in business, sports, and entertainment—and where to find more details about them in the paper.

In addition, a newspaper's space is flexible; the length of a radio program isn't. Although papers do budget the amount of space they devote for news, they can add pages—or even whole sections—when events demand it. When the news is thin, they can also fill up the paper with photographs or with stories from wire services, or just run fewer pages. With some exceptions for the biggest national and international events, radio programs are the same length on busy news days and on dull ones. *Morning Edition* is two hours long, *Day to Day* an hour, *Talk of the Nation* two hours, and so on, both when there is a lot of news to cover and when there isn't.

As a radio journalist, in other words, you are working both in sound—and in time. You have listeners, not readers. So here are a few things to keep in mind.

There are no headlines. That means that we don't have a way to catch a potential listener's ear the way a big headline at a newsstand catches the eye; to get *our* news, people have to make the effort to turn on the radio and tune to a specific station. At NPR, we do write "billboards" or "opens" to tell people what's coming up each hour. But each billboard is always fifty-eight seconds long—whether the hour it previews is loaded with hard news or mostly softer features. As a rule, we can't stretch a billboard when we have more we want to say or shorten it when we have less.

Important stories come first and get more airtime. A billboard may list four or five stories on a typical day. But when there's big news—after a presidential election, a devastating storm, or some other important event—we may devote most or all of the billboard to a single story. Similarly, when there's a major story of the day, a twelve-minute segment that usually comprises three or four pieces or interviews may focus instead on several different aspects of the same story.

There is no "front page"; the beginning of any program is the moment someone tunes in. While we generally will put the most important stories of the day at the top of an hour, we know that people listen to the radio when it's convenient for them. So even though we mention at 8:10 a.m. that there's been a plane crash in Kentucky, we may give an update on that story ten minutes later—and again twenty-five minutes after that—for people who have joined the program in progress.

A radio news magazine may not have readily identifiable "sections." Some programs try to offer listeners certain types of news at predictable days or times—sports on Fridays, or business at the end of a particular hour. But the latest developments in sports or business or any other subject can show up almost anywhere in a show. As a result, it is often harder to know "where you are" when you listen to a radio program than when you read a newspaper. If you want to read commentaries in the newspaper, you turn to the op

ed page. A commentary in a radio news magazine may come up in any program segment—which makes it especially important to identify it clearly as a commentary, so listeners don't mistake it for a news report.

Radio listeners, unlike readers, can't skip a story or segment of a program. If you're not interested in sports or business, you probably don't read those sections of the newspaper; and if you listen to NPR or other radio news media on the Web or through podcasts, you can pick and choose the items you want. But when you get your news from the radio, you have to listen to—or at least sit through—arts or economics or foreign stories to get to the subjects you might care about more. If listeners get bored with an item, they'll mentally tune it out, or select a different station, or turn off the radio altogether. For that reason, we try to write and produce our stories to keep the attention of people who are not *already* interested in the topics we're reporting on.

In radio, editorial decisions are often intertwined with production decisions. A correspondent may be given only four minutes for her report, even if it is the top story of the day—so if she wants to add more detail or include another voice, she will have to cut something else from her story. And if she is somehow able to wangle an extra thirty seconds, some other piece or interview will need to be trimmed by the same amount. Producing a radio program is a zero-sum game.

People can't relisten to a story, the way they can reread a newspaper article. When you're reading a newspaper, you may be interrupted, or let your mind wander, or just get confused. You may need to reread a couple of paragraphs just to grasp the crux of the story, or to make sure you understand the latest development. You don't get that opportunity on the radio. *Time marches on*—and with it, any opportunity a listener has to understand why a story is important or new, or to identify speakers or places or sounds. On the radio you get one chance to tell the listeners your story, and then there's no going back. (This is less true when people's "radio" is actually a computer, and they are listening via the Internet.)

Listeners can't "see" (or hear) what's ahead. When you read a story in a newspaper, your peripheral vision gives you an idea of the stories that surround it. You may be halfway through an account of a train crash, but you know there's a story about the discovery of a new dinosaur elsewhere on the same page. On the radio, someone needs to tell you explicitly what's coming up.

A "hard" deadline on the radio is very hard. If you're ten minutes late filing a story at a newspaper, no one is likely to notice. But if your story is slated to be on the air at six minutes past noon and you don't get it done until six and a half minutes past, you've failed abominably. *Talk of the Nation* always starts at 2 o'clock Eastern Time—not fifteen seconds earlier or later. Two seconds can be a long time on the radio.

To be sure, there are occasions when we can pry open the time window, even on the radio. The September 11, 2001, terrorist attacks, the crash of the space shuttle in 2003, the outbreak of war with Iraq that same year, and other big and continuing stories have all justified NPR's doing away with the usual broadcast clocks, at least for a few days. On those occasions, the highly produced billboards were scrapped or made longer or shorter than fifty-eight seconds—which is possible only when the shows don't incorporate the hourly newscasts—and the programs observed few of the usual breaks between segments. For a while, the shows even lost their individual identities and blended into one another, as NPR provided special round-the-clock programming to its stations.

But these occasions are indeed rare in the radio news business. On most days, whether we are reporters, editors, producers, directors, or hosts, our working lives are ruled by the clock.

Radio and Sound Tools

All electronic forms of communication utilize specific technological tools to create and distribute stories. However, for radio and sound production, the microphone is the most important part of the production process, and the skill to select and use the proper microphone requires experience and a basic understanding of how microphones work to amplify and alter the human voice. In the next reading, sound recording and how microphones work take center stage.

MULTIMEDIA FOUNDATIONS: CORE CONCEPTS FOR DIGITAL DESIGN

by Vic Costello, Susan Youngblood, and Norman E. Youngblood

SOUND RECORDING

There are three main components to a sound recording system—a source, something or someone creating a sound; a microphone to convert physical sound waves into an analog signal transmitted via an electric current; and a recording device to store the sound imprint.

MICROPHONES

A *microphone* is a recording instrument used to convert sound waves into an electrical equivalent that can be stored, transmitted, and played back through an audio sound system. Some microphones are designed specifically for use in a studio environment, while others are optimized for field use. Likewise, some microphones are better for voice work while others are designed primarily for instrument recording. While there's often more than one clear-cut choice, it's important to understand the fundamental differences in microphone design in order to choose the most appropriate tool for the job.

HOW DO MICROPHONES WORK?

While the digital revolution has radically transformed the design of nearly all of the production assets in the multimedia toolkit, professional microphones remain largely analog devices that have changed very little in design over the past 30 years. The microphone's job is to convert the acoustical waveform signature of the sound wave into an electrical voltage signal bearing the amplitude and frequency imprint of the recorded sound, a process called *transduction*. The signal coming out of a microphone is called an *analog signal*, because it is analogous to the variations in sound pressure and frequency present in the original sound wave. And like the original sound wave, analog recordings provide a continuous and uninterrupted representation of the original sound.

Figure 4.1 A boom arm and shockmount are used to support the microphone during this recording studio session. A pop filter is placed in front of the microphone to reduce plosives, vocal artifacts like those infamous "popping Ps."

Microphones are generally classified according to three main features or characteristics: (1) Transduction Method, (2) Polar Pattern, and (3) Form Factor.

CLASSIFYING MICROPHONES BY TRANSDUCER TYPE

Microphones use a *transducer* element to capture sounds. The transducer contains a moving diaphragm or ribbon that vibrates when exposed to a sound and encodes a sound wave's strength and frequency into electricity by modulating the current. The most common types of microphones, based on transduction methods, are dynamic microphones, moving-coil microphones, ribbon microphones, and condenser microphones.

Dynamic Microphones

Dynamic microphones use acoustical energy and mechanical vibration as the means for producing the electromagnetic signal required for analog recording. Dynamic microphones do not require a power source. They are durable, relatively inexpensive, and moisture- and shock-resistant. Moving-coil and ribbon microphones are two of the most common types of dynamic microphones. Both rely on electromagnetic induction, which

uses magnets to produce an electric current (see Figure 4.2-A).

Moving-Coil Microphones

In a *moving-coil microphone*, a diaphragm is attached to a coil (a metal core wrapped with copper wire) suspended in a magnetic field between the north and south poles of a fixed magnet. The diaphragm is a thin, circular membrane, typically made of paper, plastic, or metal. As the diaphragm vibrates, the coil oscillates in the magnetic field, producing a tiny current that's transmitted via copper wire to the microphone cable. The electromagnetic signal modulates in unison with the amplitude and frequency of the sound pressure wave, producing a copy of the original waveform.

A. Dynamic Microphone

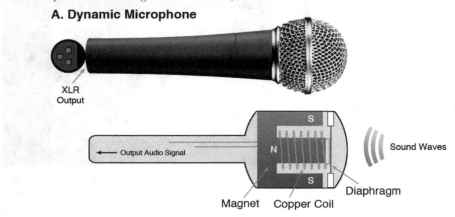

B. Condenser Microphone

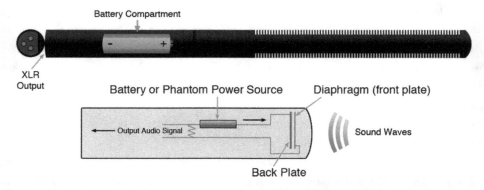

Figure 4.2 (A) A dynamic microphone is less sensitive to sound because the transducer is self-powered by the sound of the subject's voice. (B) A condenser microphone is more sensitive to sound because the transducer is powered by a battery or phantom power source.

Figure 4.3 Vintage radio microphones like this one often have a ribbon transducer.

Ribbon Microphones

A *ribbon microphone* uses a thin metal ribbon of corrugated metal, usually aluminum, as the transduction element. The ribbon is suspended in a magnetic field between the opposite poles of a fixed magnet and generates an electromagnetic current when it pulsates in the magnetic field. Ribbon microphones are technically superior to moving-coil designs because they respond to sound bidirectionally, from both the front and the back of the element. While ribbon microphones are relatively expensive, broadcasting and recording professionals value them for their superior performance and natural sound reproduction. The metal elements in early ribbon microphones were quite delicate, and ribbon microphones had a reputation for being easy to damage. Newer ribbon microphones are more robust, though as with their predecessors, you need to be careful about picking up wind noise when using them outdoors (see Figure 4.3).

Condenser Microphones

Condenser microphones use a capacitor to record variations in amplitude and frequency. The capacitor has two parts, the back plate (containing the electric charge) and the diaphragm. As the diaphragm vibrates, the distance between it and the back plate changes, thus modulating the intensity of the voltage signal. Condenser microphones are much more sensitive to sound than dynamic microphones, and as a result can be positioned further from the source of the sound. Condenser microphones are separated into two groups based on diaphragm size. Large diaphragm condensers have a bigger form factor and are more often used in a studio recording environment, while small diaphragm condensers have a slender body profile and may be found in both field and studio environments (see Figure 4.2-B).

Condenser elements require an external power source to supply the electric charge to the back plate. For this reason, condensers are often equipped with an attached battery pack or built-in power module. A single AA battery is usually all that's required. As an alternative, condensers can receive phantom power directly from a connected mixer or recording device. Phantom power supplies a 48-volt (+48V) electric current to the capacitor through the attached microphone cable. Professional audio mixers and video cameras usually include this feature (see Figure 4.4).

CLASSIFYING MICROPHONES BY POLAR PATTERN

Microphones are also classified according to their *polar pattern* (or *pickup pattern*). Polar pattern refers to how well a microphone picks up sound within 360° of its central axis. Polar patterns are three-dimensional, so in effect, the sensitivity field includes the area above and below the microphone as well as to the right, left, front, and back. The narrower the pickup pattern is, the more directional the microphone will be, and the more effective it will be

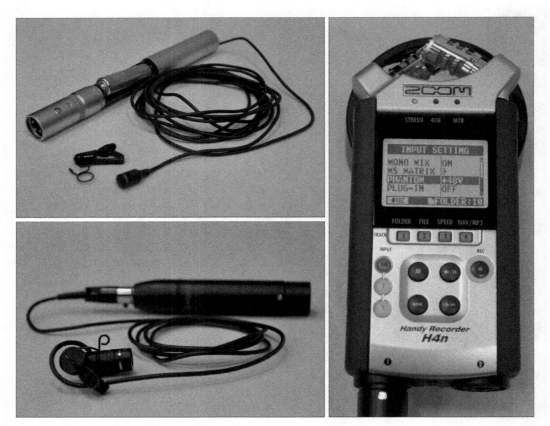

Figure 4.4 The two microphones on the left are condensers. However, the one pictured at the top can be powered with either a battery or phantom power. The microphone on the bottom does not have a battery compartment and must be powered by the camera or recorder it is connected to. Most professional recording equipment can provide phantom power, but it must be turned on to work. The phantom power switch may be located on the outside of the unit or, as shown on the right, within the menu system of the device.

in sensing sounds along the central axis. In short, the polar pattern of a microphone impacts how you use it and under which circumstances the microphone will function at its best (see Figure 4.5).

Omnidirectional

The pickup pattern of an *omnidirectional microphone* is a sphere around the microphone, though not an entirely perfect one. In theory, these microphones respond equally to sound in all directions. In practice, however, the microphone body, particularly on handheld microphones, can block or obscure the path of a sound wave. This can shield the microphone a bit from some frequencies. The smaller

the microphone's body, the less of a problem this is. Because they pick up sound from all around, omnidirectional microphones are best used in situations where there is little to no ambient sound. You may also hear these microphones called *nondirectional.*

Bidirectional

Bidirectional microphones pick up sound equally from the front and rear of the element. Most ribbon microphones are bidirectional. As a broadcast performance microphone, these are ideal for interviews where the host and guest are seated on opposite sides of a table or in situations where two people are required to share a single microphone.

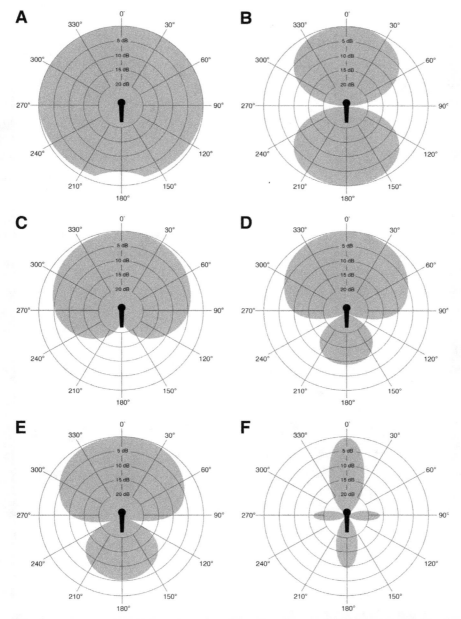

Figure 4.5 Six of the most common polar patters. (A) Omnidirectional. (B) Bidirectional. (C) Cardioid. (D) Supercardioid. (E) Hypercardioid. (F) Ultracardioid (or shotgun).

Cardioid (Unidirectional)

As the name implies, a *unidirectional microphone* picks up sound from only one direction. This makes it well suited for working in situations with lots of ambient (background) noise. There are a number of variants of this type of microphone. *Cardioid microphones* have a unidirectional polar pattern with a heart-like shape (hence their name). This pickup pattern favors sounds coming from the front and sides up to 130°. Cardioid microphones boast a relatively narrow pickup field and do a good job of rejecting ambient sound from the rear of the microphone. Cardioid microphones are ideal for recording single subjects and vocalists. Other members of the unidirectional family include *supercardioid*, *hypercardioid*, and *ultracardioid* (or *shotgun*) *microphones*. Each progression comes with a narrower pickup field and an expanded area of sound rejection from the rear of the microphone. The narrower the pickup pattern, the more proactive the operator needs to be in aiming the microphone directly at the sound source during recording.

CLASSIFYING MICROPHONES BY FORM FACTOR

Microphones come in many different shapes and sizes, but in terms of practical application, there are four microphone styles that you will run into more than all the rest put together: handheld, lavalier, shotgun, and boundary microphones. If you are familiar with these, you will be ready to handle the vast majority of the recording challenges with ease and confidence.

Handheld Microphones

Handheld microphones are designed for the talent or performer to hold during a recording session. Dynamic handheld microphones are ideal for rugged use and heavy handling, but they need to be held close to the mouth (3–6 inches) in order to generate enough sound pressure for a good recording (see Figure 4.6). The rugged construction of dynamic handheld microphones minimizes noise caused by sudden movement, rough handling, or when passing the microphone along from person to person. Reporters rely on this type of microphone most often when recording a standup interview or conducting field interviews. If you are interviewing someone using a directional handheld microphone, remember that you need to angle it toward the other person when he or she is talking.

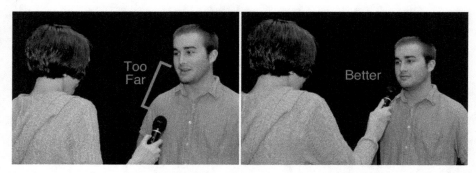

Figure 4.6 Reporters often use handheld microphones for conducting field interviews. Because handhelds are usually dynamic, they should be positioned a few inches in front of the subject's mouth.

Ethics in the Sound-only Story

All of the disciplines discussed in this book connect along the lines of ethics. In radio and sound production, which lack the visual elements used in film and television storytelling, it's very easy to change the focus or meaning of the story that an audience hears through clever editing. In addition, poor interviewing skills and whether a story is **live** or **prerecorded** inform the unique ethical considerations author Johnathan Kern writes about in the final article of this chapter.

PRODUCTION ETHICS

by Johnathan Kern

In the Soviet Union, photographs were often doctored for blatantly political purposes. A murdered commissar was removed from a photo where he had once appeared next to Stalin; a postcard showing a 1917 Bolshevik rally was altered to turn a sign advertising jewelry into a banner with a Communist slogan; Trotsky was airbrushed out of photos in a book about Lenin. And that was in the days when retouching a photograph could require hours in a darkroom, not a few seconds on a computer.

Responsible photo editors at American newspapers don't purposely change photographs. But they do occasionally print one without realizing it has been altered.[1] And they always have to decide how to crop each picture. Sometimes those decisions raise questions about the objectivity of the newspaper: Did the published photo make the demonstration look smaller than it was? Were the police purposely cropped out of the picture?

---

1 In 2007, the *Toledo Blade* discovered that one of its top photographers, Allan Detrich, had been digitally altering photographs. In a column titled "A basic rule: Newspaper photos must tell the truth," the paper's editor, Ron Royhab, described what had happened: "The changes ... included erasing people, tree limbs, utility poles, electrical wires, electrical outlets, and other background elements from photographs. In other cases, he added elements such as tree branches and shrubbery. Mr. Detrich also submitted two sports photographs in which items were inserted. In one he added a hockey puck and in the other he added a basketball, each hanging in midair. Neither was published." Detrich subsequently resigned.

Does the photo make the confrontation seem more violent than it appeared to people who were there?

As a radio reporter, editor, or producer, you will have to deal with analogous situations almost every day—to "crop" the audio, as it were. You will often be called on to decide which parts of a recorded interview will be broadcast, and which parts thrown away. You may want to shorten some of the guest's answers, and leave others at their full length. You may decide to clean up some actualities—editing out ums and stumbles and hesitations—and not others. As a producer, you may be inclined to rearrange the order of questions in an interview, or even the order of sentences in an answer. Usually radio professionals take these steps for what they consider to be production (as opposed to editorial) reasons. That is, they want to make a news report or conversation easier to listen to—they're trying to improve the pace of the interview, tighten an answer to make it more coherent, or keep an actuality from ending abruptly.

But the fact that these things *can* be done—and digital audio editing makes it easier than ever to manipulate someone's words—doesn't always mean they *should* be. And like the decisions concerning newspaper photographs, some audio production practices have serious editorial consequences. While NPR doesn't have a comprehensive set of ethical rules for mixing pieces or editing interviews or cutting actualities, the "NPR Journalist's Code of Ethics and Practices" does set out some general principles:

> NPR journalists make sure actualities, quotes or paraphrases of those we interview

are accurate and are used in the proper context. An actuality from an interviewee or speaker should reflect accurately what that person was asked or was responding to. If we use tape or material from an earlier story, we clearly identify it as such. We tell listeners about the circumstances of an interview if that information is pertinent (such as the time the interview took place, the fact that an interviewee was speaking to us while on the fly, etc.). Whenever it's not clear how an interview was obtained, we should make it clear. The audience deserves more information, not less. *The burden is on NPR journalists to ensure that our use of such material is true to the meaning the interviewee or speaker intended.* (emphasis added)

There is no easy way to ease that burden; in the end, there's no substitute for editorial judgment. But producers and others should take time to consider some ticklish production issues, in hopes that a hasty decision does not have undesired consequences.

THE UNKINDEST CUTS

On live radio, a host's interview airs as it is being conducted (or, in the case of some call-in shows, within a few seconds). The interview is not—in fact, it cannot be—edited. Occasionally a line producer will suggest a question to the host through his headphones, or let the host know that he or she is running out of time, but that doesn't change the fact that the conversation taking place in the studio is exactly the same one that the listener hears.

However, with the exception of some talk shows, most public radio news programs rely much more heavily on recorded interviews than on live ones. And those interviews often have to be edited to a fraction of their original length. On one day selected at random, some of the raw interviews for *Morning Edition* and *All Things Considered* ran twenty,

thirty, and even forty-five minutes; none was any longer than about seven minutes when it was broadcast, and most were considerably shorter.

If you're a producer assigned to edit an interview like that, where 75 percent of the questions and answers will have to be deleted, it will be difficult to stay true to the meaning and spirit of the original—no matter how much skill and experience you have. Also, you don't want guests to be shocked—or feel they were misled—when they hear themselves on the air and discover that most of what they said has been cut out. That's one reason hosts should routinely tell their guests that their remarks will be edited, and if possible give them a sense of the degree to which the interview will be shortened. This sort of fair warning gives the producer license to make the kinds of cuts required to get an interview on the air in a timely fashion.

But it doesn't absolve him of the need to exercise good judgment, or to consider the editorial ramifications of the editing process.

For example, if you're cutting an interview, it's understood that you may need to drop questions and answers, or shorten answers, or tighten up questions. But you may be tempted to go too far—collapsing two answers into one, rearranging the order of questions, and so on. When you make such extensive changes, the result may not reflect what actually happened in the studio.

Consider the highlighted sections of this interview on a proposal to cut federal funding for community development block grants—government programs designed to provide affordable housing, create jobs, and increase business opportunities. The host is speaking with a professor of urban affairs, who turned out to be a supporter of the grants. The version below aired in the first play of *All Things Considered*, before it was reedited for later feeds of the program.

HOST: Now what might be an example of a problem and a specific solution that was developed through the block grants?

PROFESSOR: Some of the problems were very prosaic. A crumbling water or sewer line in an old neighborhood would need to be replaced, and so these funds would be used to provide new infrastructure. Another example might be that the housing stock was decaying to the point of being unsafe for lower-income residents, so subsidized housing was built. In other circumstances, the moneys were used to provide community centers for recreation or to provide health-care services. The list covers the gamut of all sorts of goods and services and activities you could provide for needy neighborhoods.

HOST: The President's budget says that existing programs now are duplicative, that they're spread out over a number of agencies—he wants to put them all together—and, also, that this new approach would include what they re calling "rigorous accountability measures." Has there been a problem with oversight and accountability, making sure money's being put to good use?

PROFESSOR: I believe that the potential problem of waste or fraud is very overstated, because you have accountability at every local level with different branches of government. And I think that kind of checks and balance at the local level simply has to be trusted. And there's no reason to suspect that that kind of local check and balance would be any more or less effective as an oversight tool than stricter federal regulations and oversights in Washington.

HOST: You mentioned that the block grant program began in earnest in 1974. Who are its biggest supporters?

PROFESSOR: I think that virtually all the mayors in the country, regardless of their political stripes, like them because it's extra revenue that they have reasonable flexibility over spending.

The host here is trying to play devil's advocate by asking whether the money for these grants is put to good use. The guest responds that there are local checks and balances that are as effective as federal oversight.

But that's not how he actually answered the question. When the same interview was reedited to more closely approximate the conversation that took place in the studio, it became clear that the guest did not directly answer the host's question the first time around. What he said instead—that the use of federal money did not trigger private investment, as it was expected to—might be heard as an indirect admission that the program was not working as intended. And the host's follow-up question—which was cut out the first time the interview was broadcast—acknowledges that her first question had not been answered, or at least not answered completely. The host's tone in the second exchange is considerably tougher—and appropriately so. (The sentences in boldface were reinstated when the audio was recut.)

HOST: The President's budget says that existing programs now are duplicative, that they're spread out over a number of agencies—he wants to put them all together—and, also, that this new approach would include what they're calling "rigorous accountability measures." Has there been a problem with oversight and accountability, making sure money's being put to good use?

PROFESSOR: I think that the moneys have not necessarily always been put to the most strategic use. By strategic, I mean that cities have often spread their CDBG funds very broadly across lower-income neighborhoods—so broadly that there weren't significant concentrations of revitalization funds in any single neighborhood to trigger a change in confidence on the part of private investors there. And as a consequence, private investors didn't put their money in on top of the federal money.

HOST: What about oversight, though? This is federal money. Who makes sure that the housing project is, on paper at least, actually is built and is built without corruption and without kickbacks? There are all sorts of things that can go on when there's a big pot of money to be had.

PROFESSOR: I believe that the potential problem of waste or fraud is very overstated because you have accountability at every local level with different branches of government. And I think that kind of checks and balance at the local level simply has to be trusted.

HOST: You mentioned that the block grant program began in earnest in 1974 ...

The two versions also raise questions about the propriety of moving the answer to one question so it appears to be the answer to a *different* question. Producers sometimes do this when the host has to repeat herself to try to get a more complete response from the guest; the person editing the audio may take the first version of the question and tie it to the second, more coherent answer. In the case above, the producer justified the edit by saying the two questions were *effectively* the same. But the result gives the impression that the professor answered the question the first time it was asked—that is, it makes his answer seem more straightforward than it actually was.

This sort of unintentional editorializing can happen whenever an answer is shortened. In an effort to get time out of interview or actuality, producers or reporters frequently excise what appear to be irrelevant comments—asides, digressions, parenthetical phrases, and extra details. Most of the time, these sorts of "internal" cuts are not controversial. But look at what could happen by editing out the "digression" in the following fictional excerpt.

HOST: Senator Jones thinks the administration's plans for the new weapons system will not make it through his committee.

JONES: No—no way. The only possibility I can imagine is if the President cut funding for the D-X Missile program by fifty percent—and I can't believe that's going to happen. The administration has as good as said it isn't going to happen. This committee is not going to let the President run roughshod over us. We have the Constitutional responsibility—the obligation—to make decisions that are fiscally sound and responsible.

Take out the middle of the actuality, and the Senator sounds a lot more adamant:

> No—no way. This committee is not going to let the President run roughshod over us. We have the Constitutional responsibility— the obligation— to make decisions that are fiscally sound and responsible.

A reporter could argue that the excised portions don't need to remain in the actuality because the senator immediately dismisses the possibility he has just raised—that the administration will cut its budget proposal for the DX Missile. But in the original cut, one can almost hear the senator asserting himself, then backing off, and then reasserting himself. That moment of hesitation is lost in the second version. Through our editing, we seem to be making the senator take a stronger stand than he actually did.

Of course, some actualities *do* need to be cut down, and producers shouldn't become paralyzed out of fear of making an inadvertent journalistic blunder when they make internal edits. Many interviewees include more details than even the most patient listener could absorb. Here's another fictional actuality where a producer could safely cut any number of words and phrases without sacrificing the meaning or tone of the original:

HOST: Charles Johnson says it was actually a copier company that gave birth to the PC.

JOHNSON (48 seconds): Xerox invented, improved, or conceived of a lot of things we associate with modern computers. Look at a Macintosh computer today, or any machine running Windows—or Linux for that matter—any computer today will probably have a screen with folders, windows, menus, icons, a desktop, a trashcan, a cursor … blank "pages" that are white so they look like paper, fonts you can change, drawing tools…and the user will be selecting things with a mouse, and using a laser printer, and sending information over ethernet cable, which is used to link workstations together in a network. Even the idea of a stand-alone personal computer rather than a mainframe that people shared using dumb terminals—all of these things came out of Xerox's Palo Alto Research Center, and nearly all of them were on display as early as 1974. That's ten years before Apple came out with the Macintosh.

While the details of Xerox's achievement might be interesting, dropping a few specific examples (the whiteness of the pages, the drawing tools, etc.) or making the speaker less verbose (by trimming the mentions of Windows, Linux, etc.) would make the actuality more concise and still allow him to make his point. An edited version might look something like this:

HOST: Charles Johnson says it was actually a copier company that gave birth to the PC.

JOHNSON (25 seconds): Xerox invented, improved, or conceived of a lot of things we associate with modern computers. Any computer today will probably have a screen with folders, windows, menus, icons, a desktop, a trashcan, a cursor… and the user will be selecting things with a mouse, and using a laser printer, and sending

information over Ethernet cable. All of these things came out of Xerox s Palo Alto Research Center, and nearly all of them were on display as early as 1974.

The following actuality—again, this is a fictitious example—would pose a bigger editing problem, both because of its subject and its structure.

HOST: James Johnson is a deputy assistant secretary of defense.

JOHNSON (53 seconds): I think we can see the results of the administration's Mideast policy in a number of ways. First we have had elections in Afghanistan, and we have had elections in Iraq, and in both cases, things went much more smoothly than our critics predicted, and the turnout was bigger and more enthusiastic than many people predicted. We have seen the first municipal elections in Saudi Arabia in forty years, which amount to a small but important step toward democracy in a country that hasn't known it. In Egypt, President Mubarak has called on parliament to amend the constitution to allow for open and competitive presidential elections, potentially presenting him with the first real challenge since he came to power in 1981. And in Lebanon, we're seeing demonstrations calling for Syria to remove its troops from that country. It is not a coincidence that these are the same countries the President singled out in his State of the Union speech as being in need of democratic reform.

Here our imaginary deputy assistant secretary is making an argument—that the President's State of the Union address somehow precipitated political change in the Middle East. He supports that assertion with several examples. Since the State of the Union speech mentioned specific countries, we can't simply cut one of them out of the actuality. And trimming the dependent clauses ("which amount to a small but important step toward democracy in a country that hasn't known it," "potentially presenting him with the first real challenge since he came to power in 1981") undermines the case the speaker is making. Whether we think the speaker's argument is cogent or specious, we owe him the opportunity to make it intelligently; if this actuality has to be edited, it should be done judiciously and with forethought. (One possibility might be for the reporter to paraphrase the beginning of the cut dealing with Iraq and Afghanistan, and begin the actuality with, "We have seen the first municipal elections... ")

You can also cross onto shaky editorial ground if you keep all the sentences of an actuality intact, but change their order. This is a trick many reporters or producers use to keep an audio clip from ending on an "up" or "rising" inflection—the result of ending an actuality before the speaker took a breath or completed a thought. (For instance, imagine that the first sentence of this paragraph were part of an interview, and you wanted—for whatever reason—to end your actuality with the words "... actuality intact." Chances are that the pitch of the word "intact" would be rising just as the cut ended.) Generally producers do whatever they can to avoid ending a phrase on a rising inflection. There's no consensus in public radio on whether this kind of audio editing is unethical. Some producers and editors object to it in principle because they feel that what is broadcast should accurately reflect the actual conversation that took place. Others insist that it's their prerogative to rearrange sentences if the speaker was forewarned that his or her comments would be edited. Still others say it depends on the particular actuality that's being edited.

Compare the two variations of the following actuality. (Again, this is an imagined audio cut.) To most producers, reordering the sentences to improve the sound of the clip would clearly alter the excerpt's mood, if not its meaning:

I have never been able to make friends with anyone in the United States. When people find out I am an Arab, they avoid me. If they did not need my skills as a computer programmer, I would probably not even be able to find work. And I have been in this country ten years! My children speak Arabic and English—so maybe things will be better in a generation. They think of themselves as American, and I think that's how most people think of them. But my experience has been difficult. [Up-inflected]

I have never been able to make friends with anyone in the United States. My children speak Arabic and English—so maybe things will be better in a generation. They think of themselves as American, and I think that's how most people think of them. But my experience has been difficult. When people find out I am an Arab, they avoid me. If they did not need my skills as a computer programmer, I would probably not even be able to find work. And I have been in this country ten years!

The first cut ends on a rather optimistic note; the second buries that sentiment between two gloomy descriptions of life in the United States. And yet they both have exactly the same words. Here's a case where a producer should hesitate to "fix" the rising intonation by changing the order of the sentences—or at the very least, seek a second opinion from an editor.

OTHER PRODUCTION ISSUES

Some other common production devices raise editorial questions. For instance, reporters frequently like to "butt-cut" two actualities to show contrasting points of view. This can be very effective and ear-catching, as in this fictional example:

REPORTER: Janet Franklin is president of the National Committee for Women and Children. She says America's children are the ones who have benefited most from changes in welfare policy.

JANET FRANKLIN: I have been to New York, I have been to Chicago, I have been to Anacostia in Washington, and I can tell you welfare reform is working. Women who used to be dependent on welfare checks now have more self-respect. Children who could only look forward to living on welfare themselves now have a positive role model at home. And families have more money overall, which is hardly insignificant.

SUSAN ROGERS: That is complete nonsense. Nothing could be further from the truth.

REPORTER: Susan Rogers heads the group, Single Mothers of America. She says her research shows many families are still struggling to get by.

SUSAN ROGERS: I think welfare reform has been an unqualified disaster, no matter what the statistics say. Essentially the government has pushed large numbers of people off welfare into low-paying and stultifying jobs. Single mothers especially are now forced to work long hours at minimum wage, and put their children in day care, because they've exhausted their allotted time on welfare. It's a disgrace.

This sort of point/counterpoint production gets a lot of information into a small amount of time, and as long as the voices of the speakers are not too similar, it can highlight the crux of a controversy very powerfully. It can also be misleading.

In the example above, it sure *sounds* like Susan Rogers is responding directly to what Janet Franklin is saying. But it's not clear who was interviewed first, or what "that" refers to in the sentence "That is complete nonsense." For example, the reporter might have elicited that response by saying to her, "Your critics say you're using the welfare issue as a political ploy because you're planning on running for state office. What do you say about that?" If that's what provoked the "nonsense" answer, it would be unethical to butt-cut the two actualities this way. It's incumbent on the reporter and editor to make sure that they don't sacrifice editorial integrity for the sake of a production gimmick. In situations like this, the reporter would always be on safe ground if he or she played the recording of one interviewee to the other to get a reaction—or at least, quoted the first speaker verbatim to the second.

No one in public radio argues that it's ethical to deceive the listener. What people are constantly trying to define is when deception occurs. After all, the production process necessarily involves a certain amount of manipulation of audio, whether it's simply picking the actualities out of a raw interview or fading the sound of a farmer's combine under a reporter's voice track. Our art depends on a certain amount of artifice. So how much is too much? Does every ambience bed suggest that the reporter is really on site, and not in the studio? Should a host always make clear to the audience when an interview has been recorded? If a live interview is rebroadcast on a "rollover" of a program, should it be preceded by an announcement that it was previously recorded? Should the entire show start with such an announcement?[2]

After a while, these questions can feel like the debate over how many angels can dance on the head of a pin. But whether you are a producer, reporter, editor, or host, it's worthwhile at least to discuss these issues, and to try to come to some agreement with your colleagues about which production techniques might be off-limits.

---

2 These and other issues were raised in John Solomon's report "Pulling Back the Curtain," broadcast in December 2004 on the NPR program *On the Media*. Solomon says, "By making everyone sound better and increasing the amount of content in the broadcasts, it would seem to be a win-win-win for the network, its sources, and most importantly, its listeners. Yet is there a small sin of omission? NPR may not be actively

misleading listeners, but we all know that they don't know how we create the cleaner and more articulate reality."

Some issues seem straightforward. For instance, public radio reporters and producers do not "man-ufacture" scenes for news programs. If you arrive at an office fifteen minutes after the employees finish holding a prayer vigil for their kidnapped boss, you cannot ask them to reconvene so you can record a *simulation* of the event. By the same token, you shouldn't ask people to pretend they are answering the phone, or typing a letter, or fixing breakfast, so that you can get sound of those activities. You should never use sound effects that could be mistaken for actualities or for ambience that has been recorded on site. For example, if you interview an environmen-talist who is trying to determine whether pesticides are causing frogs to be born with abnormalities, you cannot add the generic sound of frogs croaking when you mix your piece.[3] The only sounds that are appro-priate are those you record yourself, presumably in the field with the researcher. That rule applies even if you are producing a feature, as opposed to a hard news story. One independent producer submitted a documentary about a shipwreck that included what sounded like scratchy archival audio from the 1940s:

> Marine forecast for Newfoundland: For south coast, storm warnings. Winds north-erly, fifteen to twenty knots—increasing to northwest, thirty, this evening, and to northerly gales...

---

[3] In the late 1990s, birdwatchers were exchanging notes on the Internet about what they were hearing during the CBS TV broadcast of the Masters golf tournament in Augusta, Georgia—namely, the sounds of birds that shouldn't have been so far south in early spring. For example, one writer said he heard the distinctive call of a red-tailed hawk on the ninth green—and then the identical call, recorded from the exact same distance, on the tenth. "A couple of things I heard made me wonder whether CBS wasn't playing a soundtrack or something," he wrote. It turned out he was right. CBS confessed it

had been adding taped birdsongs for its broadcast, and in 2001 made good on its promise to air only the sounds that were actually coming from the golf course.

When asked how he happened to have a record-ing of a radio broadcast for the very day of the shipwreck, the producer confessed he had written it himself and put it together it in his own studio. He was forced to remix his entire piece to remove this and other re-creations.

Some situations are trickier. One editor was concerned that she had allowed a reporter to write this description in her story on the economic consequences of prison labor:

REPORTER: Another state, another noisy factory —but this one in Zeeland, Michigan, is not behind bars. Men line stations churning out desktops and office cubicles. This factory be-longs to furniture maker Herman Miller. The company was hit hard by the recession. It laid off more than four thousand workers, almost half its work force. During those same years, the federal prison industry saw its furniture manufacturing grow 30 percent.

MARK SHERMAN: They pay no taxes, and they pay their employees a buck or less an hour. It's an outrage.

REPORTER: Standing just above the factory floor, Mark Sherman, head of public affairs for Herman Miller, looks around at the employees below. He says there's more at stake than com-pany profits.

Only the reporter and editor knew that the reporter never visited the factory. Her description was accu-rate, but it wasn't drawn from her own observation, as her writing implied. In retrospect, the reporter felt the passage probably *was* misleading; the audio had been recorded on site by a producer, so the quality of the sound would have led people to think she was there, and she describes where Sherman was standing as if she had seen him herself. This is hardly a serious crime, but the editor thought it crossed a line, and discouraged the same reporter from implying that she'd been on the scene in a later report that included an interview that had actually been conducted by phone.

It's natural for listeners to assume that a detailed description comes from a reporter or host's firsthand observation—and almost invariably, it does. But there are exceptions, and they often surface when producers write "tape and copy" for hosts. Most of the time this involves "public" audio—a presidential news conference, an announcement from the New York attorney general, or the National Transportation Safety Board's description of an airline accident. In these cases, the host often provides continuity and context—paraphrasing parts of the speech or briefing, repeating reporters' questions that were not recorded, or giving historical information to help the listener make sense of the day's news.

But some tape-and-copy segments—like this one from a series on immigrants' first Christmas in the U.S.—come very close to sounding like regular news reports:

HOST: Earlier this year an airplane landed in Burlington, Vermont. It was carrying a refugee from the Republic of Congo. He fled his country in 1998, when male members of his tribe were threatened by militia forces. He was sent to Vermont through the international resettlement work of the United Nations and the United States State Department... [W]e hear today from Joshua Dimina. In one way, he's like many new refugees this time of year. He's feeling alone.

[Music]

JOSHUA DIMINA: Good. You sing in the Congolese language. It helps me to remember my family. And Christmas is something for a family, to recognize that family is committed. But you see, I'm alone. I think Christmas will be good when I see again my son.

[Music]

HOST: When he fled the Republic of Congo, Joshua Dimina left his threeyear-old son behind. They haven't seen each other since, though Dimina has been told that his son is safe, living with Dimina's mother.

Pictures of Dimina's family and keepsakes, like his father's Bible, fill his one-room garage apartment in Burlington, Vermont, which is where he likes to practice his guitar. The thirty-eight-year-old says he's grateful for the resettlement staff that helped bring him to Vermont...

The same report goes on to include a clip from Dimina's case manager, ambience from a hospital and actualities from a doctor who talks about getting Dimina involved in medicine in the U.S. But in this case, the host not only didn't go to Vermont; he didn't conduct the interviews. The piece was reported and written by a producer.

Does it really matter? Again, this was hardly a controversial topic, so few listeners would be outraged to find out that the host served here primarily as a narrator, as opposed to a reporter. They may assume that's the way broadcast news works. Indeed, many TV producers *expect* to write for their hosts or correspondents, and are surprised to discover that public radio reporters come up with their own questions, do their own interviews, usually gather sound by themselves, and always write their own scripts.[4] But it's precisely because radio reporters and hosts are working journalists and not just announcers that a piece like this poses problems; it blurs the line between reporting and performing. "When I read an intro to a reporter's piece, I'm performing a fairly recognizable role of continuity reader," says

---

4 In 1998, CNN was forced to retract an investigative report alleging that U.S. forces used nerve gas during the Vietnam War. The producer responsible for the report was fired, but the "on-camera reporter" was not. In fact, he was able to defend himself by saying he had "contributed not one comma" to the piece.

All Things Considered host Robert Siegel. "But when I go to the Gaza Strip for NPR and do a report, I hope it's widely assumed that I have written what I have written—it's been edited, but I wrote it. And then there's this strange area in between, where somebody does a couple of phoners, writes copy to go around it, brings it in the studio, and I read it. I would think, if I were a listener and heard that, that the host had done this reporting. I don't want to be in that situation." Once listeners know the host wasn't the author of the report, they have a right to wonder how much of what else they hear on the air is what it appears to be.

The simple solution to this, and to many similar cases, is to reveal enough of the production process to make it clear that the host was not on site. Explaining at the top of the story that "We sent producer Joe Burgess to Vermont"—or even inserting a phrase like, "As Dimina told an NPR producer" before the first actuality—lets listeners know how the audio was obtained without undermining the effectiveness of the report.

For the same reason, it's important to be explicit about how any audio is acquired if the circumstances are unusual or could raise questions. If the only available cuts of a politician under investigation come from a two-year-old interview, you should say when and where the interview was originally conducted. (After all, a politician might well answer questions one way when he's just been elected and a completely different way when he's been accused of a crime and his popularity is sagging.) If your report includes excerpts of an author's works, you should include a track explaining whether they're read by the author or by an actor. If a foreign language speaker's actualities are heard only in translation, you should explicitly say so in the script. And if your piece relies on man-on-thestreet comments, it's a lot more honest to tell the audience, "We asked tourists outside Union Station in Washington what they thought" than to say, "Here's a random sample of what people think."[5]

Similar issues arise when a news story includes music. "At NPR, certain feature stories and mini-documentaries—on rare occasions—use music when it is clear to the audience that the music is being used to enhance the listening experience," Jay Kernis says. "But in most cases—especially for news stories—the source of music should be authentic and identified." For instance, if you're interviewing people in a diner and the jukebox is on in the background, you could include music from the jukebox; if you profile a baseball player and you ask him to play jazz guitar for you, you should make it clear that you coaxed him to do the performance; if you interview a doctor who says he likes to play Mahler during surgery, you could ask him to take out his favorite CD and play it for you, but you shouldn't mix it in as if it were part of a scene, if in fact it wasn't. In short, Kernis says, "the audience should not be led to think music was present where it was not, unless it is told why."

For better or worse, public radio has relatively few hard rules about how to mix and edit audio; these and most other tricky cases are judgment calls. It may be a sign that we're doing things right that very few guests complain about how their interviews are edited. Or it may simply mean that most people don't remember precisely what they said, or don't hear the interviews or pieces that feature them. In any case, the same ethical principles apply to producers as to reporters: Be fair and responsible, never mislead or deceive people—and always aim for the truth.

---

5 Pieces that rely heavily on "vox"—a montage of actualities without a reporter's voice tracks in between—often pose editorial problems. One NPR music feature did not disclose the fact that its sample of opinions came from people at the same radio station where the reporter worked. In another piece, a commentator included actualities of her friends and even family members, again without identifying them as such.

Interview with a Professional—Sound Design

Tom Scott, Academy Award-winning Sound Designer.
Interviewed by Matt Crick, Spring, 2017.

Tom Scott has been involved with sound for motion pictures since 1978, employed at Dolby Laboratories, American Zoetrope, Saul Zaentz Film Center, and Skywalker Sound. He has been the recipient of two Oscars, Academy Awards for Best Sound, on the films *The Right Stuff* and *Amadeus*.

Why are good communication skills important in your field?

Mixing Sound for movies is very much a team effort. Being able to clearly and succinctly speak and support your views makes for great team work. Being able to write well is also fundamental.

The creative back-and-forth process requires organizing your thoughts and presenting them quickly.

What specific skills do you use the most?

This may sound strange, but the one year of Latin that I took in high school I find myself using more than all the (many) years of math that I took in college. It helps me spell, choose words correctly, and after college, I spent two years in Latin America, and I was able to learn Spanish much more quickly.

What skills do you find lacking in others?

Spelling … and Spanish (particularly useful in California).

How has the knowledge you gained in a college or university been useful to you in terms of your career?

I have an engineering degree and an electronics background, but most of the skills I use professionally were learned on the job from colleagues, mentors, and employers.

What advice would you give to Communication majors?

Try to be as diverse as possible in your studies and interests. You may "follow your bliss" only to discover that time has obsoleted the thing that you thought you'd spend your career on. One skill I never learned in school was NETWORKING. I was a science wonk and not particularly social. I see now that being outgoing, even when it it is uncomfortable, is key. Reach out to make more acquaintances, keep track of them, check in with them from time to time … you will never know when one of your network folks will prove useful, may need your help on a project, know somebody else who can help find a job, a mate, a cure, seed-money … you just never know.

Thinking back on your career choices, what decision are you most proud of?

Not giving in to depression the first time I was laid off from a job I liked. The key was to keep busy. The next opportunity WILL come along.

Interview with a Professional—Radio

Dr. Rob Quicke is Professor of Communication and General Manager of WPSC 88.7 FM at William Paterson University and Founder of College Radio Day.

Why are good communication skills important in your field?

Radio is very much a verbal medium whereby the emphasis is placed on what people say and the way that they say it. So you have to be a very good communicator to understand what people want of you as well as to listen to what people are saying or communicating to you. Listening in radio is crucial, so you need to be able to develop a 'critical' ear for what you are hearing so that you can identify material that would be suitable for on-air broadcast. The other thing, of course, is having a good voice! Radio is all about conveying information in a way that is easy to understand and is entertaining and/or informative. Radio is also such an intimate medium; your voice is something that the audience will be looking to connect with. You should always be authentic in who you are and the voice that you use on air.

What specific skills do you use the most?

In terms of producing radio content, you have to develop a keen sense of what the editorial heart of your story is. If you are doing an interview, you should realize in real time whether the answers you are getting are good content for your story or piece. Never leave an interview feeling uncertain that you have the content you need. As radio is an aural medium, you should also be willing to experience and capture some of the environments and atmosphere to help your audience imagine the scene.

What skills do you find lacking in others?

I often find that young reporters or audio producers have not developed their listening skills enough so that they can completely miss and fail to follow up an incredible statement or admission in an interview. Often, a radio broadcaster can be so preoccupied with what her/his next question is going to be that she/he misses a remarkable answer that's being given to her/him.

In terms of your career trajectory, what benefits and/or value did your college/university education provide?

I can honestly say that my involvement with college radio was the best preparation for my current career. It was at college radio that I learned how to do a live radio show, how to do interviews, and how to edit a package for on-air broadcast. It was a great starting point, and college radio is a training ground for many who want to eventually work in the professional media.

In your field, how best can universities and colleges aid in a student's career plans?

A well-rounded graduate who has a clear grasp on how the world works and is technically trained in media production will be able to create compelling content professionally. A degree in media production also exposes a student to the many facets of the mass media, so she/he should have a certain degree of versatility when it comes to working on a variety of projects. Students should also grab as many opportunities as they can for hands-on experience, such as external internships and getting involved with on-campus media activities. All these experiences inform and improve one's craft.

What advice would you give to Communication majors?

Be open minded! Life after graduation will never be predictable, and it's sometimes those experiences you had at college that you thought would never be useful that actually can make a difference. You need to have as many different skills as possible so that you can be as useful as possible in a media organization.

Thinking back on your career choices, what decision are you most proud of?

I'm proud that I moved beyond just producing music radio and dived into producing speech content, as well. It's much more difficult in many ways to produce speech content that is compelling and connects with an audience. But that simple move took me to many countries around the world and allowed me to have my work broadcast on the BBC in the UK, NPR in the USA, and work in Indian radio, as well. The lesson is that you should always be looking to stretch yourself to see what you are capable of!

Conclusion

As a broadcast **medium,** radio's technological history dates back to the 1840s, and its popular shows during radio's **"golden age"** shaped the format and design for entertainment in television programming for years. Using important tools like high-quality microphones and editing software, coupled with the lack of any visuals, make sound production uniquely suited to capture the human voice and in ways film and television cannot. However, ethically, radio and sound production can arguably be more easily manipulated to present fabricated, misrepresented, or misinterpreted views of our world. Finally, the legal and regulatory history discussed briefly in this chapter demonstrates how in one case—conservative talk radio—a shift in technological distribution of the radio broadcast signal and the abandonment of a key broadcasting regulation–meant to protect all forms of expression–forever changed how and who we hear on the radio.

Using your knowledge from this chapter, complete the following classroom activity within 45 minutes using only your mobile phone.

Activity Specifics

You'll be randomly placed in teams of two. Each person in your team will be responsible for deciding on three interview questions. You will have 15 minutes to decide on questions. After 15 minutes, each team member will ask her/his own interviewee the predetermined questions. These questions and the interviewee answers will be recorded on each team member's mobile phone. This part of the activity should take no more than 20 minutes.

When the team returns, each team member will compare and contrast the interviewee answers and how effectively the questions were asked.

Questions you might ask about your handling of the interview:

1   Were the questions clear to begin with?

2   What was the technical quality of your recording? For instance, how did each person's voice sound?

3   What was hard or easy about this activity?

4   Did you pick a specific audience your interview might interest?

DISCUSSION

1   In the article on microphones, how might the concept of **polar pattern** be useful when determining proper microphone placement?

2   In your own words, describe what's meant by the phrase "theatre of the mind?"

3   In Kern's article on *production ethics,* he suggests that whether the audio production is live or pre-recorded can influence listener understanding and interpretation. What does he mean by this?

KEY TERMS

AM—the process of broadcasting a radio signal using *amplitude modulation.* AM is widely used and is credited with being the first form of modern, commercial radio broadcasting.

Audion—invented by American engineer Lee De Forest, the audion was a glass tube that "hears" and amplifies radio signals. This invention made it easier for people to receive radio signals in the form of voices and music on home radio receivers.

DJ's—a common acronym for *disc jockey*, DJ's became popular in the early days of radio and were responsible for choosing and playing music on radio stations. DJ's would provide dialog between songs to bridge the moments when songs were changed or live.

Electromagnetic Spectrum—visually represented as a scale, the electromagnetic spectrum displays high and low frequencies of electromagnetic waves.

Electromagnetic Waves—electronic impulses impossible to see with the naked eye. Similar to visible light, these waves contain electricity and broadcast signals, among other phenomenon.

Fairness Doctrine—an FCC policy that ensured that broadcast license holders, like radio stations, would present controversial issues important to the public in a "balanced, honest, and equitable" way. The Fairness Doctrine was repealed and eventually completely dismantled during massive governmental deregulation.

Federal Communication Commission—regulates communication sent using radio, television, satellite, cable, and wire in the United States. The FCC is an independent government agency overseen by the United States Congress.

FM—the process of broadcasting a radio signal using *frequency modulation*. FM reproduces high quality sound and is used by most commercial radio stations.

Golden Age—a term that refers generally to the 1930s and 1940s when radio dramas where at the height of their mass audience popularity coinciding with the Great Depression in the United States.

Medium—a word referring to the particular form electronic communication takes, such as radio, film, or television.

Morse Code—a system of sending electrical coded signals. These signals appear as dots and dashes on the receiving end of the electrical signal and are then translated into words.

Podcast—refers to the digital audio file that can be downloaded to mobile devices and computers. A podcast can easily be produced by individuals as an entertainment or informational series provided to subscribers on demand.

Polar Pattern—the specific sensitivity pick-up pattern in a microphone relative to where the sound is coming from. Each microphone has a specific polar pattern used to determine how sound will be "heard" by a microphone from different directions.

Podcasts—the digital form of serialized audio content, in the form of a dramatic story, an interview show and various other styles. Typically, a user can access a podcast and download it to a computer or mobile device, listen to it streamed live and receive subsequent podcast shows as a subscriber.

Pop Filters—sometimes called *pop shields*, these nylon-mesh screens clip to professional microphone stands and help eliminate microphone popping sounds formed when voice-over artists and performers pronounce words with "b" and "p" sounds.

Radio—a portion of the electromagnetic spectrum utilized by early inventors and companies to send signals from one point to another. Later, the term *radio* became synonymous with content such as live music and talk programs provided over the air and received by radio receivers.

Radio Stations—groups of technologically linked organizations which produce audio-only content, broadcast that content within a certain radius, and purchase audio programs from other sources for broadcast. Radio stations are considered local entities and operate within established governmental broadcasting guidelines. Radio stations broadcast digital signals through the air for reception in cars, offices, homes, or mobile devices.

Ribbons—this word refers to the electrically conductive material found in high-quality microphones. So-called "ribbon mics" tend to reproduce warm tones in the human voice well and are highly sensitive to sound. Ribbon microphones are not meant for outdoor use.

Stereo—when sound is sent through two or more speakers so that it seems to surround the listener.

Telegraph—a device invented in 1837 in the United States that sent electrical signals through a cable to a transmitter and then to an endpoint for reception.

Wave Transmitter—this electronic device generates radio waves which contain information such as sound data in the form of a human voice or music.

REFERENCES

Archer, G. L. 1971. *History of Radio to 1926*. Arno Press.

Campbell, R., C. Martin, and B. Fabos, 2014. *Media & culture: Mass communication in a digital age*. Bedford/St. Martin's, NY, NY.

Hanna, N. 2017. Why the human voice is so versatile. Retrieved March 3, 2017, from https://phys.org/news/2017-01-human-voice-versatile.html.

Jensen, K. B., ed. 2013. *A handbook of media and communication research: Qualitative and quantitative methodologies*. Routledge. 5 Howick Place, London SW1P 1WG. Registered in England and Wales

Kern, Johnathan. 2008. *Production Ethics, Sound Reporting: The NPR Guide to Audio Journalism and Reporting*. University of Chicago Press, 232–237.

Kern, Johnathan. 2008. *Sound and Stories, Sound Reporting: The NPR Guide to Audio Journalism and Production*. University of Chicago Press, 1–7.

Matthews, D. 2013. Everything you need to know about the Fairness Doctrine in one post. Retrieved on March 3, 2017, from https://www.washingtonpost.com/blogs/ezra-klein/post/everything-you-need-to-know-about-the-fairness-doctrine-in-one-post/2011/08/23/gIQAN8CXZJ_blog.html?utm_term=.c0005c9d795d.

Wallace, D. F. 2005. "Host: Deep into the mercenary world of take-no-prisoners political talk radio.". *The Atlantic*. Retrieved on March 3, 2017, from https://www.theatlantic.com/magazine/archive/2005/04/host/303812/.

Youngblood, C. S., and N. E. Youngblood. 2012. *Audio Production, Multimedia Foundations: Core Concepts for Digital Design*. Routledge. 5 Howick Place, London SW1P 1WG. Registered in England and Wales.

CHAPTER 5

Citizen Journalism

INTRODUCTION

magine that you have the ability to research, write, produce, edit, and record a newsworthy story that a professional news agency might use on air or on its sister website. You probably have the skills and tools to do that right now. This is called **citizen journalism,** or **participatory journalism,** and refers to digital content created by individuals who are not part of any professional news organizations. However, what you're less familiar with are the types of training and judgment that are required when creating a newsworthy story for the public and this training and judgment are what professional journalists can do.

Journalists who produce content for a variety of outlets are often called **digital journalists.** These professional storytellers create content for "multiple platforms (e.g., print, online, mobile) as part of their daily work" (García-Avilés 2014), and for them, a citizen journalist isn't a professional but is rather someone to share the Internet with. Sometimes a citizen journalist's results are even more impressive than a professional journalist's work (Hawkins-Gaar 2013). That said, citizen journalists do have limitations by virtue of not being trained professionally or required—as part of their paid, full-time job—to work under the types of restrictions, deadlines, and economic constraints professionals' work with every day.

Professional journalism has changed for a variety of reasons, but one of the fairly recent changes—the mainstream journalist's imperative to coexist with citizen journalists, bloggers, and other participants in the social media sphere—has presented challenges for traditional newspaper and television outlets. In response to new challenges, some news sites have linked to websites like Facebook to track viewer/reader comments on stories (Hille and Bakker 2014), however, many of the comments are not taken seriously because of the tone or critical nature. Thus, unless the news agency manages how comments are made on its news site through a strict format and process, reader/watcher comments aren't taken very seriously.

User Generated Content (UGC)

News organizations like CNN, ABC, CBS, and NBC all have **UGC (User Generated Content)** as part of the broadcast in the form of a video or an interview, and certainly, UGC is integrated into mainstream network-branded websites. UGC can be a photo, or blog, too. Keep in mind that professional news organizations exert a great deal of care and control when selecting UGC for mass media consumption. However, in the case of live news, especially when the story involves important events in other countries, the broadcast and print networks will use whatever is available to tell the story and simultaneously ensure the story's authenticity and consistency with mainstream news. This was the case with the Arab Spring and various uprisings in 2010–11. These events were "broadcast" via Facebook and YouTube, and then this UGC content aired on traditional media networks. These examples of citizen journalism were powerful and dramatic and became deeply embedded into the fabric of mainstream news stories. Scholars have pointed out that UGC is also subjected to the kind of practices, scrutiny, routines, and vetting traditional news outlets use in their own production of news stories (Ali and Fahmy 2013) and, in fact, traditional gatekeeping practices in mainstream news haven't changed despite new technologies designed to "open up" the news storytelling landscape.

Have the mainstream media "gates" opened the communication landscape for citizen journalists? If those citizen journalists are essentially telling the same stories as mainstream media why open the gates? Let's compare the differences between citizen journalism practices and traditional journalism practices.

Citizen Journalism versus Traditional Journalism

Citizen journalism, powerful as it is, doesn't have the same authority, reach, and audience that traditional mainstream journalism has cultivated over the last century. On a daily basis, audiences are more engaged with traditional news outlets than content from citizen journalism, especially online video news. However, there's one exception: **breaking news**. According to the 2016 **Reuters** report on online news video based on evidence from the **BBC** related to the Paris bombings on November 13, 2015, "the percentage of users accessing video per visit doubled from around 10% on a normal day to 22% immediately after the attack (Kalogeropoulos, Cherubini and Newman 2016).

News media scholars and practitioners recognize the potential citizen journalism represents in its various forms—online video news and blogging as prime examples of citizen journalism. In fact, print journalism has embraced participatory journalism and many print journalists support the idea that everyday citizens would work side-by-side, in partnership, with professional journalists. However, online broadcast and print news sites are still resistant to a true synergy between journalists and citizens (Paulussen and Ugille 2008). However, some news agencies will use UGC video, still photos, or authentic content to help tell the news story written by their professional journalist.

Author C. W. Anderson points out that one morning in Philadelphia—the number four market out of over 230 in the country—a car crash became big news. No media were allowed on the scene. But, an amateur photographer/reporter was able to get to the scene, and an online desk reporter and a veteran news reporter for the *Philadelphia Inquirer* took care of the rest. From his notes, Anderson recalled what the amateur reporter and photographer said about the car crash, "So I went up to the scene. And it was so minimal; I only got three pages of notes. Most of it was just me standing there, telling the onlines (professional reporters back at the *Inquirer*) what I saw (Anderson, 2013)."

In the twenty-first century, there are many digital tools and outlets for the citizen journalist, and stories happen everyday on which she/he can report. The professional relationship can be a formal or loose partnership with a professional news outlet. Maybe you contribute photos or other content or you've decided to start you own sports news blog. Regardless, the work you do is valuable training for a larger professional role—provided you learn the skills, understand the law, and prepare right now as if you were a professional journalist.

CITIZEN JOURNALISM AND THE APPLIED COMMUNICATION MODEL

Take a look at your social media feeds and notice how many people are commenting on videos, photos, news videos, **GIF's**, and **Memes** that are uploaded by complete strangers. These digital bits of culture are oddly compelling. Now, carefully read some of the comments people make. Do you notice any spelling mistakes, perhaps emoji's instead of words are used, or maybe the post is just written using poor grammar? A good citizen journalist or someone intending on making a living doing the work of a citizen journalist should have a mastery of as many digital tools as available. You'll need to learn new processes and practices and the skills associated with them. Learning how to write, like a professional journalist, is required. You'll find in the first reading that a fantastic future awaits the budding citizen journalist and companies like CNN might just be interested.

READING 5.1

WE THE PEOPLE: PART I: CITIZEN JOURNALISM

by Brian Carroll

UNDERSTANDING "WE" MEDIA

So-called "we" media are reshaping the journalistic landscape. The ease and low cost of personal publishing via the Web and the very human impulse to network socially explain why Google acquired Blogger.com in 2003, then the video-sharing site YouTube in 2006. The seemingly irrepressible need for Internet users to express themselves and to share these expressions with one another also explains why in 2005 News Corp acquired social network MySpace for $580 million, and why in the same year Yahoo snapped up the photo-sharing site Flickr. What began as an internetworked computer system for national defense, the Internet, has become a thoroughly social phenomenon.

Natural disasters such as Hurricane Katrina in Louisiana and Mississippi in 2005, the Myanmar uprising in 2007 and a catastrophic earthquake in southwest China in 2008 spawned several citizen journalism initiatives that have shown us how social the news can be. In the aftermath of Katrina, CNN.com launched iReport that solicited and published on the news Web site's home page photos and video captured by ordinary citizens. The New Orleans *Times-Picayune*, which had to go completely digital during and after the storm, also very aggressively sought contributions, reports, video and photography from Louisiana residents, contributions that helped the newspaper (and Web site) win a Pulitzer Prize for hurricane coverage.

People globally relied on participatory journalism to follow China's earthquake and rescue efforts in May 2008, disaster "coverage" that included widespread use of the microblogging software twitter to produce a steady stream of on-the-ground reporting from the affected areas. Text messages, instant messages, microblogs and blogs provided a visceral source of first-hand accounts of the disaster in what was a remarkable development for a country known for its censorship of media and of news reporting.

WHAT JOURNALISTS DO

Journalists gather and share information, applying a discipline of verification in order to maximize truth, minimize harm and provide a fair and comprehensive account [...]. By this definition, a great number of people who would not necessarily self-identify as journalists are, in fact, doing journalism. Technology-driven changes, including the near-zero cost of publishing via the Internet, are democratizing the profession, expanding the nature of civic discourse and putting the tools of the craft into the hands of everyday people.

So if the key differentiator isn't what a person is doing, perhaps it is how or why. How a person goes about gathering and sharing information and why someone writes and publishes remain key distinctions online, just as they have always been for older, traditional media. Professional journalists, for example, are called upon to act independently, according to the Society for Professional Journalists' Code of Ethics. They are to be accountable for what they write and publish. They are supposed to provide readers with the information needed to be free and self-governing. People have always craved news. As journalism experts Bill Kovach and Tom Rosenstiel wrote, people

> need to know what's going on over the next hill, to be aware of events beyond their direct experience. Knowledge of the unknown gives them security; it allows them to plan and negotiate their lives. Exchanging this information becomes the basis for creating community.
>
> (Kovach and Rosenstiel 2007: 15)

JACKS OF MANY TRADES

Today's journalists are being asked to be jacks of many trades rather than masters of any one. Online journalists are almost invariably more than merely writers or photographers or graphic designers. They are content producers and as such are being asked to learn XHTML, RSS, XML, FTP, Flash, video editing software, SoundSlides and a grab bag of other software tools and computer languages and protocols. They are being asked to deliver content to socially networked mobile devices, which place an ever higher priority on concise writing. The display spaces continue to shrink. As Eric Hoffer (2006) wrote, "In a time of drastic change it is the learners who inherit the future."

Despite the new egalitarianism of Web publishing, the skills that have characterized the guild of journalism remain valuable and important. The inverted pyramid style of presenting information, for example, a style that has so dominated newspaper reporting and that is partially credited with producing objectivity as a goal or news value, remains useful in ordering information for online presentation. The pyramid style is one of several reasons journalists are perhaps best equipped to make the transition to online from other media.

STORY STRUCTURES

The inverted pyramid orders information from most important to least, making stories easier to produce, easier to edit or cut to fit or fill a space, and it emphasizes the "who, what, when, where" fact-based approach to presenting information. As such, the inverted pyramid often is appropriate online, where information should be structured to facilitate scanning or drilling down. (The inverted pyramid also accommodated wire service feeds, which came into the newsroom much as blog posts are published, in reverse chronological order. The style has been common because it also helps to satisfy the print requirement that stories jump or continue from one page to another.) Already notoriously short, reader attention spans are even shorter online, so providing the key information immediately, up top, will be rewarded.

CNN.com's custom of providing story highlights is another way of layering information, making obvious how the story is ordered. [...] CNN's articles most often employ the inverted pyramid, interspersing multimedia options and presenting similar content around the main story.

The inverted pyramid also facilitates frequent updating because the top of an article can be replaced, with older information pushed deeper into the article. Readers can get what they want and bail out, or keep drilling and reading deeper into the coverage. CNN.com is also a model for the way it uses headers and visuals to break up the pages. At many news organizations, through staffing problems or simply a lack of motivation, too often articles are not treated as specifically online content or content that should change and develop over time, but rather as merely print poured into a new container. Articles are dumped onto the Web site and ignored until the next day's dump.

Other common story structures in print and online are chronological, narrative and thematic.

STORY HIGHLIGHTS

- Federal judge sentenced Bernard Madoff to 150-year prison term last month

- Judge: "Fraud was staggering" and "breach of trust was massive"

- Madoff's attorney says his client won't appeal prison sentence

- Madoff, 71, awaits decision on where he'll be imprisoned

- **Chronological stories** are perhaps the easiest to write because they follow a timeline, or chronology. This structure makes sense when the story being told takes place over time, though often the climax or point of the story is presented first. Live blogging uses this structure, for example, a structure that is perfect for continuing or breaking stories.

- **Narratives,** by contrast, set the scene, then draw readers into that scene. Narratives follow a story arc that unifies a discrete beginning, middle and end. Inverted pyramid stories do not, necessarily. Narratives rely on vivid description and detail common to the novelistic style. These characteristics make the narrative style problematic online unless sparingly and expertly employed.

- **The thematic approach** organizes a complex story by theme or topic, dividing up the story into discrete pieces. For example, in a preview story leading up to the National Football League's Super Bowl, the thematic approach might first compare the two football teams' offenses, then the defenses, then the kicking games, and so on. This sort of chunking makes the thematic approach a useful one online.

CROWD-SOURCED JOURNALISM

Just prior to Katrina, in London, the Underground and bus bombings served as powerful catalysts for what has since become known as the "citizen journalism* movement," if we can call it a movement. For hours after the explosions, photos taken by passengers using their mobile phones were the only pictures the world could get of the scenes inside the subway system. The first-hand accounts by passengers, and the prominent placement of the video, audio and photography from passengers on the world's news sites, boosted the profile of participatory journalism certainly in the United States and in Europe, but elsewhere in the world, as well. (*The term "citizen journalism" is problematic. Most U.S. journalists are also U.S. citizens; many "citizen journalists" are not. "Doing" journalism does not necessarily make someone a journalist any more than writing a letter or postcard makes someone a writer. Both terms, then, are imprecise. Participatory journalism and pro-am journalism are more accurate terms in their reluctance to label individuals while still describing the activity.)

In the same year as both the bombings and Katrina, riots on the outskirts of Paris in Fall 2005 boosted blog-driven journalism. With reporters struggling to find a way to tell the story of Paris's immigrant-crowded industrial suburbs, a Swiss magazine sent a squad of bloggers to one of these suburbs, Bondy. Working in shifts, the reporter-bloggers reported, wrote and posted photography from a local soccer club (http://www.hebdo.ch/bondyblog.cfm). The Swiss blog team stayed months, long after the riots calmed down and the network news cameras moved out. For magazine writers used to writing, revising, polishing, and writing some more, the new format gave them the chance to provide a visceral, albeit tentative narrative of life in the suburb during the chaotic fight for control with French police. The writers also engaged readers in live discussion online, and they used reader feedback and readers' posts to the blogs to inform and shape their writing and coverage.

The shootings at Virginia Tech in April 2007, too, showed the power of crowd-sourcing, albeit in an unlikely place for original reporting. Wikipedia's entry on the shootings was immediate, and the entry grew exponentially in the days and weeks following the horrific day in May. In this event, crowd-sourced, distributed, networked journalism had another defining event, and the Wikipedia entry reflected it, with more than 2,100 contributors to the post as of late May and 119 footnotes. As an artifact of journalism, the online encyclopedia entry succeeds in providing a useful account of what happened at the university and how people were reacting to those events, and in the days just after the shooting modeled for the world how crowd-sourced reporting *and editing* can produce smart journalism. The more people contributed, the smarter the entry got, generating yet better contributions and links from those who followed. The entry became its own filter, or in some ways its own editor, as contributors self-screened and added yet more nuance, layers of information and perspectives on the events and on coverage of the events.

To call the entry its own filter is not to discount, however, the heroic efforts of the many editors that rode herd on the information as it flowed in, editing for content, tone and taste. It is a bit like taking a standard newsroom model and expanding it out until the reporters number in the thousands and the editors in the hundreds, all disparately located, all working on no deadline, on all deadlines, on one story.

An ongoing question for journalists is whether participatory journalism is part of the problem of the decline of traditional news media or part of the solution. It is probably both. User-generated content raises questions of libel liability, quality standards, and accuracy and fairness, among others. But pro-am marriages of professional journalists and regular folks with blogs, video cameras and recorders can produce involvement and participation that get more people interested in the news. "The more that citizens participate in the news, the more deeply engaged they tend to become in the democratic process," wrote communication researchers Cecilia Friend and Jane Singer (2007: 153).

The Wikipedia entry for the Virginia Tech shootings.

SOURCES

Chris Anderson, *The Long Tail* (New York: Hyperion Books, 2006).

Hal Berghel, "E-mail—the Good, the Bad, and the Ugly," *Communications of the ACM*, 40, no. 4 (April 1997): 11–16.

Mark Briggs, *Journalism* 2.0 (Knight Citizen News Center, 2007), available: http://www.kcnn.org/resources/journalism_20/.

"Creative Destruction: An Exploratory Look at News on the Internet," Joan Shorenstein Center on the Press, Politics and Public Policy (August 2007), available: http://www.hks.harvard.edu/presspol/research/carnegie-knight/creative_destruction_2007.pdf.

Cecilia Friend and Jane B. Singer, *Online Journalism Ethics: Traditions and Transitions* (Boston: M.E. Sharpe, 2007).

Cecilia Friend, Don Challenger, and Katherine C. McAdams, *Contemporary Editing*, 2nd ed. (New York: McGraw Hill, 2005).

Jolene Galegher, Lee Sproull, and Sara Kiesler, "Legitimacy, Authority, and Community in Electronic Support Groups," *Written Communication*, 15, no. 4 (October 1998): 493.

Lee Gomes, "Why We're Powerless to Resist Grazing on Endless Web Data," *Wall Street Journal*, March 12, 2008: B1.

Rich Gordon, Beth Lawton, and Sally Clarke, *The Online Community Cookbook* (Arlington, VA: Newspaper Association of America, 2008).

Frederick Hertz, "Don't Let Your Case Get Lost in an E-Mail: Be Careful What You Say in an E-Mail, Because You Never Know For Sure How Far the Forwarding Process Might Take It," *New Jersey Law Journal* (September 2, 2002): 30.

Eric Hoffer, *The Ordeal of Change* (London: Hopewell Publications, 2006).

John B. Horrigan, "Seeding the Cloud: What Mobile Access Means for Usage Patterns and Online Content," Pew Internet & American Life Project (March 2008), available: http://www.pewinternet.org/Reports/2008/Seeding-The-Cloud-What-Mobile-Access-Means-for-Usage-Patterns-and-Online-Content.aspx.

Jeff Jarvis, "Argue with Me," *BuzzMachine* (November 2004), available: http://www.buzzmachine.com/archives/2004_11_11.html#008464.

Bill Kovach and Tom Rosenstiel, *The Elements of Journalism: What Newspeople Should Know and the Public Should Expect* (New York: Three Rivers Press, 2007).

"The Latest News Headlines—Your Vote Counts," Journalism.org (September 12, 2007), available: http://journalism.org/node/7493.

Charlene Li, *Social Technographics: Mapping Participation in Activities Forms the Foundation of a Social Strategy* (Cambridge, MA: Forrester Research, 2007).

Jenny Preece, *Online Communities: Designing Usability, Supporting Sociability* (New York: John Wiley, 2000).

Jay Rosen, "The People Formerly Known as the Audience," PressThink.org (June 27, 2006), available: http://journalism.nyu.edu/pubzone/weblogs/pressthink/2006/06/27/ppl_frmr.html.

As mentioned in several chapters, a good journalist has good judgment whether it's in print or broadcast news. This is vitally important. For citizen journalists who might be inexperienced and perhaps very comfortable with the idea of pulling photos down from Google without **attribution** or reediting a story from ABC to put on their personal **blog,** be very careful. Our next author provides you with valuable tools to help you understand basic copyright and trademark law, and you don't have to be a lawyer to understand it. That said, the general wisdom is that if you ever feel like you need a lawyer, hire one. Copyright law is complex and often not what you expect. For instance, did you know that copyright is meant to prohibit copying, not *prevent* someone else from creating a similar work?

READING 5.2

COPYRIGHT AND TRADEMARK

by Michael G. Parkinson and L. Marie Parkinson

INTRODUCTION TO COPYRIGHT

Article I, Section 8, Clause 8 of the U.S. Constitution grants Congress the power to promote science and the arts by giving authors and inventors exclusive rights to their writings and discoveries. The rights of inventors to their inventions are called *patents* and the rights of authors to their writings are called *copyrights.* Collectively, patents, copyrights, and trademarks are called **intellectual property.** The very words used to describe these rights are significant. Copyright is a right to prohibit copying. It is not the right to prohibit another author from independently creating a similar or identical document. Intellectual property is property. It can be bought and sold just like other kinds of property. It is called intellectual property because it is the product of intellectual creativity, not simply hard work. Each of these ideas is explained in more detail later in this [reading] but it may facilitate understanding to keep the concepts of *copy*, *property*, and *intellectual* in mind as you read this [reading]. It may also help to note that the notions of *author* and *writing* have been expanded to include *artists* and their *art.* Therefore, the work of graphic artists, musicians, and photographers can all be protected by copyright. As we introduce the section on trademark, we explain why trademarks are not covered under copyright law.

The first U.S. copyright laws were passed in 1790. They were revised in 1831, 1870, 1909, and 1976. In addition, when the United States ratified the **Berne International Convention** in 1989, that action modified some of the copyright laws, particularly those dealing with the requirements for notice. As we discuss copyright law, we focus on the law as it exists as of this writing, but some copyrights created prior to the 1976 act and prior to the 1989 accession to the Berne Convention are still in effect. Materials copyrighted prior to 1976 and between 1976 and 1989 have different protections and requirements than do materials copyrighted in 2005.

CREATION OF COPYRIGHTS

Before an author or artist can protect work from being copied he or she must create a copyright. The requirements to create a copyright are listed in Exhibit 5.1. Generally, a **copyright** is created the instant an original work is reduced to a tangible form and the author can prohibit others from copying his or her work by either an actual or implied notice.[2] Registration is not required to create a copyright. However, it is necessary to register a copyright before the author can obtain statutory damages and attorney fees in an infringement suit. For this reason, we include registration in our discussion of the requirements for copyright creation.

Exhibit 5.1. Requirements to Create and Enforce a Copyright. (Registration not required to create copyright but is required for enforcement.)

Original Work
Reduced to Tangible Form
Notice – Implied or Actual
Registration

WHAT IS AN ORIGINAL WORK?

There are two major limitations on what is legally an original work. First, the work must be creative.

Second, the work must be intellectual and not **utilitarian.** If they involve significant intellectual creativity, some reproductions or copies are treated as original works.

Original Work Must Be Creative

The key to intellectual originality is **creativity.** Works cannot be copyrighted simply because the author was the person who originated them. The work must have been creatively original, not simply the product of hard work. It may help you understand this concept to remember the idea that copyrights are *intellectual* property. Time, sweat, and effort are not intellectually creative. In 1991, the U.S. Supreme Court delivered an opinion that emphasizes the distinction between effort and the creativity required to make something an original work. A commercial publisher of telephone books simply copied the listings from a rural telephone company's directory and the telephone company sued for copyright violation. It is difficult to imagine a written work that takes more time and effort than the creation of an accurate telephone directory, but the Supreme Court ruled the listings in such a directory cannot be copyrighted because they are not original works. The Court said, "The *sine qua non* of copyright is originality. To qualify for copyright protection, a work must be original to the author."[3] The Court ruled the Feist Directory could legally take the work of the telephone company and republish the same information without violating copyright laws because there was nothing creative in the creation of the original directory. In order to be creative, a directory or database would have to be organized in some creative way or include novel language or material. Following this general rule, collections of court cases cannot be copyrighted nor can typefaces.[4]

Utilitarian Items Are Not Original

There is an historic distinction between utilitarian objects and the creative works that can be copyrighted. This distinction arises primarily from the separate references in the Constitution to authors and writing in one clause and to inventors and discoveries in another. Many courts have ruled that objects that can be patented should not also enjoy copyright protection.[5] This philosophical and legal distinction had little meaning to those of in mass communications until technology began to merge utility and creativity in the form of computer programming. Because some works may involve computer programming or application, we briefly describe when such utilitarian works may or may not be copyrighted.

Dealing with a low-technology work, the U.S. Supreme Court described how utility and creativity might merge in the case of *Mazur* v. *Stein* in 1954.[6] The case dealt with an attempt by a sculptor to use copyright law to protect statuettes he designed for use as bases for lamps. The courts below rejected his claims, saying the lamps were utilitarian and therefore could not be copyrighted. The Supreme Court ruled the statues themselves could enjoy copyright protection even though they were designed to be used as lamp bases. Art incorporated into the moving parts on a watch face has also been permitted a copyright.[7]

The fact that utilitarian works were denied patents led many to think that computer programs could not be protected by copyright. Congress resolved this concern with the 1980 amendments to the Copyright Act. Those amendments added language protecting computer programs as original works and defined programs with the following language: "[A] set of statements or instructions to be used directly or indirectly in a computer to bring about a certain result."[8] Furthermore, the U.S. Court of Appeals for the Third Circuit said that even when embedded in a utilitarian chip, a computer program is a copyrightable creative work if it is original and meets the definition given by the 1980 amendments to the Copyright Act.[9] Some of the difficulty deciding how to deal with programs embedded in computer chips was resolved

when Congress passed the Semiconductor Chip Protection Act in 1984. That act mixes principles from copyright and patent law to protect products that may be both utilitarian and creative.[10]

Even with these decisions and laws, courts are occasionally confronted with programs, not in chips, that incorporate both utilitarian and creative components. For example, a program that produces outlines may have utilitarian components such as pulldown menus or printing commands and these may not be copyrightable, but the same program may have specific language or instructions that can be copyrighted.[11] Some other components of computer programs, like what is often called the use and feel of the programs, have been denied copyright protection. These aspects are not reduced to written codes[12] and may be denied protection because they are utilitarian and therefore not original work. They may also be denied copyrights because they have not been reduced to a tangible form.

Copies or Reproductions May Be Original

One form of original work that seems contrary to common sense is the reproduction or copy. Courts have consistently held that a copy can be an original work if the reproduction introduces interpretation or elements of originality. This view of original work arose at a time when hand copying was the usual form of reproduction. It was solidified in application of copyright law to photography. Ours is not the first time in which courts have attempted to apply old law to new technology. Just as contemporary courts are trying to find how to separate utility and creativity in computer programs, courts in the past had to wrestle with then new technology like photography. One of the first cases applying copyright law to photography was *Barrow-Giles Lithographic Co.* v. *Sarony.* The plaintiff had taken a portrait of Oscar Wilde and the defendant copied that photograph. The facts of the case were not disputed. The defendant admitted copying plaintiff's work but defended his actions by saying that a photograph was merely a mechanical copy of a natural image and lacked the originality required for copyright. In other words, the defendant said that one cannot copyright a photograph because it is not an original work. The Supreme Court ruled photographers, by posing their subjects, arranging background and costume, and selecting lighting, do add their own originality and creativity to photographs.[13] Working from this logic, a later Circuit Court case said, "no photograph, however simple, can be unaffected by the personal influence of the author, and no two will be absolutely alike."[14] In short, a photograph, even though it is only a copy of nature, has enough creativity to be an original work and can be copyrighted.

Because of the principles established for photography, we know that some copies can be copyrighted. But the element of creativity must be more than just a trivial modification. In 1951, the U.S. Court of Appeals ruled that an engraver's copy of an old art master had enough creativity to be copyrighted but that simple colorization of the engraver's work was too trivial to justify a new copyright. The court said that an author must contribute "something more than a merely trivial variation. ..." He must contribute "something recognizably his own."[15]

For those in mass communications, this means that news photographs, video, or audiotape of news, and courtroom sketches may all be copyrighted.[16] Probably more important to most mass communications practitioners, it also means an original interpretation or new expression of facts can be copyrighted. The copyright of news reports or expressions of facts are somewhat complicated by the requirement that copyrighted material must be reduced to a tangible form so that **pure ideas** or information cannot be copyrighted. That distinction between expression and ideas is addressed in the next section.

REDUCED TO A TANGIBLE FORM

In order to copyright any work, that work must be in some **tangible form.** The form can be any medium including writing, painting, sculpture, photography, or magnetic recording.[17] The Copyright Act even includes language saying works may be "fixed in any tangible medium of expression now known or later developed."[18] The act also says materials are protected by copyright as soon as they are reduced to a tangible form.

The requirement for a tangible form means ideas, facts, or pure information cannot be copyrighted because they are not tangible. What can be copyrighted is the physical expression of the ideas, facts, or pure information. For example, if an individual has an idea for a word-of-mouth public relations campaign, even if that campaign is implemented, the idea or concept cannot be copyrighted. What could be copyrighted is the written plan or instructions for the campaign.

If a reporter invests his or her time and energy in research to identify information for a groundbreaking story on political corruption, he or she cannot copyright the facts in the story. Only the tangible form of the story itself can be copyrighted. Another reporter could read the story, rewrite it, and add his or her own elements of creativity in the way the facts are expressed.

Copyright is available for the form of expression of an idea but not for the idea itself.[19] The principle that ideas cannot be protected by copyright was made obvious by the U.S. Supreme Court in a ruling involving an author who developed a unique accounting system and described the system in a book he copyrighted. The Court ruled other accountants could use his system or ideas; they just could not use the expression or the language he had used to describe the system in his book.[20] What is protected by copyright is not an idea but the exact tangible form in which it is expressed.

Furthermore, if there is only one way to express an idea, one may not even be able to copyright one's tangible writings. For example, Frank Morrissey developed an idea for a sales promotion contest based on customers' social security numbers. He even wrote the rules for the contest and registered those rules for copyright. After attempting to sell his idea to several companies, one of those companies began to use the promotional scheme without paying him. Morrissey sued for copyright infringement because a promotion for Tide soap used a copy of the rules he had registered. The court held that the promotional contest idea was not tangible and could not be protected by copyright. Even more damaging to Morrissey, the court held that the rules for the contest could only be expressed in a limited number of ways and therefore even the rules could not be copyrighted because they were simply an idea, not a form of expression.[21] In a more contemporary case, the U.S. Court of Appeals ruled the Windows system used on most personal computers cannot be copyrighted. The court ruled the system of "icon-driven" computer controls originated by Macintosh is a pure idea and there are only a limited number of ways computer controls and screen images can express the idea. Therefore, Microsoft Windows programs are free to adopt ideas and control features developed by Macintosh without violating any copyright laws.[22]

NOTICE

Notice simply means including markings, language, or specific admonitions to the viewers of material that the author does not intend to surrender his or her rights to the intellectual property. Without notice, a person seeing a document or photograph might innocently assume the work is available for public use. In the United States, the requirements for notice were fairly formal and rigid until 1976. Specifically, a notice had to include three elements: (a) the word *copyright*, the abbreviation "C" or "Copr.," or the symbol ©; (b) the date of publication; and (c) the name of the copyright holder.[23] Each of these

elements serves a simple and logical function. First, the word or abbreviation for copyright tells the reader or viewer that the author prohibits unauthorized use of the material. Second, the date allows a reader to determine if or when the copyright will expire. Third, the name of the copyright holder helps the reader locate the copyright holder in order to seek permission to use the copyrighted material.

From 1976 to 1989, the requirements for notice gradually eroded. The date of the most recent Copyright Act was 1976; the date the Berne Convention on intellectual property was implemented in the United States was 1989. If there is reason to determine the requirements for notice for material first published between those dates, one would be advised to consult an attorney.[24] Prior to 1976, the rule was straightforward. Formal notice was required.

Since 1989, the rule has been consistent if not quite so simple. An original work published today is still protected by copyright even though it does not include formal notice. However, the absence of notice does make it more difficult to pursue an action for infringement. If a work is published without notice, a viewer who copies it may claim a defense called *innocent infringement*. An innocent infringer is one who uses the material without knowing it was copyrighted.

Copyright infringement can be prosecuted either as a civil matter between the copyright holder and the person making unauthorized copies or as a criminal matter in which the government asserts its authority. The penalties for criminal copyright are greater and obviously there are advantages to having the government pursue someone who has improperly taken one's materials. However, criminal copyright violation must be "willful."[25] Someone who can claim innocent infringement will probably escape the government's involvement. Furthermore, even in civil cases, the defense of innocent infringement may reduce the amount of damages a defendant is ordered to pay a wronged copyright holder.[26] In summary, a notice statement may not be legally required but it costs virtually nothing to add and provides both some legal protection and convenience.

REGISTRATION

As noted previously, registration is not a requirement to create a copyright. The copyright is created the instant an original work is reduced to tangible form.[27] However, registration is required before an author may sue someone for infringing on that copyright[28] and there are limitations on damages that occur prior to the date of registration. For example, if someone copies and sells your work after the date of registration, you may be entitled to attorneys' fees and statutory damages. If that person copies and sells your work prior to the date you register the copyright, you will not be able to recover your attorneys' fees and you cannot recover the statutory damages. You will have to prove the amount of your loss to establish the damage the defendant will be required to pay you.[29]

For most works, the requirement to register a copyright is simply the completion of a form, the payment of $30, and submitting one copy of an unpublished work or two copies of a published work. The procedure is outlined and the forms are available from the U.S. Copyright Office online at www.copyright.gov. If you believe you have written a Pulitzer Prize-winning article, a Clio-winning advertisement, or a Silver Anvil-winning public relations campaign, it certainly seems worth the minor expense of protecting your rights by registering the work.

OWNERSHIP OF COPYRIGHT

Remember that copyrights are intellectual property and property can be sold, inherited, or simply given away. Therefore, the copyright holder is often not the author of the copyrighted work. However, the **duration** of the copyright is, in many cases, a function of the life of the author rather than the copyright holder. Since the first

Copyright Act in 1909, the duration of copyright ownership has been gradually increased. Most copyrights established today are valid for the life of the author of the copyrighted material, plus 75 years.[30] If the work is co-authored, the copyright is enforceable for the life of the last surviving author, plus 75 years.[31] One exception, which is explained later in the practice notes, applies to works for hire. Works for hire are written by an employee or are written under contract for another person. The copyright for works for hire can be valid for as long as 120 years.[32] An excellent summary of copyright duration is online at http://www.copyright.Cornell.edu/training/hirtle_public_domain.htm.

If one is negotiating for the purchase or sale of a copyright, he or she should note that any contract to transfer a copyright must be in the form of an express and written contract.[33] It should also be noted that simply buying a work does not give the new owner a copyright in the work. The copyright must be sold separately.[34] This means, for example, that purchasing an original Mark Twain manuscript does not give the purchaser the right to copy or to publish that manuscript.[35]

Even a bona fide purchaser may not have perpetual ownership of the copyright. The 1976 Copyright Act created a right to "terminate transfer."[36] Under this provision, an author who sells his or her copyright can terminate the transfer during a 5-year period that begins 35 years after the copyright is sold. This right even extends, in some cases, to relatives of the author who may inherit the right of **termination of transfer.** The provision was created to help authors who sell rights to literature or songs early in their career and only later learn that they will be worth much more than was originally paid. This right to terminate transfer does not apply to works for hire.

Ownership of co-authored works is somewhat complicated and we can only present a simplified summary of the rules governing them here. Generally, the copyright is owned by the author who wrote or created the first part of the work, unless there was some intent on the part of the authors to create a **joint work**.[37] Also, where one person compiles the works of several other authors into one piece, copyright of the resulting compilation is owned by the compiler.[38] Where the authors intended to create a joint work, the co-authors are owners "in common" of the copyright. Owners in common, in this context, have a duty to report any use of the copyright to the other authors, to share any profits, and not to do anything that would damage the rights or interests of the other co-authors. […]

TRADEMARK

Copyrights are intellectual property, as are trademarks, service marks, and trade dress. Trademarks are the logos, icons, symbols, or even titles associated with products in trade. Trademarks can also include short slogans associated with products in trade.[39] For example the white script "Coca-Cola" on a red background is a trademark of the famous soft drink company. So too the phrase "things go better with Coke" could be a trademark for the company. **Service marks** are like trademarks, but they are associated with services rather than products for sale. An example of a service mark might be the word "Kelly" in green, associated with the Kelly temporary services company. **Trade dress** refers to elements of packaging or product modification that are associated with particular brands or companies. To qualify as trade dress, these modifications or elements must be done solely for the purpose of product identification. The pink color of OwensCorning fiberglass and the familiar shape of a Coca-Cola bottle are examples of trade dress. Trade dress cannot include functional elements of packaging. A handle on a paint can, for example, is not trade dress. Trademarks, service marks, and trade dress are all governed by the same basic rules. For the sake of simplicity here, we collapse all three under the one label of *trademark*.

Although copyrights, patents, and trademarks are all intellectual property, some very significant differences exist between the laws that govern patents and copyright on one hand, and trademarks on the other. Copyrights and **patents** are governed by federal law, while trademarks are primarily regulated by state law. Copyrights can be bought and sold like other property, but **trademarks** are rights "appurtenant" to products and cannot be sold without affecting the product or business with which they are associated.[40] Finally, a copyright is created simply by reducing an original idea to a tangible form while the creation of a trademark requires the creation of an association between the trademark and a product in the public mind.

The U.S. Constitution makes specific provisions for copyright and patents and most copyright and patent law is consolidated under federal authority.[41] Trademarks are not mentioned in the Constitution and attempts to create federal laws to regulate trademarks have been declared unconstitutional.[42] As a result, trademarks are controlled by a combination of state laws and some federal laws. The federal laws only control how trademarks are used in interstate commerce. The federal government's registry of trademarks is only a listing of state-recognized trademarks.

PURPOSE OF TRADEMARKS

Originally, trademarks were created to give notice to customers about the origin of the goods they purchased.[43] However, they have evolved to do more than identify the manufacturer; they now are markers of company goodwill and often are representative of the public's attitude toward a product or company.[44]

Particularly important to practitioners in public relations and advertising, courts have ruled that trademarks are (a) indications of product origin, (b) guarantees of quality, and (c) marketing and advertising devices.[45] In effect, a trademark can be the symbol of a company's goodwill and the quality of its products. Advertising campaigns are often based on the consumers' identification of a trademark with a quality product and public relations campaigns may use the public's positive perception of a trademark associated with a company that has been a good corporate citizen. Both advertising and public relations professionals, therefore, benefit from protecting their clients' trademarks.

HOW TRADEMARKS ARE CREATED

Until recently, in order to create a trademark legally, it had to be used. Some association had to be created in the public mind between the trademark and the product or service before anyone had the right to prohibit others from using the trademark.[46] Today, it is possible to register an "intent to use" a trademark.[47] However, this registration depends on the registrant submitting a sworn statement that no other company or person has established a right to use the trademark and that she or he will actually begin using the trademark. In other words, one has to swear that no one else has a common law right to the trademark and that one will establish a common law right very soon. Again, the common law right to a trademark is established by its actual use and the creation of an association between the product and the trademark in the collective mind of the public.

Registration of trademarks, by itself, does not establish a right to the trademark. The registry is administered by the U.S. Patent and Trademark Office but rights to trademarks are established by state laws. The registry is only a listing of trademarks that have been established under state laws.[48] In most states, the right to a trademark is established by use of the trademark and the establishment of an association between the mark and a product or service.[49] Although registration with the federal government does not create a right in the trademark, it does have some significant advantages. First, registration provides notice to any future user of the trademark. If a trademark is registered, no one can later begin using the same trademark and argue that they did not know it had already been used. The registration and subsequent publication of the trademark in the government's "Official Gazette" is legal notice to everyone of a claim to that trademark.[50] Other advantages of registration are (a) access to the federal court system for enforcement of the copyright, (b) use of the registry to help establish the trademark in foreign countries, and (c) assistance from the U.S. Patent and Trademark Office in challenges to use of the trademark by foreign companies. Instructions for registering a trademark are available at www. uspto.gov.

It should also be noted that registration of trademarks must be renewed every 10 years. This requirement helps identify marks that have been abandoned and may be available for use by a new company or product.[51]

NOTES

1   *Burrow-Giles Lithographic Co. v. Sarony*, 111 U.S. 53, 55 (1884).

2   17 U.S.C.A. § 102(a) (2002).

3   *Feist v. Rural Telephone Service Co., Inc.*, 499 U.S. 349,345 (1991).

4   *Matthew Bender & Co. v. West Publishing Co.*, 158 F.3d 693 (1998); *Adobe Systems v. Southern Software, Inc.*, 45 U.S.P.Q.2d 1827 (1998).

5   U.S. CONST. art. I,§ 8; *Brown Instrument Co. v. Warner*, 161 F.2d 910 (1947).

6   *Mazur v. Stein*, 341 U.S. 201 (1954).

7   *In re Yardley*, 439 F.2d 1389 (1974).

8   17 U.S.C.A. § 101 (2002).

9 *Apple Computer, Inc. v. Franklin Computer Corp.,* 714 F.2d 1240, 1245 (3d Cir.1983), *cert. dismissed* 464 U.S. 1033 (1984).

10 17 U.S.C.A. § 902 (2002).

11 *Brown Bag Software v. Symantec Corp.*, 960 F.2d 1465 (9th Cir. 1992).

12 *Computer Associates International, Inc. v. Altai, Inc.*, 982 F.2d 693 (1992).

13 *Burrow-Giles Lithographic Co. v. Sarony*, 111 U.S. 53, 55 (1884).

14 *Jewelers Circular Publishing Co. v. Keystone Pub. Co.*, 274 Fed. 932,934 (S.D.N.Y. 1921).

15 *Alfred Bell & Co. v. Catalda Fine Arts, Inc.*, 191 F.2d 99, 102 (2d Cir. 1951).

16 *Time Inc. v. Bernard Geis Associates*, 293 F.Supp. 130 (1968).

17 *Goldstein v. California*, 412 U.S. 546 (1973).

18 17 U.S.C.A. § 102(a) (2002).

19 *Johnson Controls, Inc. v. Phoenix Control Systems, Inc.*, 866 F.2d 1173 (1989).

20 *Baker v. Selden*, IOI U.S. 99 (1879).

21 *Morrissey v. Proctor & Gamble Co.* 379 F.2d 675 (1st Cir. 1967).

22 *Apple Computer, Inc. v. Microsoft Corp.* 35 F.3d 1435 (9th Cir. 1994), *cert. denied* 513 U.S. 1184 (1995).

23 17 U.S.C.A. 401(b) (2002).

24 17 U.S.C.A. § 405(a) (2002).

25 17 U.S.C.A. § 506 (2002).

26 17 U.S.C.A. § 504 (2002).

27 17 U.S.C.A. §§ 102(a), 408(a) (2002).

28 17 U.S.C.A. § 41 l(a) (2002).

29 17 U.S.C.A. § 412 (2002).

30 17 U.S.C.A. § 302(a) (2002).

31 17 U.S.C.A. §302(b) (2002).

32 17 U.S.C.A. § 302(c) (2002).

33 17 U.S.C.A. § 204 (2002).

34 17 U.S.C.A. §§ 202, 204 (2002).

35 *Chamberlain v. Feldman*, 300 N.Y. 135, 89 N.E.2d 863 (Crt. App.N.Y. 1949).

36 17 U.S.C.A. § 203 (2002).

37 *Shapiro, Bernstein & Co. v. Jerry Vogel Music Co.*, 221 F.2d 569 (2d Cir. 1955).

38 17 U.S.C.A. § 201 (2002).

39 *Coca-Cola Co. v. Seven-Up Co.*, 497 F.2d 1351, 1354 (Cust. & Pat.App.Bd.1974).

40 *Hanover Star Milling Co. v. Metcalf*, 240 U.S. 403 (1916).

41 U.S. CONST. art. I, § 1

42 *U.S. v. Steffens*, 100 U.S. 82 (1879).

43 *Time, Inc. v. Motor Publications, Inc.*, 131 F.Supp. 846 (D.Md. 1956).

44 *Scott Paper Co. v. Scott's Liquid Gold Inc.*, 439 F.Supp. 1022 (D.Del.1977), *reversed* 589 F.2d 1225 (3d Cir. 1978).

45 *Reddy Communications v. Environmental Action Foundation*, 477 F.Supp. 936 (D.D.C. 1979); also see, *Allied Maintenance Corp. v. Allied Mechanical Trades, Inc.* 399 N.Y.S.2d 628 (N.Y. 1977).

46 15 U.S.C.A. § 1051 (2002).

47 15 U.S.C.A. § 1051(b) (2002).

48 www.uspto.gov, retrieved June 5, 2004.

49 See, e.g., *Thrifty Rent-A-Car System v. Thrift Cars, Inc.* 831 F.2d 1177 (1st Cir. 1987).

50 15 U.S.C.A. § 1062 (2002).

51 15 U.S.C.A. §§ 1058, 1059 (2002).

Writer Lauren Stevens recently wrote in the *Huffington Post* about so-called "mommy blogging." She bemoaned the fact that "I've seen virtual altercations and shaming occur over a variety of parenting topics ..." (Stevens 2014), and her concerns echo across the Internet when it comes to blogging. Blogging technology has made significant technological advancements, like embedded audio and video content and sophisticated do-it-yourself blogs. But much of the blog content out there, while personal, isn't journalistic. The next author introduces the concept of blogging and how to blog journalistically. This is sage advice for the citizen journalist.

READING 5.3

INVESTIGATIVE JOURNALISM AND BLOGS

by Paul Bradshaw

INTRODUCTION

This [reading] will look at the relationship between investigative journalism and blogs, beginning with a brief history of the technology and its journalistic uses, before exploring three areas in which blogs and new media technologies have become important tools in investigative journalism: in sourcing material; in disseminating the results of fieldwork; and as a source of funding.

In the course of addressing these areas we should recognise how blogging's history has shaped its contents, while being wary of falling into technological determinism. No technology is neutral, and all technologies have their own cultural histories that influence the content, cultures and uses that grow up around them, histories that are influenced by the actors who play a part in their development. This [reading] provides a brief overview of those histories, while also recognising that the blog genre and technologies are still in flux.

The question of who can call themselves journalists, and the value of 'amateurism' in reporting, have been recurring themes during the rise of citizen journalism. The second part of this [reading] deals with that 'professional versus amateur' debate, arguing that amateur bloggers perform a useful role outside the commercialised, bureaucratised work processes of professional journalists, simultaneously noting how the blog form has been 'co-opted' by the mainstream media.

The section on sourcing looks at the rise of *reader contribution* and *crowdsourcing*[1] as methods of gathering, refining and checking information, and notes the related potential for increased reader engagement from a journalism that previously 'reduced publics to spectators' (Bromley, 2005: 321). The section on publishing then looks at how the potentially limitless time and space of new media technologies have opened up new possibilities for publishing source material and escaping the time-bound nature of traditional news. It is argued that the conversational and iterative nature of new media technologies offers an opportunity to rebuild public trust in journalism through transparent working practices, while networked digital distribution technologies offer a way to circumvent censorship and build international audiences. However, readers should be wary of becoming technologically determinist by falling for the idea that 'everyone is a journalist' or, indeed, no one is.

A final section looks at how the already creaking economic bases for traditional journalism have been further weakened by new media technologies, and how investigative journalists are turning to the internet for new ways of funding—some directly through reader donations or sales of related products; others through foundations, advertising and licensing; most through a mix of all of the above. Finally, the conclusion addresses the strengths and weaknesses of investigative journalism in a new media age, and proposes that its future lies along a number of paths, but that in the end it is the organisational culture, ways of doing things that are entrenched and not likely to simply disappear because of a new technology, and the economic pressures on the boardroom that will dictate what happens next, rather than the technology.

BLOGGING AND JOURNALISM

To ask whether blogging *is* journalism is to mistake form for content. Blogs—like websites, paper, television or radio—can contain journalism, but may not. They are platforms, albeit, like other media platforms, with certain generic conventions. Like all conventions, these have advantages and disadvantages for journalism, which this [reading] aims to address.

As platforms, blogs are a type of website which is normally built to a template, using content management software, on which entries are dated and arranged with the most recent entry (post) uppermost. Despite their extraordinary range and number, there are shared qualities to blogs which derive from their technology and history. These include a most-recent-post-top structure, a 'blogroll'[2] of related sites, an often personal or subjective writing style, brevity, and, related to brevity, a tendency to link to any source mentioned (which the user can click to find out more).

When they first began to spread in the late 1990s, blogs tended to be lists of links to similar sites, and this 'blogroll' element still remains in many blog systems and templates today. Blog posts, meanwhile, often hinged around a single link, where:

> An editor with some expertise in a field might demonstrate the accuracy or inaccuracy of a highlighted article or certain facts therein; provide additional facts he feels are pertinent to the issue at hand; or simply add an opinion or differing viewpoint from the one in the piece he has linked. Typically this commentary is characterized by an irreverent, sometimes sarcastic tone. More skilful editors manage to convey all of these things in the sentence or two with which they introduce the link … Their sarcasm and fearless commentary reminds us to question the vested interests of our sources of information and the expertise of individual reporters as they file news stories about subjects they may not fully understand. (Blood, 2000)

Although the first blogs were programmed by their authors, it was the launch of free content management systems such as Pitas, Blogger and Groksoup (all in 1999) which facilitated an explosion in blogger numbers as the barriers to entry were lowered to those without HTML coding skills. Rebecca Blood (2000) argues that this change, and Blogger's interface and culture in particular, resulted in a change in the medium itself, in favour of more diary-like blogs, with accompanying cult of personality focusing on the author as a 'star' blogger. It was during this time that blogs received much of their initial exposure in the mainstream media.

The years since, however, have seen a number of supplementary technologies develop that have made the blog more similar to journalistic enterprises. One is the rise of RSS as a distribution method. RSS (*Really Simple Syndication* or *Rich Site Summary*), now routinely included in blog services such as Blogger and Wordpress, is a technology which allows readers to subscribe to a blog through an 'RSS reader', by which they create a personal webpage which 'pulls' the feed from the blog, so that they do not have to visit it.

This removes the requirement for readers to check the blog itself for any new postings, and means they can instead include the blog feed as one among a number to form their personal news service. It also means feeds can be aggregated by publishers or journalists.

A second factor is the rise of *linkbacks* (also known as trackbacks, refbacks or ping-backs). These 'ping' a blogger to notify them when another blogger has linked to their post, while a brief extract of the referring website and a link is often included as part of the comments on a particular post, enabling the blogger to address any response or debate, as well as allowing readers to follow discussion that has taken place on other blogs since the original post was written. This combination of reverse referencing and notification adds to blogging's conversational nature, making bloggers aware of their readers' identities and opinions, and allowing them to correct errors or clarify and refine arguments. Notably, articles which are not written on a platform using *trackback* technology, i.e. most traditional news websites, do not get included in this discussion.

Thirdly, because of the tendency for blogs to link frequently, and because of the importance of incoming links to a webpage's ranking on search engines such as Google, blogs have become a major factor in the profile of particular stories. A story that is heavily blogged benefits from a high visibility on search engines—particularly blog-specific search engines which monitor popular terms and sites. Economically, the advent of services such as *AdSense* and *BlogAds* meant some journalistic bloggers who began as amateurs were able to commercialise their operations and employ full-time staff, as popular blogs such as *Boing Boing* and the *Daily Kos* enjoyed visitor numbers higher than most mainstream news organisations.

Perhaps partly as a result of the significance of blogs to search engine ranking, and therefore readers and online advertising revenue, and partly because of the threat that blogs pose in taking away their audiences, the blog format has been increasingly adopted by news organisations, who have either co-opted the technology for their own journalists, employed bloggers on their staff, teamed up with blogging and citizen journalism operations (Gant, 2007), or targeted them for takeovers (The Outlook, 2007). With this shift into the mainstream media, the pre-existing generic qualities of blogs have, in many cases, been diluted, with some journalists writing blog entries in the same way as a column, disabling comments or linkbacks, or failing to link to their sources (in some cases because of legal concerns or the technical limitations of the content management systems). The blog, in these cases, sometimes becomes a new platform for traditional print content ('shovelware[3]'), or a defensive act of what Susan Robinson describes as 'news repair'. In other cases, however:

> They are now achieving what Gans called for in an 'indirect sharing of responsibilities' with journalists [and] represent the multi-perspectival news that will end up setting more and different agendas as desired by Gans. (Robinson, 2006: 80)

THE AMATEUR–PROFESSIONAL DEBATE

Blogs have attracted criticism for being susceptible to mob rule (Allan, 2006), for containing ill-informed and biased opinion, for being an 'echo chamber' of homogenous voices (Henry, 2007), for lack of editorial rigour, and as representing the rise of the 'cult of the amateur'. At the same time, professional journalism itself has been under attack for the rise of a commercial culture (Gant, 2007), with many journalists seeing 'their autonomy diminishing as newsroom standards of ethics, rigour and balance lost out to management goals of saving money and trivializing the news' (Beers, 2006: 113), while under-resourced newsrooms have faced criticism for running unedited PR videos (Henry, 2007), or relying on only one source (Ponsford, 2007), and investigative journalism specifically has been criticised for allowing sources to set agendas (Feldstein, 2007).

Underlying many of these debates are tensions between amateurism and professionalism. By its nature, professional journalism is commercial, required to make money. In order to do this it must either attract very large audiences, or relatively affluent ones that are attractive to advertisers or willing to pay high cover prices. It must also keep costs low where it can, meaning newsgathering is generally routinised, and bureaucratised.

Herman (2005) illustrates this in identifying five things which condition information as it is processed into news: the size, ownership and profit orientation of news operations; the dominance of advertising; dependence on 'official sources'; attempts at control; and ideological pressures.

Herman's framework is useful in illustrating how few of those pressures are applicable to blogs. Most journalism blogs are written by one person, who does not make a profit from their blogging. Advertising, if any exists, is typically sold through a third party such as Google AdSense, and the blogger is rarely dependent on the revenues generated

from that—although commercial blog networks are increasing in number.

However, while 'official sources' are not used in the same way that journalists rely on press releases and spokespeople, there is a well-documented reliance on the mainstream media itself for second-hand information, albeit often complemented with reference to alternative versions, deeper information and original documents.

The amateur nature of blogs is often seen as a counterpart to the professional nature of journalism. This is what Axel Bruns calls 'gatewatching' (Bruns, 2005), or Jane Singer describes as an 'antidote to journalistic group think' (Friend and Singer, 2007: 119). As Skinner points out:

> They are guided by a purpose or mandate other than the profit motive and they are often organized to facilitate a broader range of input into production than their corporate cousins [and] provide ways of seeing and understanding that are marginalized or not available there. (cit. in Beers, 2006: 115)

For instance, a Pullitzer-nominated blog, Michael Yon's reporting from Iraq, expressly rejects commercial assignments in order to remain independent:

> Not as a rabble rouser or as pugnacious individualist reflexively bucking 'the system', merely someone who could buck the system when it needed bucking. (Yon, 2007)

The subjective quality of blogs is compensated for by their sheer number: objectivity, some commentators argue, is no longer essential in an age and on a platform where publishing monopolies do not exist, and the opposing view is only a click away (Gillmor, 2005), while objectivity as an aspect of professional journalism was motivated by commercial pressures to attract advertisers and large audiences (Friend and Singer, 2007; Gant, 2007). Indeed, objectivity as a value within mainstream journalism is losing its appeal, with some organisations dropping it from their codes of ethics (Friend and Singer, 2007).

Blogs' appearance of being 'unchecked' is misleading. Whereas professional journalism employs editors to check reports before publishing, blogging tends to reverse the process: publishing, then checking. Editing, in this case, takes place 'from the margins', as readers and other bloggers check the facts presented in a process of 'iterative journalism' (Bruns, 2005). This can result in legal problems when erroneous or libellous information is published and distributed without correction. Unlike mainstream journalism, however, which produces a time-bound product that seeks to be definitive, or at least a 'first draft of history', the products of blogging and other forms of new media journalism are forever unfinished: open to comments, rewrites, updates and, in the case of wikis,[4] editing and redrafting by users themselves.

SOURCING MATERIAL

While the opportunity that blogs provide for anyone to publish has undoubtedly led to a proliferation of new sources and leads, in particular 'Insider' blogs produced by experts and gossips working within particular industries (Henry, 2007) and even 'YouTube whistleblowers' (Witte, 2006), it is the very conversational, interactive and networked nature of blogs which has led journalists to explore completely new ways of newsgathering.

One of the biggest changes that blogging and new media have brought to journalism is the rise of 'crowdsourcing', whereby individual elements of a particular project are spread (or 'outsourced') between members of a particular community. Typically these take one of two forms: tapping into a range of experience and expertise; or simply tapping into distributed manpower.

Attempts to tap into the 'wisdom of crowds' (Surowiecki, 2004) draw on blogs, wikis, social networking, mailing lists and the ideas of the open source movement. These enable journalists to tap into a wider range of knowledge or manpower than exists in the newsroom and to pursue stories that might otherwise not have been covered, or which would have taken longer to cover.

Talking Points Memo, one of the most successful investigative journalism blogs, frequently draws on its readership to pursue big stories. In December 2006 the blog posted a brief piece about the sacking of a US Attorney from the State of Arkansas and, noting that several other US Attorneys were being replaced, asked its readers if they knew of anything similar happening in their area. As the blog, along with sister blog *TPM Muckraker*, accumulated evidence from around the country, the rolling story led to the resignation of a senior Justice Department official and to the cause being taken up by Democrat politicians.

NOTES

1 Crowdsourcing—drawing on the knowledge or manpower of readers to pursue a story or, 'outsourcing' to the 'crowd'.

2 A blogroll is a list of links to other blogs.

3 Shovelware—software that 'shovels' content from print onto the web, without any changes.

4 Wiki—a webpage or collection of webpages that anyone can edit.

5 BAE is Europe's biggest arms company. The story concerns alleged corruption and bribery in selling arms overseas.

BIBLIOGRAPHY

Allan, S. (2006) *Online News*. Maidenhead: Open University Press.

Andrews, P. (2003) 'Is blogging journalism?' *Nieman Reports*, *57* (3), Fall 2003, http://www.nieman.harvard.edu/reports/03–3NRfall/V57N3.pdf

Ante, S. E. (2003) 'Commentary: have web site, will investigate', *BusinessWeek*, July 28, 2003, http://www.businessweek.

com/magazine/content/03_30/b3843096_mz016.
htm

Beckett, C. (2007) 'Networked journalism: for the people
and with the people', *Press Gazette*, 18 October 2007,
http://www.pressgazette.co.uk/story.asp?sectioncode=
1&storycode=39147&c=1

Blood, R. (2000) 'Weblogs: a history and perspective', Rebecca's
Pocket, September 7, 2000, http://www.rebeccablood.
net/essays/weblog_history.html

Bowman, S. and Willis, C. (2003) *We Media*, http://www.
hypergene.net/wemedia/ weblog. php

Bradshaw, P. (2007) 'Blogs and journalism', 8th Vienna
Globalisation Symposium, May 31, 2007, http://
onlinejournalismblog.files.wordpress.com/2007/06/
vienna _speech_postdraf.doc

Bromley, M. (2005) Subterfuge as public service, in Stuart
Allan (ed.) *Journalism: Critical Issues*. Buckingham: Open
University Press.

Bruns, A. (2005) *Gatewatching*. New York: Peter Lang.

Center for Investigative Reporting. Bi-annual Report: Reveal:
Results, 2004, http://centerforinvestigativereporting.org/
files/2004report.pdf

Center for Public Integrity, 'Katrina Watch: How We Did It',
August 31, 2007, http://www.publicintegrity.org/katrina/
report.aspx?aid=884

Electronic Frontier Foundation (2005) 'How to blog safely
(about work or anything else)', May 31, 2005, https://
www.eff.org/Privacy/Anonymity/blog-anonymously.
php

ePluribus Media. KATRINA Timeline, 2006, http://timelines.
epluribusmedia.org/timelines/index.php?table_name=tl_
katr&page=0&function=search&execute_ search=1

Feldstein, M. (2007) 'Dummies and ventriloquists: models of
how sources set the investigative agenda', *Journalism*, 2007,
8, 499.

Friend, C. and Singer, J. (2007) *Online Journalism Ethics*. Armonk,
NY: ME Sharpe.

Frola, L. (2007) 'watchdogs at work', Poynter Online,
January 3, 2007, http://www.poynter.org/column.asp?
id=83&aid=115844

Gannes, L. (2007) 'Alive in Baghdad: can citizen journalism
done right pay the bills?' *NewTeeVee*, August 28, 2007.

Gans, H. (2003) *Democracy and the News*. Oxford: Oxford
University Press.

Gant, S. (2007) *We're All Journalists Now*. New York: Free
Press.

Gillmor, D. (2004) *We The Media*. Sebastopol, CA: O'Reilly.

Gillmor, D. The End of Objectivity (Version 0.91), 'Dan
Gillmor on Grassroots Journalism, etc.', January 20,
2005, http://dangillmor.typepad.com/dan_ gillmor_on_
grassroots/2005/01/the_end_of_obje.html

Habermas, J. (1989) *The Structural Transformation of the Public
Sphere*. Cambridge, MA: MIT Press.

Henry, N. (2007) *American Carnival: Journalism Under Siege in an
Age of New Media*. Berkeley, CA: University of California
Press.

Herman, E. (2005) Media in the US political economy. In
J. Downing, A. Mohammadi and A. Sreberny-Mohammadi
(eds) *Questioning the Media: A Critical Introduction*, 2nd ed.
New York: Sage.

Howe, J. (2006) Gannett to Crowdsource News, Wired, March 11
2006. http://www.wired.com/software/webservices/news/
2006/11/72067

Howe, J. (2006) 'The rise of Crowdsourcing', *Wired*, June 2006,
http://www.wired.com/wired/archive/14.06/crowds.
html

Howe, J. (2006) 'Gannett Roundup: The Blogs', *Crowdsourcing.
com*, November 7, 2006, http://crowdsourcing. typepad.
com/cs/2006/11/gannett_roundup.html

Jones, L. (2007) 'Independent journalist blazes a trail from
Afghanistan', Freelance Writing Tips, September 13,
2007, http://www.freelancewritingtips.com/2007/09/
independent-jou.html

Journeyman Pictures (2007) Journeyman Profile, http://www.
journeyman.tv/?lid=4

Kirkpatrick, M. (2007) 'What are the top investigative journalism video series online? How do they pay their bills?'
SplashCast, September 7, 2007, http://splashcastmedia.
com/investigativejourno

Knightley, P. (2004) 'Media: investigative journalism—a great
reporter is dead. Who are', *Independent on Sunday*, July 25,
2004, http://findarticles.com/p/articles/mi_qn4159/is_
20040725/ai_n12757697

McDermott, T. (2007) 'Blogs can top the presses', *Los Angeles
Times*, March 17, 2007, http://www.latimes.com/news/
nationworld/nation/la-na-blogs17mar17,0,4018765,full.
story?coll=la-homeheadlines

Meyer, P. (2004) *The Vanishing Newspaper*. Columbia, MO:
University of Missouri Press.

Norton, Q. (2007) 'Wikileaks spilled', *Wired*, January 12, 2007
http://blog.wired.com/27bstroke6/2007/01/wikileaks_
spill.html

Outing, S. (2005) 'Investigative journalism: will it survive?'
AllBusiness, November 16, 2005, http://www.allbusiness.
com/services/business-services-miscellaneousbusi-
ness/4685406-1.html

Outlook, The (2007) Blogs: the next takeover target? Octo-
ber 23, 2007, http://outlook.standardandpoors.com/
NASApp/NetAdvantage/i/displayIndustryFocus
Editorial.do?&context=IndustryFocus&docId=12491873

Ponsford, D. (2007) 'Survey criticises dailies for single-sourcing',
Press Gazette, October 19, 2007, http://www.pressgazette.
co.uk/story.asp?sectioncode=1&storycode=38881

Revkin, A. C. (2006) 'A young Bush appointee resigns his
post at NASA', *New York Times*, February 8 2006, http://
www.nytimes.com/2006/02/08/politics/08nasa.
html?pagewanted=print

Reynolds, G. (2005) Instapundit.com, September 18, 2005.

Robinson, S. (2006) 'The mission of the j-blog: recapturing
journalistic authority online', Journalism, 7(1): 65–83.

Rosen, J. (2004) 'The legend of Trent Lott and the weblogs',
PressThink, March 15, 2004, http://journalism.nyu.edu/

pubzone/weblogs/pressthink/2004/03/15/lott_case.html

Rosen, J. (2007) 'They're not in your club but they are in your league: firedoglake at the Libby Trial', PressThink, March 9, 2007, http://journalism.nyu.edu/pubzone/weblogs/pressthink/2007/03/09/libby_fdl.html

Rosen, J. (2007) 'The journalism that bloggers actually do', *Los Angeles Times*, August 22, 2007, http://www.latimes.com/news/opinion/la-oew-rosen22aug22,0,4771551.story

Sandburg, B. (2005) 'Lawyers flock to mystery web site's coverage of SCO-IBM Suit', *The Recorder*, September 9 2005, http://www.law.com/jsp/law/LawArticle Friendly.jsp?id=1126170313067

Shane, S. (2007) 'For bloggers, Libby trial is fun and fodder', *New York Times*, February 15, 2007, http://www.nytimes.com/2007/02/15/washington/15bloggers.html?_r=1&pagewanted=print&oref=slogin

Smith, P. (2007) Guardian investigators share BAE bribery exposé on the web, *Press Gazette*, July 23, 2007.

Surowiecki, J. (2004) *The Wisdom of Crowds*, London: Abacus.

Sweeney, J. (2007) 'Row over Scientology video', *BBC News*, May 14, 2007, http://news.bbc.co.uk/1/hi/world/americas/6650545.stm

Thompson, C. (2006) 'A timeline of the history of blogging', *New York Magazine*, February 20, 2006, http://nymag.com/news/media/15971/

Thompson, B. (2007) 'Who stands to gain from Wikileaks?', *BBC News*, March 13, 2007, http://news.bbc.co.uk/1/hi/technology/6443437.stm

Tomlin, J. (2007) 'From the frontline to the Frontline Club … and back', *Press Gazette*, September 28, 2007, http://www.pressgazette.co.uk/story.asp?storycode=38934

Weise, E. (2007) 'Pet-food scandal ignites blogosphere', *USAToday*, June 4, 2007, http://www.usatoday.com/tech/webguide/internetlife/2007-06-04-petfood-scandal_N.htm?loc=interstitialskip#

Wikileaks (2007) Wikileaks: About, http://www.wikileaks.org/wiki/Wikileaks:About

Witte, G. (2006) 'On YouTube, charges of security flaws', *Washington Post*, August 29, 2006, http://www.washingtonpost.com/wp-dyn/content/article/2006/08/28/AR2006082801293.html

Woodard Maderazo, J. (2007) 'YouTube, Flickr become forces for cultural change', *MediaShift*, September 28, 2007, http://www.pbs.org/mediashift/2007/09/breaking_government_blockadesy.html

Yon, M. (2007) 'How this project is funded, Michael Yon', *Online Magazine*, 2007, http://michaelyononline.com/wp/how-this-project-is-funded

Interview with a Professional

Jackie Califano is a Senior/Line Producer at Cheddar. She has over six years of professional experience in television news and a degree in Communication from William Paterson University in Wayne, NJ.

Interviewed by Matt Crick, Spring, 2017.

Why are good communication skills important in your field?

Communication is the backbone for everyday life but especially in live television. When you're relaying a story or headline, from source to broadcast, there are often 4–8 handlers of that information before it reaches the audience. The communication between them has to be impeccably concise otherwise you might report something inaccurate. In live television, even the slightest bit of inaccuracy is unacceptable. There is no room to make a mistake or edits after the fact.

What specific skills do you use the most?

The first skill I use most is the ability to multitask. You have to be prepared to step in at any given moment for any given job. You work on a team, and sometimes that team needs some extra support somewhere it wasn't expecting. Live television has a lot of moving parts. It's really exciting, actually, and never boring, but you have to be on your toes and at the ready. There's an old adage that claims you never want to be the jack of all trades and master of none, but it's actually quite the opposite in television. Now it's more along the lines of, "BE the jack of all trades, and you'll never be out of a job."

In terms of Broadcast Journalism, what skills do you find lacking in others?

Patience. It's almost certainly impossible to find anyone with patience in a newsroom. I think the one thing that people forget most often is the fact that getting frustrated or angry won't change anything. If you're a good communicator, the chips will fall where you want. If, however, you're not a good communicator, the chips will be scattered all over the place and turned upside down. The point is, be patient and make sure you gather your thoughts so you can clearly communicate what you want accomplished.

How has the knowledge or skills you gained at a college or university been useful to you in terms of your career?

Everything I learned in the university has helped me throughout my career. I began my career in technical operations checking radio satellite schedules and logging video. Now I'm an editorial producer for the #1 business news network, traveling for conferences, and meeting Fortune 500 CEOs and senior executives. I learned every job in our university control room and live studio and still relate to a lot of those roles on a daily basis. It's so important to know what each position requires and how long it takes to carry out a task. You're more respected as a show producer but also as a human being.

What advice would you give to Communication majors? Pitfalls to avoid, that sort of thing.

Maintain and build professional relationships. There will come a point in your career when you'll be happy you did. Having that familiarity with someone, especially in your industry, will prove to be invaluable at one point or another. First impressions are the most lasting. Don't be rude, do ask questions, and, most importantly, appreciate all the little things people do to help along the way.

Thinking back on your career choices, what decision are you most proud of?

I'm most proud of having the desire and enthusiasm to keep moving forward. People in our industry tend to get comfortable very quickly; they're too complacent. I like to keep moving and learn new things to better myself and my career. When you're given an opportunity to do something that you think is near impossible, take it; don't even think twice.

Conclusion

Citizen journalism is an active and growing segment of the mass communication landscape. Reuter's Digital News Project reports that **off-site news** consumption, like online news stories viewed on Facebook, can get as much 75–100 million views for certain stories. But, the study also found that the most successful online news videos were short and "focused on soft news, and have a strong emotional element" (Kalogeropoulos, Cherubini and Newman 2016). Most likely, networks like CNN and the *New York Times* will only want a small percentage of "soft news" content.

Generally, the growth of online video is a positive trend for citizen journalists. It means that more and more websites, especially social networking sites, will take advantage of original content. However, as you probably realize now, creating an online news story doesn't automatically mean a radio or television network will select your story or hire you as a **freelance stringer**. It's important to note that research shows that the majority of online video content in the United States isn't news content as a professional journalist might imagine. This is problematic for a citizen journalist or for anyone making UGC because professionals will expect the journalistic standards that they practice daily in a newsroom will be followed.

For instance, as a citizen journalist, you'll be expected to know something about copyright and how to work within the boundaries of U.S. law regarding the use of photos, video, and other content. If you're a blogger, your writing needs to meet a recognizable journalistic standard, as well. Finally, if you do make contact with a professional news agency or they reach out to you, expect that you will not be considered a "professional journalist" until you meet the expectations within the organization and deliver the story on budget—if there's a budget—and on deadline.

CLASSROOM ACTIVITY

Using your knowledge from this chapter, complete the following classroom activity within 45 minutes using only your mobile phone.

Activity Specifics

You'll be randomly placed in teams of two. Each person in your team will be writing three questions for a news story that must be approved by your instructor, acting in the role of Assistant Editor, Digital Tools and Platforms. Once approved, you will spend 20 minutes getting at least two interviews and will record the interviews on your mobile phone. In the last 25 minutes of this activity, you'll be transcribing the answers to your questions and will write your story.

Questions you might ask about yourself before writing your story:

1   How can I use the Inverted Pyramid model to guide my story?

2   What will be the biggest challenge in getting my story?

3   Where might my story be published?

4   What was hard or easy about this activity?

DISCUSSION

1   In the Carroll article, what does the author mean by "jacks of many trades?"

2   In the article on copyright law, what's meant by "fixed in any tangible medium"?

3   In the article on investigative journalism and blogging, would the author argue that blogging technology can't be journalistic? Why or why not?

KEY TERMS

BBC—this acronym stands for the British Broadcasting Corporation. The BBC is a public service broadcaster. The BBC is unique when compared with U.S. television networks in that the BBC is funded primarily through a television license fee that is charged to all British households. The BBC does not use commercials in television programs.

Breaking News—a term used by professional radio and television news organizations that describes a story being broadcast that has just begun or new information which adds to an earlier reported story. Breaking news is typically delivered to audiences live.

Citizen Journalism—a type of journalism that uses the Internet as the primary distribution of news content to the public. Citizen journalists often use social media platforms to distribute.

Digital Journalists—a job title and general description of a person who uses digital tools to create news stories for distribution over the Internet. Digital journalist is a term that has been appropriated by mainstream media as well as everyday citizens.

Freelance Stringer—a freelance journalist. Typically, *stringers* are used when it's not economically viable for a news organization, like NBC, to pay for a full-time staff member to cover the news during a specific event or at a specific location far from the newsroom.

GIF's—a digital file extension that stands for graphic interchange format. Recently, GIF's have gained in popularity, especially on mobile phones, because they can be created quickly, are very short, and require very little drive space.

Memes—another form of visual communication that is popular, particularly on social media platforms. Memes are typically humorous and involve a culturally recognizable image or text that can easily be adapted to suit or satirize current events.

Off-site News—refers to websites that provide online video that often originates from traditional news organization websites, like CNN.com. Off-site news websites, like Facebook, are responsible for the majority of online news stories viewed by the public.

Participatory Journalism—another term for citizen journalism but one that incorporates the ideas that the citizen journalist is part of the mainstream news creation process or somehow working with professional journalists to tell a news story.

Reuters—one of the largest news organizations in the world. Reuters provides news content to the public and news organizations.

UGC—this acronym stands for user generated content and refers to any content created by the average user. UGC content doesn't typically incorporate professional journalistic standards in the ways mainstream news media stories do.

REFERENCES

Ali, S. R., and S. Fahmy. 2013. "Gatekeeping and citizen journalism: The use of social media during the recent uprisings in Iran, Egypt, and Libya." *Media, War & Conflict 6* (1), 55–69.

Anderson, C. W. 2013. A Day in the Life of 21st Century Journalism. *Rebuilding the news: Metropolitan journalism in the digital age.* Temple University.

Carroll, B. 2010. We the People, Part I: Citizen Journalism. *Writing for Digital Media.* Routledge, 169–175. 5 Howick Place, London SW1P 1WG. Registered in England and Wales.

De Burgh, H. 2008. *Investigative Journalism and Blogs.* Investigative journalism. Routledge, 1–6. 5 Howick Place, London SW1P 1WG. Registered in England and Wales.

García-Avilés, J. A. 2014. "Online Newsrooms as Communities of Practice: Exploring Digital Journalists' Applied Ethics." *Journal of Mass Media Ethics 29* (4), 258–272.

Hawkins-Gaar, K. 2013. "36 stories that prove citizen journalism matters." Retrieved on March 12, 2017, from http://www.cnn.com/2013/04/03/opinion/ireport-awards-hawkins-gaar/.

Hille, S., and P. Bakker. 2014. "Engaging the Social News User: Comments on News Sites and Facebook." *Journalism Practice 8* (5), 563–572.

Kalogeropoulos, A., F. Cherubini, and N. Newman. 2016. The Future of Online News Video.

Parkinson, M. G., and M. L. Parkinson. 2006. *Copyright and Trademark. Law for Advertising, Broadcasting, Journalism, and Public Relations: A Comprehensive Text for Students and Practitioners.* Routledge, 298–304. 5 Howick Place, London SW1P 1WG. Registered in England and Wales.

Paulussen, S., and P. Ugille. 2008. "User generated content in the newsroom: Professional and organisational constraints on participatory journalism." *Westminster Papers in Communication and Culture 5* (2).

Stevens, L. 2014. "The Dark Side of Mommy Blogs." *The Huffington Post.* Retrieved on March 12, 2017, from http://www.huffingtonpost.com/lauren-stevens/the-dark-side-of-mommy-bl_b_6033224.html.

CHAPTER 6

Broadcast Journalism: Writing, Speaking, and Presenting the News

INTRODUCTION

The academic discipline and profession of broadcast journalism represent an evolution of traditional print journalism practices like fact checking and the **inverted pyramid** represented in the form of daily news that's published electronically and distributed through technologies like radio and television. Current technologies have always influenced newsgathering and reporting, and certainly technologies like the printing press, photography, the telegraph, television, and the Internet continue to influence the way daily news is collected and written about. For instance, Internet sites like YouTube represent an "existential threat" (Ryfe and Blach-Ørsten 2011) for some professional broadcast journalists. News audiences have changed, as well; half of Americans aged 18–49 get their news through online content, (Mitchell, Gottfried, Barthel and Shearer 2016) and not television, print, or radio. However, recent research suggests that much of the online information accessed for news consumption is often "similar or identical" to journalism created in traditional news outlets like television or radio (Forde and Johnston 2013).

All broadcasters face the challenge of determining whether the news story is factual, valuable, and compelling. These challenges bring into sharp relief the difficulties widely written about in the 2016 presidential campaign regarding **fake news.** When emotions run high, even with massive amounts of good information at our fingertips, maintaining a critical and suspicious posture when evaluating news sites is tough. One can argue we need the professional broadcast journalist, specially trained in how to determine **newsworthiness** and able to facilitate and curate truthful and valuable stories that impact our daily lives. In fact, based on recent research from the Pew Research Center, in one study, Americans used two paths to get news: social media and direct visits to news organization websites (Mitchell, Gottfried, Barthel and Shearer, 2017).

Newsworthiness in the Age of Fake News

In late 2016, a new term was introduced into American culture: fake news. This term is particularly problematic for broadcast journalists because, as some have argued, journalists were the alleged source of so-called fake news in the 2016 U.S. Presidential campaign. At the time of this writing, real news stories about fake news are almost a daily part of the **news cycle** and beg the question, "What is real news," or to put it in broadcast journalism terms, "What is newsworthy?"

Over time, journalists have developed a set of criteria (Campbell, Martin and Fabos 2016) that frame how a journalist should behave professionally. These criteria provide the core guidelines for journalists and are integral to deciding whether a story is newsworthy. The criteria are: timeliness, proximity, conflict, prominence, human interest, consequence, usefulness, novelty, and deviance. If you were to examine a local news story using these criteria, you would, perhaps, begin to see the difference between a story that's newsworthy and one that's fake news. But, if you want a less complex way of determining whether an online news source is fake or not, take a look at a recent list of fake news sites CBS news recently posted on the main CBS.com website at http://www.cbsnews.com/pictures/dont-get-fooled-by-these-fake-news-sites/.

Deciding what's newsworthy, whether to write the story, managing the deadlines for the story, and finally presenting the story yourself to thousands or even millions of radio listeners and television viewers isn't just your job to do alone. But, the decision-making begins with you, and that's part of being a professional broadcast journalist.

Defining a Broadcast Journalist

For purposes of this book, a **broadcast journalist** is someone who produces and/or reports news in radio or television. A broadcast journalist can also be described as someone who possesses a set of particular qualities that compliment and strengthen credibility and authority with viewers and listeners. One of the individual qualities that employers expect from a broadcast journalist is commitment—no doubt you've heard this word before—especially in the context of a job search or career decisions. Many broadcast professionals suggest that a college degree in journalism or a related media discipline, along with "wit, charm, subtlety, persistence—and heaps of talent" (Boyd 2001), is necessary. Broadcast journalists should also display several other weightier characteristics: (1) the ability to demonstrate a broad base of knowledge related to history, geography, and names; (2) process new information; (3) demonstrate an "ethical compass"; (4) command of grammar, syntax, tone, and storytelling; and (5) an ability to understand all the tasks and technology involved in creating a professional broadcast (Geisler 2011). Of course, there are many more characteristics and expectations for broadcast journalists. One final characteristic a broadcast journalist possesses, **ethics,** can be taught in a classroom but is also a function of how you're parented, your personal decision-making process, and the way you see the world.

BROADCAST JOURNALISM AND THE APPLIED COMMUNICATION MODEL

You might have noticed that so far almost every professional interviewed for this book mentioned something about the importance of writing regardless of the specific discipline or career under discussion. This was pure coincidence, and we didn't ask our professionals to emphasize writing when answering questions. But, they did. It's true, writing is one of the keys that unlocks success in all the careers and will most likely make you invaluable if you become good at it. In broadcast journalism, your story begins with a **news script,** and there are some special considerations when writing for television and radio. Thompson's article in the next section provides valuable tips for successful storytelling in broadcast journalism and reminds you to "**K.I.S.S.**"

Ethics

As you'll recall, ethics is one of the core components of the Applied Communication Model. For broadcast journalists, more than some other professions, the public as well as professional colleagues will scrutinize daily a broadcast journalist's ethical choices. Broadcast journalists must adhere to a **code of ethics,** which is clearly described by the **Radio Television Digital News Association (RTDNA),** the largest professional organization for electronic journalism in the world. Following RTDNA guidelines, a television news story should be written, produced, and broadcast using the following guiding principles: (1) Truth and accuracy above all; (2) Independence and transparency; and (3) Accountability for consequences (RTDNA 2015).

Ethical decision-making is so important for a broadcast journalist that many respected professional journalists have been reprimanded and even fired for what is essentially a lack of ethical behavior and decision-making. Two famous instances of this in broadcast journalism come to mind. First, Brian Williams, former NBC Nightly News anchor, who was caught "exaggerating his experiences" in covering the Iraq War in 2003 (Stanglin 2015), was fired as anchor and demoted. Lara Logan, a correspondent for *60 Minutes*, was suspended from *60 Minutes* and publicly vilified regarding how she and CBS handled an interview with a former security contractor (Maloy and Gertz 2013) as part of the now infamous Benghazi attacks.

Thinking about the historical connections between print and broadcast journalism, a story's newsworthiness, the characteristics defining a broadcast journalist, and, finally, the importance of journalistic ethics will help guide you on the path to a career in journalism. Along the way, you'll gain a better understanding of how news is created and how to make sense of the news you see and hear. But, you really need to *create* the news yourself and that begins with practicing some of the skills and thinking involved. In the next several readings, the authors discuss the importance of writing and interviewing in broadcast news and offer some thoughtful and strategic ways to plan and prepare for your career in broadcast journalism.

WRITING BROADCAST NEWS SCRIPTS

by Rick Thompson

People think I can teach them style. What stuff it all is! Have something to say and say it as clearly as you can. That is the only secret to style. (Matthew Arnold, *Collections and Recollections*)

THE PRINCIPLES

Having established that broadcast journalists should aim to write as they would speak to an individual member of the audience, using a clean and accurate version of the spoken language, and avoiding journalese, the question then arises whether it is possible to learn techniques for writing against the clock, or whether good writing comes naturally. Some editors seem to believe that journalists have their talent genetically embedded somewhere in the anatomy: maybe in the blood, maybe in the nose ('He has a nose for a story, that one'); maybe in the bladder ('I have a feelin-in-me-water about this one'); or in the abdomen, home of the gut feeling. Many more distinguished editors believe no such thing.

We can all teach ourselves to write better. Techniques can be developed by younger journalists to subdue the panic induced by a close deadline, and to ensure a comprehensible story. And the best experienced writers are always working on their technique, and seeking new ways of telling their stories. Of course there are a million ways to write any script, and there is no universal formula. But there are principles and practices which give any writer a rock-bed of certainty on which to build his or her personal style.

CLARITY, SIMPLICITY AND CONCISENESS

In writing, hence in style, the primary consideration is comprehensibility—therefore, clarity. (Eric Partridge, 'Style', *Usage and Abusage*)

> Simplicity is the key to happiness in the modern world. (The 14th Dalai Lama, *Happiness, Karma and Mind*, 1969)

The first and overriding principle is that we want our scripts to be understood easily by the audience. The World Service's Bob Jobbins says: 'If I were to give one word of advice to a young journalist, it would be *clarity.*' And it is clear that, for most editors, this clarity is coupled with *simplicity* and *conciseness.* Broadcast journalism is very much the art of précis: it is the technique of paring down the information to its essentials. A typical television news report may be only ninety seconds long, of which only forty seconds might be the reporter's own voice. That's the equivalent of about four column inches in a broadsheet newspaper. A local radio report may be even shorter than that. Seconds are precious and cannot be wasted. So no words can be a waste of time. Richard Sambrook, who for several years was a lead writer on the flagship BBC Nine O'Clock News, emphasises the need for scripts to be crisp and concise:

> You have to write as you would speak to someone, but you also have to pare it down. Less is more. Take out the superfluous words. Take out the unnecessary adjectives. At the same time keep it conversational to engage people. It's very different from the written text.

At ITN, Sir David Nicholas created a style which was known for its clarity. He summarises it like this:

> Writing for broadcast news should be composed of short sentences, it should be direct, and it should be tightly, tightly edited. No excess baggage—like an airliner! Be absolutely tough. Go over the script if you have the chance and see what you can expunge without losing any meaning.

Sir David relates that he would practise his own scriptwriting by taking a column in the *New York Times*, and trying to reduce it to half its length without losing any facts.

In schools of journalism in the United States, you will hear tutors urging their students to 'Kiss! Remember to kiss!'. This refers to the now well established advice from a veteran editor to a junior journalist wanting to know how to treat a story. 'Keep it simple, stupid!' In Britain, where we like to think we are a little more polite and sympathetic, KISS is said to stand for 'Keep it simple and straightforward'.

SHORT SENTENCES WORK BETTER

> A sentence is more likely to be clear if it is a short sentence communicating one thought, or a closely connected range of ideas. (Harold Evans, *Essential English*)

In broadcasting, writing in a simple and straightforward manner usually means writing sentences that are not too long. You do not want to have to take a breath in the middle of a sentence when broadcasting live or recording a report. Spoken English is generally composed of short sentences. In fact when talking to each other we sometimes use phrases that are not complete sentences. (Writing this way is certainly acceptable for some television news commentaries, but much less acceptable on radio […].) Over three decades, ITN's main news presenter Sir Alastair Burnet made short sentences his trademark. Spare words were cut. Those left

carried more emphasis. His scripts were orderly. They were easy to follow. But there's no need to be that rigid. There will be times when a more rounded, flowing sentence is appropriate to the subject matter, lending variety to the rhythm and permitting more expression in the voice. Either style will become monotonous without the other. But as a general rule, short sentences work better.

I would recommend any young broadcast writer to become comfortable with the shorter sentence style. It makes it easier to write the story when you feel under pressure, and it will always work on the air. Clearly it should not degenerate into a sequence of unrelated staccato statements. But when it becomes second nature to write crisply and simply, it is easier to break out into a flowing sentence when the occasion arises. For example, the following sentence has forty-three words, so it would be difficult to read it out loud without having to take a breath:

> The online search engine, Google, is turning up the pressure on its main Internet rivals, Microsoft and Yahoo, by launching a free email service called Gmail, which it says will block spam and will have five hundred times more storage capacity than Hotmail.

It's easy to break up the sentence:

> The online search engine, Google, is turning up the pressure on its Internet rivals Microsoft and Yahoo. Today it launches a free email service called 'Gmail'. Google says it will block spam—and has five hundred times the storage capacity of Hotmail.

If you listen carefully to broadcast news, you will notice that many of the most experienced and most respected correspondents use short sentences, especially when they want to convey a sense of tension or expectation. Here is a section of television commentary by the BBC's John Simpson, as he reported on the fall of Kabul in November 2001. Presumably it was written under some pressure:

'It was just before dawn that the wild dash for Kabul developed. Thousands of soldiers intent on capturing the capital. It seemed to take no time at all to cover the twelve or so miles. As we drew nearer to Kabul, the grim evidence of battle. These were former members of the Northern Alliance who'd switched sides and joined the Taliban. No mercy for them. Then we saw they had captured another man. The presence of our camera probably saved his life. He was paralysed with terror. By now there were no Taliban left to resist. Then came the critical moment. Would the Northern Alliance simply race on and pour into Kabul itself, even though they'd undertaken not to? The commander in charge was determined not to let it happen. He ordered the armoured vehicles to block the way. The great advance was stopped in its tracks. But Kabul lay temptingly close below us now. The small BBC team decided to head on.'

Of course on air it was not as staccato as it looks on paper. Simpson's delivery included pauses for the natural sound, and the pictures provided a flowing continuum of the military advance. Here he prepares to spend the night with a Belgrade family in their air-raid shelter:

'This is a city Tito built. New Belgrade. A dormitory suburb for the post-communist middle class. On a day like this everyone likes to get out into the sun. It's only at night that clear skies mean heavy bombing. Each part of New Belgrade has its air-raid shelter. Tito thought they might be needed against attacks from Russia. Never conceivably from NATO.'

The most striking difference between reporting for broadcast news and reporting for newspapers is the use of very short and simple sentences or phrases.

WHAT'S THE STORY?

Obscurity of expression generally springs from confusion of ideas. (Thomas Babington Macaulay, *English Essays*)

Unfortunately, simplicity isn't all that simple! Clear writing will only be possible if you have a clear idea of the essentials of your story. Good writing is not a display of dexterity, like calligraphy or accurate typing. It happens in the mind. So it is worth reflecting for a moment on what we mean by a 'story'.

In Britain we tend to take for granted the idea that our journalism is composed of a series of these so-called stories. The question 'What's the story?' is asked scores of times every day in every newsroom. But in many other countries, the concept is far from clear. After the collapse of the Soviet Union, I organised training courses for producers and reporters in many former communist countries, where for two or three generations there had been very little independent or enquiring journalism. So-called journalists had been simply reprocessing official information. I soon discovered that in the new climate of a free press, some writers found it difficult to identify 'stories' because this required a process of analysis and decision-making which was unfamiliar to them. Many would confuse events with stories. 'My story is that there is a meeting of the Baltic Environmental Alliance, with representatives of all the countries bordering the Baltic who are discussing how to clean it up.' But what's the *story*? It may be that the clean-up will cost ten billion Euros and take fifty years. It may be that a Polish chemical factory is defying the agreements and poisoning Sweden's fisheries. Very often stories emerge from events, but they should not be confused with the event itself. The opening of an art exhibition (still a favourite subject for television news magazines in former Soviet states) is a story only if there is something about it that is novel and interesting to the viewers.

It seems that in other languages there is no precise equivalent of the English word 'story' meaning a piece of journalism, which is probably why so many journalists working in other languages use the word. The French 'histoire' does not quite mean the same thing. To some students of journalism from overseas, 'story' seems an odd choice of a word, suggesting fiction or fairy story. Of course a journalist's story is rooted in fact and related with accuracy. But it is still a narrative, and the word indicates quite neatly the idea that the reader will want to know what happens next or how it concludes. Journalism in the free world has developed as a series of short stories because it works. People want to read stories. Stories sell newspapers. In broadcasting the listeners and viewers certainly want to hear or watch stories. 'Please will you read this document' is a much less appealing invitation than 'Listen, I'm going to tell you a story'.

SUBJECTS AND EVENTS ARE NOT NECESSARILY STORIES

But even in Britain, where there is a long tradition of enquiring journalism presented in narrative form, it is still possible to hear scripts that put the event at the beginning, and leave it to the listeners to find for themselves the main point of interest—the story. You, the journalist, should make the decision about what the story is. That is the essence of journalism. Your employer pays you to make those decisions. If you have a host of facts and a number of possible implications which you would like to report, sit back for a moment and consider which will be the one point to attract the attention of the audience and encapsulate the subject of the piece.

In my view, newspaper journalists are better at doing this than broadcasters. Perhaps that is because of the unforgiving discipline of writing the newspaper headline. Once committed to the presses, a boring headline is banged out in black and white perhaps millions of times, seeming more and more boring each time—certainly to

the hapless sub-editor who wrote it. So newspaper headline writers are extremely unlikely to decide that the story is, for example: 'David Hockney opens new exhibition'; or 'Colin Powell arrives in Jordan on the latest stage of his Middle East shuttle'; or 'Tory Party Conference opens in Brighton'. But broadcasters quite regularly use such headlines. They are *diary items*, not news.

In his book, *The Television News Handbook*, BBC News Executive Editor, Vin Ray, says:

> Think how you would tell a friend what the story is in one sentence and bear that in mind as you put the piece together. Too much information will make your writing style tortuous and cramped … Bear in mind the difference between the subject of a story and your treatment of it.

STORY FOCUS IN THE TREATMENT OF SUBJECTS

Even experienced correspondents sometimes write like this:

> The engine, an RB-211C Whisperjet, designed for the new short-range European Airbus commuter-liner, and said to be twenty per cent quieter than equivalent engines, is to be built at Rolls-Royce factories in Derby and Coventry.

It's the kind of script which has plenty of facts, probably lifted from a company press release, but no story focus. The most interesting aspect of the story may well be that this is to be the quietest airliner of its size, and the story would then develop by mentioning new tougher noise limits being imposed by the EU. It might go on to explain that new carbon fibre blades in the engines reduce friction and are therefore quieter. That's why Rolls-Royce have called the engine the 'Whisperjet'. If the story was being written for a regional service in the Midlands, or a local radio station in Derby, the focus would be on the number of local jobs created or secured. For example:

> Five thousand workers at the Rolls-Royce aero-engine factories in Derby and Coventry have been told their jobs are safe for at least six years, because of an order to supply engines for the new European Airbus. The company says one of the reasons they won the contract was because the engine, the RB211C, operates well below the EU's tough new noise limits for short-range aircraft. They've called the new engine the 'Whisperjet', because it's said to be twenty per cent quieter than its rivals. The works convenor at the Derby factory, Daniel Black, said the Airbus contract was 'great news for all the people at Rolls-Royce who've worked so hard to turn the company round'.

And whatever the story focus, as a general rule, the information will be taken in more easily in shorter sentences.

Trying to cram in too many pieces of information in the same sentence is one of the main faults in broadcast scripts. If you hurl out too many facts and figures, the people listening at home or on the motorway simply cannot follow the narrative, or remember much of it a few seconds later. Writers are strongly advised to keep to the essential facts that support the key point of the story, and to deliver them one at a time.

WRITING THE KEY POINT OF THE STORY FIRST

As another general rule, when writing a bulletin story or the introduction to a full report, try to put the key point of the story first, preferably in the top line.

> At a news conference this afternoon, the Chief Constable of the West Midlands Police, David Jones, announced that …

is much less effective than:

> A new police unit is being set up to fight the spread of crack in the West Midlands. Announcing the move at a news conference this afternoon, the Chief Constable, David Jones, said …

We should not confuse the 'peg' with the most interesting point of the story. As most readers of this book will know, the peg is journalists' slang for the topical development on which we hang our story about an interesting issue. It is the reason for doing the story today. The peg may be a conference, or the publication of a report, or the start of a hearing, or no more than an anniversary. It should certainly be mentioned early in the story, but not necessarily in the opening phrase. The Sky News presenter, Julie Etchingham, says:

> My real pet hates are any links which begin 'A report out today …' or 'According to latest figures …'. They're dreadful in any news bulletin, but are particularly inappropriate for 24-hour news, which is supposed to be constantly fresh and appealing.

Sometimes there can be several stories in the same news programme stemming from various government initiatives, and the effect can be to make your output sound like the official pronouncements of a state broadcaster: 'The Prime Minister has announced that … the Department of Health is to … The Foreign Secretary has arrived in …'. Putting the story first avoids this rather dull and formal approach, and will interest your viewers and listeners much more.

In regional television and local radio, where on some days quite a number of bulletin stories can originate from the police calls, the danger is that too many stories can begin with 'Police in …': 'Police in Stirling …' or Police in Dumbarton …'. It's much more interesting to put the key subject of your story in the first line. And incidentally it should be '*The* police in …' (see 'The definite article', pp. 31–2).

Of course there will be occasions when you want to build up to the story, either to make sure the significance or context of the latest development is clearly understood, or simply to attract the attention of the listener. The section on writing studio introductions (pp. 101–11) develops the idea that an inviting opening line is extremely important. Sometimes this will be in the form of a question directed at the listener or viewer, for example: 'Should schoolchildren be forced to wear uniforms?' (Radio Four Today programme). This introduction then went on to the new angle, which was a report from a head teachers' association.

But introductions that are obviously teasing should be used sparingly, and usually on less serious stories. The formula of 'Jane Williams thought it was just another quiet Sunday when she took her Yorkshire terrier, Lucky, for his morning walk …' can very easily become a stroll into cliché land. In general terms, it is good practice to get into the habit of identifying the key point of interest in your story, and putting it first. Teachers of journalism often summarise this advice as: 'The first sentence must *interest*, the second sentence must *inform*.'

THE DIRECT STYLE

NOT TOO MANY SUBORDINATE CLAUSES

It is not very good practice to start with a subordinate clause, for example, 'Following his pledge at last week's party conference to reduce taxes for poorer families, the Chancellor has …'. By definition, people expect the news to be new. To attract their interest, it's usually best to put the new development in a running story first, for example, 'A new tax credit for low-income families is likely to be a key part of next month's budget …'.

In fact subordinate clauses should be used sparingly throughout broadcast news scripts. The crisp, tight, simple style which avoids long sentences, and which is advocated by all leading editors, has little room for hanging ideas, of the

'*following … after … due to …*' variety. You would be unlikely to say: 'Needing some milk, I went to the corner shop.'

Here is the opening paragraph of a *Guardian* front-page article, written by their Political Editor, Michael White, an experienced correspondent who is widely regarded as an acute observer of the world of politics and a fine writer:

'Tony Blair last night won a respite in the battle to restore his troubled premiership after delivering a sombre mid-term conference speech which impressed mainstream Labour activists for its candour but failed to win over his more unforgiving critics.'

It's a concise summary of the story as interpreted by the correspondent, packed with information. But this single sentence, without a single punctuation mark, would be difficult to read on the air without running out of breath or losing the audience's attention. We seldom talk to each other that way; and remember that many people in your audience may be listening a little casually. Presenting them with one idea at a time makes it much easier to follow the news. So if you find yourself writing, as in the above example, '*after … which … but*' in the same sentence, try dropping in a few full stops.

THE ACTIVE VOICE

In a similar way, the simple, direct style of spoken English is much more comfortable with the use of the active voice rather than the passive. So we tend to say 'Dad bought the paper', rather than 'the paper was bought by Dad', even when replying to a question about who had bought the paper. The active voice suits broadcast news. It is usually a more logical line of thought, it is a more direct and muscular style, and it is more in line with normal speech.

The passive will be more appropriate when the focus of the story that you want to emphasise is someone or something that has been on the receiving end of an action. For example, you would probably write 'fifteen thousand patients were taken to hospital by taxis in London last year, an increase of fifty per cent …' rather than 'taxis took fifteen thousand patients …'. You would probably report, for example, that a wild kangaroo attacked a British tourist. But if the tourist happened to be Prince Harry, you'd almost certainly write 'Prince Harry was mauled by a deranged kangaroo …'. As ever, there are no firm rules. But there is a strong tendency towards using the active tenses for the clearest, crispest writing. The direct style also expunges all redundant words, and has surprisingly few adjectives and adverbs.

In the next article, the authors provide some excellent checklists and resources to get you started on telling the best story possible. For instance, ask yourself "who is this story about?" Maybe the answer isn't obvious. Research is vital to writing and **producing** a good story but what kind of research is best?

READING 6.2

CONDUCTING AN INTERVIEW

by Jerry Lazar

In addition to learning the technology of recording video and audio, videojournalists also need to master the techniques of interviewing. Being a good interviewer requires more than just holding a microphone in front of someone's face. Being a good interviewer means knowing what questions to ask.

This symbol indicates when to go to the *Videojournalism* website for either links to more information or to a story cited in the text. Each reference will be listed according to chapter and page number. Links to stories will include their titles and, when available, images corresponding to those in the book. Bookmark the following URL, and you're all set to go: http://www.kobreguide.com/content/videojournalism.

TELLING THE STORY FROM MANY POINTS OF VIEW

A good story needs a central protagonist—a hero, if you will. So start by asking yourself, "Who embodies the essence of this story?"

Sometimes this choice will be obvious and sometimes not. At times, a decision to deliberately gravitate toward a less obvious choice can set your story apart from others on the same topic.

For instance, instead of experts or opinionmakers typically called upon by journalists to give the "official" word, you might pursue interview subjects less accustomed to being in the public eye. These people will probably not be as comfortable or as polished in front of a camera as the former, but that slightly rough quality often turns out to be an asset.

For Djamila Grossman's story about heroin addiction, he found a convicted addict who actually had asked for a maximum prison sentence. Of course, the videojournalist could simply have interviewed drug experts, rehabilitation professionals, social workers, and police officers. Instead, he decided to interview this particular drug addict who was trying to get clean.

Heroin Addict Finds Hope. The story's producer focused on an addict to convey a more realistic vision of problems of going straight. (Video by Djamila Grossman, *Standard-Examiner*)

Here's a checklist of what to look for when selecting the central character in your story:
- Knowledgeable? Informed? Involved?
- Affected/impacted by the story?
- Primary mover/shaker in the story?
- Strong feelings and opinions about the subject?
- Articulate and willing and able to speak candidly on camera?
- Reputable? Credible? Reliable? Trustworthy?
- Cooperative?
- Representative of a larger group, trend, or perspective?

But one person does not a story make! Think how boring a book or movie would be with only one character in it. The same is true of videojournalism and multimedia storytelling. An alarming number stories fail because they feature only one character source.

Constantly ask yourself, "What other perspectives are there? Who can best represent and articulate them?"

As you research and gather information for your story, search for names of individuals in previous accounts in newspapers, magazines, books, and on the Web. As you start contacting them, via phone or email, always ask them, "Who else should I talk to?" That's one way to cultivate fresh perspectives—and perhaps even find the ideal "hero" for your story.

CONTRASTING POINTS OF VIEW

Whenever you can show a contrast between two sides of an issue, two points of view, two opposing characters, you have the potential for a good story.

Mel Melcon of the *Los Angeles Times* built a clever story by contrasting a Marilyn Monroe imitator and a Marilyn Monroe wax figure from Madame Tussaud's Wax Museum. Interviews with the lookalike and the museum's PR person representing the wax Marilyn provide the contrasting points of view.

The best stories, in fiction and in real life, are those with intrinsic drama that is the result of showing two or more people in conflict. So always try to explore individuals' motives—and then find someone who represents a competing interest or point of view.

Three years ago, Monica Long was told that a mammogram indicated ductal carcinoma in situ, or D.C.I.S., an early form of breast cancer. As a result, she had a quadrantectomy, in which about a quarter of her breast was removed. When Long's medical records were reexamined later during a routine checkup at a different facility, she was told that she had never had cancer at all. Experts say that her case is not all that unusual. Videographers Stephanie Saul and Shayla Harris, working for the *New York Times*, not only interviewed the doctor who caught the mistake but also allowed the doctor who gave the original diagnosis a chance to respond.

Pathology of Errors. Besides interviewing the central subject, the producers of this video interviewed doctors on both sides of a controversy over whether the patient really needed to have a breast operation for cancer. (Produced by Stephanie Saul and Shayla Harris, *New York Times*)

For another example that requires multiple points of view, consider the debate over a proposed city council measure that requires restaurants to provide health insurance for all their employees. Rather than featuring only the politician who sponsored the legislation, your story might center on a popular waiter at a local restaurant. But will you just follow him about his day and let him explain how important it is to have health care coverage? Well, that may be part of the story, but let's also hear from the supporting and opposing lawmakers. Let's hear from restaurateurs who favor the measure, and those who oppose it. What

pop•u•LA•tion
Stories from the sidewalk

0:02 / 3:11

Battle of the Blondes. This multimedia piece presents a synchronized sparring match between two Marilyn impersonators—one live, one a wax model—who spend their days on Hollywood Boulevard. Melissa Weiss has played Marilyn Monroe on Hollywood Boulevard for the past nine years. Interviews with Weiss and a PR representative for Madame Tussaud's provide the contrasting narration. (Produced by Mel Melcon, *Los Angles Times*)

do they think the impact will be on their business? Let's hear from the rest of the wait staff and the kitchen crew. Are any of them opposed to the legislation? During your sleuthing, keep your eyes and ears open for unexpected sources that may be directly or indirectly affected by the matter at hand, even customers, for example.

As you pare down your potential interview subjects, here are some other questions to ask yourself:

- How and why is this person knowledgeable about this subject?
- Can this person's information be independently confirmed through other sources?
- Who does this person speak for, or represent?
- What is this person's reputation?
- Why is this person willing to talk? Does his eagerness to participate affect his or her credibility as a reliable source?

HOW WILL INTERVIEWS BE USED IN YOUR STORY?

As you plan and prepare for your interviews, think about how they will be used in your video story. In typical TV news reports, for example, the subject and interviewer are on camera together, and we see and hear both of them during the interview—either in the same frame or, preferably, in alternating sequences.

Extreme Couponers Get Groceries for (almost) Free. In a story about clipping coupons for supermarket discounts, Treasure Phillips tells her tale. However, the viewer never hears the original interview questions that stimulated the answers. (Videojournalist: Jacob Templin. Supervising Producer: Craig Duff, *Time.com*)

But for telling stories in short documentaries, the following situations are the better options:

- Subject is on-camera, and we see and hear her responding to questions. The original questions being answered, however, have been edited out.
- Subject is on-camera, but we hear the interviewer's questions off-camera.
- Subject's voice responds to questions while we see B-roll footage of what the person is talking about.

Each interviewee may be used once or twice in the final story. Or they may appear throughout the video. You will most likely use some combination of these alternatives to weave your story together. Sometimes the central character's voice narrates the entire video, essentially describing the footage as it's shown.

BACKGROUND RESEARCH

The most critical aspect of interview preparation is researching your topic and your subject. Research not only helps you prepare excellent questions, but provides you with a high level of comfort and authority while you're conducting your interview.

Nobody expects you to become an overnight expert, but your interview subjects will generally be more cooperative if they feel you've done your homework and are taking them, and their pursuits, seriously. Some talk-show hosts claim they like to know as little as possible about their guests, so that they can ask "average person" questions. But they're usually being disingenuous, as their producers provide them with well-researched questions on file cards. And those who really do pride themselves on their ignorance frequently stumble and look foolish when they pose questions that reflect their lack of preparedness. Asking "average-person questions" is time-wasting and insulting to their guests, as well.

The best interviewers—such as NBC's Bob Costas and NPR's Terry Gross—are, as you can readily tell, exceptionally well prepared. They're able to steer in-depth discussions in unexpected directions.

The purpose of all your research is to ask good questions, so begin by envisioning specifically what kinds of information you're hoping to glean from your interview. You will be looking for someone who can describe an issue or an event or a process in a clear and engaging way. You'll want to try as discreetly as you can to extract opinions and attitudes. You'll also need to make sure in advance that your subject's responses will be lucid and complete. And with the subtlest approach possible, you also will want to get the person to respond to other perspectives—even the most contrary or competing ones, if applicable.

The more you know, the better your questions will be. The better your questions, the better their answers will be. The better their answers, the better your story will be. In short—if you want to end up with an excellent story, you must set out to obtain excellent information before you ever start.

FINDING THE FACTS

When it comes to research, web search engines are your best friends. There is no excuse these days to conduct anything less than an exhaustive exploration of the person you're interviewing and the ideas and areas you'll be discussing. Search the general topic and see what comes up. There will probably be so much data that you'll have to narrow the search. Do make sure your web information comes from reliable sources such as original research in journals, government sites, and data available in the public record, including published reports in the *New York Times*, the *Wall Street Journal*, and other news organizations that typically explore multiple sides of topics.

Don't stop with online research. Libraries are still valuable reference centers, and reference librarians can be invaluable in helping narrow research. Don't forget books and video.

You'll also be calling sources for facts and figures necessary for the story. Although they themselves may not warrant on-camera interviews, sources such as these can often lead you to others who may be camera-worthy. Be discreet. But don't be afraid to pick peoples' brains for references.

If you're working on a story about a resurgence of sales of vinyl record albums, a record-industry trade association spokesperson may provide a valuable statistic. Using that statistic may not warrant an on-camera interview, but you may be able to use the data in a voice-over narration, on-screen text, or graphics. Also, you might ask that first person to recommend a record company executive for an interview.

What are some of the things you need to know before you can develop the questions for your interviews about the comeback of vinyl?

- **History.** What's the story behind vinyl records? When were they invented? How long were they in use? When did they fall out of general use? Why are people buying them again?
- **Controversial issues.** Find out anything regarding the medium's longevity. What devices played the music? How was the quality of sound?
- **Follow the money.** Does vinyl cost more or less than CDs to produce?
- **Contrarian point of view.** Who thinks vinyl is outdated and gone for good?
- **Who has the facts?** People in academia study all kinds of wondrous things. Are there professors of history or popular culture to query? What about canvassing musicians themselves? Or finding out who is developing new recording/storage technologies?

A far more serious, tragic story required extensive research that provided *New York Times* reporters Gabe Johnson and Michael Moss entrée into the loosely regulated meat-packing industry, where lax safety precautions have led to a surge in food poisoning cases in recent years. Consuming a home-cooked hamburger containing a virulent strain of E. coli bacteria nearly took the life of a young dancer, Stephanie Smith, and left her brain damaged and paralyzed.

By focusing on the numerous stops along the trail—from stockyards to your dinner plate—this

John Knowlton, Journalism professor, Green River Community College

- Have I made clear the purpose of my interview—both to myself and to my subject? (What do you really want from this interview and how eager are you to obtain this information? The more specific your purpose and the more apparent your enthusiasm, the more likely you are to gain cooperation.)

- Have I made it clear (to myself and to the subject) why I want information from this particular individual? (A source may be flattered to be singled out.) Have I eliminated my own preconceived biases and eliminated my emotional barriers to communication?

- Have I done preliminary research on the person and the topic to be discussed—read things about him or her, done preliminary interviews so that I can develop new areas of inquiry?

- Has my research included preparation for "small talk" or "icebreaker" kinds of commentary? (For example, review news accounts of recent Supreme Court decisions when preparing to interview a lawyer.)

- Before requesting the interview, have I prepared a few "sample" questions cold-bloodedly calculated to be both provocative and ego-reinforcing?

- Am I prepared to use my listening "down time" effectively? (Your mind runs three to four times faster than people's speech, so you can tune in and out of the conversation. You can make effective use of the "nonlistening" time to evaluate what is being said, make comparisons with other data, take notes, and to think up new questions.)

- Am I (or will I be by the time of the interview) well-rested, well-nourished, and sober with all my mental faculties alert so that I can catch the fine nuances of meaning or things left half-expressed or even unsaid—in short, am I ready to listen between the lines?

investigative video piece provides a clear explanation of what can, and has, gone terribly wrong with our food regulatory systems. By bookending the story with one woman's heartbreaking consequences of unwittingly eating an E. coli–infested hamburger, it turns a scientific story into a personal—and *frightening* story.

PLANNING THE INTERVIEW

Thoughtful interviews are well planned. Planning means contacting your subjects, explaining your story and why you need their input. It also requires detailing who your story is for and how and where it will be used. Good preparation also demands you arrange a mutually suitable time and place for the interview. And it means preparing questions that will elicit the most informative and engaging responses. Never just show up on someone's doorstep unannounced, expecting a thoughtful and cooperative subject to be waiting for you.

There's no need to go into exhaustive detail in your initial contact. You want to offer just enough information so your subject will be prepared for the interview, but won't give them the opportunity to rehearse responses. Offer general areas of conversation you'll be exploring, but don't provide a list of specific questions, as that will ruin any chance for spontaneity.

Choose a time and location that will provide minimal distraction and noise. Ideally, you can shoot your subject in his or her "natural habitat"—at work or at home, or in a location that's appropriate for the story itself. Make sure to schedule enough time—and remember to include time for setting up your location for recording optimal audio and video.

Pullman Porter and Family Patriarch. Mel Melcon of the *Los Angeles Times* interviewed and photographed Lee Wesley Gibson, who turned 100 in July 2010 and worked for the Union Pacific Railroad for 38 years. The *LA Times* staffer interviewed the centenarian in a quiet place with little distracting noise but took pictures of Gibson in a number of locations, including an old Union Pacific railroad car, the subject's house, and at a funeral. (Produced by Mel Melcon, *Los Angeles Times*)

You don't want to be rushed. Depending on the nature and complexity of your story, you may need to make multiple visits, at a variety of locations—especially if you're following a process over a period of time. Or things can become more complicated as you unearth new information that requires an on-camera response or rebuttal from other sources. Let the subject know that.

How much time should you request for your interview? That really depends on too many factors for us to generalize. TV news reporters are accustomed to getting in and out fast. They have frequent and rigid deadlines to meet and they know that only a short sound bite—a telling comment or observation extracted from a longer interview—will be used for their minute-long story. They realize there is no point in burdening the editor (most likely themselves) with wading through a half-hour conversation for the "money" quote. Instead, they fire off three quick questions, and they're good to go.

Videojournalists face fewer such constraints. But at the same time, busy audiences do expect and appreciate economy. Even though stories can

be told more expansively, nobody has the patience to sit through rambling monologues, especially when so many other online distractions beckon.

WHAT IF THE PERSON DOESN'T WANT TO TALK WITH YOU?

If someone does not want to be interviewed, that's certainly his or her right. Plenty of people are wary of strangers in general and journalists in particular. Even a public official is not obligated to grant an interview. But if a source is important to your story, here are some tips for enticing him or her to cooperate:

- Don't use the word "interview"—it can be off-putting. Say you'd like to talk or chat. It sounds less intimidating. (But be clear that your conversation will be on camera.)
- Like a good salesperson, try to intuit what's causing the resistance and overcome specific objections by anticipating and accommodating the person's concerns.
- If it's a question of the person not having enough time right then, offer a more convenient time or place—perhaps in the person's car on the way to work.
- If someone is afraid of looking bad or sounding stupid, explain why his or her perspective is so vital and necessary for your story.
- If the person claims to have nothing to say, reiterate the information you are seeking. If he or she still feels uncomfortable, at least ask for suggestions of other possible sources.
- If you're having trouble getting access to a source, particularly one in an official capacity who may be surrounded by protective underlings, be persistent. Call, write, email, or just show up. Find a mutual acquaintance (or another source) to serve as intermediary.
- Be clear that the story will be told with or without the person's cooperation—and so to be fair, you want to provide an opportunity to tell his or her side of the story.
- Appeal to the person's vanity. Each person has something special and important to

contribute to your story. Emphasize the person's unique contribution.

WHAT IF THE PERSON ASKS YOU WHAT TO WEAR?

Sometimes your subjects will ask what to wear for the interview. If the story is about a retired soldier, you might suggest his or her uniform. A costume might be appropriate for a stage actor before or after a performance.

More general useful advice is that blue is a color that shows well on screen and is not distracting, as are pastel colors. Most critical is what *not* to wear for a video interview:

- Bright white reflects the maximum amount of light and can throw off exposure.
- Black is too harsh, can suck up all the light, and throw off exposure.
- Bright red "bleeds" on screen and is distracting.
- Stripes, herringbone patterns, small intricate designs, and checks can actually pulsate on screen. Hats, sunglasses, or tinted glasses tend to hide the face and be hard to light. Large, dangling earrings distract and can make noise or hit the microphone during head movements. Logos make the interview look like an advertisement. Shiny objects, including ties, can end up looking like plastic or mirrors.

DEVELOPING YOUR QUESTIONS

The two most important things you will be bringing to your interview (besides your equipment) are your list of questions and your sense of curiosity.

You'd be amazed at how many would-be interviewers leave those things at home, and instead think that the most important thing to bring is themselves—their own sparkling wit and personality. They somehow forget that the interview is about the other person.

Your curiosity is probably what got you impassioned about storytelling in the first place. Good interviewers are curious about the world and are sincerely interested in other people and what makes them tick.

As you're preparing your questions, invite interested friends and associates to contribute as well. Nowadays, the Web makes it especially easy for journalists to solicit questions for upcoming interviews, especially via social media such as Facebook or Twitter. You can invite input from total strangers who may share an interest (and even some expertise) either in your topic or in your interviewee.

Now that you've learned all you can in advance about your subject, and have determined what fresh information, ideas, and emotions you'd like to see shared with you and your audience, you need to structure a conversation designed to elicit all that. Even though some interviewers smugly pride themselves on their provocative or challenging questions, in truth, a question is only as good as the response it evokes. This fact is doubly true in videojournalism, where you're unlikely to include the questions when editing.

Remember: you're a journalist, not a talk-show host.

CORE QUESTIONS

In addition to standard biographical background questions, nearly all your inquiries will focus on:

- What your subject has done, is doing, or plans to do
- What your subject thinks about _____
- How your subject feels about _____
- What your subject knows about _____
- What your subject has experienced regarding _____

Tami Tushie's Toys. Just as their mothers may have done, women still give parties in their homes to sell merchandise to friends and neighbors. These days, plastic containers or candles aren't the only things being sold. Tami Tushie is a working hostess of "Pure Romance" parties, where she hawks sex aids—lotions, potions, and toys designed to perk up a woman's sex life. Notice how the story answers the who, what, where, when, and why questions readers have. (Produced by Melody Gilbert, Kiersten Chace, Adrian Danciu and Emily Rumsey)

What people remember most about a story is usually not factual. Rather, a viewer recalls the emotions the story stirs up and the senses it awakens. That's why asking how a subject feels, in every "sense," is a completely useful and valid interview tactic.

"Describe what it was like to _____" is a good phrase for teasing out how a subject feels about something without asking "How did it feel to _____?"

Allow flexibility, so that the conversation can follow a natural course and go down unexpected but fruitful paths.

Keeping in mind that your story will follow a narrative arc—rising action, conflict, and resolution—you'll want to ask questions that lend themselves to that dramatic structure:

• How did you get started?
• What is your goal?
• What drives you? Why are you passionate about this?
• What are the obstacles or hurdles preventing you from reaching that goal?
• How have you overcome them? How do you plan to overcome them?
• What does the future look like?

TIP Remember to listen to your subject's answer, not prepare for the next question. Your next questions could expand on what the interviewee just said before you change topics and take the interview in a new direction.

TYPES OF QUESTIONS

There are two general types of interview questions—closed-ended and open-ended. What's the difference? A closed-ended question can be answered with a "yes" or a "no" or a one-syllable word, whereas an open-ended question cannot. The best questions are open-ended because they lead to expansive responses. Look at the difference:

Closed-ended: Do your teenage kids respect you?
Open-ended: Tell us about your relationship with your teenage kids.
Closed ended: Are you going to vote in favor of this legislation?
Open-ended: What do you think about this proposed legislation?
Closed-ended: What's your favorite hobby or activity?
Open-ended: What do you do on weekends?

QUESTIONS TO CLOSE

Here are some other tried-and-true "closers" that you can adapt for your purposes:

• What is the significance of what you've told us today?
• What have you learned from this experience?
• What would you like our audience to do about this?
• Is there anything you would have done differently, knowing what you now know?
• What are your plans for the future?
• What obstacles and challenges lie ahead?

It's also a good idea to ask whether you can call on the subject again if you need further information.

Finally, always ask your subject, "Is there anything else you would like to add?"

STRUCTURE YOUR QUESTIONS IN THEMES

So that you're not hop-scotching all over the place, structure your questions to be clustered around themes. (Editing will also be easier.) Know well ahead where you plan to begin, and where you hope to end.

The first question should be nonconfrontational—just to get everyone relaxed and rolling. Save tougher questions for later in the interview, especially if they're confrontational in nature. The final question might be an open-ended summation, along the lines of, "So what's the most important thing we should remember about _____?"

Organize the Questions with Bullet Points and Key Words

Instead of writing specific detailed questions, consider writing a list with bullet points and memory-jogging keywords. That way, you won't fall into the trap of reading the questions verbatim, like a spelling bee moderator, or worse, a police interrogator. You'll also be more inclined to pursue the interview as a conversation, which is conducive to the subject's sharing stories. Conversation is preferable to Q&A, which more often produces clipped, lifeless responses. To make sure you aren't leaving out important themes you intend to explore, or information you need to get on-camera, do, of course, consult your list.

CONDUCTING THE INTERVIEW

Respect other people's busy schedules by arriving punctually and prepared. Dress professionally, or at least appropriately for the setting. Your appearance affects how people relate to you. You want to do everything you can to win your subject's trust and confidence.

BEFORE YOU START

If you think there is any possibility you will need them later, take care of signing release forms first.

If you're at your subject's home or office, look at the surroundings to get a sense of what the person is like. A picture on the desk or wall may lead to small talk with your subject, serving as an "icebreaker" before the formal interview begins. Look for personality clues and identify any items that might be relevant to the discussion and might be used as visual props.

Take charge of the shooting circumstances:
* Find a suitable spot, with even, non-fluorescent lighting and a minimum of ambient noise.
* Arrange your seats so that you are relatively close and facing each other.
* Ask everyone present to mute their phones, and everyone other than the subject not to speak.
* Unplug noisy appliances.
* Mic the subject, and, if your questions also need to be recorded, perhaps yourself.
* Record some sound and check the audio quality.

PREPPING THE SUBJECT

Put your subject at ease. Begin with a bit of casual small talk—traffic, weather, sports, and the like. Be sure to say "thank you" in advance for the time being generously shared with you.

Popular Science. David Frank and Natalie Angier put the forensic science teacher and his students at ease during an interview for a story about what maggots reveal about decomposing bodies—and the popularity of this new high school science topic. (Produced by David Frank and Natalie Angier, *New York Times*)

SOME DON'TS AND DOS TO REMEMBER WHILE YOUR SUBJECT IS TALKING

DON'T:

- **Don't kid yourself into thinking that sharing your personal secrets will entice them to share theirs.** It won't. It only makes them think you're wasting their time. Nobody cares about you. Even famous interviewers like Oprah Winfrey and Barbara Walters succeed in ferreting out private insights without tipping their own hand or heart.
- **Don't do all the talking.** Again, it's not about you. You're not there to impress anyone. And don't clear your throat—just ask your question.
- **Don't preface questions with** "I'm wondering if..." or "I'd like to ask you this ..." or "Here's a question ...." Also, don't offer your opinion as an opening statement. Get to the point. Pretend it's a 140-character tweet.
- **Don't interrupt.** Your voice will ruin the subject's audio track.

DO:

- **Do heed the power of silence.** If your subject answers a question tersely, incompletely, or unsatisfactorily, just sit quietly and look at the person instead of moving on to the next question. The silence may seem uncomfortable, but before long, he or she is likely to jump in and fill it. Your silence also conditions subjects to avoid simplistic or pat answers, and it shows them that you expect them to work a little harder and think things through. Psychotherapists use this moment of silence technique on their "subjects" all the time. You can do it too.
- **Do listen! Listen! Listen!** And show that you're listening (and not just getting ready to pounce on the next question on your list). Otherwise, you might miss the revelation of a key piece of information that begs further exploration.
- **Do use body language to change the interview's direction.** If you're getting an unusable long-winded answer, use body language (e.g., raising an index finger) to subtly but silently interrupt, and then say, "I understand, but...." And then pose your next question.
- **Do resist the urge to say "mmm-hmm" or "yeah"** or emit other reflexive responses that are likely to intrude into the final audio. Instead, nod in acknowledgement, or use approving facial expressions (smile, raise eyebrows, and so on).
- **Do guide the interview** by using your list of topics and questions, but be open to possibilities. If you're listening carefully, you'll find plenty of opportunities for unanticipated follow-up questions that take you down unexpected yet fruitful paths.
- **Do repeat the question** if you don't get a satisfactory answer to a question; don't be afraid to rephrase it and try again.

Ask the person to look into the camera and say and spell his or her first and last name distinctly and to say, for example, "My name is _____ , and I'm a [profession] for the [name of company, etc.]."

To make the interview easier to edit, ask your subject to incorporate your questions into the answers. Provide an example. "For instance, if I ask, 'Where did you grow up?' it would be good if you could respond, 'Where did I grow up? I grew up in Philadelphia.' By including the questions in the answer, you will avoid a one-word response, like 'Philadelphia.'" Rehearse with your subject by asking the person's favorite ice cream flavor. If he gives a one-word answer like "Chocolate," then ask him to respond in a complete sentence that incorporates the question: "What kind of ice cream do I like? I like chocolate ice cream."

For another example, if you ask, "What went through your mind when the winds and water of Katrina came roaring through your neighborhood?" the answer might go like this: "What went through my mind when Katrina hit? I thought the wind was going to blow us away!" When you get back to the editing suite, you'll be able to use that quote anywhere, because it's a complete statement.

DURING THE INTERVIEW

Remember that being interviewed is not a natural activity for most people, so it's up to you to put them and keep them at ease. Your body language speaks volumes. Maintain comfortable eye contact and lean forward in a manner that says, "I'm interested" without seeming overly intense.

Some videojournalists take notes during an interview. Note taking allows them to see the answers to their questions and make sure they have follow-up responses. Notes also help when it's time to edit. Other videojournalists find that interviewing the subject, checking the focus and framing on the camera, making sure the sound has no interfering hisses, and so on, is enough of a job, so they don't add note taking to the list. You will find your own method of working after your have tried several one-on-one interviews.

HOW TO ASK QUESTIONS TO GET THE BEST RESPONSE

The single most important follow-up question is: **"Why?"**

The single most important follow-up question to a follow-up question is: **"Why?"**

Try a psychotherapeutic technique. "Mirror" your subject by **repeating the tail end of his or her response** as a method of eliciting an expanded answer as well as verifying your understanding of the response. **Subject:** "I think global warming is a fraud and climate scientists have deceived us for years.' **You:** 'Climate scientists have deceived us?' **Subject:** 'Yes, climate scientists were afraid of losing their grant money, so they rigged their data … .'

Ask **one question at a time**. Multi-part questions are too confusing and don't lend themselves to coherent, cohesive responses.

Keep the questions **short**. It's the answers that are important.

If anyone starts reeling off statistics, or any abstract concepts, ask for **concrete, real-world examples.**

Prod the storyteller who lives within all of us: **"What happened next?"**

Be unfailingly **polite**. Take the high road.

COMMON PROBLEMS AND DILEMMAS

Despite the best research and preparation, even the best interviewers are sometimes confronted with problems and dilemmas during an interview.

What should you do if the subject offers only monosyllabic responses? Skilled interviewers often follow up with questions such as …

Q: "Why?"

Q: "Can you expand on that, please?"

Q: "If you had to explain it to _____, what would you say?"

Q: "Tell me more."

Ask questions that call for a story:

Q: "What motivated you to become active in environmental causes?"

A: "My mother"

Q: "How so?"

A: "She took me to a rally when I was 12."

Q: "Really? Take me back to that event, and walk me through it. What were you thinking and feeling?"

What if the subject offers a lot of long-winded responses? Preface your next question with …

> Q: "Briefly, Miss Jones, before the (video) battery dies, I want to make sure I get these few quick questions in …"

Feign disinterest.

Put down your list of questions or your notebook.

What if the subject is dodgy and evasive or outright lying?

Don't ever call anyone a liar or even suggest that he or she is not telling the truth.

Re-ask:

> Q: "But XYZ has another perspective on that …"

> Q: "For those who say [the opposite], how would you respond?"

Catch the lie on camera. Then unravel it when you interview other sources.

CONFRONTATIONAL INTERVIEW

What's the best way to conduct a confrontational interview, without losing the subject's participation or cooperation?

There's no better case history of this than David Frost's historic adversarial interview with Richard Nixon, available on DVD. (Or you can enjoy the dramatic re-creation in the movie 'Frost/Nixon').

Writing in *American Journalism Review* and using Frost/Nixon as an example, CNN's Mark Feldstein offers a "how-to" primer for confrontational interviews that includes these suggestions:

- **Take charge** immediately by interrupting self-serving filibusters and by carefully avoiding pleasantries that might weaken the necessary resolve to go for the jugular.
- **Go for the tight shot.** Prepare to zoom in slowly on the interviewee's face when the exchange grows heated. This cinematic effect visually reinforces the editorial goal of zeroing in on the quarry.
- **Use props.** As every good trial lawyer knows, tangible exhibits such as video, photos, and documents not only help buttress a cross-examination but also add theatrical flair.

- **Set up targets to lie.** You can't force anyone to do so, of course, but it is always better to provide an opportunity to tell a falsehood on-camera before (not after) you pull out the smoking-gun memo that proves culpability. A single lie captured on-camera shakes the foundation of everything else the subject says afterward.
- **If you've the luxury of having a second camera,** keep it rolling no matter what. That way, if your subject rips off his microphone or storms out of the room, you have footage of his defensive tantrum. Also, the second camera comes in handy if interviewees blurt out embarrassing comments during a lull when they think they are not being recorded.

Are any of these tactics unfair? Not at all, Feldstein says. "No more so than the carefully coached evasions, posturing, pontificating, stonewalling and outright lying that your target has perfected over a lifetime."

AFTER THE INTERVIEW

After the interview is over, you may be tempted to breathe a sigh of relief, pack up your gear, say "Thanks," and head out the door. But hold on— your work isn't quite done yet:

- Confirm that your video and audio functioned throughout the interview.
- Exchange contact information, and invite the subject to call you if he or she thinks of anything pertinent after the interview.
- Arrange for future interviews, if needed.
- When you get back to your work space, tie up any loose ends by doing the following:
- Transcribe and organize your handwritten notes while they're fresh in your memory.
- Write down any observations made during the interview, including questions for other sources, and ideas for additional video, that will support or refute what the person has just said.
- Verify facts, dates, statistics, and quotes.

HOW A VIDEO INTERVIEW DIFFERS FROM A PRINT INTERVIEW

Unless you're following your subject over a period of time, or in a variety of locales, you'll probably get only one shot at an in-depth video interview. If you forgot to ask a question, or later think of a follow-up question you wished you'd asked, it's probably impractical to go back for another formal shooting session to capture that one quote. Besides, the subject will probably be wearing different clothing from the original shoot, the lighting conditions may differ, and so on.

Now, if it were a print interview, you could just phone, ask your question, and insert the response wherever it fits best in your story. Not so easy with video. Instead, you would need to add missing information with your voice-over (VO) narration (if there is one) or perhaps with text that runs over the footage.

ON THE RECORD

By definition, a video interview is "on the record," whereas the subject of a print interview can try to negotiate conditions before imparting information (e.g., "off the record" or "not for attribution" or "confidential").

If the subject of a print interview mispronounces a word, or uses faulty grammar, or has a strong accent or even a speech impediment, all that may go unnoticed or get "cleaned up" in print. A video interview, by contrast, hides nothing. Certainly, some sections may be edited out, but otherwise what you see (and hear) is what you get.

TIP Learn from the best. Watch how the masters conduct interviews. Find journalists you enjoy watching, and study their techniques.

Better yet, as you're watching an interview on television or on the Web, imagine you're in the interviewer's chair. Listen carefully, and think about what question you would ask next.

If you're watching a video story in which the subject does all the talking, with the questions edited out, write down what questions might have elicited those responses.

What more would you like to learn? What other questions would you have asked?

Our final author provides very clear steps for successful job preparation and planning. For instance, if you're willing to move and work in a smaller television **market**, your path to future success might be shorter and even more satisfying than holding out for the "perfect job." If you've not thought about the importance of on-the-job training (OJT) professional journalists are expected to take advantage of OJT as part of the profession. There are many professional networking organizations and important industry groups available to guide you and your career if you take the time to find these groups.

READING 6.3

CAREER AS A NEWS REPORTER: JOURNALIST

More writers are now becoming self-employed freelancers, although the challenges of running their own small business and providing their own health insurance can be daunting.

Journalism is generally a safe career with few injuries, although war correspondents and reporters covering news like protests, fires and floods sometimes are in physical danger. The job

---

is stressful, which can lead to various health issues. For all writers, frequent computer use can lead to eyestrain, back pain, and repetitive motion injuries such as carpal tunnel syndrome.

On the other hand, reporters at small town papers sometimes become bored because the pace is slower and there is not much exciting news to cover. Staffs are smaller, so reporters are expected to do everything— cover a number of beats, take their own photographs and write their own headlines. Small and mid-sized newspapers and magazines provide a broad training ground, but they can also provide more challenges to a new journalist to learn a variety of skills and beats.

EDUCATION AND TRAINING

A Bachelor's degree in Journalism, media studies, English, or communications is generally required to enter the field. Some smaller newspapers or online media outlets may accept a good writer with a high school diploma, but most hiring editors require a four-year degree before they will consider a candidate.

There are more than 1,500 colleges and universities that offer degrees in journalism and related fields. About 100 of those programs are accredited by the Accrediting Council in Journalism and Mass Communications (ACEJMC). The council states that it does not specify which courses should be taught, but rather evaluates institutions against their own objectives and ACEJMC standards for "preparing students for professional careers in journalism and mass communications."

Some of the best-known journalism schools (also called J-schools) include:

Columbia University
University of California-Berkeley
University of Missouri-Columbia
Northwestern University
Indiana University-Bloomingdale
Ohio University
Syracuse University
University of Florida
University of Georgia

University of Maryland-College Park
University of North Carolina at Chapel Hill

A number of these schools also have highly regarded journalism graduate schools. While a master's degree is not typically required to start your career, it can help you move into top editorial or management positions. Columbia, Northwestern, Syracuse, Cal-Berkeley and UNC-Chapel Hill are among those with leading graduate J-school programs.

With so many choices, how can you pick the right J-school for you? Start with national rankings of colleges and universities. There are general school rankings, such as those issued by US News and World Reports each year. Make sure you also get a copy of the current Cox International Center survey. The center, located at the University of Georgia, conducts an annual survey of journalism and mass communications undergraduate and graduate programs. If the cost of attending a prestigious J-school is beyond your budget, you can still get a great journalism education at a lesser-known school if the curriculum matches your plans.

Use these surveys to narrow down your field of higher education choices, and then visit the websites of individual schools to learn more details. Look for professors who have working experience as reporters or editors, because those with real-world experience can best help you prepare for a career. Some schools are stronger in newspapers or magazines, while others are more focused on mass media and broadcasting.

Having current technology available is important—particularly if you plan to become an online or broadcast journalist. Is there a robust student newspaper with opportunities for you to contribute? Talk to the faculty to determine how well the school fits your needs and your anticipated career path.

In journalism school, take advantage of every opportunity to create work samples to add to your portfolio. Volunteer for the school newspaper, literary magazine, radio and TV stations, or online news site. Vigorously pursue internships on and off campus that will provide working experience as a reporter, editor or news commentator. The more work samples you can accumulate–printed pieces, edited magazines, television appearances and radio broadcasts–the better positioned you will be to get that critical first job after graduation. The more news pieces you produce, the better journalist you become. Actively seek out mentors–professors, local journalists, guest speakers, even talented fellow students who can share tips for building a career.

Once you are working in the journalism field, there will be ample opportunities for continuing education. State press associations can provide training in areas such as libel laws and local sunshine laws (which provide public access to government meetings and decisions). The Reynolds Center for Business Journalism provides free online and in-person training to help all reporters cover business news more effectively. The Society for Professional Journalists focuses on issues around press rights, open records laws, and using the Freedom of Information Act to access federal government information that may not be readily available. Online media is constantly evolving, so the more skills you can learn–from video blogging to social media to website construction–the more options you will have as your career evolves.

No matter what type of career you select, there is always a need for continuing education to stay abreast of new trends. The need to keep learning and growing is particularly keen in the highly competitive world of journalism. No matter how good a writer you may be, there is always room for improvement through continual practice. There is always a new interviewing technique to learn, new technology to master, and new media outlets to consider.

EARNINGS

Salaries for news analyst reporters, correspondents and editors vary widely. Median annual earnings of reporters and correspondents are about $35,000. The lowest 10 percent earn about $20,000, and the highest receive more than $75,000 a year.

In one detailed recent study, median annual salaries for reporters and correspondents are $34,000 in the newspaper, periodical, and book publishing sector, versus $38,000 in radio and television broadcasting. Broadcast news analysts earn about $55,000. Their salaries can range from $40,000 to almost $150,000.

For editors, annual wages are about $50,000, and range from $30,000 to $100,000. Median annual pay is about $50,000 for those working in the newspaper, periodical and book publishing fields. For salaried writers and authors (a category that includes both fiction and non-fiction writers in a variety of fields and employment settings), median annual wages are about $55,000.

Pay for reporters and editors declined slightly in recent years, while salaries increased for radio and television journalists. However, salary is not the only consideration when evaluating employment opportunities. The types and amounts of benefits vary widely among employers. In fact, at a large corporation, benefits may be worth an additional 30 percent beyond your base salary. A benefits package may include medical, life and other insurance coverage; paid time off for vacation, holidays or sick leave; and pensions and other retirement considerations. Comp time–paid time off to compensate for working extra overtime–is also common at some news organizations.

OPPORTUNITIES

The career outlook for journalists is mixed, with growth seen in broadcast and online outlets, while traditional print markets are continuing to cut back. The number of jobs for editors is expected to remain roughly the same. Competition will be keen for fewer jobs in traditional media such as newspapers and magazines, although some job losses will be offset by new opportunities emerging with online media. Declines in job openings are expected because of the consolidation of news organizations, and decreases in the readership of newspapers.

Employment of broadcast news analysts is expected to grow by 10 percent. News agencies are turning from traditional reporters to analysts who can provide in-depth insights and commentary about current news. However, employment of reporters and correspondents is expected to drop in the coming decade. One trend contributing to that projection is the increased consolidation of the news industry. As larger organizations acquire smaller news agencies, they often reduce the number of journalists employed. The increase in demand for online news will offset some of the downsizing.

As a result of these trends, reporters, correspondents and broadcast news analysts face increased competition for fewer positions. Prospects should be best for those with experience in the field, often gained through internships or by working on school papers, stations, and websites. Competition will be even tougher at national newspapers, network TV stations and in large metropolitan areas. Opportunities will likely be better in small local newspapers and television and radio stations.

GETTING STARTED

Are you ready to pursue a career as a journalist? Begin by gathering more detailed information about the role of a journalist and how you can begin working towards your goal. Written information about careers in the communications profession is widely available at libraries; from colleges and universities; and through your school's guidance counselors. The Internet has a broad range of easily accessible data from media companies, government agencies, professional associations, and recruiters who help candidates find employment. The websites of newspapers, magazines and broadcasters may offer tips on their job openings and how they evaluate potential new hires.

Before college, find ways to start getting experience as a reporter. Volunteer for your school paper, or contribute local items to a website like Patch or Examiner. There are many other websites that accept columns and articles from writers with no prior experience (typically for little or no pay). Actively seek out internship opportunities with local media outlets. Any article that appears in print or in an online outlet will add to your collection of clips and build up your portfolio as you progress from high school to college, and eventually into the work force.

It's never too early to start taking classes. There are online and live classes that will help—not just with being a reporter, but also in photography, blogging, digital video, and similar online media skills that are highly prized by employers.

You will need a four-year degree in journalism or communications to get started, so investigate which colleges and universities can provide the required training. Also think about how you will get some preliminary experience to help land that first job. Are there internships or volunteer opportunities available near your school? You may be able to find an entry-level position on a part-time basis that will put money in your pocket while enhancing your résumé.

Spend some time talking to people who already work as journalists, or who work closely with that profession (such as city officials or corporate public relations officers). Ask them what skills are valuable to help applicants find a position and advance along their career path. You can find these individuals through professional associations—or simply by looking in your local newspaper to see who the editors and reporters are. Associations can be helpful—not only for learning about the profession and local conditions, but also for internships, training programs, and scholarships. Most states and metropolitan areas have active press associations. Many of these groups have outreach programs that specifically target students who are interested in journalism careers, while others let students join or attend sessions at a reduced cost.

Call on your personal network for support and advice. Discuss your plans with family and friends for input on whether becoming a journalist seems an appropriate choice for your personal strengths and interests. Also include your school counselor, for helpful information about local educational opportunities, employment prospects, and networking venues.

Once you gather your data, it is time to give careful thought to whether a career as a journalist feels right for you. Are you comfortable with the educational requirements? Would you be content working long hours—including nights, weekends, and holidays—to cover breaking news? Do you work well under pressure? Can you write quickly, concisely and accurately? Can you see yourself happily pursuing a successful career as a reporter? If so, start taking those first steps today towards a rewarding, fulfilling career!

ASSOCIATIONS

- American Society of Journalists and Authors http://www.asja.org
- Association of Capitol Reporters and Editors http://capitolbeat.wordpress.com
- Association of Young Journalists and Writers http://www.ayjw.org
- International Press Association http://internationalpress.com
- Investigative Reporters and Editors http://www.ire.org
- Journalism Education Association http://jea.org
- National Association of Black Journalists http://www.nabj.org
- National Association of Broadcasters http://www.nab.org
- National Education Writers Association http://www.ewa.org
- National Federation of Press Women http://www.nfpw.org
- National Freedom of Information Coalition http://www.nfoic.org
- National Press Club http://press.org
- National Press Foundation http://national-press.org
- Newspaper Association of America http://www.naa.org
- Online News Association http://journalists.org
- Reporters Association for Freedom of the Press http://www.rcfp.org
- Society of American Travel Writers http://www.satw.org
- Society of Environmental Journalists http://www.sejarchive.org/pub\/index.htm
- Society of Professional Journalists http://www.spj.org
- State Press Associations http://www.gebbieinc.com/presasns.htm

PERIODICALS

- American Journalism Review http://www.ajr.org
- American Press Institute http://www.naafoundation.org
- American Society of Business Publication Editors http://www.asbpe.org
- Columbia Journalism Review http://www.cjr.org
- Current http://www.current.org
- Editor and Publisher www.editorandpublisher.com
- Editors Only www.publishinghelp.com/editors
- Online Journalism Review http://www.ojr.org
- Poets & Writers http://www.pw.org/magazine
- The American Editor http://www.asne.org/kiosk/editor/tae.htm
- The Writer http://www.writermag.com
- Writers Digest http://www.writersdigest.com
- Writers' Journal http://www.writersjournal.com

WEBSITES

- Associated Press http://www.ap.org
- Copyediting http://www.copyediting.com
- Dow Jones Newspaper Fund http://www.newsfund.org
- HARO (Help A Reporter Out) http://www.helpareporter.com
- Huffington Post http://www.huffingtonpost.com
- Journalism Jobs http://www.journalismjobs.com
- Magazine Journalism Internships http://www.internships.com/intern/journalism/magazine
- People and the Press: http://www.people-press.org
- Poynter Center for Media Studies http://www.poynter.org
- Reynolds Center for Business Journalism http://businessjournalism.org

Interview with a Professional

Marc Dorian is a long-time Producer with ABC Television network's *20/20.*
Interviewed by Matt Crick, Spring, 2017.

Why are good communication skills important in your field?

Communicating with your boss—Often an idea for a story never makes it out of the incubation stage unless you can convince your boss that it is a worthwhile investment in time and money. Pitching your story well is paramount to getting the green light. Being able to boil down the essence of a story in 90 seconds or less and present it effectively is the ever important first step. Beyond that, managing expectations and implementing feedback from higher-ups is essential to the process.

Communicating with your team—As a TV news producer, I often find myself trying to get a story shot, written, and edited under severe deadline in unpredictable environments. Hundreds of elements have to come together quickly to make the story work. ... Shoot schedules, travel logistics, getting subjects to appear on camera, media management, graphics, editing. It's all in the details, and if they are not communicated effectively to the team, the smallest things could ultimately cost missing a deadline, or worse, airing a story that is simply not accurate. Quick and precise communication with each team member is vital.

Communicating with the story subjects—A very important aspect of putting a story together is establishing a relationship with the subjects of each story. It is essential that each subject feels comfortable sharing their story and that it is done in a manner that is accessible for the audience.

Communicating with the viewer—Communicating the story effectively to the viewer requires a great sense of storytelling. The producer should do this in an economical style while making sure the tonality is true to the subjects you are reporting on. Adding a cinematic style will also keep the viewer engaged.

What specific skills do you use the most?

Writing—I write most of my own stories, and the art of storytelling is the essence of what we do

Research—Being able to quickly get read-in on a story is very important. You need to find solid sources of information.

Organizational skills—With so many moving parts in the production of a news magazine broadcast, it is of upmost importance to have organization strategies in place so you don't lose that phone number, camera card, shot, soundbite.

Technical know-how—I shoot a lot of my own stories, and I find that being technically proficient to the point that it becomes secondhand allows me to focus on content rather than fumbling with my equipment.

In terms of Broadcast Journalism, what skills do you find lacking in others?

Producers often set out with a preconceived notion of what a story is, or they are trying to fulfill their boss's concept of that story. In the end, those producers often find themselves not only promising something they can't deliver but also they might miss the essence of the real story. Often stories reveal themselves once you are in the field, and the producer who is open to letting the story unfold will most often have the best final product.

How has the knowledge or skills you gained in college or university been useful to you in terms of your career?

I learned most of the technical aspects of broadcast journalism on the job, not in college. I think having a well-rounded education gave me a better foundation to tackle a myriad of different subjects that I have covered over the years.

What advice would you give to Communication majors? Pitfalls to avoid, that sort of thing.

I find too many people enter the field of broadcast journalism focused on trying to become the archetype of what they think a TV producer or on-air talent should be. Often lost or ignored is the story. Storytelling is the most important skill you can have as a journalist, and adding your own unique voice to that story will allow more people to connect with your work, and you will ultimately cut through the noise.

Thinking back on your career choices, what decisions are you most proud of?

The decision to follow my passion and choose journalism as my career leaves me with few regrets. My job has taken me around the world and exposed me to a constantly changing variety of people, places, issues, and wonders. Each story I have worked on has been different and important in its own unique way … I've helped highlight wrong-doing, set the record straight, allowed the powerless to have a voice, and even helped a wrongfully imprisoned person go free. It has allowed me to share my experiences with millions of others and hopefully leave them a little bit wiser.

Conclusion

Broadcast journalism is an exciting profession but will require some unusual sacrifices if you want to stay in the field for the long term. The hours are long, weekend work is the norm, and holidays are especially hard because worthy news stories are even harder to find. On the other hand, the skills you learn as a broadcast journalist translate into everyday use: good organizational skills, strong writing and verbal communication skills, a personal set of ethics, and a wide variety of knowledge about the world are just a few examples. A broadcast journalist connects with her/his audience, tells good stories, demonstrates excellent writing and presenting skills, and accomplishes all of these things while abiding by a clear set of ethical standards of practice. Don't forget all of this happens, everyday, under strict broadcast regulations and newsroom deadlines.

CLASSROOM ACTIVITY

Using your knowledge from this chapter, complete the following classroom activity within 45 minutes using only your mobile phone.

Activity Specifics

You'll be randomly placed in teams of two. Each person in your team will be responsible for locating two websites you feel qualify as *fake news* websites. Once you've found the websites, spend 30 minutes writing down the reasons and evidence why the sites are fake news sites. For the last 15 minutes of this activity, each student will present her/his findings to the class.

Questions you might ask about your website:

1   Is the website part of a known and vetted professional news source?

2   If not, what clues about how the site is designed make you think it's a fake news site?

3   What is the purpose of your fake news website?

4   What was hard or easy about this activity?

DISCUSSION

1   In the Thompson article, what does the author mean by "write how you speak?"

2   In the article on conducting interviews, what are open-ended questions, and why are they generally better than closed questions when interviewing?

3   According to the *Career as a Reporter* article, many jobs in large news organizations are disappearing.

4   The author suggests this will continue into the near future. What can you do personally and professionally to prepare for this?

KEY TERMS

Broadcast Journalist—a person who writes and/or produces and presents news stories for airing on radio or television.

Code of Ethics—refers to the ethical and agreed upon standards broadcast journalists apply and practice when creating news stories.

Fake News—a new term in broadcast and print journalism that refers to information that is presented as authenticated and verified news. Fake news providers create propaganda in order to distract, misinform, and redirect website visitors and viewers. Research shows that fake news is most often spread via social networks like Facebook.

Inverted Pyramid—refers to the classic storytelling structure for a news story: the pyramid shape is upside down with the most newsworthy information at the top, important details about the story are in the next section, and the least important information—background, general information, etc., are at the bottom of the pyramid.

K.I.S.S.—an acronym that stands for Keep it Simple Stupid. British broadcasters have changed K.I.S.S. to mean Keep it Simple and Straightforward, referring to how news scripts should be written and news stories should be told.

Market—this term refers to a geographical location in the United States where the population can receive the same television and radio station signals. Television and radio stations decide on what types of events and stories to cover based, in large part, on the market in which the most people view them.

News Cycle—refers to a period of time from a single news broadcast to the next. The news cycle is 24 hours for cable television news.

News Script—a specific type of written script designed to tell stories effectively within the constraints and professional practices in television and radio news.

Newsworthiness—comprises a set of conventions used to establish whether a story is important and relevant enough to be researched, written, and broadcast or printed for release to the public.

Producing—a term in broadcast journalism for the person who develops and organizes stories for air. Depending on the size of the market, a producer might also be responsible for booking guests, securing locations, writing, editing, and shooting a news story.

Radio Television Digital News Association (RTDNA)—the professional organization that serves and guides broadcast journalists and news management in the ethical application of duties associated with a broadcast journalist's daily job.

REFERENCES

Boyd, A. 2001. Broadcast journalism: techniques of radio and television news. Taylor & Francis., NY, NY.

Campbell, R., C. Martin, and B. Fabos. 2014. Media & culture: Mass communication in a digital age. Bedford/St. Martin's. 480–481. NY, NY.

"Don't get fooled by these fake news sites." Retrieved on March 11, 2017, from http://www.cbsnews.com/pictures/dont-get-fooled-by-these-fake-news-sites/.

Forde, S., and J. Johnston. 2013. "THE NEWS TRIUMVIRATE." Journalism Studies 14 (1), 113–129. doi:10.1080/1461670X.2012.679859.

Geisler, J. 2011. "8 Essential skills for anchors (& any journalist) covering breaking news." Poynter.org. Retrieved on March 11, 2017, from https://www.poynter.org/2011/8-essential-skills-for-anchors-any-journalist-covering-breaking-news/118945/.

Institute for Career Research. 2016. Career as a News Reporter: Journalist. 23–34.

Lazar, J., and K. Kobre. 2012. Conducting an Interview, Videojournalism: Multimedia Storytelling. Waltham: Focal Press, 155–166.

Maloy, S., and M. Gertz. 2013. "A Comprehensive List Of the Problems With 60 Minutes' Benghazi Segment." Retrieved on March 9, 2017, from https://mediamatters.org/blog/2013/11/15/a-comprehensive-list-of-the-problems-with-60-mi/196922.

Mitchell, A., J. Gottfried, M. Barthel, and E. Shearer. 2016. "The Modern News Consumer: News Attitudes and Practices in the Digital Era." Pew Research Center, Journalism & Media. Retrieved on March 10, 2017, from http://www.journalism.org/2016/07/07/the-modern-news-consumer/.

Mitchell, A., J. Gottfried, M. Barthel, and E. Shearer. 2016. "How Americans Encounter, Recall and Act Upon Digital News." Pew Research Center, Journalism & Media.

Retrieved on March 11, 2017, from http://www.journalism.org/2017/02/09/how-americans-encounter-recall-and-act-upon-digital-news/.

Ryfe, D. M., and M. Blach-Ørsten. 2011. Introduction. Journalism Studies 12 (1), 3–9. doi:10.1080/14 61670X.2010.511939.

https://www.rtdna.org/content/rtdna_code_of_ethics.

Stanglin, D. 2015. "Brian Williams apologies, blames his ego for telling false tales." Retrieved on March 9, 2017, from http://www.usatoday.com/story/news/nation/2015/06/19/brian-williams-nbc-today-anchor-apologizes/28971565/.

Thompson, R. 2005. Writing Broadcast News Scripts, Writing for Broadcast Journalists. Routledge, 39–47. 5 Howick Place, London SW1P 1WG. Registered in England and Wales.

PART TWO

INTRODUCTION
BY KELLI JEAN K. SMITH

I n Part Two of this book, we move into the areas of study that include fewer technical skills and are more academic and theoretical in nature. The content of these chapters is meant to help you develop a greater understanding of human interaction that can be useful in your personal and professional lives. My goal is to provide you with information that will help you empathize with others, understand how your behavior affects others, and adapt your behavior to fit different situations. In connection to the core principles of the Applied Communication Model, the information in these chapters should help you to improve your ability to tailor your stories to different audiences and present information in an ethical manner. These skills are important, no matter which line of work you choose to go into.

CHAPTER 7
Communication Studies

INTRODUCTION

According to the National Communication Association (NCA), "At its foundation, Communication focuses on how people use messages to generate meanings within and across various contexts" (https://www.natcom.org/about-nca/what-communication). Why study Communication? College graduates with Communication degrees have the knowledge and skills that employers are looking for. They demonstrate strong verbal, nonverbal, and written communication skills and have considerable expertise in speaking well in front of small and large audiences (https://www.natcom.org/academic-professional-resources/why-study-communication). They also develop strong critical thinking and research skills. In fact, *The Princeton Review* lists Communication as one of the top ten college majors (https://www.princetonreview.com/college-advice/top-ten-college-majors).

The NCA website describes several areas of specialization you can choose from, depending on your interests. Here are just a few examples: Applied Communication, International and Intercultural Communication, Interpersonal Communication, and Small Group and Team Communication.

COMMUNICATION STUDIES AND THE APPLIED COMMUNICATION MODEL

The courses you take in the Communication Studies major are aimed at improving your **communication competence**. Communication competence refers to your ability to accomplish your goals in a socially appropriate manner (Spitzberg and Cupach 1984). There are three components of communication competence: knowledge, skill, and motivation. You must know what behaviors are called for in a given situation, have the ability to convert that knowledge into action, and be willing to communicate in an effective and appropriate manner. The more competent you are as a communicator, the more likely it is that you will achieve your personal and professional goals.

Impression Management and Self-disclosure

One of the most common standards by which we evaluate a person's communication competence is **adaptability** (Spitzberg and Cupach 1989). Adaptability refers to your ability to adjust your behavior so that it is appropriate to the environment, the situation, and the audience (Dura, 1983). When you want to make new friends, begin romantic relationships, get a job, etc., you behave in a way that's consistent with how you want to be seen and share the information that you believe will help you accomplish these goals. Put another way, you tell stories about yourself to let people know who you are.

We use communication to influence the perceptions people have of us. This is called **impression management**. For example, you might want to be seen as friendly, intelligent, or capable, so you behave in a way that will give others that impression of you. Erving Goffman (1959) describes our everyday interactions as theatrical performances. According to his **dramaturgical perspective**, we are all actors who play different roles for different audiences. We have scripts for many events and perform on a variety of stages. In other words, we display different aspects of ourselves (tell different stories about ourselves) depending on the situation and our goals. Being adaptable allows you to tell your stories in the most effective way.

Self-disclosure is another part of telling your story. When you engage in self-disclosure, you share information about yourself with others. This can include your likes and dislikes, past experiences, future goals, fears, etc. Part of being a competent communicator is knowing what information to share, how much of it to share, and when it is appropriate to share it. Generally, when we begin a new relationship, our disclosures start out as superficial and gradually become more personal and cover a wider range of topics (Altman and Taylor 1973). Relationships develop as we reciprocate disclosures, meaning that we match the content and intimacy level of the information our partners share. Sharing too much information too soon can make your partner uncomfortable and hinder the development of the relationship. Sharing too little information can be interpreted as a lack of interest.

Emotional Intelligence

Emotional intelligence is the ability to recognize emotions in yourself and others, determine appropriate expressions of emotion, and manage emotions accordingly (Salovey and Mayer 1990). The following reading describes the components of emotional intelligence and explains why it is important for success in your personal and professional life.

EMOTIONAL INTELLIGENCE: THE NEW SCIENCE OF SUCCESS

by Jeff Feldman and Karl Mulle

IN THIS CHAPTER, YOU WILL LEARN

- why emotional intelligence is so important for success
- the definition and components of emotional intelligence
- the basic framework for discussing emotional intelligence […]
- how this [reading] can help you *EQuip Yourself* for success.

Jimmy's mom glanced at his report card and frowned. "Look at these grades! Do you realize that this is going into your permanent school record?" The dreaded parental warning played over and over again in Jimmy's 10-year-old mind. "Have I really just blown my opportunity to be successful in life?" he wondered.

Do you recall your school report cards? If you attended grammar school before the 1980s you likely would not have received quarterly progress updates via the electronic, computer-generated version so familiar today. Certainly grades for each course were issued, but they were handwritten in black, blue, or red ink. The long journey home from school even found some youngsters frantically trying to find the right color ink, so that the C in Social Studies could be converted into a B, or possibly even an A. Of course the hope was to avoid whatever the inevitable punishment was going to be for achieving grades lower than expected. Unfortunately, these report cards contained something much more difficult for these children to deal with, something that no one could change or avoid—the teacher's comments scrawled in the margins of the report.

Who knew then, that the most important predictor of young Jimmy's success had little to do with the grade itself, but was more a factor of those handwritten notes in the margin?

Jimmy plays well with all the students and is the most popular boy in school. He is a natural leader. Unfortunately, he is using his popularity to influence other children to stay late on the playground during lunch, instead of coming to math class on time. His grade in math has slipped to a "C."

If Jimmy was slightly more precocious and allowed to get away with it, he could turn to his parents and say, "Did you know that getting along well with others is a component of emotional intelligence, which research shows is more important for success than my 4th grade math scores?"

Unfortunately, Jimmy can't quite pull that off, and his low grade in math may lead him to be grounded from playing with his friends for a few days. The truth is that the life skills Jimmy learns on the playground are just as important as his academic training in helping him to successfully achieve his goals and get what he wants out of life. When Jimmy is older and enters the workforce, he will discover that a basic level of technical skill and academic achievement are necessary to get his "foot in the door." He will realize that in some ways school never ends. *All* employees are expected to develop expertise by learning and improving on the job. But beyond these basic, *threshold* requirements, the crucial skills that are necessary for his achievement and success are all related to *emotional intelligence* (Goleman, 1998):

- listening and oral communication
- adaptability and creative responses to setbacks and obstacles
- personal management, confidence, motivation to work toward goals, a sense of wanting to develop one's career and take pride in accomplishments
- group and interpersonal effectiveness, cooperation, and teamwork; ability to negotiate disagreements
- effectiveness in the organization, wanting to make a contribution, leadership potential.

Daniel Goleman (1998), who has conducted studies in over 200 large companies, says: "The research shows that for jobs of all kinds, emotional intelligence is twice as important an ingredient of outstanding performance as ability and technical skill combined. The higher you go in the organization, the more important these qualities are for success. When it comes to leadership, they are almost everything."

Emotional intelligence then, is the *x-factor* that separates average performers from outstanding performers. It separates those who know themselves well and take personal responsibility for their actions from those who lack self-awareness and repeat the same mistakes over and over. It separates those who can manage their emotions and motivate themselves from those who are overwhelmed by their emotions and let their emotional impulses control their behaviors. It separates those who are good at connecting with others and creating positive relationships from those who seem insensitive and uncaring. It separates those who build rapport, have influence, and collaborate effectively with others from those who are demanding, lack empathy, and are therefore difficult to work with. Above all, emotional intelligence separates those who are successful at managing their emotional energy and navigating through life from those who find themselves in emotional wreckage, derailed, and sometimes even disqualified from the path to success.

EMOTIONAL INTELLIGENCE: THE DIFFERENCE BETWEEN SUCCESS AND DERAILMENT

Two stories will be presented. One ends successfully; the other does not. Both of these stories represent emotionally charged situations in which the primary difference between one's success and the other's derailment is *emotional intelligence*. In each situation, emotional arousal offers two possible outcomes:

Success = Being aware of your emotions and managing them so your behaviors are intelligently and proactively driven, resulting in intentional and successful outcomes.

Derailment = Losing control of your emotions so your behaviors are impulsively and reactively driven, resulting in unintended and potentially costly outcomes.

A SUCCESS STORY

Sarah was 22 years old and had somewhat limited business experience. She was now living on her own, so finding a job (and a source of income) was very important to her. After a series of four interviews for an inside sales and customer service position with a new company, she finally got the call that offered her the position. In her own words she describes the experience:

"I was very excited! This was a new industry in an area of computer technology I was unfamiliar with. It would be an exciting new challenge. Five days before my official start date, I unexpectedly received a plane ticket in the mail from the CEO of the company. I contacted him and asked what it was regarding and was told he would like me to go to Washington, D.C., and assist him with selling the company's computer software at a major tradeshow.

"Initially, I was taken aback with the proposition. I had never met the CEO. I hadn't yet set foot in the office to do even a minute of training. I had no idea how to sell software I had never seen … much less fly to D.C. and sell it there!

"I was nervous. My emotions were telling me to figure out some way to avoid this trip. My gut feeling, however, told me that my decision to go on this trip as requested would set the tone for the rest of my career with this company. It would also establish the CEO's perception of me. Despite feeling scared and quite unprepared for this role, I determined to make the best of it and told the CEO I would be happy to assist him.

"I only had four days to get ready and did not even own a decent business suit. I was on a very limited budget, so I went to a thrift shop to look for an appropriate business outfit. I found the perfect suit. Then I went to the dollar store and found some fake jewelry that looked real enough. I put it all together and managed to look very professional for less than $15.

"When the big day arrived, I flew to D.C. Taking my first taxi ever, I headed downtown to one of the most upscale hotels in Washington. Feeling way out of my league, I checked in and called the CEO to let him know I had arrived. We met at a restaurant in the lobby of the hotel. He was tall and dressed perfectly. My impression was that he set high standards for how he expected others to look. He was professional, friendly, and extremely intelligent. I could tell immediately that he had a low tolerance for incompetence.

"We had a nice dinner meeting, but he offered little in the way of training or information about what I was expected to do. As our dinner ended, he handed me a folder that contained information about the products I would be selling the next morning. It was 11 p.m. I was exhausted and had to go right to bed without time to look over the materials.

"The show started at 7:30 a.m. and I was up at 5 a.m. to give myself enough time to get ready. With little time to spare, I propped up the papers he gave me in front of the bathroom mirror and managed to study the materials while blow-drying my hair! I did the best I could to learn about the software and its features, compatibility issues, technical support solutions, and other details. I relieved some of my nervousness by reminding myself that the CEO would be there to work with me.

"When we met in the tradeshow hall, there were several thousand professionals ready to ask us questions. As it turned out, there would be no "us." The CEO said I would have to run the show on my own because he had to attend meetings all day. In that moment, I actually wanted to cry! I had no idea what I was doing, and these people all wanted answers.

"By about mid-morning, I began to feel more confident. My crash course with hairdryer in hand turned out to be very helpful. Most of the tradeshow attendees showed understanding if I didn't have an exact answer to their questions, and accepted my offer to follow-up with them later.

"At the end of the day when my new boss came back, I was full of smiles. I was proud of myself for all of the accomplishments—arriving, quickly learning the job, and actually selling some software! He inquired, "How did it go?" "Excellent," I replied. "I did great and we made a lot of money!" His face lit up and he was eager to hear the details. I told him that I sold a $200 piece of software. His face formed a funny smile, the way a parent smiles when a child does something wrong but is too cute to reprimand.

"Now, 10 years later with the same company, I know that $200 for a day is a terrible show. The goal is about $5,000 a day. But in my blissfully ignorant excitement, the CEO was too nice to burst my bubble. It was the foundation for a wonderful 10 years at his company. I am now Director of Operations and oversee a multimillion-dollar business.

"I learned many lessons from that experience in Washington, D.C. Perhaps the most important being that no matter who you are, stretching outside your comfort zone is a formula for success and confidence. Even if I had failed (which in terms of sales numbers I did), I would always be proud that I got on the plane and with a positive, optimistic attitude tried my best! Doing so then and since has ultimately led to a level of achievement I had only imagined."

A DERAILMENT STORY

Ron Artest Jr. was born and raised in the largest public housing development in the United States, the Queensbridge Projects of Long Island City, New York. His success in basketball provided him with his ticket out of the projects. After becoming an NCAA All-American in 1999, he joined the professional ranks, and by 2004, was considered one of the best defensive players in the National Basketball Association. In fact, he was voted the NBA's Defensive Player of the Year for the 2003-2004 basketball season. Unfortunately for Artest, his on-court success has often been be overshadowed by his reputation for having a short fuse.

On November 19, 2004, Artest took center stage in arguably the most infamous brawl in professional sports history. With less than a minute left in the game, Artest's Indianapolis Pacers were well on their way to victory with an insurmountable 97-82 lead over the Detroit Pistons. The brawl began when Artest fouled Piston's Ben Wallace. A frustrated Wallace, upset at being fouled so hard when the game was effectively over, responded by shoving Artest hard with both hands, accidentally hitting him in the nose. A number of Pacers and Pistons squared off, but Artest actually walked away from the fracas and lay on the scorer's table in order to calm himself down. At this point *cooler heads could have prevailed*, but Wallace continued to instigate. He walked over to the scorer's table and threw his armband at Artest. One of the Piston's fans followed suit by throwing a cup full of ice and liquid that hit Artest on the chest and in the face.

One could argue that Artest was *provoked*. In his own words, Artest said: "I ... was lying down when I got hit with a liquid, ice and glass container on my chest and on my face. After that it was self defense." In self-defense mode, Artest snapped to attention and jumped into the front-row seats,

confronting the man he believed to be responsible. But in the chaos of the moment, he actually confronted the wrong man. The situation quickly erupted into a brawl between Piston's fans and several of the Indiana Pacer players. Artest returned to the basketball court, where he managed to deck a Piston's fan, who apparently was taunting him. The mayhem ended with Detroit fans throwing chairs, food, and other debris at the Indianapolis players while they walked back to their locker room.

In the aftermath, each participant could easily replay the blow-by-blow details that explained and even provoked each successive act of aggression. A flagrant foul provoked a push, a soda-and-ice shower, and some name-calling. A push, a soda-and-ice shower, and some name-calling provoked a brawl in the stands and a fan getting punched. Maybe on some level of playground justice, everybody got what he deserved; perhaps all of the impulsive, uncontrolled emotional behaviors should cancel each other out. After all, it is much easier to critique the actions of others than it is to actually do the right thing in the heat of battle. In moments of honesty we all must admit times when our emotions have unraveled us. It hardly seems fair to single out one player or fan's lack of self-control as being more egregious than the next.

The NBA, however, has rules, and the brawl became a classic case of *two wrongs do not make a right*. Players are expected to use emotional self-control and rational behavior to maintain the immutable boundary that separates the fans from the court. Given this expectation, the list of guilty participants was indeed extensive. But when the penalties were finally doled out, Artest's penalty was the most severe because of his past history of losing control. He was suspended for 73 games plus playoff appearances, the longest nondrug- or gambling-related suspension in NBA history. NBA Commissioner, David Stern, administered the penalty, stating: "I did not strike from my mind the fact that Ron Artest had been suspended on previous conditions for loss of self-control."

Regardless of how harsh or unfair this penalty may seem, it serves as a poignant reminder to those who are interested in the field of emotional intelligence. Unmanaged emotional behaviors can be very costly and can derail you from fulfilling your true intentions.

Not only did Ron Artest confront the wrong guy, at the wrong time, and in the wrong way, but that one impulsive act turned out to be tremendously costly. Financially, the suspension cost him $5 million in salary as well as potential endorsement earnings. Emotionally, the suspension cost him an opportunity to compete for a possible NBA championship with a team that might have made it to the finals.

> ## GUIDING PRINCIPLE
>
> Unmanaged emotional behaviors can be very costly and can derail you from fulfilling your true intentions.

In our success story, Sarah not only recognized the affect that her feelings of anxiety, fear, and insecurity were having on her, but she also managed these emotions in a way that helped her to gain confidence as well as valuable experience in her new job. Had anxiety taken control, she might have missed her flight, offered excuses, pretended that there was a death in her family, or created any number of other reasons for avoiding the very thing that she needed to do in order to be successful.

In our derailment story, Ron Artest actually did recognize that he was agitated and tried to manage his emotions by resting on the scorer's table. This worked until a fan threw a drink on him. Artest defended his actions by claiming self-defense, but there is one significant flaw to

this argument—*being hit in the face with a cold liquid is not really a severe threat*. In fact, many coaches can testify that they have safelysurvived being doused by an entire bucket of ice-cold liquid. There was actually a lesson to learn from this incident and a much more emotionally intelligent way for Artest to have handled this situation. He could have continued to manage his anger and then ask security personnel to escort the offender out of the stadium. Perhaps this alone would have been sufficient to satisfy his anger, but if his anger required even more justice, then he still had the option of pressing charges in a court of law.

There are at least two significant differences between these two stories. First, it is more difficult to manage your emotions when someone is deliberately hostile or offensive as opposed to when someone is simply challenging you to step outside of your comfort zone. Second, there will always be a healthy debate about how ethically right or wrong it is to lose control of your emotions in certain situations. In fact, there is often understanding, not punishment, when you lose control of your emotions because a projectile is thrown at you. At any rate, this [reading] is not concerned with either difference. In other words, it makes sense to live your life in an emotionally intelligent way: *No matter how intensely difficult it may be to manage your emotions in certain situations, and no matter how justified you believe it is to lose control of your emotions in certain situations*.

> ## GUIDING PRINCIPLE
>
> Out-of-control emotions can have a tremendous affect on your performance, on how others perceive you, and on how those in power ultimately judge you.

Out-of-control emotions can have a tremendous affect on your performance, on how others perceive you, and on how those in power ultimately judge you. The more successful outcome is accomplished when emotional intelligence is applied. This book, then, is all about understanding how to develop into a more fully emotionally intelligent person. […]

COMPONENTS OF EMOTIONAL INTELLIGENCE

Describing an emotionally intelligent person is like describing a wonderful teacher, an effective counselor, or a successful politician. An entire range of qualities, skills, and behaviors need to be delineated to fully comprehend what the individual is really all about. After all, emotional intelligence, like teaching, politics, or counseling, is *a way of being*. Concise definitions are possible, but not adequate. We have concisely defined emotional intelligence as:

> *Using your emotions intelligently to gain the performance you wish to see within yourself and to achieve interpersonal effectiveness with others.*

This definition is sufficient as a starting point for understanding EI, as long as one places special emphasis on each component of the definition. *Emotional intelligence* therefore is

- *Using your emotions*—implies both awareness of and the ability to manage your emotions.
- Using your emotions *intelligently*—implies that you can consciously reflect on your emotions and then choose appropriate responses.
- To *gain the performance you wish to see within yourself*—implies that our emotional energy can serve a special purpose in both motivating and helping us to achieve our goals.

- To *achieve interpersonal effectiveness with others*—implies that our intelligence and sensitivity about emotions can help us achieve better results when relating to others.

There is both a personal and interpersonal or social component to emotional intelligence. Daniel Goleman, Richard Boyatzis, and Annie McKee (2002) have introduced a model for understanding emotional intelligence that divides personal and social competence into four basic domains. The first two domains are *self-awareness* and *self-management*. These domains relate to personal competence. The second two domains are *social awareness* and *relationship management*. These domains relate to social competence. According to this model, each domain contains a set of behaviors that can be developed in order for one to become more emotionally intelligent (see Figure 7.1).

EI	**Personal Competence (Self)**	**Social Competence (Others)**
Recognition	**Self-Awareness** • Emotional Self-Awareness • Accurate Self-Assessment • Self-Confidence	**Social Awareness** • Empathy • Organizational Awareness • Service Orientation
Regulation	**Self-Management** • Emotional Self-Control • Transparency • Adaptability • Achievement • Initiative • Optimism	**Relationship Management** • Developing Others • Inspirational Leadership • Influence • Change Catalyst • Conflict Management • Teamwork & Collaboration

Figure 7.1 Goleman, Boyatzis, and McKee's four domains of emotional intelligence; each domain contains a set of emotional competencies.

UNDERSTANDING AND GROWING YOUR OWN EI

This four-domain model of understanding emotional intelligence will serve as a basic framework for how emotional intelligence is discussed […].

These four domains of emotional intelligence do not stand alone, independent of one another. Rather, they are interdependent, fitting together like puzzle pieces to present a complete portrait of what an emotionally intelligent person looks like. Emotional intelligence is therefore a comprehensive model that is used to understand how cognitions and emotions affect both personal and interpersonal behaviors. The development of emotional intelligence requires an integration of the competencies and behaviors that make up each domain of this model (see Figure 7.2). [...]

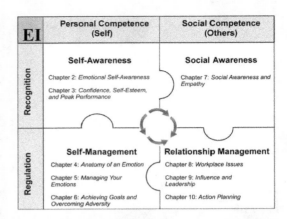

Figure 7.2 The framework for understanding emotional intelligence. Self-awareness affects self-management and social awareness; self-management and social awareness affect relationship management.

Listening Skills

Listening is an important skill to develop in both our personal and professional lives. We engage in several different types of listening. You can listen for enjoyment, to give support, to learn something, or to evaluate a message to decide whether to accept or reject it (Wolvin and Coakley 1995). Listening isn't always easy. Internal and external distractions can prevent you from listening carefully. The next reading demonstrates the importance of being an effective listener and provides tips to improve your listening skills.

READING 7.2

LISTENING PAYS OFF

by Chris Battell

In *Listening Leaders™: The Ten Golden Rules to Listen, Lead, and Succeed,* Lyman K. Steil and Richard K. Bommelje ask the question: "Who holds the major responsibility for successful communication? Is it the sender or the receiver?" If you compare the training available for becoming a better speaker and giving presentations with the training available for learning to listen better, you might assume that responsibility rests squarely with the sender or speaker. But the truth is that communication is a two-way street: The responsibility rests with both parties.

Listening, however, tends to get shortchanged in terms of development because people assume that they already know how to listen. After all, the mechanics of listening appear so simple. One individual speaks; another individual hears and responds.

But there is a big difference between hearing and listening. Hearing refers to the physical perception of sound, while listening is a complex combination of hearing, seeing, comprehending, and interpreting communication.

In the world of business, poor listening skills can be costly and affect performance. Some of the results of poor listening skills include

- wasted meeting time
- inaccurate orders and shipments
- lost sales
- inadequately informed, misinformed, confused, or angry staff and customers
- unmet deadlines
- unsolved problems
- wrong decisions
- lawsuits
- poor employee morale.

Alternatively, listening with full attention and commitment leads to greater productivity, excellence, smoother relationships, collaboration, sharing, and innovation.

Fortunately, listening effectively is an acquired skill. Just as a person can improve his or her speaking skills with conscious, deliberate practice, so too can he or she improve poor listening skills.

This [...] will guide you in the development of effective listening skills by providing

- a solid understanding of the basic principles of effective listening
- techniques, advice, and development activities to improve your listening skills for better performance
- new skills you can apply today to dramatically improve your position as an organization leader, department manager, or team leader.

LISTENING 101

Research on how humans communicate is vast. The facts and conclusions are often surprising and sometimes dismaying. Here are just a few to consider:

- One study showed that 70 percent of many people's days is spent in communication.
- In turn, that 70 percent is made up of nine percent writing, 16 percent reading, 30 percent talking, and 45 percent listening.
- The U.S. Department of Labor estimates that of total communication time, 22 percent takes the form of reading, 23 percent speaking, and 55 percent listening.
- A study by Sperry Rand showed that 45 percent of a manager's time is spent listening.
- Some research shows that 75 percent of oral communication is ignored, misunderstood, or quickly forgotten.
- Some experts believe we can only listen effectively from one-third to two-thirds of the time.
- The typical speaker talks at a rate of 140 words per minute.
- The typical listener can hear at a rate of 280 to 560 words per minute.
- Most people can think three times faster than the typical speaker can talk.
- By some estimates, in classroom training, the learner retains only 15 percent of what is written or spoken.

Clearly, people spend a great deal of time listening, but often do not understand, remember, or act on what others are saying. In fact, most conversations are not true conversations at all. Instead, they are two monologues in which both participants just wait for the other participant to stop talking. Listening, however, requires discipline and commitment.

KINDS OF LISTENERS

Experts use various, overlapping descriptions for the many kinds of listening:

- **appreciative:** listening for aesthetic enjoyment of sound
- **active:** listening as a willing act of attending to and interpreting with an open mind the words and feelings a speaker expresses
- **comprehensive:** listening to learn
- **critical:** listening to make decisions such as when one listens to a political debate
- **defensive:** listening to discover arguments for oneself and against a speaker
- **dichotic:** listening to two things at once
- **discriminative:** listening to distinguish the significance of one sound from another
- **empathic or empathetic:** listening to put yourself in another person's place to understand, but not necessarily agree with what's being said and why
- **reflective or responsive:** listening to paraphrase, summarize, and clarify a message
- **selective:** listening only to what one wants to hear
- **therapeutic:** listening to help someone talk through a problem.

KINDS OF LISTENING

Harvey A. Robbins, in *How to Speak and Listen Effectively*, suggests that listeners come in four behavioral styles:

1 Analytical.
2 Amiable.
3 Driver.
4 Expressive.

To communicate effectively, you must understand how the listener prefers to receive information and adjust your communication style appropriately.

Analyticals tend toward perfectionism and deal in logic and details. They tend to keep feelings to themselves. In talking with them, prepare your case in advance and be accurate and realistic. Provide tangible evidence to support your points.

Amiables put a high value on people and friendships. They go out of their way to avoid offending anyone. They have their opinions, but are not inclined to tell you what's on their mind. Ask "how" questions to draw out their opinions.

Drivers can appear to be pushy, making demands on themselves and others. They tend to keep emotions under wraps and resent those who gossip and waste time in idle conversation. They are decisive and results oriented and like to give guidance to both those who need it and those who don't. Be brief, specific, and to the point when dealing with drivers.

Expressives are looking for a good time. They are enthusiastic, creative, and intuitive, but have little tolerance for those unlike themselves. Easily bored, they tend to go off on tangents. Stick with the big picture when relating to this type. […]

25 TIPS TO BE A BETTER LISTENER

Listening well takes a lot of mental preparation. Consider these tips to prepare yourself to be a better listener.

1 Consider the speaker a valuable and worthy person who is offering you the gift of his or her ideas, feelings, and experiences.
2 Turn UP the volume of your self-talk so you can let go of mental roadblocks to listening: prejudice, like, dislike, ego, preconceived ideas, opinions, and solutions.

3   Think of yourself as the host or hostess to the speaker, which means that while the speaker is sharing, you are serving; the focus is on the speaker, not you.

4   Recognize that powerful listening begins with deciding to really listen; listening is an inside-out job.

5   Write some positive self-talk statements for listening before the most difficult conversations.

6   Recognize that the more you understand your own thoughts, feelings, and actions the more you will understand other people. Self-knowledge is the way to deeper empathy.

7   In all conversations, notice your own feelings and the body sensations associated with those feelings.

8   After a challenging conversation that did not go so well, use the "left-hand column" exercise to reflect on what happened and what you might do next time.

9   Pay attention to your inner voice (self-talk). When it becomes clear, you are open to challenging that voice to a more positive position.

10 Recognize that you cannot fake listening and always strive to be genuine.

11 Even when you do not necessarily like or agree with someone, view that person in the light of "unconditional positive regard."

12 Put yourself in the speaker's shoes to the best of your ability. Empathy fuels listening and is "the ability to really see and hear another person and understand him or her from his or her perspective" according to Robert Bolton in *People Skills*.

13 Recognize that listening is healthy for both the speaker and you.

14 Be aware that powerful listening does not imply agreement or giving in. According to Stephen Covey in *The Seven Habits of*

Highly Effective People, listening means seeking to understand before seeking to be understood.

15 Before any important conversation, imagine the other person's concerns, questions, and issues. You can even list those and tentatively test one or two of your ideas during the conversation.

16 Recognize that if you are genuinely listening, your nonverbal communication will convey that. You will maintain good eye contact, an attentive body position, supportive hand gestures, and so forth.

17 Rephrase what you hear the speaker say to check understanding, show that you are listening, and be a strong sounding board.

18 Recognize that every time you really listen, you strengthen your relationship with the speaker.

19 As the listener, practice reflecting feelings and reflecting meanings as appropriate.

20 Ask open-ended questions to encourage the speaker to share relevant facts, ideas, opinions, and feelings.

21 Summarize the other person's views before sharing your own.

22 In a conflict situation, use listening whenever the other party is emotional. When emotions run high, problem solving becomes difficult until the other party feels truly heard.

23 Understand that one of the most important leadership skills is listening. Great leaders listen to everyone, searching for the best information and ideas to forge into the future.

24 Current sales practices promote listening to prospects as a way to deeply understand needs and provide truly viable solutions.

25 Strive to listen because it is one of the most powerful ways to develop yourself and others.

Communicating Ethically

In 2007, Nev Schulman began an online relationship with someone named Megan. They met on Facebook and talked and texted each other for seven months before he discovered that Megan was not who she claimed to be. The story was made into a documentary, *Catfish* (2010), followed by *Catfish: The TV Series* in 2012. "Catfishing" has come to refer to the act of creating a false online identity to trick someone into a relationship. Although some people question the authenticity of Nev's story, catfishing does happen and can lead to embarrassment, emotional damage, identity theft, and even blackmail. This brings us to the role of ethics in communication.

Ethics should guide your communication in your interactions with others. William Neher (2017) identified several principles of ethical communication in interpersonal relationships. First, you and your partner should be truthful with each other. A relationship can't grow without trust. Second, you should both be fully engaged in the conversation and *really* listen to each other. Third, both participants should focus on the other person rather than on themselves. By following these principles, you let your partner know that you value and respect them, and your relationship, whether personal or professional, can continue to develop.

CLASSROOM ACTIVITY

15–20 minutes

In groups of 3–4, list some people, fictional or real, that you think of as competent communicators. Why do you think that they are competent? What do they have in common? List some people that you think are not competent communicators. What makes you think that they lack competence? Come up with a list of guidelines to help people improve their communication competence based on the strengths and weaknesses of the people you listed. Discuss your lists as a class, and come up with a final list of guidelines.

DISCUSSION QUESTIONS

1   Think of a time when you wanted to influence someone's perceptions of you. How did you want them to see you? What did you do to get them to see you that way?

2   Do you generally find it easy to self-disclose to others, or does it take a while for you to open up? What factors influence your willingness to share information about yourself with others?

3   Review the skills related to emotional intelligence. Which skills do you think are your strengths? Which skills do you have to work to develop? Explain.

4   Which of the "25 Tips to Be a Better Listener" do you find most useful? Why?

KEY TERMS

Adaptability—the ability to change your behavior so that it is appropriate in different situations with different audiences and goals.

Communication competence—the ability to accomplish your goals in a socially appropriate manner.

Dramaturgical perspective—a theoretical framework that uses theatre as a metaphor to explain our behavior in everyday interactions.

Emotional intelligence—the ability to recognize emotions in yourself and others, determine appropriate expressions of emotion, and manage emotions accordingly.

Impression management—a person's attempts to influence the way that she/he is perceived by others.

Self-disclosure—voluntarily sharing information about yourself with others.

REFERENCES

Altman, I., and D. Taylor. 1973. Social penetration: The development of interpersonal relationships. Austin, TX: Holt, Rinehart, & Winston.

Duran, R. L. 1983. Communication adaptability: A measure of social communicative competence. Communication Quarterly 31, 320_326.

Feldman, J., and K. Mulle. 2008. Emotional intelligence: The new science of success. Danver, MA: ASTD Press.

Goffman, E. 1959. The presentation of self in everyday life. New York: Anchor Books.

National Communication Association. n.d. What is communication? https://www.natcom.org/about-nca/what-communication.

Neher, W. 2017. Communicating ethically (2nd ed). New York: Routledge.

Princeton Review. n.d. Top 10 college majors. https://www.princetonreview.com/college-advice/top-ten-college-majors.

Salovey, P., and J. D. Mayer. 1990. "Emotional intelligence." Imagination, Cognition and Personality 9, 185–211.

Spitzberg, B. H., and W. R. Cupach. (1984). Interpersonal communication competence. Newbury Park, CA: Sage.

Spitzberg, B. H., and W. R. Cupach. 1989. Handbook of interpersonal competence research. New York: Springer-Verlag.

Wolvin, A., and C. G. Coakley. 1995. Listening (5th ed.). Madison, WI: Brown/Benchmark.

CHAPTER 8

Media Studies

INTRODUCTION

Media Studies deals with the social, economic, political, cultural, aesthetic, legal, and ethical dimensions of communication media. Students in Media Studies examine media representations of race, ethnicity, gender, class, and sexual orientation and explore how media representations of the social world compare to the "real" world. They also investigate the social impact of media and media globalization and familiarize themselves with media technology.

Theories: agenda-setting, exemplification, spiral of science, McLuhan the media is the message, media ecology, uses and gratifications.

Media Studies and the Applied Communication Model

The Media Studies major features a mix of theory and practice that teaches students how to understand and evaluate the impact of media on individuals and society. You will learn about historic and contemporary media practices and approaches, which will allow you to go from being a passive consumer of information to a critical thinker who is able to analyze media and media messages. The curriculum will help you develop **media literacy**, the ability to evaluate news and distinguish it from propaganda and opinion. This issue has become more important recently, and the spread of "**fake news**" can have serious outcomes. Students also learn about **media effects**, the impact that media have in our everyday lives.

Classic and Contemporary Theories of Media Effects

Researchers have investigated how media use affects the audience. One of the early media effects model is the **hypodermic needle** (or magic bullet) **model**. It suggests that the media "shoot" their message into a passive audience that is immediately affected by the message. Research has not supported this model. This was followed by the development of the **Uses and Gratifications theory** which assumes that people are active media users who choose and use media to satisfy specific needs. Although it answered the question, "Why do we use media?" it didn't address the effects it has on us. Contemporary theories include **Social Learning theory** which states that we learn behavior through observation, **Cultivation theory** which claims that heavy television viewing causes people to believe the world depicted on television is consistent with the real world, and **Spiral of Silence theory** which predicts that people who believe that their views on an issue put them in the minority will keep their views to themselves to avoid rejection.

Language and Content of the Media

One of the areas that Media Studies focuses on is what content is distributed to local, national, and international audiences. Governments regulate media to varying degrees, which means that they can control which topics receive coverage and whose point of view is presented. In December 2017, the *Washington Post* reported that the Trump administration had prohibited the Centers for Disease Control and Prevention (CDC) from using a list of seven words or phrases in official budget documents. The words are "vulnerable," "entitlement," "diversity," "transgender," "fetus," "evidence-based," and "science-based." There was an immediate and intense negative response on social media. Scientists feared that this was part of a larger attack on science that would prevent them from conducting their research. The Department of Health and Human Services and the director of the CDC denied that the words were banned. The list was meant to provide guidance for how to phrase budget requests strategically in order to improve the likelihood of getting funding for projects from a conservative Congress. Whether the word ban was mischaracterized or not, the story illustrates how censorship (or perceived censorship) can affect which issues we are able to address.

News Media Literacy

As stated previously, one of the skills that you will develop is the ability to analyze and evaluate media content. Seth Ashley, Adam Maksl, and Stephanie Craft (2013) developed a news media literacy scale that measures three dimensions. First, there is the understanding that authors are motivated to create messages for profit or to influence people, and they target specific audiences. Second, messages contain value judgments and can be interpreted differently by different people. The messages are constructed using multiple techniques to influence attitudes and behaviors. Third, messages can filter out or omit information, thereby affecting audiences' perceptions of reality. Knowing how the news media system works allows you to be a more critical consumer of information.

Multitasking

Technological advances have given us unprecedented access to different media. We have smart phones, tablets, and laptops that allow us to watch movies and shows while working on class assignments and chatting with friends. As a result, our ability to focus decreases. The next reading discusses **multitasking** and the implications for us if we continue to do it.

THE MULTITASKING MYTH

by Devora Zack

I'm great at multitasking.

Multitasking is neurologically impossible.

"No man is free who is not master of himself." —Epictetus

Multitasking fails us.

Let me take that one step further. Multitasking doesn't even exist. We'll circle back to this alarming yet scientifically backed claim later.

Why are so many people drawn into the albatross of multitasking? We are collectively thwarted by modern-day plagues such as:

- Too much to do, too little time
- Cluttered life, cluttered mind
- Growing piles of daily demands
- A whirlwind of distractions

Nooo! [Cue eerie Halloween music.]

This list is the tip of the iceberg. Go ahead; brainstorm a few dozen examples of your own. I'll wait here, tapping my foot, growing ever more anxious that I'm wasting my irreplaceable time.

When you return, check out how one guy I interviewed described multitasking in daily life: "What is the impact of multitasking when looking at text messages while driving? Reading the newspaper while talking on the phone to colleagues? Watching *NFL Live* when your wife wants to talk about schedules? You run into the car ahead of you, agree to finish a project before it can possibly be done, and schedule a business trip on your father-in-law's birthday."

In a fruitless effort to compensate for the tsunami we call our lives, we try to tackle several tasks at once … making distracted living rampant. We lose concentration, heighten stress, and senselessly fret over items unrelated to the task at hand. We are relentlessly disrespectful to the people right in front of us—colleagues, customers, vendors, employees, cohorts, and our own family.

Fragmented attention (aka multitasking) fractures results and foils relationships.

A MONSTER IN OUR MIDST

What makes multitasking so enticing?

We know of the dangers of texting and driving, yet many of us still do it. How can we circumvent distraction? Why is it so difficult to immerse ourselves in a single task at a time? Because lurking around every turn is what I call the multitask monster. Many are thwarted by this compelling creature.

One of his primary tricks is pulling our attention toward unrelated obligations as we work. He looms over our desks, lumbering around our workplace, two heads recklessly swinging in opposite directions, daring us to focus on one over the other. As we stare in despair at our stealthily expanding in-box, the multitask monster soothingly whispers into our ears the Sole Solution: "Tackle two, three, four at once! It is your *only hope*."

Worse, seemingly everyone else has taken on the multitask monster as a revered guide, responding to his every beck and call.

Resist! Stop the madness! Gather your resilience and kick that multitask monster out the door. Multitask monsters are like ocean sirens luring sailors to disaster—though notably less well groomed.

What if I asked you to banish the multitask monster for one day? Could you do it? What would stop you? Can you give it a go? What results will you reap?

One client reflected, "I've always prided myself on being a multitasker over the years, but if I were to do honest self-evaluation today, I realize there are pitfalls to all this madness!"

Another acknowledged, "When I do more than one thing at a time I never do anything particularly well."

The hard fact is that attempting to multitask correlates with low productivity.[1] By definition, doing more than one thing at a time means you are distracted. The only way to do anything particularly well—or, let's raise the bar, *spectacularly* well—is through full task engagement. As I heard a father sagely explain to his son, a newly minted college grad, "At any given time, you can do one thing well or two things poorly."

THE ALLURE OF DISTRACTION

We are distracted. This does not serve us well.

Don't blame yourself entirely. Cultural expectations—based on technological advances—have resulted in unrealistic demands. We are expected to absorb a torrent of information from a plethora of media without pause. We are to be constantly accessible.

Many of us react to the alarming pile of demands by splitting our focus among tasks. We are in the midst of an increasing trend toward what Linda Stone calls "continuous partial attention"—giving superficial, simultaneous attention to competing streams of information.[2] Living in our own personal big bang, we feel unable to keep pace with the frenetically expanding universe encircling our lives. Again and again I hear,

"The more I try to keep up, the more overwhelmed I become."

A slew of people suffer from the misconception that multitasking is necessary to cope with task overload. This always backfires.

Multitasking is misleading. Rather than mitigating demands, it magnifies our problems. Our brains are incapable of honing in on more than one item at a time.

Multitasking blocks the flow of information into short-term memory. Data that doesn't make it into short-term memory cannot be transferred into long-term memory for recall. Therefore, multitasking lowers our ability to accomplish tasks.

We are losing our ability to focus. We are scattered. We are impolite. We cause—and suffer from—accidents. We are unproductive. We relinquish control. We pretend to multitask.

Why did I say "pretend"? Because multitasking doesn't exist! I'll keep sneaking in this factoid until you're ready to hear it. It's make-believe! Think Zeus throwing lightning bolts. Or Casper the Friendly Ghost.

EVERYBODY LOVES A NEUROSCIENTIST

As any neighborhood neuroscientist will attest, the brain can only focus on one thing at a time.

Allow me to expand. The brain is incapable of simultaneously processing separate streams of information from attention-demanding tasks. What we conversationally reference as multitasking is technically called task-switching—moving rapidly and ineffectively among tasks.

As Dr. Eyal Ophir, a neuroscientist at Stanford University, explains, "Humans don't really multitask, we task-switch … switch[ing] very quickly between tasks." Although this feels like multitasking, the brain is incapable of focusing on two things at once. Plus, performance suffers as attention shifts back and forth.[3]

Not only that, get a load of this from Dr. Earl Miller at the Massachusetts Institute of

Technology: "You cannot focus on one [task] while doing [an]other. That's because of what's called interference between the two tasks. … People can't multitask very well, and when people say they can, they're deluding themselves. The brain is very good at deluding itself."[4]

To recap, actual multitasking is not possible, and what is commonly labeled as multitasking is really task-switching. We task-switch within tenths of a second; we don't consciously notice delays. So from here forward I will alternatively reference multitasking as task-switching, "attempts to multitask," or "so-called multitasking." Occasionally I'll just say multitasking, although you and I both know that is just shorthand. Most defenders of multitasking do not have a grasp of its actual meaning. I don't intend this as a slam. Multitaskers are only halfway paying attention to what I'm saying anyway.

Even electrical synapses short-circuit over so-called multitasking. As one client shared with me, "I met up with my boss as I walked in this morning. He was talking to me as I entered my PIN into the door lock. I said to him, 'I can't multitask,' meaning I couldn't listen to him and enter my number at the same time. He told me multitasking also backfires in the context of electrical engineering, the way circuits are designed. If you try to make a circuit do more than one thing, its efficiency is reduced."

My client's boss has a doctorate in electrical engineering. In fact, according to the Oxford English Dictionary, the word *multitasking* is derived from computer processing, emerging in the English lexicon at the time of the first computer.

> **Multitasking:** [noun] 1. Computing simultaneous execution of more than one program or task by a single computer processor. 2. Handling of more than one task at the same time by a single person.

Replacing rapid-fire shifts with attention on one task at a time enables us to achieve more in less time. We wind up ahead.

WHEN MULTITASKING ISN'T MULTITASKING

Some folks angrily retort, "I can hold a conversation and empty the dishwasher. I can listen to the radio and drive! That's multitasking."

Allow me to begin by saying that I admire your feisty spirit. That said, Dr. David Meyer can clear things up: "Under most conditions, the brain simply cannot do two complex tasks at the same time. It can happen only when the two tasks … don't compete with each other for the same mental resources."[5]

Multitasking means combining two or more activities, potentially causing at least one to receive inadequate attention. Activities that require virtually no conscious effort can be performed in conjunction with primary tasks and do not fall in the bandwidth of multitasking. "Simple" tasks are automated, low-level functions, including rote activities that do not require concentration.

Engaging in two unrelated tasks at the same time when at least one does not demand conscious effort is not multitasking. Activities in this category vary based on one's experience and surroundings. For example, driving to the local grocery store is a basic, mundane event for many, yet a new driver must give her full attention to the same event. Doing dishes takes no conscious effort, unless this is an atypical chore for you. Most of us can drive and chat with a passenger or listen to the news and tidy up.

Although autopilot tasks vary based on background and intention, activities that may fall into this category include:

- Listening to music
- Filing papers
- Basic food preparation
- Simple repair or craftwork

It's a slippery slope. Unexpected distraction could cause a favorite passage to be missed, a document to be misplaced, a meal to burn, or glue to spill. We can be driving along a familiar route, space out, and miss a usual exit. The actual cause is a brain that temporarily disengages from our actions. The unruly mind spaces out, goes somewhere else entirely, and fails to synchronize with the current mission. It was multitasking.

There is a fine line between engaging in a largely reflexive activity and maintaining awareness of an unexpected twist. Perhaps you can drive to work without thinking ninety-nine percent of the time. But if a car unexpectedly swerves into your lane, are your reflexes ready to react?

Another danger is confusing automated and attention-demanding tasks. For example, people mistakenly believe they can text and walk, remaining fully aware of their surroundings. We will soon discover the fallacy of this belief.

Although there are instances when engaging in two *noncompeting* activities can be beneficial, choose carefully. Squeezing a stress ball while on a conference call can be a positive release, whereas checking email is a distraction. Stretching while watching a television show is far more beneficial than just sitting on the couch. Listening to upbeat music while exercising can heighten the effectiveness of a workout, although conversing or reading while on a treadmill typically reduces calories burned. Engaging in two noncompeting activities when at least one is automatic is generally harmless; pursuing competing tasks can exact a very high toll.

THE PRICE WE PAY

Raise your hand if you have observed people doing any of the following:

- Colliding with others while looking at a phone
- Not driving when the light turns green
- Playing games on handheld devices at professional events
- Not noticing when arriving at the front of a line at a shop or café

These minor irritations are the tip of the iceberg. Multitasking takes a terrible toll.

In the United States, distracted driving kills tens of thousands of people each year, with an economic toll from injury and loss of life amounting to $871 billion annually. Distracted driving and driving under the influence (DUI) are nearly tied as the top two causes of deadly car crashes. DUI accounts for 18 percent of deaths in motor vehicle crashes, with distracted driving a factor in at least 17 percent of fatal vehicular accidents. The true percentage is likely much higher. Distracted driving is under-reported, because police have difficulty identifying whether distraction has been a factor.[6]

TEXTING WHILE DRIVING

The American Automobile Association (AAA) Foundation for Traffic Safety cites handheld phones as a major safety problem. According to a 2014 AAA study, more than 67 percent of U.S. drivers regularly talk or text behind the wheel, despite acknowledging the associated risks.

But, as AAA Director of Traffic Safety Jake Nelson notes, "Using your phone while driving may seem safe, but it roughly quadruples your risk of being in a crash. ... None of us is immune to the dangers of distracted driving. The best advice is to hang up and drive."[7]

TEXTING WHILE WALKING

Texting while walking also poses a serious safety issue. A major danger stemming from texting and walking is that pedestrians believe they have it under control. In reality, "when texting, you're not as in control with the complex actions of walking."[8] Paying attention to the phone instead of one's surroundings can be catastrophic.

The most common categories of typical pedestrian distractions include:

- Manual—physically doing something else
- Visual—seeing something that distracts you
- Cognitive—mulling over thoughts in your head

Conduct an experiment next time you are strolling with a colleague using his handheld device. (You, obviously, are walking unhindered, well adjusted, and blissful, thanks to this [reading].) Gently suggest that he put the device away so as not to step accidentally into oncoming traffic or bash into an innocent passerby.

Does your colleague gratefully reply, "Cheers, mate! Thanks for the helpful reminder. You just saved my life! Lunch is on me!"

Or does he mutter distractedly under his breath, "Relax. Don't worry. I'm fine. I know perfectly well what's going on around me."

When a walker gets whacked upside the head, it's always the other guy's fault. Regardless of who's to blame, the fact remains that the number of injuries involving pedestrians on their mobile phones more than tripled from 2004 to 2010.[9]

Accidents stemming from being distracted, such as texting and walking, result in a particularly high percentage of head injuries and fatalities. As a public service campaign in Washington, DC, reminds drivers, "Pedestrians don't come with airbags."

Preoccupied people fall down stairs, trip on uneven pavement, and walk into traffic.[10]

DISTRACTIONS WHILE LEARNING

Multitasking weakens our ability to concentrate. We are collectively losing the ability to sustain prolonged attention, and distraction results in knowledge less flexibly applied in new situations.[11] The capacity to apply knowledge from one context to another is called transference. Attempts to multitask reduce this ability.

In his book *The Shallows*, Nicholas Carr argues that the Internet has changed how we process information.[12] Although the Web enables us to find data with greater ease than when we perused periodicals at the local library branch, it hurts how we absorb and retain data. Scanning a screen has largely replaced reading a page, yielding shallow learning and poor retention.

[…]

WORKING WHILE DISTRACTED

Repeatedly dropping and picking up a mental thread results in greater mental fatigue and more mistakes than deep immersion in a single task. When we are distracted, the brain processes and stores information ineffectively. Multitasking—constantly switching between tasks—negatively affects concentration. Task-shifting is the antithesis of concentration. Multitaskers exhibit a lower ability to concentrate and are correspondingly less efficient.[13]

Wait, there's more. Multitasking also exacts a toll in three additional areas:

- Quality of life
- Relationships
- Everything else that matters to you

No big deal.

GENERATIONAL EDGE?

I am frequently asked whether young people have an edge when it comes to multitasking. Does growing up in a high-tech world make one better equipped to do several things at once? It does not. As Douglas Merrill put it, "Everyone knows kids are better at multitasking. The problem? Everyone is wrong."[14]

College and high school students have the same memory limitations as adults. Regardless of age, we understand and recall less when task-shifting. Poorly acquired information results in a weak ability to transfer and apply concepts. Learning to concentrate is a life skill.

As a University of Vermont study revealed, non-course-related software applications on student's laptops are open and active more than 42 percent of the time they are engaged in schoolwork. The level of distraction among university students is epidemic.

The younger generation has a wildly inflated idea of how many things they can attend to at once.[15] Young people who attempt to perform two challenging tasks at once are deluded, because complex brain functions compete for the same part of the brain—the prefrontal cortex. It is difficult for individuals to self-evaluate how well their mental processes are operating, because the processes are unconscious.[16]

Texting, messaging, and being online while in class or doing homework has a negative effect on grade point averages because, as a Harvard study revealed, divided attention hinders our ability to encode information. The result is we remember less, or nothing at all. So-called multitasking behavior "leads to a lower capacity for cognitive processing and precludes deeper learning."[17]

SHE BLINDED ME WITH SCIENCE

Efforts to multitask require the brain to switch focus extremely quickly, in less than a tenth of a second. These delays and losses of concentration add up to a poor use of time and drain our brainpower.

If we know the drawbacks of attempting to multitask, why do we keep crawling back for more?

For starters, we are pursued by a plethora of tantalizing distractions, 24/7. We can't even watch television without seeing another show advertised in a giant scroll on the bottom quarter of the screen.

Another allure of multitasking is the craving for novelty. This helps explain why we are tempted to multitask even when we know it is wrong. When stimuli signal a change to the status quo, dopamine is released. Adrenaline races through the bloodstream, regardless of whether these changes are perceived as positive or negative. This surge contributes to the attraction of new tasks over what we are currently doing.[18]

Help is on the way. The brain's executive system in the frontal lobe can assist in suppressing irrelevant information. Our executive system determines what input is extraneous and where to direct our attention.

We can achieve our goals by learning to reduce distractions. Bonus! This is an acquirable skill, one that you—Hey! I'm talking to you!—can achieve. Read on.

NOTES

1 Gigi Foster and Charlene M. Kalenkoski, "Measuring the Relative Productivity of Multitasking to Sole-tasking in Household Production: New Experimental Evidence," IZA Discussion Paper no. 6763 (July 2012).

2 Linda Stone, "Beyond Simple Multi-Tasking: Continuous Partial Attention" (November 30, 2009). http://lindastone.net/2009/11/30/beyond-simple-multi-tasking-continuous-partial-attention.

3 Eyal Ophir, Clifford Nass, and Anthony D. Wagner, "Cognitive Control in Media Multitaskers," *Proceedings of the National Academy of Sciences* 106, no. 37: 15583–15587.

4 In Jon Hamilton, "Think You're Multitasking? Think Again," National Public Radio (October 20, 2008). http://www.npr.org/templates/story/story.php?storyId=95256794.

5 In Annie Murphy Paul, "The New Marshmallow Test: Resisting the Temptations of the Web," *The Hechinger Report* (May 3, 2013). http://hechingerreport.org/content/the-new-marshmallow-test-resisting-the-temptations-of-the-web_11941.

6 National Highway Traffic Safety Administration, *The Economic and Societal Impact of Motor Vehicle Crashes, 2010* (Washington, DC: National Highway Traffic Safety Administration, May 2014). DOT HS 812 013.

7   In Michael Green, "Teens Report Texting or Using Phone While Driving Significantly Less Often than Adults," *AAA News Room* (December 11, 2013). http://newsroom.aaa.com/2013/12/teens-report-texting-or-using-phone-while-driving-significantly-less-often-than-adults.

8   Marcene Robinson, "Think It's Safe to Type a Quick Text While Walking? Guess Again," *University of Buffalo News Center* (February 26, 2014). http://www.buffalo.edu/news/releases/2014/02/022.html.

9   Jack L. Nasar and Derek Troyer, "Pedestrian Injuries Due to Mobile Phone Use in Public Places," *Accident Analysis & Prevention*, 57 (August 2013): 91–95.

10 Robert Glatter, "Texting While Walking? Think Twice," *Forbes* (July 31, 2012). http://www.forbes.com/sites/robertglatter/2012/07/31/texting-while-walking-think-twice.

11 Karin Foerde, Barbara J. Knowlton, and Russell A. Poldrack, "Modulation of Competing Memory Systems by Distraction," *Proceedings of the National Academy of Sciences* 103, no. 31: 11778–11783.

12 Nicholas Carr, *The Shallows: What the Internet Is Doing to Our Brains* (New York: W. W. Norton, 2010).

13 Institute for the Future and Gallup Organization, *Managing Corporate Communication in the Information Age* (Lanham, MD: Pitney Bowes, 2000).

14 Douglas Merrill, "Why Multitasking Doesn't Work," *Forbes* (August 17, 2012). http://www.forbes.com/sites/douglasmerrill/2012/08/17/why-multitasking-doesnt-work.

15 Larry D. Rosen, L. Mark Carrier, and Nancy A. Cheever, "Facebook and Texting Made Me Do It: Media-Induced Task-Switching While Studying," *Computers in Human Behavior* 29, no. 3: 948–958.

16 Paul, "The New Marshmallow Test."

17 Reynol Junco and Shelia R. Cotten, "No A 4 U: The Relationship Between Multitasking and Academic Performance," *Computers & Education* 59, no. 2: 505–514.

18 Gregory Burns, Satisfaction: *The Science of Finding True Fulfillment* (New York: Henry Holt, 2005), p. 43.

Ethical Issues in Media Studies

Students in media studies analyze various forms of media from an ethical perspective and explore audience perceptions of what is ethical and what is not. Marshall McLuhan coined the term "global village" to describe how the use of electronic media connects us. We have instant access to information from around the world through electronic media. This has the effect of "shrinking" the world so that it's one big community, rather than a collection of smaller communities. This feeling of community should foster the desire to increase your awareness of global issues and become more involved with each other.

Because we have the ability to share words, images, and video so quickly and widely, it is important to be sure that the information we share is accurate. According to a study by Maksym Gabielkob, Arthi Ramachandran, Augusting Chaintreau, and Arnaud Legout (2016), social media users appear to retweet news without reading the actual stories. Fifty-nine percent of the people in their study shared news stories without clicking on the link themselves. Headlines do not give you the complete story, and you (or the people you share it with) may misinterpret the story. You may also be sharing misrepresentations or completely false information. A responsible member of the global village must read information with a critical eye and consider the source of the information before sharing it.

Another cause for concern is harassment, hate speech, name-calling, and personal attacks—also known as trolling. Anonymity can encourage negative behavior because a troll can act without fear of consequences. The targets of trolls can suffer from depression, anxiety, lower self-esteem, and may even be driven to suicide. Artificial intelligence and human moderators can prevent or remove some of the inappropriate comments, but filtering comments may restrict free speech.

A final consideration has to do with the ability of media to influence our attitudes and behaviors. According to the Pew Research Center, about 70% of American adults have at least one social media account. We use platforms such as Facebook, Instagram, Snapchat, and Twitter to keep in touch with friends and family members, but we also follow celebrities. We are curious about them, and following them gives us the chance to be part of their lives in a small way. Celebrities often have millions of followers. Their popularity gives them the ability to influence their followers, so they are paid to endorse products and brands. The Federal Trade Commission (FTC) guidelines state that endorsers must clearly indicate that their post is an ad if there is a connection between the endorser and the brand, but celebrities sometimes do not disclose that their posts are actually ads. They may therefore exercise undue influence over their followers.

Conclusion

The media studies curriculum teaches you about the history, content, and effects of mass media. It encourages you to think critically about news content and understand how media content can (and can't) influence you. By examining media with ethics in mind, you can become a more competent communicator. Media studies prepares you for careers that require strong communication skills. You may also consider graduate school.

CLASSROOM ACTIVITY

Purpose: to get students to think critically about their media use and how it affects them.

Recommended time: 15–20 minutes.

Working in groups of 3–4 people, think of some examples of media content that had a strong effect on you. It could be a positive effect or negative effect. Discuss why you believe it had so much of an influence on you. Were there commonalities in the examples you thought of? As a class, discuss messages that you believe are important for college students. How would you get the messages to your audience? Which media would you use to reach them?

DISCUSSION QUESTIONS

1 How do you determine whether a news story you see on social media is true? Have you ever shared or retweeted a story before checking if it was true?

2 Which of the theories described in the chapter do you think is the most accurate description of media effects? Why?

3 How do you multitask? What effect do you think multitasking has on your life?

4 Memes are humorous items such as images or videos that are shared by Internet users. Some of them make fun of the person in the image or video. What would you do if you saw a mean-spirited meme that targeted you or someone you are close to?

KEY TERMS

Cultivation theory—a media effects theory which argues that heavy television viewers believe that the real world and television portrayals of the world are consistent.

Fake news—fabricated news stories; deliberately spread misinformation.

Hypodermic-needle model—an early media effects model that sees people as passive audiences who the media inject with messages that have an immediate effect on them.

Media effects—how media influence an audience's thoughts, attitudes, and behavior.

Media literacy—your ability to analyze and evaluate media.

Multitasking—splitting your attention between two or more tasks at the same time.

Spiral of silence theory—a media effects theory that predicts people will keep their views to themselves if they believe they are in the minority.

Social learning theory—a media effects theory that says we learn behaviors through observation.

Uses and gratifications theory—a media effects theory which argues that people are active rather than passive and choose and use media to satisfy their needs.

REFERENCES

Ashley, S., Maksl, A., & Craft, S. (2013). Developing a news media literacy scale. *Journalism & Mass Communication Editor, 68(1)*, 7-21.

Gabielkov, M., Ramachandran, A., Chaintreau, A., & Legout, A. (2016) Social clicks: What and who gets read on Twitter?. *ACM SIGMETRICS / IFIP Performance 2016*, Antibes Juan-les-Pins, France.

Sun, L.H., & Eilperein, J. (2017, December 15). CDC gets list of forbidden words: Fetus, transgender, diversity. *The Washington Post*. Retrieved from https://www.washingtonpost.com/national/health-science/cdc-gets-list-of-forbidden-words-fetus-transgender-diversity/2017/12/15/f503837a-e1cf-11e7-89e8-edec16379010_story.html?utm_term=.dd0b3946731b.

Zack, D. 2015. *Singletasking: Getting more done—one thing at a time*. Oakland, CA: Berrett-Koehler Publishers.

CHAPTER 9

Journalism

INTRODUCTION

The Journalism curriculum prepares students for careers in the news industry. Students learn to become critical consumers of news media and develop their skills in news writing, reporting, and editing. They study the rights and responsibilities that media professionals have under the First Amendment and learn the boundaries of constitutional protection in relation to privacy, defamation, and obscenity. Jobs related to this degree include reporter, columnist, layout and page designer, editor, publicist, news director, grant writer, and market researcher.

JOURNALISM AND THE APPLIED COMMUNICATION MODEL

Journalism comes in a variety of forms. For example, investigative journalism refers to in-depth reporting with the goal of uncovering the truth about a particular topic. News reporting relays factual information in a straightforward manner. Feature writing involves a more thorough exploration of a topic than news reporting. It includes interviews and offers new perspectives on the topic. Columns are another type of journalism in which authors expresses their own opinions in their own personal styles. Reviews include both facts and opinions. They describe the subject being reviewed and give an informed opinion on it based on the author's research and experience. Editorials are opinion pieces on topics of public interest that represent the position of the editors of the publication.

Principles and Practices of Journalism

According to the American Press Institute, "Journalism is the activity of gathering, assessing, creating, and presenting news and information. It is also the product of these activities." (https://www.americanpressinstitute.org/?s=what+is+journalism).

Bill Kovach and Tom Rosenstiel's 2014 book, *Elements of Journalism*, describes the "theory and culture of journalism". Based on a comprehensive examination of newsgathering that included surveys, hundreds of hours of interviews with journalists, and content studies of news reporting, they state that "the purpose of journalism is to provide people with the information they need to be free and self-governing" (p. 6). They identified nine essential principles and practices that allow journalists to accomplish this.

1   **Journalism's first obligation is to the truth.** People need accurate information presented in context to make good decisions. Journalists should gather and verify information and be clear about their sources and methods so the audience can make their own judgments of the information.

2   **It's first loyalty it to citizens.** Journalists' must put the public interest ahead of their own self-interest or assumptions.

3   **Its essence is a discipline of verification.** Journalists must use objective methods to assess and test information. This includes finding multiple witnesses, getting comments from different sides of an issue, and disclosing as much as possible about sources.

4   **Its practitioners must maintain an independence from those they cover.** Journalists should not be influenced or intimidated by sources or allow their own class, ethnicity, religion, gender, etc. to limit their view of what they cover.

5   **It must serve as an independent monitor of power.** Journalism acts as a watchdog over people who are in positions that allow them to affect citizens. Journalists inform the public about what the powerful few are doing and how it affects them.

6   **It must provide a forum for public criticism and compromise.** Journalism should not only provide an outlet for discussion. It should represent different interests and points of view fairly and provide verified information that the public can use when making decisions.

7   **It must strive to make the significant interesting and relevant.** Journalists should provide information on topics that people want to know about and topics that they should know about in a way that makes people want to receive it.

8   **It must keep the news comprehensive and proportional.** Journalism should not sensationalize some stories while neglecting others. The news should cover everyone affected by events and take different experiences into account when telling stories.

9   **Its practitioners must be allowed to exercise their personal conscience.** It is important for journalists to have a strong sense of ethics to prevent incomplete or inaccurate information from being published.

GATHERING INFORMATION

One of the most important skills that you develop in journalism is the ability to gather information. The information can be obtained from human sources, databases, public records, and directories. Human sources make your story interesting and relevant. Conducting successful interviews requires you to do some preparation ahead of time. Before you interview someone, you need to decide what information you want from them and prepare questions that will get you the answers you need. Ask open-ended questions that allow the interviewee to provide details. Ask follow-up questions to get more information. Be an effective listener. You may need to deviate from your original set of questions if the interviewee brings up another topic or skip questions if the interviewee answers them while responding to earlier questions. Be a skilled notetaker. Write down key words and phrases and make note of details such as the interviewee's facial expressions, speech rate, tone of voice, etc. It's much better to have more information you need than to be missing information.

Writing the Story

Another important skill that you develop in journalism is the ability to write clearly. Gathering information is only part of the process. Once you have the information, you need to structure the story and write it in a way that gains and maintains the reader's attention. Start with a **headline** that makes readers stop and look at the story. A common organizational structure is the **inverted pyramid**, which provides the most important facts at the beginning of the story followed by nonessential information in order of importance so that the least important details are at the bottom of the pyramid. The opening paragraph of a story is called the **lead**. The subsequent paragraphs are called **nut graphs**. In a relatively short period of time, we've seen mass media take the form of newspapers, radio broadcasts, television broadcasts, and, most recently, online news. Each additional form of mass media came with its own changes. The following reading discusses the effect that the growth of social media has had on storytelling.

STORYTELLING IN THE AGE OF SOCIAL NEWS CONSUMPTION

by Steve Rubel

Social media is having a dramatic, perhaps out-sized impact on how digital news is produced, distributed, consumed and ultimately monetized. As mobile and social technologies reach critical mass, it is fueling a footrace to create highly shareable, yet informative news stories that generate traffic. More critically this is changing how journalists approach their craft.

To address this dynamic further, Katie Scrivano and the Edelman Media Network (a team of earned media specialists) teamed with two start-ups, *NewsWhip* and *Muck Rack* to study U.S. social news consumption.

Working with NewsWhip, we identified the 50 overall most-shared, English-language articles, and in six key topics – general news, food and beverage, energy, health, technology and finance. Edelman Intelligence then analyzed each story to identify significant commonalities. This helped shaped a survey of more than 250 working journalists that Edelman conducted in collaboration with Muck Rack.

This research revealed that:

- More than 75 percent of journalists say they feel more pressure now to think about their story's potential to get shared on social platforms.
- To make their stories more shareable, journalists are infusing their stories with five key ingredients: video/images, brevity, localization, more use of human voice and a proximity to trending topics.
- Nearly 3/4 of journalists are now creating original video content to accompany their stories. However, very few journalists (13 percent) are relying on sourcing consumer-generated video and only 3 percent are using corporate video.
- Journalists see five key trends impacting their profession this year: more mobile friendly

content, faster turnaround times, more original video, smaller newsroom staff and social media growing in influence.

Additionally, the NewsWhip data revealed a wealth of information about which networks influence the news we read, and which publishers and writers are having success in adapting to a world where social sharing behaviors influence what stories stick to screens.

Later [...] Edelman will publish a more detailed analysis of this data to map the "genome" of a shareable news story broadly and across the aforementioned sectors. However, this top line analysis revealed that:

- Facebook dominates all other social platform interactions.
- Non-legacy media publishers make up the majority of the most-engaged sites on Facebook (top sources: *The Huffington Post, BuzzFeed, Mashable, PlayBuzz*).
- *The Huffington Post* featured more video than any other news site; emerged as top shared news outlet on Facebook overall.
- BBC, *The New York Times* and *Mashable* posted the most amount of shares on Twitter.
- *Forbes, The New York Times* and *Business Insider* posted the most amount of shares on LinkedIn.
- Some 4 percent of the most shared articles originated from UK publishers.

Social media, on one level, has democratized news distribution: publishers, companies and journalists can now directly engage their audiences. However, these algorithms and sharing behaviors have created a new complex web of intermediaries between the media and their audiences. This is impacting how news is produced, and perhaps even which stories are selected for production and prominent distribution.

In 2015 and beyond, communicators will need to see the landscape as a whole, develop systematic thinking and a more connected way of linking up paid, earned and owned strategies to ensure they get heard. This means discovering the shareable angles on stories (the "social lede"), deepening relationships with journalists and helping them create original video content.

This is a topic I personally will be focused on studying and writing about throughout the year. It warrants quite a bit of research and thought about how communicators can now ensure their messages get heard in a world of unlimited content, yet limited time and attention. Our strategies must account for the outsized role that just a few players like Facebook have on what we see.

Steve Rubel is Edelman's chief content strategist.

Ethical Issues in Journalism

William Neher and Paul Sandin (2017) provide an overview of the types of ethical issues that media professionals face. First, the media function as **gatekeepers** who determine what information is presented to the public as well as how much information is presented. Psychologist Kurt Lewin introduced the term to refer to the people who gather, sort, select, and disseminate information. Gatekeepers have the power to influence the way that media consumers view the world by focusing public attention on some issues but not others.

A second ethical concern that Neher and Sandin describe has to do with the effects of stereotyping in the media. **Stereotypes** are "qualities perceived to be associated with particular groups or categories of people" (Schneide 2004, 24). They are overgeneralizations about what people are like based on their race, religion, sex, age, etc. Ethical professionals must be concerned with whether stereotyping can suggest that some kinds of people are more important than others or result in harm to people who are portrayed negatively.

The third type of ethical issue that Neher and Sandin discuss centers around truth and accuracy. The press has an obligation to provide the public with facts. Journalists must not fabricate, manipulate, or distort information. They must also ensure the accuracy of information before passing it on to the public. Most professional organizations have adopted codes of ethics to guide their members. The code of ethics of the Society of Professional Journalists provides a summary of ethical concerns that are common to most professional organizations.

READING 9.2

SPJ CODE OF ETHICS

PREAMBLE

Members of the Society of Professional Journalists believe that public enlightenment is the forerunner of justice and the foundation of democracy. Ethical journalism strives to ensure the free exchange of information that is accurate, fair and thorough. An ethical journalist acts with integrity.

The Society declares these four principles as the foundation of ethical journalism and encourages their use in its practice by all people in all media.

SEEK TRUTH AND REPORT IT

Ethical journalism should be accurate and fair. Journalists should be honest and courageous in gathering, reporting and interpreting information.

Journalists should:
- Take responsibility for the accuracy of their work. Verify information before releasing it. Use original sources whenever possible.
- Remember that neither speed nor format excuses inaccuracy.
- Provide context. Take special care not to misrepresent or oversimplify in promoting, previewing or summarizing a story.

- Gather, update and correct information throughout the life of a news story.
- Be cautious when making promises, but keep the promises they make.
- Identify sources clearly. The public is entitled to as much information as possible to judge the reliability and motivations of sources.
- Consider sources' motives before promising anonymity. Reserve anonymity for sources who may face danger, retribution or other harm, and have information that cannot be obtained elsewhere. Explain why anonymity was granted.
- Diligently seek subjects of news coverage to allow them to respond to criticism or allegations of wrongdoing.
- Avoid undercover or other surreptitious methods of gathering information unless traditional, open methods will not yield information vital to the public.
- Be vigilant and courageous about holding those with power accountable.
  Give voice to the voiceless.
- Support the open and civil exchange of views, even views they find repugnant.
- Recognize a special obligation to serve as watchdogs over public affairs and government. Seek to ensure that the public's business is conducted in the open, and that public records are open to all.
- Provide access to source material when it is relevant and appropriate.
- Boldly tell the story of the diversity and magnitude of the human experience.
  Seek sources whose voices we seldom hear.
- Avoid stereotyping. Journalists should examine the ways their values and experiences may shape their reporting.
- Label advocacy and commentary.
- Never deliberately distort facts or context, including visual information.
  Clearly label illustrations and re-enactments.
- Never plagiarize. Always attribute.

MINIMIZE HARM

Ethical journalism treats sources, subjects, colleagues and members of the public as human beings deserving of respect.

Journalists should:
- Balance the public's need for information against potential harm or discomfort.
  Pursuit of the news is not a license for arrogance or undue intrusiveness.
- Show compassion for those who may be affected by news coverage. Use heightened sensitivity when dealing with juveniles, victims of sex crimes, and sources or subjects who are inexperienced or unable to give consent. Consider cultural differences in approach and treatment.
- Recognize that legal access to information differs from an ethical justification to publish or broadcast.
- Realize that private people have a greater right to control information about themselves than public figures and others who seek power, influence or attention. Weigh the consequences of publishing or broadcasting personal information.
- Avoid pandering to lurid curiosity, even if others do.
- Balance a suspect's right to a fair trial with the public's right to know. Consider the implications of identifying criminal suspects before they face legal charges.
- Consider the long-term implications of the extended reach and permanence of publication. Provide updated and more complete information as appropriate.

ACT INDEPENDENTLY

The highest and primary obligation of ethical journalism is to serve the public.

Journalists should:
- Avoid conflicts of interest, real or perceived.
  Disclose unavoidable conflicts.

- Refuse gifts, favors, fees, free travel and special treatment, and avoid political and other outside activities that may compromise integrity or impartiality, or may damage credibility.
- Be wary of sources offering information for favors or money; do not pay for access to news. Identify content provided by outside sources, whether paid or not.
- Deny favored treatment to advertisers, donors or any other special interests, and resist internal and external pressure to influence coverage.
- Distinguish news from advertising and shun hybrids that blur the lines between the two. Prominently label sponsored content.

BE ACCOUNTABLE AND TRANSPARENT

Ethical journalism means taking responsibility for one's work and explaining one's decisions to the public.

Journalists should:
- Explain ethical choices and processes to audiences. Encourage a civil dialogue with the public about journalistic practices, coverage and news content.
- Respond quickly to questions about accuracy, clarity and fairness.
- Acknowledge mistakes and correct them promptly and prominently. Explain corrections and clarifications carefully and clearly.
- Expose unethical conduct in journalism, including within their organizations.
- Abide by the same high standards they expect of others.

The SPJ Code of Ethics is a statement of abiding principles supported by additional explanations and position papers (at spj.org) that address changing journalistic practices. It is not a set of rules, rather a guide that encourages all who engage in journalism to take responsibility for the information they provide, regardless of medium. The code should be read as a whole; individual principles should not be taken out of context. It is not, nor can it be under the First Amendment, legally enforceable.

Interview with a Professional

Interviewed by Kelli Smith, Spring, 2017.

Nicholas M. Bowman, Ph.D., is an Associate Professor of Communication Studies at West Virginia University in Morgantown, WV. At WVU, he studies the psychology of mass media, including the uses and effects of interactive media such as social media and video games. Prior to his research career, he was a journalist in St. Louis, MO, where he covered various beats, including sports and civil litigation. He was part of a team that founded one of the first daily law newswires in the state, as an office with Courthouse News Service, and also helped CNS establish coverage in central and western Michigan.

How have the knowledge or skills you gained at a college or university been useful to you in terms of your career?

For me, it was learning that there is a basic science to the practice of communication—that it's not a magical process that some people are just "good" at and others, "bad" at it. More than anything, learning about theories such as face negotiation theory (which deals with how to manage conflict while protecting the self-concept of both parties) and Goffman's dramaturgy (which uses a theatre metaphor to explain human behavior) allowed me to be more thoughtful in my own communication with others—sort of taking an "internal audit" of how I handled past encounters so that I would be better at handling future ones.

What specific communication skills do you use the most in your field?

As a journalist—and even as a researcher now—perhaps the single most important communication skill is mindfulness: making sure that your focus and attention are completely on the person (or people) that you are talking to. You have to show them respect, but you also have to hang on almost every detail of the conversation because you never know what you'll need to refer to later. I work very hard to make sure that when I'm in a conversation with somebody, I am completely focused on her/him. Folks forget that communication is a receiver-oriented process, so it's most important that I demonstrate that I'm an active and attentive receiver.

Related to this, people also have to learn tact—that is, how to disagree or challenge others while still maintaining their face. Folks tend to engage communication as a contest or challenge and it's really not. It's the ultimate process of sharing and compromise.

Thinking back on your career choices, what decision are you most proud of? What do you wish you had done differently?

I tend not to be a very prideful person, so it's sort of tough for me to think of decisions that I'm most proud of. However, I do remember one of my very first assignments as a Regional Editor with Courthouse News Service—working the state-level and federal-level courts in St. Louis City and St. Louis County. Part of my job was to scour recent court filings for any civil lawsuits of interest (big companies and/or large amounts of money), but we noticed that in STL City that the cases were often very outdated—we were getting filings one or two weeks late, but as a newspaper, that's just not practical: one week is no longer news.

I proposed meeting with the county clerk (Mariano Favazza, who was actually running for mayor that year) and explained the issue to him. He was initially pretty skeptical and a bit dismissive (friendly, but didn't seem to be willing to help), but after a long conversation, I was able to convince him that reporter access to the court system was a critical component of an open court system. It would have been easy to have tried to sue him for access (such as a Freedom of Information Act case) or run an exposé or opinion column bashing him to the public, but I resisted: I explained to my colleagues that let's just hear him out and talk to him as a person. By staying mindful of him and his position in the courts but politely challenging his position (he was worried that our request would create a burden on his staff), we came to an agreement—in fact, he began requiring all attorneys to file a "media copy" of their cases in the STL courts: instantly turning the 21st Circuit of Missouri into one of the most open courts in the state.

Things I could have done differently? Oh brother … there are hundreds. I don't have an isolated story that I'd like to share (some are pretty embarrassing) but in general, I can think of so many times that I got into unnecessary conflicts with colleagues and rivals because I was too quick to jump to conclusions rather than hearing them out and making sure that I really understood the source of our conflict.

What advice would you give to Communication majors?

COMM majors have a really bad habit of not taking their own studies seriously. They buy into a rhetoric that "COMM is easy" and "COMM isn't really a science" and as a result, they tend not to take their classes seriously. I really despise this, and I often ask them, "if human communication were so easy, then why are humans so demonstratively terrible at communicating with each other?" We're all experienced communicators, but we've all got so much to learn about the psychological, interpersonal, and sociological processes that have such a dramatic impact on how we share messages with each other. I always push my COMM students to make sure that they truly "own" their degrees and major so that they can be successful.

Conclusion

Journalism plays an essential role in a democratic society. It provides citizens with the information they need to make the best possible decisions about their lives. As a journalist, you have the responsibility to seek and report the news in an ethical manner, remain impartial, and resist attempts to influence the news you cover. The skills that you acquire as a journalism student are applicable beyond the newsroom. Strong written and oral communication skills; research and information-gathering abilities; organizational, time management, and listening skills; and the ability to work both independently and collaboratively will serve you well in a wide range of jobs.

CLASSROOM ACTIVITY

Purpose: to practice writing headlines and leads that will draw readers to your story.

Recommended time: 15–20 minutes.

Think of a significant event in your life. It could be a fun, exciting event, a scary event, an accomplishment you are proud of, etc. Write a headline and lead for this event. Be sure to provide the essential information (who, what, where, when, why, how) that the reader would want to know. Use strong nouns and verbs, and avoid overusing adjectives and adverbs. Share your headline and lead with the class. Vote for the top three stories that make you want to continue reading.

DISCUSSION QUESTIONS

1   What news sources do you turn to when you want information? Why do you choose these media outlets instead of others?

2   Citizen journalism refers to newsgathering and reporting done by public citizens rather than professional journalists. What impact do you think citizen journalism has on professional journalism? What ethical issues should be considered when producing or consuming citizen journalism?

3   According to the old cliché, "If it bleeds, it leads." Basically, this means that stories that involve violence, injury, or death get higher ratings than other stories, so they get more coverage. As a journalist, how would you distinguish between stories that serve the greater good by making the public aware of a potential danger and stories that are sensationalized to gain attention and advertising revenue?

4   Tragedies and disasters often receive a lot of attention in the news. Although showing graphic images and grieving families can potentially raise awareness and prevent future tragedies, these images can be hurtful to the people connected to the event. How would you balance the public's need for information against an individual's right to privacy?

KEY TERMS

Gatekeepers—people within a news organization who determine what information is newsworthy and relevant to their audience and control what information is presented to the public.

Headline—eye-catching title that sums up a news story.

Inverted pyramid—an organizational structure, commonly used in media writing, in which the most important information is presented in the first paragraph of the story; nonessential information is presented in subsequent paragraphs.

Lead—the first paragraph of a news story that contains the most important parts of the story.

Nut graph—paragraph that follows the lead and provides additional details, quotes, statistics, etc.; it explains the subject of the story and why it is important.

Stereotype—an overgeneralization about a characteristic associated with a group or category of people.

REFERENCES

Kovach, B., and T. Rosenstiel. 2014. *The elements of journalism: What newspeople should know and the public should* expect (3rd ed.). New York: Three Rivers Press.

Neher, W. W., and P. J. Sandin. 2017. *Communicating ethically: Character, duties, consequences, and relationships* (2nd ed.). New York: Routledge.

Rubel, S. (2015). Storytelling in the age of social news consumption. http://www.edelman.com/post/storytelling-age-social-news-consumption/.

Schneider, D. J. 2004. *The psychology of stereotyping.* New York: The Guilford Press.

Society of professional journalists code of ethics. n.d. https://www.spj.org/ethicscode.asp.

CHAPTER 10

Public Relations

INTRODUCTION

Public Relations courses and extracurricular opportunities enhance a student's knowledge and skills in critical problem solving, creative idea development, reputation management, and research and measurement. The curriculum includes integrated communication planning, digital and social media marketing, strategic multiplatform writing, event promotion, and program development and prepares students for careers in a variety of increasingly integrated marketing communications industries. Students intern and secure careers working across a variety of industry sectors including fashion, sports, consumer, healthcare, food, travel, finance, entertainment, corporate, and many more.

PUBLIC RELATIONS AND THE APPLIED COMMUNICATION MODEL

Public Relations (PR) is part persuasion and part relationship building. A PR specialist aims to create a strong, positive, mutually beneficial relationship between her/his organization and the public. Public Relations programs help support an organization's business objectives, enhance its corporate reputation, drive sales, and even build a brand.

Public relations differs from journalism in several important ways (Wilcox, Cameron and Reber 2014). Journalists are objective observers that provide the pubic with news and information. PR professionals inform people, too, but they also try to change people's attitudes and behaviors to help an organization reach its goals. Also, whereas journalists write for the general public and rely on the medium that publishes or broadcasts their work to reach their audience, PR professionals tailor their messages to specific audiences and use multiple channels to reach the audience.

PR also differs from advertising (Wilcox et al. 2014). In advertising, organizations pay for space and broadcast time. They have complete control over the content, appearance, and time and place the advertisement appears. In contrast, PR materials are prepared and submitted to a news department, and the editor determines whether to use it or not and controls the final version of the information. In addition, PR relies on a variety of tools such as brochures, posters, special events, direct mail, and feature stories to reach the audience whereas advertising is accomplished almost exclusively through mass media outlets.

Public Relations Writing

As a PR specialist, you create a narrative that builds or enhances the reputation of a company or organization. This doesn't mean lying to cover for incompetent or corrupt clients (despite what you might think from watching television shows and movies). PR specialists aim to gain public trust by providing truthful information about the client. They want to promote and protect the client's image but not at the expense of the public's well-being.

There are several ways PR professionals can get information to their target audience. One way is by using mass media such as newspapers and television broadcasts to report the information. A **news release** is sent to news outlets and provides them with information that the company wants to make the public aware of. This could include announcements of events, new products or services, and policy changes. **Media alerts**, memos designed to inform reporters and editors about upcoming newsworthy events, are another tool PR professionals use to get information to audiences. This is more of an invitation to reporters and editors to get them to go to an event and write a story about it. A **pitch** is a short note sent to an editor along with a news release or media alert to get her/his attention and make her/him want to cover your story. Other channels for getting information to the target audience include brochures, newsletters, feature stories, annual reports, and letters.

Digital storytelling is another method that PR professionals use to transmit information to large audiences quickly and in a cost-effective manner. Digital storytelling is telling stories with a variety of multimedia tools. The following reading provides tips for writing stories that will be shared online.

THE ROLE OF STORYTELLING IN A DIGITAL AGE

by Barbara Bates

(http://www.prnewsonline.com/wp-content/uploads/2014/01/small-pg-6-SB-HS-Barbara-Bates.jpg) Companies spend an inordinate amount of time and money on creating exhaustive and fancy messaging matrices that often times sit on a shelf. But messaging is just the starting point. The corporate narrative is where the magic happens and for companies that get this right it can mean the difference between obscurity and breakthrough market leadership.

When former longtime *Barron's* reporter Mark Veverka and I first discussed collaborating on a new marketing practice built on the power of digital storytelling, we struggled with the word "content" because it has become so ubiquitous and lost some of its value as a descriptor.

One mistake that companies' make is to embark on content development without a narrative strategy in place.

Why is a narrative so important for companies to develop? The main reason is to capture your desired audience's attention.

People are drawn in by stories; they remember stories more than just facts and they are more likely to share a story, and thereby amplify your reach, via the most effective way possible: word of mouth.

The explosion of communications channels has created more storytelling opportunities, but it's also created some challenges. Not all story formats work through all channels, so matching your story length and type to the best channel improves readership.

Photographic stories work well on **Twitter**, short stories on blogs, longer features in print, etc. A few more key tips to keep in mind:

1 **It takes a combination** of good journalistic skills and creative writing to build compelling narratives.

2 **Think visually**. The old adage of a picture telling a thousand words really does ring true. And with today's information overload, visuals can often breakthrough the noise better than the written word.

3 **Follow the journalistic practices** of drawing from compelling story arcs that match your own story; the phoenix rising from the ashes, David vs. Goliath, the "can they make it," story or the ones with unexpected consequences. These are storylines that contain drama, and drama entertains.

4 **Take a page from your creative writing class** (or from Nancy Duarte's highly regarded book, "Resonate") and leverage the power of "the hero's journey." Based on the psychology of Carl Jung and the mythology research of Joseph Campbell, the hero's journey reveals the basic structure of numerous stories, myths and movies.

5 Think about breaking your "story" into separate chapters. Avoid the need to tell everyone everything all at once.

I mentioned the brilliant work of visual storyteller Nancy Duarte and her organization above. She just released her newest book, titled "Slidedocs." It covers the new paradigm of "shorter is better" business communications.

A "slidedoc" is a document created using presentation software, where visuals and words unite to illustrate one clear point per page.

One point Duarte makes early on in her book is that the Web and mobile communications have reconditioned people to prefer consuming information in small chunks.

And, not surprising considering her body of work, she underscores the importance of visuals. According to Duarte, the benefits of consuming clear and concise prose, combined with helpful visuals, include:

- Space limitations force a slidedoc's author to boil down the material to its essence. Done correctly, this makes the material clearer to the reader.
- Visualized ideas help the audience "see" what you're saying. When critical business decisions need to be made quickly, visually articulated concepts reduce the time to reach consensus.
- Time savings are achieved by allowing the audience to read the material instead of listening to it be presented.
- Consensus building is accomplished when people have time to discuss the material. After reading a slidedoc, people can gather to have conversations about it that create movement toward objectives.
- Shorter time to understanding happens with material that's been parsed, structured, and visualized.

While storytelling has been around for thousands of years, new rules are starting to emerge.

Since these are still early days for many of the newer storytelling disciplines, don't be afraid to experiment.

CONTACT:

Barbara Bates is CEO and founder of Eastwick Communications. She can be reached at barbara@eastwick.com (mailto:barbara@eastwick.com). This article originally ran in the March 3, 2014 issue of **PR News**. Read more subscriber-only content by becoming a **PR News** subscriber today (http://www.prnewsonline.com/about/info).

Other Essential Skills

Anyone who plans to have a career in PR should develop her/his skills in several key areas. In addition to the ability to write clearly and concisely, you need strong research skills. You must have the ability to gather information and keep up with current events to be knowledgeable about a subject. Strong organizational skills and time management are also important as you will have multiple clients and projects going on at the same time. This will require you to coordinate communication between the relevant parties, plan and coordinate activities and events, and make sure that materials are distributed on time all while staying on budget. Problem-solving ability is another skill that a PR specialist must have. You will be called upon to think of new, creative approaches to old ideas, so you need to be imaginative. Additional skills that you should develop include flexibility, attention to detail, and emotional intelligence.

Public Relations Ethics

PR professionals need to take the public interest, their employer's interests, and the standards established by the profession into consideration when making ethical decisions. They must also consider their personal values. The Public Relations Society of America has a code of ethics that should guide your professional behavior.

PUBLIC RELATIONS SOCIETY OF AMERICA (PSRA) MEMBER CODE OF ETHICS

Public Relations Society of America Member Code of Ethics 2000

- Professional Values
- Principles of Conduct
- Commitment and Compliance

This Code applies to PRSA members. The Code is designed to be a useful guide for PRSA members as they carry out their ethical responsibilities. This document is designed to anticipate and accommodate, by precedent, ethical challenges that may arise. The scenarios outlined in the Code provision are actual examples of misconduct. More will be added as experience with the Code occurs.

The Public Relations Society of America (PRSA) is committed to ethical practices. The level of public trust PRSA members seek, as we serve the public good, means we have taken on a special obligation to operate ethically.

The value of member reputation depends upon the ethical conduct of everyone affiliated with the Public Relations Society of America. Each of us sets an example for each other—as well as other professionals—by our pursuit of excellence with powerful standards of performance, professionalism, and ethical conduct.

Emphasis on enforcement of the Code has been eliminated. But, the PRSA Board of Directors retains the right to bar from membership or expel from the Society any individual who has been or is sanctioned by a government agency or convicted in a court of law of an action that is not in compliance with the Code.

Ethical practice is the most important obligation of a PRSA member. We view the Member Code of Ethics as a model for other professions, organizations, and professionals.

PRSA MEMBER STATEMENT OF PROFESSIONAL VALUES

This statement presents the core values of PRSA members and, more broadly, of the public relations profession. These values provide the foundation for the Member Code of Ethics and set the industry standard for the professional practice of public relations. These values are the fundamental beliefs that guide our behaviors and decision-making process. We believe our professional values are vital to the integrity of the profession as a whole.

ADVOCACY

We serve the public interest by acting as responsible advocates for those we represent. We provide a voice in the marketplace of ideas, facts, and viewpoints to aid informed public debate.

HONESTY

We adhere to the highest standards of accuracy and truth in advancing the interests of those we represent and in communicating with the public.

EXPERTISE

We acquire and responsibly use specialized knowledge and experience. We advance the profession through continued professional development, research, and education. We build mutual understanding, credibility, and relationships among a wide array of institutions and audiences.

INDEPENDENCE

We provide objective counsel to those we represent. We are accountable for our actions.

LOYALTY

We are faithful to those we represent, while honoring our obligation to serve the public interest.

FAIRNESS

We deal fairly with clients, employers, competitors, peers, vendors, the media, and the general public. We respect all opinions and support the right of free expression.

PRSA CODE PROVISIONS
FREE FLOW OF INFORMATION

Core Principle Protecting and advancing the free flow of accurate and truthful information is essential to serving the public interest and contributing to informed decision making in a democratic society.

Intent:

To maintain the integrity of relationships with the media, government officials, and the public.

To aid informed decision-making.

Guidelines:

A member shall:

Preserve the integrity of the process of communication.

Be honest and accurate in all communications.

Act promptly to correct erroneous communications for which the practitioner is responsible.

Preserve the free flow of unprejudiced information when giving or receiving gifts by ensuring that gifts are nominal, legal, and infrequent.

Examples of Improper Conduct Under this Provision:

A member representing a ski manufacturer gives a pair of expensive racing skis to a sports magazine columnist, to influence the columnist to write favorable articles about the product.

A member entertains a government official beyond legal limits and/or in violation of government reporting requirements.

COMPETITION

Core Principle Promoting healthy and fair competition among professionals preserves an ethical climate while fostering a robust business environment.

Intent:

To promote respect and fair competition among public relations professionals.

To serve the public interest by providing the widest choice of practitioner options.

Guidelines:

A member shall:

Follow ethical hiring practices designed to respect free and open competition without deliberately undermining a competitor.

Preserve intellectual property rights in the marketplace.

Examples of Improper Conduct Under This Provision:

A member employed by a "client organization" shares helpful information with a counseling firm that is competing with others for the organization's business.

A member spreads malicious and unfounded rumors about a competitor in order to alienate the competitor's clients and employees in a ploy to recruit people and business.

DISCLOSURE OF INFORMATION

Core Principle Open communication fosters informed decision making in a democratic society.

Intent:

To build trust with the public by revealing all information needed for responsible decision making.

Guidelines:

A member shall:

Be honest and accurate in all communications. Act promptly to correct erroneous communications for which the member is responsible. Investigate the truthfulness and accuracy of information released on behalf of those represented.

Reveal the sponsors for causes and interests represented.

Disclose financial interest (such as stock ownership) in a client's organization. Avoid deceptive practices.

Examples of Improper Conduct Under this Provision:

Front groups: A member implements "grass roots" campaigns or letter-writing campaigns to legislators on behalf of undisclosed interest groups.

Lying by omission: A practitioner for a corporation knowingly fails to release financial information, giving a misleading impression of the corporation's performance.

A member discovers inaccurate information disseminated via a website or media kit and does not correct the information.

A member deceives the public by employing people to pose as volunteers to speak at public hearings and participate in "grass roots" campaigns.

SAFEGUARDING CONFIDENCES

Core Principle Client trust requires appropriate protection of confidential and private information.

Intent:

To protect the privacy rights of clients, organizations, and individuals by safeguarding confidential information.

Guidelines:

A member shall: Safeguard the confidences and privacy rights of present, former, and prospective clients and employees.

Protect privileged, confidential, or insider information gained from a client or organization.

Immediately advise an appropriate authority if a member discovers that confidential information is being divulged by an employee of a client company or organization.

Examples of Improper Conduct Under This Provision:

A member changes jobs, takes confidential information, and uses that information in the new position to the detriment of the former employer.

A member intentionally leaks proprietary information to the detriment of some other party.

CONFLICTS OF INTEREST

Core Principle Avoiding real, potential or perceived conflicts of interest builds the trust of clients, employers, and the publics.

Intent:

To earn trust and mutual respect with clients or employers.

To build trust with the public by avoiding or ending situations that put one's personal or professional interests in conflict with society's interests.

Guidelines:

A member shall:

Act in the best interests of the client or employer, even subordinating the member's personal interests.

Avoid actions and circumstances that may appear to compromise good business judgment or create a conflict between personal and professional interests.

Disclose promptly any existing or potential conflict of interest to affected clients or organizations.

Encourage clients and customers to determine if a conflict exists after notifying all affected parties.

Examples of Improper Conduct Under This Provision:

The member fails to disclose that he or she has a strong financial interest in a client's chief competitor.

The member represents a "competitor company" or a "conflicting interest" without informing a prospective client.

ENHANCING THE PROFESSION

Core Principle Public relations professionals work constantly to strengthen the public's trust in the profession.

Intent:

To build respect and credibility with the public for the profession of public relations. To improve, adapt and expand professional practices.

Guidelines:

A member shall: Acknowledge that there is an obligation to protect and enhance the profession.

Keep informed and educated about practices in the profession to ensure ethical conduct. Actively pursue personal professional development.

Decline representation of clients or organizations that urge or require actions contrary to this Code.

Accurately define what public relations activities can accomplish.

Counsel subordinates in proper ethical decision making.

Require that subordinates adhere to the ethical requirements of the Code.

Report practices not in compliance with the Code, whether committed by PRSA members or not, to the appropriate authority.

Examples of Improper Conduct Under This Provision:

A PRSA member declares publicly that a product the client sells is safe, without disclosing evidence to the contrary.

A member initially assigns some questionable client work to a non-member practitioner to avoid the ethical obligation of PRSA membership.

PRSA MEMBER CODE OF ETHICS PLEDGE

I pledge:

To conduct myself professionally, with truth, accuracy, fairness, and responsibility to the public; To improve my individual competence and advance the knowledge and proficiency of the profession through continuing research and education; And to adhere to the articles of the Member Code of Ethics 2000 for the practice of public relations as adopted by the governing Assembly of the Public Relations Society of America.

I understand and accept that there is a consequence for misconduct, up to and including membership revocation.

And, I understand that those who have been or are sanctioned by a government agency or convicted in a court of law of an action that is not in compliance with the Code may be barred from membership or expelled from the Society.

_____

Signature

_____

Date

Interview With a Professional

Interviewed by Matt Crick, Spring, 2017.

Armando Triana is Social Media Director at Coyne Public Relations in New York. Armando has more than a decade of integrated marketing experience.

Why are good communication skills important in your field?

To have a successful career at a PR firm and in social media, you must have good communication skills. From writing emails to colleagues, speaking with vendors over the phone, and making presentations to clients, PR professionals must be concise and convincing.

What specific skills do you use the most?

I use interpersonal, public speaking, and writing skills every day. On an interpersonal level, I collaborate with colleagues on campaigns and must clearly talk through my ideas. I must convey those campaign ideas to clients to get their buy-in and must compile a written plan, speaking presentation, or both. I must then implement the campaign to the masses, developing such things as social media content, website landing pages, and influencer outreach materials, to ensure audiences engage with the campaign and it's a success.

I think it's advantageous for PR professionals to have a working knowledge of other disciplines, including marketing, advertising, and digital. Public relations is a much broader industry now. It's important for PR professionals to understand the larger picture of how earned, shared, and owned media work together to achieve business results.

What advice would you give to Communication majors?

Internships are a must. There are many different segments of PR, such as in-house, agency, consumer, business-to-business, and college internships are useful to explore these areas and help determine where you want to start your career. To best succeed in this ever-changing industry, have a plan and be persistent but also be flexible to new opportunities.

Thinking back on your career choices, what decision are you most proud of? What do you wish you had done differently?

I have an interest in the latest technology and jumped in as social media networks were first forming. I used these channels personally at first and quickly became the go-to person on how to leverage for client business. My career path has aligned with the growth of social media and it's importance in communication and marketing. I'm proud to have followed my passion and be able to do what I love every day.

Conclusion

Working in PR is challenging and rewarding. There are diverse career opportunities in education, nonprofit organizations, politics, entertainment, and corporations. The knowledge and skills you acquire are applicable in virtually all industries and interest areas. It's not all parties and schmoozing, but it gives you a chance to make a difference in an area that is meaningful to you.

CLASSROOM ACTIVITY

Exercise Objective: Create a pitch to increase sales of a product by attracting a NEW customer base.

1   Find a partner or work in a group of three, then, have someone from each pair or group select one object from the options provided by the instructor. (Instructors may provide items such as pens, lip balm, gum, wallets, a bottled beverage, etc.)

2   List potential "new" target audiences for the object you have selected. Potential target audiences may be identified by age, geography, income, interests, personality, etc.

3   How will you reach and influence your audience? What type of channel or platform would you use (e.g., media, social media, events, etc.)?

4   Come up with three strategies (the ways you will reach the audience) and three goals those strategies will help achieve. This information comprises the pitch. **STUDENTS MUST NOT RECOMMEND ADVERTISING IDEAS! NO PAID MEDIA!**

5   One person from each pair or group will present their strategies and goals (the PR Plan) to the class, and the class determines if it would "hire" that PR Group to be the PR firm to promote the product.

DISCUSSION QUESTIONS

1   What type of organization or individual would you most want to do PR for? Why?

2   How can using the Internet as a tool be beneficial to public relations professionals? What drawbacks might there be?

3   Imagine you work for a company whose reputation has been damaged because its employees were recorded making racist statements. What would you do to repair the company's image?

4   Which of the professional values described in the PRSA Code of Ethics do you believe is the most important? Why?

KEY TERMS

Digital storytelling—using computer-based tools such as images and audio and video clips to tell stories.

Media alert—an announcement that lets news outlets know of an upcoming event that you want them to cover.

News release—a document that is sent to news outlets containing the information that your client wants to share with the public.

Pitch—a letter that accompanies a news release or media alert that gains the attention of the reporter or editor and makes them want to cover your story.

REFERENCES

Bates, B. 2014. *The role of storytelling in a digital age*, from http://www.prnewsonline.com/the-role-of-storytelling-in-a-digital-age-by-barbara-bates/.

Public Relations Society of America. n.d. *PRSA member code of ethics*. http://www.prsa.org/resource-library/ethics/code-of-ethics/.

Wilcox, D. L., G. T. Cameron, and B. H. Reber. 2014. *Public relations: Strategies and tactics* (11th ed.). Boston, MA: Allyn & Bacon.

CHAPTER 11

Theatre and Comedy

INTRODUCTION

Theatre and Comedy students study both academic and artistic aspects of theatre and comedy. They learn to appreciate and understand performance history and theory as they read, critique, write, direct, and act in staged plays or comedy routines and skits. They also gain experience in production such as scenery construction and design, lighting and sound, costume and makeup, and backstage crew assignments. Theatre and Comedy courses prepare students for careers in the performing arts, of course, but they also prepare students for any career that requires strong communication skills.

THEATRE AND COMEDY AND THE APPLIED COMMUNICATION MODEL

There are similarities between dramatizations on stage and on screen. Just as in film and television, stage performances have actors, scenery, and costumes, and they elicit many of the same feelings as screen performances. Unlike in television and film, however, theatre takes place before a live audience. The actors influence the audience, but the audience also influences the actors.

Elements of Theatre

There are several basic elements that are common to all theatre events (Wilson and Goldfarb 2015). First, the **audience** and the **performers** are essential elements. The performers play characters and create the illusion of another place and time, and the audience accepts the illusion. Because theatre is a live performance, the audience and performers influence each other and shape the theatre experience. The next element is the **script**, which is the story that is performed. The **director** oversees rehearsals and gives guidance to the performers so that they have a shared interpretation of the script. The director also coordinates the work of the production team to ensure a quality performance. Another necessary element is the **theatre space**, which must include a stage and a place for the audience to sit or stand. **Design elements** include the scenery, costumes, lighting, and sound that complete the performance. Performances are divided into **acts**, major divisions between parts of the story. Each act features several **scenes**, which are shorter action sequences that occur in a single place and time.

Dramatic Genres

The two main dramatic genres in theatre are **tragedy** and **comedy**. Tragedy refers to plays that are serious in tone. *Oedipus Rex* and *Antigone* by the Greek playwright, Sophocles, and *Romeo and Juliet* and *Macbeth* by William Shakespeare are some famous tragedies. Comedy refers to plays that are light in tone and are meant to make the audience laugh. Shakespeare is also known for comedies such as *A Midsummer Night's Dream* and *Much Ado About Nothing*. Contemporary comedies include Neil Simon's *The Odd Couple* and Samuel Beckett's *Waiting for Godot*. Another form of theatre is **musical theatre**, which combines songs, spoken dialogue, and dance. They can be tragedies, comedies, or a combination of both. Famous musicals include *Oklahoma!* (1943), by Richard Rodgers and Oscar Hammerstein II, Claude-Michel Schonberg and Alain Boubil's *Les Miserables* (1985), *Rent* (1996), by Jonathan Larson, Stephen Schwartz and Winnie Holzman's *Wicked* (2003), *and* Lin-Manuel Miranda's *Hamilton* (2015).

Acting Skills Onstage and Offstage

Adapted from *Making Use of the Actor's Skills*

Theatre students learn a variety of skills that are not only essential in the performing arts but they can also be useful in your personal and professional lives. If you practice these skills in your everyday life, you can become more adept at reaching your communication goals.

Vocal skills: We can communicate a great deal of information by varying the rate, volume, pitch, resonance, and intonation of our voices. For example, you can use louder volume to convey power or a strong emotion and a faster speech rate to communicate excitement. You can emphasize important parts of your message with your voice to let people know that they should focus on them. By practicing control of these vocal qualities, you can become more effective at expressing your meaning and influencing your audience.

Physical skills: We can use our posture, body position, gestures, facial expressions, and level of eye contact to communicate messages to others. For example, a relaxed, open body position along with smiling and making eye contact with others can convey confidence and make you look approachable. Through practice, you can become more aware of your body and facial expressions and control them to project the image of yourself that you want others to see.

Concentration and relaxation skills: We have gotten used to multitasking and switching rapidly from one task to another. This can make it difficult for us to really focus on one thing for a long period of time. There are many times, however, when events, jobs, and relationships demand sustained concentration. Relaxing your mind and body prepares you to concentrate on the moment and the people you are with.

Improvisational skills: Improvisation involves speaking, moving, thinking, and acting without any planning or rehearsal. You can plan for the expected, but improvisational skills allow you to deal with the unexpected while still appearing confident and poised.

Empathy, the ability to take the perspective of others and to feel compassion for them, helps us to understand the people we interact with. It encourages our desire to help them and lets us think of potential ways to improve our interactions with them. The following skills help you develop empathy.

Observational skills: We learn a great deal of information by observing others. Observational skills allow us to gain insight into why people behave the way they do and develop greater empathy as we begin to understand each other better.

Imaginative skills: Imaginative skills allow us to create new ideas, solve problems in new ways, and visualize the experiences of another person. Like observational skills, imagination skills help us look at things from different perspectives and cultivate compassion for others. If you can understand another person's point of view, you can imagine potential ways to communicate with her/him successfully.

Character skills: Portraying a character that is different from yourself lets you consider things from another person's point of view. Acting as that character, you think, act, and respond to others differently than you normally would. Taking another person's point of view allows you to understand her/his situation, feelings, and behaviors so you can improve the quality of your interactions with her/him.

Comedy Studies

A growing number of universities are offering courses and even degrees in comedy. At first, it might seem a little strange to think of comedy as an academic pursuit. What do you study? Can you learn to be funny? What can you do with a degree in comedy anyway? Well, comedy courses are anything but frivolous. Students learn about comedy theory along with historical and cultural aspects of comedy. They also get a lot of practice in writing and performing comedy.

The following reading provides a brief overview of some theories of comedy and discusses the structure of comedy writing.

WRITING THE SIMPSONS: A CASE STUDY OF COMIC THEORY

by Edward J. Fink

Photo 11.1: *The Simpsons*, courtesy of Twentieth Century Fox, used in agreement with "FOX Network Sites Term of Use."

THERE HAS BEEN MUCH DEBATE OVER the reasons for the enduring success of Fox Television's long-running animated, prime-time comedy series *The Simpsons*, now in its twenty-fourth season (1989-present). The program satirizes contemporary American life, allowing us to see ourselves in the mirror of the absurd. It explores topics of the day, poking fun at the sitting president, going green, and the latest fads. It parodies our culture, including movies, TV shows, and pop songs, offering us laughs at inside jokes along the way. It is written tightly, with every word and action setting

up or delivering a joke or gag while moving the plot speedily from scene to scene, sometimes barely lingering long enough for viewers to get a joke (e.g., the sermon titles on the marquee in the cover shots of the church before cutting to the interior scenes). The list of reasons for its success goes on.

This article argues that another reason for the lasting popularity of *The Simpsons* can be found in comic theory. In an era of technological change and audience fragmentation, the prolonged success of this series reveals that theories of comedy still operate effectively for writers. Specifically, this article demonstrates that the show's writers incorporate every element of comedy in one way or another in every episode. The result is that each episode contains at least some humor to fit everyone's comic style. Everyone can laugh at *The Simpsons*, regardless of what that person normally finds to be funny.

It is doubtful that the writers of *The Simpsons* actually keep a list of the many types of humor that make up comic theory (e.g., incongruity, superiority). Certainly they do not consult a laundry list of how to write jokes (e.g., running gags, rule of thirds) when they hit writers' block. Rather, their years of creativity and experience as comedy writers in general, and for *The Simpsons* in particular, have resulted in their understanding comedy at a tacit level. They know the world of the imaginary Springfield so well, their characters in such depth, and the culture they are satirizing so thoroughly that they almost automatically include all types of humor in their scripts week after week.

EDWARD J. FINK is professor and chair of the Department of Radio-TV-Film at California State University, Fullerton.

To make the case that the writers of *The Simpsons* utilize the full gamut of comic theory in each episode, even if subconsciously, this article presents a case study of a single episode, though the argument can be applied to any episode. The episode selected for this analysis is "There's Something about Marrying" (season 16, episode 10, originally broadcast 20 February 2005).[1] This episode is somewhat representative in upholding the tradition of satirizing contemporary culture. It also contains many of the regular cast of characters. Additionally, it is noteworthy because it is the only episode that ever aired with a parental advisory, warning viewers, "This episode contains discussions of same sex marriage." The advisory does not air online, in syndication, or on the DVD series.

Act 1 opens with young Bart Simpson and his friend Milhouse attempting a prank, only to realize that the town folk are wise to their mischief. They need "fresh meat." A turnip truck drives by, and a man falls off, introducing himself as Howell Huser, a happy-go-lucky country bumpkin who travels about. The boys prank him multiple times, and he leaves, shaming the town. Howell next appears on television. He does travel features, and in this segment he gives Springfield a bad review. Immediately, the town's tourism dries up. The mayor calls a town meeting to discuss the problem. It is decided to legalize same-sex marriage to bring tourist dollars back to town.

Act 2 begins with Springfield's TV commercial for gay marriage. The cars roll in. The local pastor, Reverend Lovejoy, refuses to marry gay couples. Bart's father, Homer Simpson, realizes an opportunity to cash in and becomes an instant minister via the Internet. He moves beyond gay weddings, marrying anyone to anything, and is featured on the TV show *Smartline*. His wife's sister, Patty, appears at the Simpsons' home to announce that she is gay, asking Homer to marry her to the woman she loves. Her sister Marge, Homer's wife, has conflicting feelings about this.

Act 3 starts with tea as Marge unconvincingly attempts to come to grips with her sister's lesbian union. Patty brings her fiancée, Veronica, to meet the family. Veronica is a professional golfer, and the two met when Patty was a spectator at a tournament. Marge is less than enthusiastic. Patty asks Marge to accept her and to come to the wedding. Before the ceremony, Patty's identical twin sister, Selma, expresses her sorrow that she will now be alone. Patty comforts her, contrasting her with their sister Marge, who might not even show up for the wedding. Meanwhile, Marge happens by the bathroom with the door ajar, where she sees the toilet seat up and Veronica shaving her face. Veronica is a man! Marge attends the wedding, and all goes well until she finally objects. Patty is angry, thinking Marge cannot accept her marriage to a woman, but Marge points out the reason for her objection: Veronica's real gender. Veronica confesses all, stating that he disguised himself as a woman to play in the golf tournament, but that he really is in love with Patty and still wants to marry her. Patty declines, remaining true to her sexual orientation, reconciling with sister Marge, and walking off into the sunset with twin sister Selma.

This article analyzes this episode of *The Simpsons* by reviewing the theories of high and low comedy, incongruity, superiority, psychoanalysis (relief) of humor, and the structure of comedy writing. It is demonstrated that the writers of this episode apply each of these elements of comic theory in some way, as they do in all episodes of this series. The result is laughs for everyone, showing that the theories of comedy continue to be relevant for writers in today's technological society.

HIGH AND LOW COMEDY

Comic theory has its documentable origins in the ancient Greek theater. Aristotle analyzed dramatic poetry in his well-known *Poetics*, which focused on tragedy but which has relevance to comedy as well. His discussion of the six elements of drama set the stage for dramatic criticism: plot, character, theme, dialogue, music (sound), and spectacle. A host of analysts through the centuries have built on Aristotle's foundation and contributed much to the literature.

In the late nineteenth and early twentieth centuries, a modern theory of comedy began to take shape. Theorists looked at Aristotle and the classical comedies of the Greeks and Romans. They studied the works that followed, including the Renaissance traditions of the famed *commedia dell'arte* and its derivative characters, such as Harlequin, Pantalone, and Punch and Judy (Katritzky). They read the new comedies of their own era from writers such as Oscar Wilde (1854–1900), George Bernard Shaw (1856–1950), Anton Chekhov (1860–1904), and later Noel Coward (1899–1973). They began to view humor in two types: high and low comedy (Charney).

HIGH COMEDY

High comedy is sometimes referred to as the "comedy of manners," a term first applied to a genre of late-seventeenth-century British plays called "Restoration comedy" (Nettleton, Case, and Stone 149). This type of humor generates laughter through its sophistication, witty dialogue, subtle nuances, and character idiosyncrasies. It satirizes the upper class or "high society." The characters are usually wealthy, do not engage in much physical work, and have time to sit around and exchange educated banter. This high-brow comedy exposes the everyday foibles and quirks of the rich. We laugh because they are no better than we are, and maybe worse. We delight in their comeuppance. Their lives of ease turn out to be futile and silly.

Although *The Simpsons* is best known for its low comedy (next section), each episode contains some elements of high comedy as well. In this case study of "There's Something about Marrying," we hear some witty repartee in this brief exchange between Moe the Bartender and Sideshow Mel at the town meeting:

MOE: What's in a martini?
MEL: Gin and vermouth.

MOE: And that makes a what?
MEL: A martini.
MOE: Never heard of it.
A short time later …
MOE: Okay, now let's say I put a Lean Cuisine in a blender and I pour some beer on it. What do you call that?
MEL: A Lean Cuisiney?
MOE: Wrong.

Additionally, high comedy requires some intelligence on the part of the viewers to appreciate the humor. In *The Simpsons*, the audience needs to be knowledgeable of cultural references. For example, for the opening prank, Bart and Milhouse place a sign that reads "free beer" above a beer bottle, which is tied to a string that is secretly tied to a watermelon in the tree above. They hide while town drunk Barney approaches, but instead of falling for the prank, he remembers the "twelve steps." We understand this to mean the twelve steps of Alcoholics Anonymous. But instead, Barney takes twelve literal steps backward, runs to the bottle, and snags it while doing a flip, causing the watermelon to land harmlessly on the sidewalk. He then tells Bart and Milhouse, "Nice try, boys. Now, as the roadrunner said to the coyote, beep beep." This is an inside joke for those who know the Looney Tunes' Roadrunner and Coyote cartoons.

LOW COMEDY

In contrast to high comedy, low comedy involves more physical humor than dialogue. It often incorporates aggression and violence (Keough), but in a funny or "slapstick" context so that the characters are not truly or permanently harmed (more on that later) (MacHovec). Low comedy showcases burlesque, horseplay, and sight gags. It satirizes the uneducated "lower class." The characters fall down, hit each other, and exert great physical energy to get things that, of course, they fail to get. They demonstrate acts of stupidity. We laugh because we know we are better than these low-brow rubes, and when they suffer temporary pain, we enjoy their misery.

The idea of laughing at others' pain is codified in the German theory of *schadenfreude*, literally "harm joy" or "damage joy." It is our "pleasure in the misfortunes of other people" (Portmann 3), sometimes defined as "malicious glee" (28). We feel a mischievous satisfaction when we witness others suffer (as long as the harm is not lasting). We delight when others "fall from grace" (Takahashi et al.). The characters of low comedy endure physical pain and misfortune for the viewers' enjoyment. Their low life of physical suffering, like the high comedy life of ease, results in their comeuppance—to the delight of the audience. The old *Punch and Judy* puppet shows[2] and *The Three Stooges*[3] are examples of entertainment fare that relies heavily on low comedy, or slapstick, to please the viewers through schadenfreude.

It is worthwhile to note that some scholars discuss "mudita" as the opposite of schadenfreude. *Mudita*, from the Pali and Sanskrit languages, means "joy" and is often translated as "sympathetic joy" or "appreciative joy" (*Buddhist Studies*): the joy we experience from others' good fortune rather than misfortune. This joy is one of four "immeasurables" in the Buddhist tradition, along with love, compassion, and equanimity: positive attitudes to be cultivated toward others (*A View on Buddhism*). Applied to comic theory, mudita posits that we can experience joy not only when characters suffer (schadenfreude) but also when they succeed. Obviously, although mudita has applications to comedy, it is not exclusive to comic theory. Viewers can experience sympathetic joy at others' success in all types of storytelling, including tragedy, melodrama, and other types.

Returning to the broader concept of low comedy, every episode of *The Simpsons* is filled with physical, low-brow antics, including—but not always—some pain that lets the viewers experience schadenfreude, as well as some gain that elicits mudita. Examples of mudita in this "Marrying"

episode come when Homer successfully rakes in the cash as a minister who marries gay couples and when Marge, realizing her lesbian sister's fiancée is a man, dances a jig of joy because her sister will not marry the wrong person after all. For schadenfreude, Howell Huser (a parody of Huell Howser, host of a public TV series in California) literally falls off a turnip truck and is beaten with a stick by the *Creature from the Black Lagoon* (1954), tricked by finger-snapping gum, and stoned as he leaves town. Patty puts her cigarette out on Homer's hand and then in his eye, and then he stabs his own hand trying to kill a fly. Some nonviolent low comedy includes the sight gag of a salty sea captain who has an unholy alliance with a stuffed swordfish, a musical TV ad for Springfield's gay-friendly culture, and Homer's chapel sign announcing that he "will now marry anything to anything else—diaper fee for chimp brides." In brief, *The Simpsons* utilizes a great deal of low comedy while also incorporating elements of high comedy.

INCONGRUITY THEORY

Today, comic analysts generally cluster the many things that make us laugh into three broad categories. These are sometimes referred to as the three grand theories of comedy: incongruity, superiority, and psychoanalysis or relief (Berger, *Anatomy of Humor*; Meyer; Raskin; Scharrer et al. 619). Each is examined here in turn.

Incongruity theory encompasses humor that juxtaposes things in new or unusual ways. Often, a character faces a situation for which he or she is totally unprepared—a "fish out of water"—or some other match-up of things that do not belong together occurs. Whatever the incongruity, the unusual juxtaposition often catches viewers off-guard with visual or spoken jokes or gags that they did not see coming. They are surprised by something unexpected, illogical, absurd, or exaggerated (Berger, *Anatomy of the Joke*; McGhee). *The Simpsons delivers*.

FISH OUT OF WATER

When a character faces elements outside his or her normal world, the person becomes a "fish out of water." The fun ensues when the character attempts to deal with the new situation, by trying to adapt to it, overcome it, or get away from it. The characters in *The Simpsons* often find themselves in this predicament. In this episode, Howell Huser—normally happy-go-lucky—is beaten down by the boys' pranks. Reverend Lovejoy deals with same-sex marriage by turning a deaf ear. Homer becomes an ordained minister. Marge deals with conflicting feelings at the news that her sister is gay. In each instance, a character has to deal with something new, something with which he or she has no prior experience. In the hands of experienced comedy writers, these situations generate laughs.

UNEXPECTED SURPRISE

An element of surprise often lies behind the laughs of incongruity. In the "Marrying" episode, we do not anticipate town drunk Barney's athletic ability as he snags a beer out of a watermelon trap. We are surprised when newly ordained minister Homer prints out a punch-out clerical collar. We do not expect Lisa to obey her father's instructions to take over choking her brother Bart, and we laugh when she unenthusiastically does so.

SELF-REFLEXIVITY

Sometimes surprises include self-reflexive jokes: observations about a program within the program itself. For example, Homer telephones the Fox network, which he has on speed dial (another unexpected bit), to pitch a weak program idea, only to get a voice mail message poking fun at Fox TV shows. The self-reflexive gag is that *The Simpsons* is a Fox show. Another comic bit of self-reflexivity is the sight gag of Homer's map to stars' homes in Springfield, which holds on the screen for a whopping seven seconds of silence before Homer says directly to the viewers, in an incongruous breaking

of the normal third-person dialogue, "Have you read them all? Okay, good."

ILLOGICAL

Included in incongruity theory is the illogical. We laugh when something happens that we know just does not make sense. In this episode, Homer becomes a minister simply by typing his name into the e-Piscopal Church Web site, and out prints a clerical collar. Later, he has a fantasy in which he is married to himself, has babies, and makes out with himself—pure, delightful nonsense.

ABSURD

Related to the illogical is the absurd: the utterly silly or ridiculous. Howell Huser gets his revenge on Springfield for the pranks played on him by shaming the town and then giving it only a six out of ten on his rating scale of cities. The mayor opens the town meeting by saying, "As usual, I will open the floor to all crazy ideas that jump to people's minds." Different voices in the crowd respond with "stronger beer," "gladiator fights," "poetry slam," and "giant rats." It is a theater of the absurd in an animated sitcom.

EXAGGERATION

Comedy of exaggeration is part and parcel of incongruity theory. A three-eyed fish appears in the lake next to the nuclear power plant, only to stand up as the creature from the black lagoon. After Huser's scathing review of Springfield airs on the Soft News Network, Springfield is reduced to a ghost town within a superimposed time frame of only "one month later." Patty's supposedly lesbian fiancée, Veronica, turns out to have not one but an exaggerated three stereotypical gay names: Leslie Robin Swisher.

LOGICAL EXTREMES

Incongruity also means comedy of logical extremes. The sea captain, in his extreme loneliness, seems ready to marry anything, be it a stuffed swordfish or, in the closing tag, the wooden maiden from his ship's bow. In Homer's quest to "marry anything to anything else," he marries the Reverend Lovejoy to his Bible.

STEREOTYPES

Stereotypes also fit into incongruity theory. Comic writers rely on stereotyping when they need a quick gag and have neither the time nor the need in a story to create nuance through dialogue or subtle characterization. The stereotyped characters often appear quickly, with the incongruity stemming from their juxtaposition with other story elements. In this episode, the gay television commercial that opens act 2 relies on a host of homosexual stereotypes (e.g., a same-sex couple holding hands while skipping) that are incongruous with what we normally expect to see in a TV ad. Marge's flashback montage to Patty as a young girl shows Patty engaging in stereotypical lesbian behavior: she dresses up in construction clothes; she puts up a poster of the androgynous Miss Hathaway from *The Beverly Hillbillies*; and she makes out with a girl at the movies. In brief, *The Simpsons* is loaded with all types of incongruous humor.

SUPERIORITY THEORY

Another of the three grand theories of comedy is superiority. We laugh, outwardly or inwardly, openly or suppressed, when we feel better than or triumphant over others (Berger, *Anatomy of Humor*; Feinberg; Grotjahn; Gruner, *Understanding, Game*; Meyer; Morreall, *Taking*; Rapp; Ziv). *The Simpsons'* writers engage comic superiority theory in every episode.

META-TEXTUAL

Superiority theory works on the levels of both meta-text and context. On the meta-textual level, we viewers—standing outside the world of *The Simpsons*—look into that world and feel superior. We laugh at Homer's buffoonery because we know we are all smarter than he is. In fact, nearly every character in town, with a few exceptions such as

Lisa, is a fool. In this episode, no one can be as stupid as the mayor with his absurd running of a town meeting and his ad-libbed warning in the gay commercial to avoid the Jefferson Avenue exit ("For God's sake, do not take that exit!"). None of us would marry our own sister, as stereotypical hillbilly Cletus marries his (maybe) sister, Brandine. Who among us would be so foolish as to go on television and admit we used "non-diseased meat from diseased animals" in our "whatcha-ma-carcass" sandwich, as Krusty the Clown does?

CONTEXTUAL

In addition to the meta-textual viewers laughing through their superiority at the inferiority of *The Simpsons* characters, those characters within the context of *The Simpsons* world often generate laughs via superiority theory as well. At this contextual level, Lisa Simpson, eight years old and moved up from the second to third grade, is arguably the smartest person in all of Springfield. In this episode, she demonstrates her superiority to the viewers as the only person at the town meeting who has a plausible idea to bring back tourists: legalize same-sex marriage. Kent Brockman, the news anchor for *Smartline*, sometimes has moments of intelligence and sometimes not. Here, when "Reverend" Homer requests that the newsman call him "Your Holiness," Brockman's relative intelligence compared with Homer's leads him to respond, "I can't; I just can't."

Often Marge Simpson demonstrates intelligence superior to that of others, with the laughs coming from her exasperation when no one will listen. In this episode, she attempts to engage Reverend Lovejoy in a debate over the biblical context of marriage, but Lovejoy ignores her by ringing the church bell. Additionally, it is Marge's conflict and character arc that ultimately make her the protagonist of this episode. She has thought through the issue of gay marriage and supports it. However, upon learning that her sister Patty is a lesbian and wishes to marry a woman, Marge is conflicted, reasoning intelligently but not convincingly, "I love you. I love gay marriage. So I'd be a super hypocrite if I didn't love your gay marriage, right?" Ultimately, she accepts Patty's lesbianism, and she does not have to give Patty up when it is revealed that Patty's fiancée is a man, whom Patty refuses to marry because she likes girls.

DIALOGUE

The humor of superiority is revealed, as all things are revealed in screenwriting, through two elements: dialogue and action. The spoken words and the characters' behaviors show who is superior and who is inferior. In this episode, we laugh as the stupid Patty engages the even stupider Homer in this witty banter (high comedy) of put-downs at the door:

> PATTY: Hey, saturated fats, I came to ask you a favor.
> HOMER: Let me get my belt sander. Maybe I can grind the ugly off your face.
> PATTY: Very funny.
> HOMER: I wasn't joking.

He reaches off screen and gets a belt sander (action resulting in visual humor, a sight gag).

In another dialogue exchange, Marge, knowing that Veronica is really a man and not wanting Patty to get hurt, stands up to object to the wedding.

> MARGE: No, I can't let this happen!
> PATTY: I knew it. You think everyone in the world should have a big dumb man—like you.
> HOMER: People, please, can we wrap this up? It's gonna rain, and I gotta get the bikes in here.
> MARGE: Patty, it's not what you think. Veronica is a man!

Marge tears the collar off the dress, revealing Veronica's Adam's apple.

In another example, Homer's inferiority and stupidity are revealed when he becomes an instant minister via the Internet and is immediately distracted by the computer screen. He excitedly says, "Now to answer all the pop-ups. Ooh, a talking moose wants my credit card number. That's only fair." Additionally, when son Bart comments that his mother, Marge, got married to "the first blimp that floated by," Homer—seemingly unaware that he is referring to himself—retorts, "Correction: the first blimp who got her pregnant."

ACTION

In terms of action, this episode, like all episodes, reveals Homer's (and others') imbecility in numerous ways. For example, Homer gives Patty a homemade wedding veil, which is just a paper bag with some lace, and when Patty comments that it smells like cheeseburgers, Homer grabs it back to take a sniff. Later, Homer uses a knife to kill a fly on his hand. In another scene, Homer chokes Bart and then has Bart's sister, Lisa, take over the choke hold while he answers the door.

Often, Homer is portrayed as inferior through helplessness. Patty puts out a cigarette on his hand in response to his joking that Marge should be more worried about his leaving her for a "sausage patty" than her "sister Patty." Patty then warns Homer, "Next time it'll be your eye." Sure enough, in a later scene, she puts a cigarette out in his eye in response to his put-down that her meeting Veronica was like a scene in the movie *Bride of the Monster* (1955).

AGGRESSION AND VIOLENCE

These examples demonstrate that aggression and violence are often part of superiority theory. Sometimes the aggression is verbal, as in the insults and put-downs quoted previously. Other times, the violence is physical, including beatings and pain, as in the cigarette gag, first on the hand and then in the eye. Humorous violence or aggression has long been a part of the superior-inferior relationships in comedy (Keough; MacHovec), even though pain and laughter rarely occur simultaneously in real life, representing "a psychologically incongruent combination" (Mustonen and Pulkkinen 183). Whether the humor is violent or not, and whether it is revealed through dialogue or action, *The Simpsons'* writers gleefully apply both meta-textual and contextual superiority theory in all their scripts.

PSYCHOANALYTIC OR RELIEF THEORY

According to the psychoanalytic or relief theory of comedy, laughter releases nervous energy, sometimes caused by forbidden feelings (Freud, *The Joke*; Schaeffer). It is catharsis theory applied to comedy. People laugh at action and dialogue that reduces their stress in some way (Berlyne 50–53; Morreall, *Comic Relief*). Shurcliff notes, "[T]he greater the subjects' anxiety prior to relief, the greater … the judged humor" (362). This theory, like superiority theory, also relates to violence. Scharrer et al. observe, "[P]eople laugh at things that make them uncomfortable (e.g., aging, violence) or guilty (e.g., sex). Freud (1922) contended that watching painful acts being inflicted on others allows for a release of one's own hostilities and hidden desires, thereby allowing for pleasure" (619). The same can be said for watching sex. *The Simpsons* is chock-full of this psychoanalytic humor, or laughter through relief.

GUILT

What secret guilt causes us to laugh at this episode? There is sex, of course—the topic is gay marriage. Psychoanalytic theory posits that we feel guilt and then release it through laughter as we watch men kissing men in the Springfield pro-gay TV ad, or Homer kissing Homer in his thought-balloon fantasy, or the girl-girl kissing of young Patty or older Patty and Veronica on the couch. Then, too, there is violence. We feel guilty and then laugh for relief as we see Howell Huser take a beating or watch the flashback in which Patty is struck in the eye by Veronica's golf club. In addition to sex and violence, other depictions can bring about feelings of guilt, such as religion. We feel guilty about and consequently laugh at Homer's sacrilege when he mockingly marries Reverend Lovejoy and his Bible, or when he prays to God to bless "another gay union that angers you so."

DISCOMFORT

Related to guilt is the broader concept of all types of discomfort. According to psychoanalytic theory, any feelings of discomfort can bring about laughter as relief. We might be a little uncomfortable at the beginning when two boys set up a prank for their next unsuspecting victim. In the middle, we might squirm a bit as Homer mocks Marge for not knowing her sister is gay by sarcastically quipping, "Hey, Marge, here's another bomb—I like beer!" At the end, we might feel a bit of discomfort as Patty and twin sister Selma plan to "go to the airport and leave a bag unattended" because that's "a good way to meet security personnel."

NO LASTING HARM

A significant part of psychoanalytic theory is the longstanding comedy rule that there can be no lasting harm. If characters are truly hurt or killed, and the pain or death is lasting, then we cannot laugh; we can only feel sympathy, or pathos. To be sure, comedy draws us into a story with sympathetic portrayals of characters who elicit pathos. In this episode, we feel for Marge as she struggles with her sister's lesbianism. But in comedy, any harm done to a principal character—someone we get to know well enough to be emotionally invested in him or her—can be only temporary and nonfatal. We laugh at Howell Huser's beating because he only gets some cuts and bruises and is okay in the end to go on TV and trash-talk Springfield. We laugh at Homer getting a cigarette on his hand and in his eye because we know his hand will be fine, and he will be able to see again in the next scene. We laugh at Patty's not getting married because she is not left devastated but is saved from marrying the wrong "man."

HAPPY ENDING

These examples of "no lasting harm" reinforce the notion that comedy must have a happy ending. To be sure, characters can suffer some temporary harm along the way, but in the end everything turns out for the best. In *The Simpsons*, at the end of each episode, life returns to normal (or what passes for normal) in Springfield. Homer ends his wedding business. Patty and Marge reconcile. Patty reunites with twin sister Selma, and they walk off into the sunset. This happy ending, in which any harm during the episode is revealed to have been only temporary, is a hallmark of comic theory. From the psychoanalytic perspective, people are able to find humor in others' pain, as well as view sex, sacrilege, aggression, or other depictions that make them feel uncomfortable or guilty, because they can laugh at these depictions to release their hidden or forbidden feelings. Comedy provides a catharsis, or relief, from their stress. The writers of *The Simpsons* provide ample situations that allow viewers to laugh through their discomfort.

STRUCTURE OF COMEDY

This article has explored comic theory, from the early notions of high and low comedy to the current categorization of humor into three broad theories: incongruity, superiority, and psychoanalytic (or relief). Although these concepts shed light on the types of depictions that make us laugh, equally significant to the comedy writer is how to structure comedy. It is important to analyze and apply the methods to set up and carry out comic dialogue and action.

SETUP AND PAYOFF

One significant notion in all writing is the setup followed by the payoff. For regular viewers of *The Simpsons*, the opening title sequence is already a setup because they know each opening has a few changes unique to that episode (e.g., the words that Bart writes on the chalkboard, Lisa's saxophone solo, and the billboard ad in the later high-definition opening). Depending on the final length of the

episode, sometimes the opening is the full sequence, opening with clouds and moving to an aerial shot of Springfield, and sometimes it is truncated (as is the case in this episode), moving from the opening clouds directly to Homer driving into his driveway. Whatever the case, the opening always ends with the couch gag, in which the Simpsons family ends up on the couch in front of the TV in some unusual and unique way. In this episode, the couch gag already pays off the audience: the Simpsons are bruised hockey players with missing teeth.

THREE-ACT STRUCTURE

Beyond the opening titles, the standard three-act structure of any teleplay or screenplay is used to set up dialogue and action in the viewers' minds and then to pay them off. All writers know that a story must have a beginning (act 1), middle (act 2), and end (act 3). *The Simpsons* delivers once again.

This "Marrying" episode, consistent with the program's tight writing style, covers lots of ground at a rapid pace in each act. The speed of the action from one scene to the next is accelerated, sometimes moving almost too fast for the viewers to get a joke (e.g., Homer's "marry anything to anything" sign with the gag at the bottom that there is a "diaper fee for chimp brides"). Each act sets up character traits and plot points that are paid off later.

Act 1 sets up Howell Huser as a gullible visitor, who gets his payback via a bad review of Springfield. That sends the town into decline, setting up the meeting at which the payoff to increase tourism is legalizing same-sex marriage. Act 2 sets up Springfield as "welcoming gays since 2005," as the street banner reads (the episode aired in 2005). However, Reverend Lovejoy refuses to participate, setting up Homer Simpson to get paid off, literally, by becoming an instantly ordained Internet minister and performing gay weddings, or weddings of "anything to anything else." Patty arrives, revealing her lesbianism, setting up a conflict in her sister Marge. Patty's request that Homer perform her wedding to Veronica sets up the climactic scene of act 3—the final gay wedding. The wedding day arrives, with the lingering question of whether Marge will accept her sister's lesbian union and attend. The payoff is that she does. Then, in a climactic turn of events, Marge reveals that Patty's fiancée, Veronica, is really a man. Patty's beloved confesses and asks Patty to marry him as a man. She resolutely refuses, remaining single but true to herself, spared a marriage to the wrong "man." In the denouement, the audience is paid off again as everything returns to normal: Patty and Marge embrace, and Patty and Selma reunite and walk off together.

DIALOGUE

Just as the three-act structure itself is carefully crafted with setups and payoffs, individual lines of dialogue and actions are also well-constructed in the setup/payoff pattern. An example of dialogue setting up a later revelation occurs when Patty introduces Veronica to the family and they later kiss. Marge covers baby Maggie's eyes and tells the lesbian pair, "Whoa, save something for your wedding night." Veronica responds, "Oh, we're saving *everything* for our wedding night." As she speaks, the animators shift her eyes mischievously three times, as if she's keeping a secret. Of course she is, and Veronica's foreshadowing line of dialogue and shifting eyes are paid off when Marge spots Veronica in the bathroom with the toilet seat up, shaving and singing "Dude (Looks Like a Lady)." Having discovered that Veronica is a man, Marge chuckles and says, "Looks like Patty's going to get something she didn't register for."

ACTION

In terms of action, an example of the setup and payoff structure is Homer's pondering how much money he could make by marrying gay couples. He quips, "These people have rights— the right to buy me a sixty-two-inch TV!" The camera perspective then widens to reveal that he is carrying an anti-gay marriage picket sign, which he throws in the trash. This visual setup and payoff uses incongruity theory. A man protesting gay marriage changes his mind instantly when he realizes he can make money, and off he runs to become an online minister.

RULE OF THREES

In addition to the classic setup and payoff structure of writing, another useful element of comic structure is the "rule of threes." This age-old convention remains current and in use because it always works and is sometimes necessary to set up the punch line of a joke or gag of a sight gag. According to the rule of threes, two items set up a pattern, and then a third item pays it off. In this episode, Homer gets wounded three times in poking accidents. The first time, Patty puts out a cigarette on his hand. The second time, she flicks a cigarette into his eye. The third time, he jabs his own hand with a knife (off-screen) to kill a fly.

RUNNING GAGS

Related to the rule of threes is the running gag (though sometimes twice is sufficient, and four or more times can work as well). A running gag is something seen and/or heard that happens once for humor and then is repeated later for a second laugh, and maybe a third time or more for an additional laugh or two. In this episode, the watermelon is a running gag, first set up as a trap for an unsuspecting drunk, at which time Milhouse clarifies that it is a seedless watermelon. When Howell Huser arrives, he sees the splattered watermelon and asks the boys if they want to plant the seeds, displaying disappointment when Milhouse explains again that it is seedless. Sideshow Mel is also a running gag. He first appears at the town hall meeting to exchange witty banter with Moe the Bartender. He appears again at the wedding to deliver an important line of dialogue, in case the viewers miss the visual. Pointing to Veronica after Marge rips off "her" dress collar, Mel exclaims, "Look at the size of that Adam's apple!" Another running gag is the sea captain, who shows up at the town meeting with a stuffed swordfish in hand and in the tag with a wooden maiden from a ship's bow.

In addition to these "intra-episode" running gags, *The Simpsons* offers some "inter-episode," or series-long, running gags. Two are in this episode. One is Homer choking Bart—a gag that recurs in a number of episodes throughout the seasons. A second is Nelson stepping into the frame to utter his mocking catch phrase, "Ha-ha." Here, he utters his "ha-ha" as a gag response to Marge's argument with Reverend Lovejoy that she thinks God does not care if two people who love each other have the same "hoo-hoo" or "ha-ha."

DOUBLE WHAMMY

Another useful structure for a comic gag is the double whammy. This is a verbal or sight gag that has two punches instead of one. A double whammy in this episode is Homer's map of stars' homes. When the map is revealed in close-up, the first whammy is the silliness of the thing: a child-like drawing of streets and houses that shows, among other things, a "Hunny Tree" (Winnie the Pooh), an X that marks a "good place for a Denny's," and a "scary rock." That first visual whammy of the map is followed seven seconds later by a second aural whammy, which is Homer's punch line directly to the viewers: "Have you read them all? Okay, good."

INNUENDO AND DOUBLE ENTENDRE

Innuendo and double entendre have been part of comic structure since the beginning. Innuendo is a veiled reference to something sexual. No actual sexual object or action is stated or depicted, but the context of the sentence hints at something sexual. In this episode, when Marge comes across Veronica in the bathroom preparing for the wedding and discovers that she's a man, Marge quips, "Looks like Patty's going to get something she didn't register for." In contrast, a double entendre is the actual statement of an object, action, or dialogue that has

a double meaning—the translation of "double entendre"—and one of the two meanings is sexual. Here, Marge says to Reverend Lovejoy, "As long as two people love each other, I don't think God cares whether they both have the same hoo-hoo or ha-ha." Though the words "hoo-hoo" and "ha-ha" have no meaning of their own, in this context they refer to male and female genitalia.

ONE-LINERS AND PUT-DOWNS

Another structure for comic writers is the one-liner: a word or a brief phrase or sentence that draws laughter. As expected, *The Simpsons*' writers use these regularly. In this episode, the reference to a Krusty fast-food product as a "whatcha-macarcass sandwich" serves as a one-liner. Another comes when Marge is surprised to learn that her sister Patty is a lesbian, and Patty declares, "You could see it from space, Marge!" Yet another is Homer's salutation at the start of Patty's wedding: "Queerly beloved." Sometimes a one-liner is also a put-down in which one character asserts superiority over another. Here, one-liner put-downs include Patty's address to Homer as "saturated fats" and his rejoinder that he will get his belt sander to "grind the ugly off [her] face."

SIGHT GAGS

Sight gags are also a useful element of comic structure. Here, one example is Homer's gift to Patty. He tells her he picked out a wedding veil just for her: a homemade "do not feed" sack with two eyeholes cut out and a veil glued on. Other sight gags include the title of Milhouse's trick gum—Troublemint—and Homer's envisioning gay couples as $100 bills. *The Simpsons*' writers regularly employ all these elements of comic structure, many of them perfected through millennia of use, because they are time-tested to set up and deliver laughs.

CONCLUSION

This article has analyzed an episode of *The Simpsons* as a case study to construct the argument that the writers of this ongoing and classic TV series utilize all elements of comic theory and structure in every episode. This explains, in part, why the show continues to appeal to a large audience. This analysis further demonstrates that all the elements of comic theory remain relevant and useful for today's comedy writers in a world marked by increasing technological innovation and fragmenting audiences.

Contemporary comic theory dates back to the nineteenth-century dichotomy of high and low comedy, which built on earlier traditions, from Aristotle to *commedia dell'arte* to Restoration comedy. The creators of *The Simpsons* employ both high and low comedic elements in "There's Something about Marrying," as well as in every other episode. The viewers laugh at the characters' occasional witty repartee and experience schadenfreude at the characters' misfortune, as well as "mudita" at their occasional good fortune.

Additionally, *The Simpsons*' writers use the current three grand theories of comedy in force. This episode and others have numerous moments of incongruity, such as when characters find themselves to be fish out of water. Unexpected occurrences, revelations, and self-reflexive jokes surprise us. The illogical and absurd entertain us. Exaggerated characters and actions, including logical extremes, drive us to laughter. Stereotypes shortcut the story, taking it directly to a punch line or gag by relying on our commonly held conceptions and misconceptions.

Superiority is used for laughs. Meta-textually, we viewers recognize our superiority over Homer and the other ignoramuses who populate the fictional Springfield. Contextually, Lisa's superior intelligence—and sometimes others' intelligence relative to the village idiots—generates humorous situations. Through dialogue and action, the writers reveal who is superior and who is inferior, frequently and deftly employing aggression and violence, all the while creating laughs.

Psychoanalytic theory, also known as relief theory, helps explain our laughter as a catharsis, or purging, of hidden and forbidden feelings and desires. We feel guilty watching same-sex couples kiss, so we giggle. We are uncomfortable at Homer's blasphemy, so we chuckle. We feel bad that Howell Huser gets beaten up, so we laugh. In the end, however, no one suffers any long-lasting harm, and the world of Springfield is happily returned to its version of normal.

The structure of this and other episodes of *The Simpsons* also employs the full gamut of comedy writing guidelines. The writers use the traditional three-act structure, with tight writing and accelerated action to maintain a fast pace, thereby delivering a number of setups and payoffs each week. The "rule of threes" regularly sets up punch lines and sight gags. Running gags, both intra-episode (within each episode) and inter-episode (across multiple episodes), add to our enjoyment. An occasional double whammy delivers twice the laughs in one joke. Innuendo and double entendre are employed for sexual humor. One-liners, including put-downs, add to our satisfaction. Sight gags regularly spice up each show. In sum, the writers of *The Simpsons* demonstrate that the elements of comic theory and structure continue to be vital to the writer's craft in this age of multiple storytelling technologies and venues.

NOTES

1   Before delving into this article, I recommend that readers view *The Simpsons* episode "There's Something about Marrying" (season 16, episode 10, original airdate 20 February 2005). A search should provide links to sites that stream this episode.

2   For more about *Punch and Judy*, visit http://www.punchandjudy.com/.

3   For more about *The Three Stooges*, visit http://www.threestooges.com/.

REFERENCES

Aristotle. *Poetics*. 335 BCE. Trans. Gerald F. Else. Ann Arbor: U of Michigan P, 1970. Print.

Berger, Arthur Asa. *An Anatomy of Humor*. Piscataway: Transaction, 1999. Print.

———. "Anatomy of the Joke." *Journal of Communication* 26.3 (1976): 113–15. Print.

Berlyne, Daniel E. "Humor and Its Kin." *The Psychology of Humor*. Ed. Jeffrey H. Goldstein and Paul E. McGhee. New York: Academic Press, 1972. 43–60. Print.

Buddhist Studies, Unit Six: The Four Immeasurables. Buddha Dharma Education Association and BuddhaNet, 2008. Web. 1 June 2012.

Charney, Maurice. *Comedy High and Low: Introduction to the Experience of Comedy*. 2nd ed. New York: Peter Lang, 2005. Print.

Feinberg, Leonard. *The Secret of Humor*. New York: Rodopi, 1978. Print.

Freud, Sigmund. *Beyond the Pleasure Principle*. 1922. Whitefish, MT: Kessinger, 2010. Print.

———. *The Joke and Its Relation to the Unconscious*. 1905. New York: Norton, 2003. Print.

Grotjahn, Martin. *Beyond Laughter: Humor and the Subconscious*. New York: McGraw-Hill, 1966. Print.

Gruner, Charles. R. *The Game of Humor: A Comprehensive Theory of Why We Laugh*. Piscataway, NJ: Transaction, 1999. Print.

———. *Understanding Laughter: The Workings of Wit and Humor*. Lanham: Rowman & Littlefield, 1979. Print.

Katritzky, M. A. *The Art of* Commedia*: A Study in the* Commedia dell'arte, *1560–1620, with Special Reference to the Visual Records*. Amsterdam: Rodopi, 2006. Print.

Keough, William. "The Violence of American Humor." *What's So Funny? Humor in American Culture*. Ed. Nancy A. Walker. Wilmington: Scholarly Resources, 1998. 133–43. Print.

MacHovec, Frank J. *Humor: Theory, History, Applications*. Springfield: Thomas, 1988. Print.

McGhee, Paul E. *Humor: Its Origin and Development*. New York: Freeman, 1980. Print.

Meyer, John C. "Humor as a Double-Edged Sword: Four Functions of Humor in Communication." *Communication Theory* 10.3 (2000): 310–31. Print.

Morreall, John. *Comic Relief: A Comprehensive Philosophy of Humor*. Hoboken: Wiley-Blackwell, 2009. Print.

———. *Taking Laughter Seriously*. Albany: State U of New York P, 1983. Print.

Mustonen, Anu, and Lea Pulkkinen. "Television Violence: A Development of a Coding Scheme." *Journal of Broadcasting & Electronic Media* 41.2 (1997): 168–89. Print.

Nettleton, George H., Arthur E. Case, and George Winchester Stone Jr., eds. *British Dramatists from Dryden to Sheridan*. 2nd ed. Carbondale: Southern Illinois UP, 1975. Print.

Portmann, John. *When Bad Things Happen to Other People*. New York: Routledge, 2000. Print.

Rapp, Albert. *The Origins of Wit and Humor*. New York: Dutton, 1951. Print.

Raskin, Victor. *Semantic Mechanisms of Humor*. New York: Springer, 1984. Print.

Schaeffer, Neill. *The Art of Laughter*. New York: Columbia UP, 1981. Print.

Scharrer, Erica, Andrea Bergstrom, Angela Paradise, and Qianqing Ren. "Laughing to Keep from Crying: Humor and Aggression in Television Commercial Content." *Journal of Broadcasting & Electronic Media* 50.4 (2006): 615–34. Print.

Shurcliff, Arthur. "Judged Humor, Arousal, and the Relief Theory." *Journal of Personality and Social Psychology* 8.4 (1968): 360–63. Print.

Takahashi, Hidehiko, Motoichiro Kato, Masato Matsuura, Dean Mobbs, Tetsuya Suhara, and Yoshiro Okubo. "When Your Gain Is My Pain and Your Pain Is My Gain: Neural Correlates of Envy and Schadenfreude." *Science* 323.5916 (2009): 937–39. Web. 1 June 2012.

A View on Buddhism. N.p., 2 Nov. 2011. Web. 1 June 2012.

Ziv, Avner. *Personality and Sense of Humor*. New York: Springer, 1984. Print.

Types of Comedy

Steve Kaplan (2013) writes, "Comedy is the art of telling the truth about what it's like to be human" (14). He points out that everyone has flaws and weaknesses. We all do stupid things and mess up sometimes. Kaplan argues that "Comedy helps us live with who we are" (20) because it reminds us that all of those things are what make us human.

Comedy comes in several different forms. In **sketch comedy**, a series of short scenes called sketches are performed by a group of comic actors. Sketches are usually less than ten minutes long. *Monty Python's Flying Circus, In Living Color, Kids in the Hall, Chappelle's Show*, and *Saturday Night Live* are just a few examples of sketch comedy shows. **Improvisational comedy**, or improv, consists of performances that are made up on the spot. Improvisation comedy clubs such as Gotham City Improv and television shows like *Whose Line is it Anyway?* feature improv performances.

Stand-up comedy involves comedians who speaks directly to the audience. Their routines usually include funny stories and some jokes and one-liners. Some comedians use props in their performances. The comedian's performance can affect the audience, but audience's reactions also affect the comedian. If the comedian fails to deliver laughs, the energy level in the room can drop considerably, resulting in an unsuccessful performance.

Storytelling is important when writing stand-up comedy. As Jared Volle in *How to write stand-up comedy with storytelling* explains, you learn how to write stand-up comedy stories by thinking of a story that you already tell people, identifying the most important parts of the story, and editing out the unimportant parts so that you are left with a story that includes only the best parts. The goal is to capture and maintain the audience's attention, build up a little bit of tension, and deliver the punch line.

Scholars and academics have begun to explore the potential social benefits of comedy. The next article discusses how comedy routines may be good for more than a few laughs.

READING 11.2

THE SCIENCE OF COMEDY: CAN HUMOR MAKE THE WORLD A BETTER PLACE?

Academics are Considering how Comedy can be Socially Beneficial

by Stuart Jeffries

"You know what's not funny?" said the comedian Chris Rock once. "Thinking about it." As if to prove the point, last weekend's Playing for Laughs symposium at De Montfort University in Leicester brought together academics, practitioners, educationalists and service providers to investigate how comedy can be used as a force for good within communities in Leicester and beyond. Laugh? Not often, but thanks for asking.

Thinking about comedy is becoming a big academic industry. Last year, Dr Sharon Lockyer set up the *Centre for Comedy Studies Research* at Brunel University, London, and even an academic journal, *Comedy Studies*, published in print for the first time later this year.

The speakers at De Montfort University included comedian and adoption campaigner *Joy Carter* discussing how comedy can be used to tackle

issues of transracial adoption; Karian Schuitema of the University of Westminster discussing the role of comedy for children with special needs; and Liselle Terret, of Coventry University, on how comedy could be used to challenge social ideas on women and the mental health system.

Tell me a joke, I ask one of the speakers at the conference, Geoff Rowe, founder and producer of Dave's Leicester *Comedy* Festival. "I don't tell jokes," he replies. "I pay professional comedians to do that for me." Oh dear. Oh well. Here's mine: How many comedy conference delegates does it take to tell a joke? A not inconsiderable number.

I never said it'd be funny."Over the last five to eight years there's been a shift in the public perception of academics studying comedy. It's becoming regarded as a worthwhile area," says Lockyer before her symposium talk entitled Exploring *Comedy* and Disability in Live Performance. Comedian Jo Brand, the Brunel alumna who is the CCSR ambassador says it is "great to see that comedy is being taken seriously".

Perhaps it is, but what's most intriguing about Lockyer's work is that it considers how comedy can be socially beneficial. "The media fixates on comedy controversies where comedy has been deemed to be problematic or offensive," says Lockyer. "You can see that in the controversies over the Danish cartoons depicting Muhammad, the film Borat and what it did to Kazakhstan, and Jonathan Ross and Russell Brand."

Those examples seem to bear out venerable theory of comedy set out by the Chuckle Brothers of philosophy, Plato and Hobbes, namely that we're always laughing at someone else's expense. Or, as Hobbes put it in Human Nature: "The passion of laughter is nothing else but sudden glory arising from some sudden conception of some eminency in ourselves, by comparison with the infirmity of others, or with our own formerly." Thus understood, comedy isn't just Mock the Week, but invariably mocks the weak.

But must it? Psychiatric-nurse-turned-comic *Rob Gee*, one of the speakers, says: "Every joke has a target and therefore every joke has the potential to be cruel or hurtful. It also has the opposite." But what could that opposite be? Gee has organised award-winning workshops in sports centres and acute psychiatric units aimed at adults with severe and enduring mental health problems, and is often invited to schools to teach kids improvisation and sketch performances. He says: "The idea that comedy could be therapeutic or give people skills seems absurdly worthy, but that's exactly what I've been trying to do."

When Gee visits schools to give comedy workshops, he finds the best students of comedy improvisation are nine year olds. Why? "They're already a little worldly wise but they aren't yet concerned about being cool like adolescents are. So they're very creative and unafraid and savvy. Some teachers run scared of allowing comedians to teach their kids, but they shouldn't be so sceptical." Why not? "Think

of what a huge problem it is getting boys to read and write. When I teach kids about sketch comedy, they love to write down their sketch ideas. It's one of the few times you can see them enjoying writing. So learning how to do sketches helps improves their literacy, their confidence, their self-esteem."

What would Michael Gove say? "It's the antithesis of the traditionalist view of what should be happening in schools, but given that most of the jobs that our kids will be doing in the next 50 years haven't been invented yet, it seems important to train kids to be flexible, have self-esteem, be literate, rather than follow a traditional curriculum—comedy can help with those things."

But still, the idea of comedy as socially beneficial remains a stretch. "It's counterintuitive, I agree," says drama lecturer Roger Clegg, who organised the symposium. "But think of it this way. Most standup comedians started in the playground when they were bullied. It starts off as a defence mechanism and ends up as empowerment. That's why it can be a force for good."

"What I've really noticed in my research," says Lockyer, "is a rise in the bullied or demonised or oppressed taking ownership of comedy directed at them, subverting it and using it to make people laugh with rather than at them." Her latest academic paper Exploring the Potential of Disabled Comedians in Improving the Lives and Experiences of Disabled People consists of interviews with disabled comedians and their audiences. "In the past eight years there's been a rapid rise in the number of really talented disabled comedians. I think one big impetus was the foundation of a group called *Abnormally Funny People* set up by Simon Minty in 2005. They did a really successful Edinburgh run. Thanks in part to them, some disabled people have seized that sense of empowerment comedy can give them.

"That said," Lockyer adds, "I'm not saying comedy can change the world for the better."

But maybe it can. Maybe it already has. "Remember those HIV campaigns in the 1980s with TV ads showing tombstones and icebergs?"

asks Leicester comedy festival's Geoff Rowe. "When I was a teenager I didn't get my education from those ads or from government leaflets, but from comedians. It was Lenny Henry, French and Saunders, and Rik Mayall doing things with condoms and cucumbers who really educated me."

Thirty years on, Rowe runs the Big Difference Company, that similarly tries to use comedy to raise awareness of social, health and environmental issues. "We do projects to improve public health and reduce health inequalities. That can mean projects to do with quitting smoking, alcohol, healthy eating and we often work with the NHS to targeted groups—primary-school children, minority groups and men."

But isn't there an inverse relationship between funny and informative? When Rowe hires professional comedians to do comedy routines about cancer, surely it isn't the subject matter but the prospect of being subjected to improving messages that is liable to be a turn off? "You'd think so but some of the best comedy shows I have been to have tackled cancer. They're really life affirming and positive experiences."

In collaborating with the NHS, Rowe's professional comedians are often required to perform sets in front of health professionals to make sure the material is medically accurate. "They are the toughest critics and those are probably the worst gigs anyone will ever play. But they're worth it. After public gigs, members of the audience will come up to me or the comedians and say, 'I think I've got lung cancer,' and we can be a signpost, directing them to the medical people who can help."

The late Monty Python's Graham Chapman notwithstanding, Leicester hasn't exactly a reputation for comedy excellence, but now it is at the forefront of using comedy to remedy social ills. "Other cities specialise in dance, theatre, music or film. For good or ill, I hope good, Leicester specialises in comedy," says Rowe.

Mark Charlton is project manager for Square Mile, De Montfort University's programme to improve local lives with academic expertise. In one sense it's a typical outreach project of the kind that many British colleges and universities run to make themselves relevant to the local community. But one of its 40-odd projects is unusual. "We asked people in Leicester what they would like from us," says Charlton. "And quite a lot said standup comedy workshops. Why? "Some were determined to become standups but others in the group wanted to boost their confidence and self esteem and make themselves feel good about themselves."

The 15-week course is now in its second year, with DMU alumnus Alan Seaman from Leicester's Ship of Fools comedy club taking on residents with no performance skills and training them to become stars of their own show—or at least perform a 10-minute routine at a local community centre during the comedy festival.

"It's not just standups but a really diverse bunch. One's a really aggressive performance poet and another's quite a gentle poet in the Pam Ayres vein," says Charlton. "Another's a sharp-suited well-spoken Jimmy Carr-like comedian—all great in their own way."

But how can you gauge whether the course has been successful? "Only from feedback from the participants and that's been overwhelmingly positive. We're thinking of taking the course further and putting on a show in Edinburgh at some point. What really struck me is that two of the people who took part had quite severe mental health problems but the rest of the participants became very protective of them. And there were all these people from different parts of the community—different races, occupations, classes, ages—all coming together." Pro vice-chancellor and dean for art, design and humanities of De Montfort University Barbara Matthews says: "If you think about the sense of community comedy gives, then I think Leicester is benefiting from projects like this one and that will evolve over the years."

For Roger Clegg a lot of these comedy initiatives have a topical political significance. "If they're not the encapsulation of David Cameron's Big Society I don't know what is." If Britain is broken as the prime minister suggests, maybe comedy can help repair it.

Interview with a Professional

Matt Locker, Professional Actor.
Interviewed by Matt Crick, Spring 2017.

Why are good communication skills important in on-camera acting and presentations?

Well, it boils down to WHY you are on camera in the first place. In one form or another, it's to tell a story. It's all about storytelling. Someone with good communication skills is going to be a better story teller. In terms of acting, the actor's job is to serve the script- to tell the author's story as effectively as possible.

What specific skills do you use the most?

I cannot underscore enough how the core basics of "acting" are essential in story telling. It begins with script analysis, even where there is no script. What is your objective? WHY is this material important? Who is the one person you talking with? What is your specific relationship with this person? What are your obstacles and what is the best approach to get around the obstacle? It's all about relationships. For me, each camera lens I have met over the last 30 plus years is the "same person", we have built a relationship, have our in-jokes, and know each other's secrets.

What skills do you find lacking in others?

Knowing "why" we do and do not do things in the medium. Before the age of digital ease, creating a television image was an expensive, labor intensive effort which required tapping our full creative mode. The blank canvas, or "video space" was only filled with elements which assisted in telling a story. When a news anchor did a story on "X", the only elements seen and heard related to supporting that story. Today, we have anchors talking about "X", which the screen is filled with information on "Y, Z, K, Q, and P". As the human mind can only focus on one idea at a time, this is very ineffective communication. This is an extension of why radio DJ's do not talk over vocals, the brain can hear only one or the other. The "old schoolers" had a clearer understanding of the history of the medium, what worked and why. I fear that is lost in favor of digital eye candy. Tell one story at a time.

How has what you've learned on the job and as a University student helped you succeed?

In today's age where everyone who has an iPhone thinks they can be a film maker. A thorough understanding of "The Medium Is the Message" by Marshall McLuhan is a must. I can take the identical script, same actors, and shoot the same scene on three different mediums and tell three different stories. What helped me succeed was I was fortunate to enter college with a head start, having worked production at a CBS affiliate prior to school. The concept of "broadcast quality" was seared into my head. If a project fell short of broadcast quality, it did not go out. Today, my "brand" of work is known for high standards, and I have a reputation for being fiercely protective of the medium.

What advice would you give Communication majors?

First, take some acting classes, and augment with improv classes. Improv classes are scary as hell, but when you find yourself in front of a live mic or camera, and all hell breaks loose … and it will … improv classes prepare you capitalize on the situation, rather than be stammering with egg on your face. The "YES, AND" rule needs to be reflex action. Secondly, start your financial planning right away. It's a fickle business, and you need a good savings account for the lean times. Jumping from city to city is the norm, and you'll need to always have a reserve for first month, last month, and security deposit on hand. Put money away now! Third, take English and writing classes. Remember, we are in the business of storytelling.

What are you most proud of professionally and what do wish you'd done differently?

Two distinct moments of pride. At the age of 16, I showed up at our local CBS station and asked if I could watch how TV was done. I didn't leave. I was a sponge, and was eventually hired. WBNB-TV was destroyed by Hurricane Hugo in 1989, but everything I learned there still makes up a big portion of my creative soul. More recently, I landed a role in, "Powder Burns West: An Original Audio Western Drama". It's a old-school radio serial, done in a contemporary way. The audience "sees" the story through the eyes of Sherrif Burns, who is blind. The show came along when I was starting to have doubts about myself, and the next thing I know I am in the old west working with the likes of David A. Gregory (One Life To Live, The Good Fight); John Wesley Shipp (The Flash, Dawson's Creek); and a cast of supportive, like minded brethren. Very proud of that project. Differently? Wish I saved money.

Conclusion

Theatre and Comedy is a challenging and exciting major. Theatre and comedy courses provide a way for you to explore your creative side and develop technical and performance skills that you can use onstage, behind the scenes, or in a completely different line of work. Through performance, you learn to control your body and voice to present yourself in the way that you want to be perceived. Improvisation teaches you to think quickly and adapt to unexpected situations. Playing different characters improves your ability to empathize with others. The skills and confidence you gain will be helpful to you no matter what career path you take.

CLASSROOM ACTIVITY

Purpose: to practice using your imaginative, improvisational, and character skills.

Recommended time for activity: 20–30 minutes.

Find an interesting object, and bring an object to class. Get into groups of three. As a group, think of a story that involves a character seeing and/or using all three objects. Come up with a detailed description of the character. What is her/his background? Where is she/he when she/he interacts with the objects? What is she/he doing? What do the objects mean to her/him? Each group will then share its story with the class.

DISCUSSION QUESTIONS

1. Think of a live performance (play, musical, or comedy show) that you've seen. Did you enjoy it? Why or why not? How did seeing it live differ from watching a television show or movie?

2. What is empathy? Why is it important for us to have empathy for others?

3. Which of the comedy theories described in the Fink reading appeals to you the most? Why?

4. Comedians sometimes include material that makes the audience a little uncomfortable even while it is laughing at the jokes. Some people may be offended by jokes about issues such as race, sexuality, weight, class, politics, etc. Do you think "offensive" humor should be avoided? Why or why not?

KEY TERMS

Act—major divisions between parts of the story in a play.

Audience—the people who are there to watch the performance.

Comedy (theatre genre)—plays that are meant to make the audience laugh.

Design elements—scenery, costumes, lighting, and sound.

Director—the person who supervises rehearsals.

Improvisational comedy—comedy performances that are made up at the time of the performance.

Musical theatre—a form of theatre that combines songs, spoken dialogue, and dance.

Performers—the actors who play characters and put on a performance.

Scene—a short action sequence that occurs in a single place and time.

Script—the story that the actors perform for the audience.

Sketch comedy—a form of comedy in which a series of short scenes called sketches are performed by a group of comic actors.

Stand-up comedy—comedy routine in which the comedian speaks directly to the audience.

Theatre space—the location in which the performance takes place; it must include a stage and a place for the audience to sit or stand.

Tragedy (theatre genre)—plays that are serious in tone, often featuring a hero or heroine who has a tragic flaw that leads to her/his downfall.

REFERENCES

Kaplan, S. 2013. The hidden tools of comedy: The serious business of being funny. Studio City, CA: Michael Wiese Productions.

Volle, J. n.d. How to write stand-up comedy with storytelling. Retrieved from http://www.creativestandup.com/how-to-write-stand-up-comedy-storytelling/.

Wilson, E., and A. Goldfarab. 2015. Theatre: The lively art (9th ed.). New York: McGraw-Hill.

CHAPTER 12

Using the Applied Model in Your Academic and Professional Career

INTRODUCTION: THE APPLIED COMMUNICATION MODEL REDUX

You'll recall that we described a useful communication model for you in the first chapter called the Applied Communication Model. You are at the center of this model. Whether it's communicating with your sister, your boss, or writing and producing a full-day fashion show for Breast Cancer Awareness, we believe the four principles of the Applied Communication Model—story, audience, ethics, and skills—are powerful, practical and explain how communication careers connect. We also hope that we've made clear throughout this book that applying all these principles, as an expert might do, isn't really what *everyday* communication is about.

What's important is that you integrate the Applied Communication Model's core principles into your daily life and workplace, practice them in whatever form fits the job or the moment, and seek to become better at creating messages and communicating with the people you meet.

For many readers right now, there is one very important life stage rapidly approaching—the internship search. In this final chapter, we'd like to highlight internship search strategies through the Applied Communication Model "lens," offer some advice on effective email and phone strategies, and give you concrete suggestions that will help you on the road to success.

The Internship Search—Writing Emails

Other than communicating face-to-face well during an in-person interview, which is the most important step during the internship or job search process, writing a good email is an essential skill. There are many resources on how to write a good email, but we've provided several fundamental tips and a few observations in the upcoming section.

Expert Email Writing Advice: Academic

Authors Corrigan and McNabb point out that "Instead of jumping right into your message or saying 'hey,' begin with a greeting like 'Hello' or 'Good afternoon,' and then address your professor by appropriate title and last name, such as 'Prof. Xavier' or 'Dr. Octavius'" (Corrigan and McNabb 2015) and include items like a subject line. Dr. Crick asks his students to state a clear need in the email subject line and include the word *urgent* or *important* if necessary. However, he clearly defines the difference between those two words and reminds students that it's okay to not include them if it's not necessary. Avoid writing an email as if you are texting, no emojis, "idk," "lol," "jk," or :0, ☺, or elaborately designed responses like =^.^=. Also, many professors become concerned when students demonstrate a lack of caring in class or display a sense of entitlement. For instance, if you're late a lot, don't turn in work, or miss class, it *appears* as if you don't care. Now imagine being perceived this way by your professor, and she/he opens the following email from you, "Hey, I missed class last week. What did I miss?" ☹

In "Dear Student: My Name Is Not 'Hey,'" Assistant Professor Stacy Patton voices her frustration (Patton 2015), explaining that the familiarity some of her students have in email communication is more like how a friend or sister would write. She considers this a major issue, especially as a person of color, and considers that in predominantly white classrooms, "the message implies that instructors like us are more laid back … that we don't have to be shown the same respect" (Patton 2015).

Expert Email Writing Advice: Professional

There's not much difference between an academic themed email and a professional email. Most professors expect a similar level of professionalism and tone in your missive even if it's your first college or university level course. As you know, emails are a large part of professional communication, too, and poor email habits and skills can have far reaching consequences.

Poorly written emails can have influence beyond an internship or job interview. Email etiquette, or **netiquette** as it's called, can influence human lives. For instance, in 2010 during the Deepwater Horizon BP oil spill in the Gulf of Mexico, an engineer who was on Deepwater rig wrote an email to a manager about controversial decisions he needed to make regarding closing a deep water well. Unfortunately, the email message was a rambling essay that included personal (non-work related) information and was more like something you'd find on social media (Ward 2016). The engineer's manager replied that he was going dancing and would get back to the engineer the following day. The engineer should have called the manager or expressed the problem more seriously. If you don't know what happened shortly after the aforementioned email was sent, just search for "Deepwater Horizon."

When writing your internship email, avoid the pitfalls you've just read about and include the following customized approaches. First, do your research. Carefully read the internship description to find out the specific name and title of the person in charge of the department for which you'd like to work and the specific details of the internship position. For smaller companies, there may not be a human resources person, and you'll contact the person you would eventually work for, but larger companies have a Human Resources person who will be the first person to read your resume.

Second, customize your email text with the specific words that are used in the actual internship description. If the email reads, "skills in Photoshop, writing press releases, and expert Adobe Premiere editing skills required," you would carefully and cleverly weave something about Photoshop, press releases, and Adobe Premiere into your email. Don't copy what was in the job description *word for word* as that indicates you're a bit lazy.

Third, include the job description or job code in the subject line of your email along with your name.

Last, if you're applying to a large corporation and you can locate a valid email for *anyone* in the department you'd be working in, you can use the company's **naming convention.** For instance, if you know the first and last name of the contact you need at the company and the naming convention is "crickm@wpunj.edu" or "m.crick@whateverworks.com," you can just fill in the name in the correct way. Of course, you take the risk that you're clever but unsolicited email won't be received well. On the other hand, if you can't get a response from anyone, this strategy can work.

Below are some examples of well written and poorly written email examples.

A Well Written Professional Email

Dr. Crick,

I just had a few questions about the upcoming assignments.

I saw the updated due dates for the last two assignments, and I just wanted to clarify a few details.

1. Assignment one doesn't specify a particular format for the document. Do you have requirements for font style, spacing, font size, etc.?
2. I'm not sure about whether to include camera angles in my TV script or even how to do that. Can I meet with you during your office hours to discuss this?

Thanks for your time. I appreciate it.

Student Name

A Poorly Written Professional Email

Hey professor I was wondering if you think it's necessary for me to come into class tomorrow?

Sent from my iPhone

The above email was sent via mobile phone. It's a real email. This is more and more common, and having your emails **pushed** to a mobile device is great; it's an efficient way to manage your communication. However, take the time to put in your name and contact information in the body of the email. An email like the one above seems to be sent as a second thought, not well written and, frankly, a silly question.

EMAIL STRATEGY: ETHICS, AUDIENCE, STORY, SKILLS

It's not possible to cover all the great approaches to writing effective and strategic emails; there are many resources available to you. But you should approach and use the available resources and research on writing emails carefully. Stay away from nonacademic sources, i.e., "Sarah's Blog" or "BestEmailsEver.com." Remember that unless you're reading content on a professional or academic site, the source of that content may not be peer-reviewed or vetted at all. There are hundreds of legitimate and professionally scrutinized sources available; it's not in your best interest to click on the first hit Google returns.

Throughout this book, each chapter has connected one or more of the Applied Communication Model principles to a specific communication discipline and career. Along those lines, we've outlined how the Applied Communication Model can be used when writing emails regardless of the recipient. This is a smart and strategic approach to writing an email that could mean the difference between an internship or job interview or another summer working at a job you don't like, like cleaning dog cages, something Dr. Crick did one Spring Break back in the day.

Emails and Ethics

Simply put, be genuine and authentic when you write an email. Don't pretend to be someone or something you're not. Eventually, you may meet the interviewer face-to-face and whatever pretense or sham, however small, could easily be brought to light. For example, if you've presented yourself in an email as someone who has written press releases or articles, you should bring them to the interview; it's likely you'll be asked about the work you did, and concrete, "in-the-flesh" examples are powerful in an interview.

Emails and Audience

If you're applying for an internship, it's not typical the person reading the email is like you in terms of age, socio-economic status, ethnic/racial background, etc. … It makes sense to think carefully about how the person reading your email will read and understand your written words. Write the email for your audience, and talk about internship specifics. In the moment the hiring manager or producer is reading your email, the email itself is the only thing you have in common at least as far as you know. Your audience isn't 18 years old and might be as old as 50! Do you know how to communicate, in writing, with someone who might be two and half times your age? There are many examples of email communication available for you if you do the research.

Emails and Story

Many internships and also jobs don't even ask for cover letters anymore. Liz Ryan, writing for the leading business resource, *Forbes*, points out that there's not much use for the cover letter as a job hunting tool when online applications are common and "recruiters and hiring managers in their blogs … admit that they don't even glance at cover letters" (Ryan 2016). *Huffington Post* writer Harry Bradford says, "Really … most cover letters are kind of a waste of time. They tend not to give a good sense of the candidate, and they can be super boring to read" (Bradford 2015).

These days, the storytelling job, when it comes to your internship search, must begin with your email. When we use the word *story* in this context, imagine that the person looking at your email reads about 300 emails a day as part of her/his job. This person is ready for a good story! Be authentic, be honest, and be professional. A great way to start an email is to avoid anything like "I found your internship posting on. ..." You found it? It sounds like you spotted a dollar bill in the street. Perhaps you were surfing the web for the latest **DLC** for *Doom* and happened upon it? In one fell swoop, in the first sentence, you have diminished the importance of your email communication, devalued the company, and possibly demeaned a complete stranger.

Emails and Skills

Simply put, the most obvious skill you'll need for emails is the ability to write a short, clear, and interesting communication with the goal of getting an interview. That's it. If you're email is too familiar, contains spelling or grammatical errors, or isn't customized for the position you want—the person reading your email knows that you've just "copied and pasted" an email for another job.

Good internship and job search strategy, like any other kind of strategy for life success, takes time and careful attention. It's better to write five great emails for internships you really want than 20 "copy and pasted" emails with name changes that don't tell a story and aren't tailored to the specific internship opportunity. By the way, don't forget that if you send emails or resumes through online companies like **LinkedIn** or **Indeed**—before a human being even reads what you've written—the content you submit is matched to a database with specific internships or job requirements. If you don't include the right combination of words and phrases, your resume or email communiqué will end up floating in Internet space forever.

THE INTERNSHIP STRATEGY: ON THE PHONE

In *The Millennial Generation Research Review*, published by the U.S. Chamber of Commerce, 80% of millennials sleep with their cellphone next to their bed (Seppanen 2012). Even so, it might surprise you to know that for many millennials—those born between 1980 and 1999—talking on the phone can be an anxiety producing, frightening, and life-interrupting experience. Talking on the phone is quickly becoming a lost art, and many jobs, like sales professional, associate producer for a television network show, and many other professions, require interaction on the phone. In the workplace, if you ignore a phone call or choose to email someone instead (Hofschneider 2013), this can hurt a business or even a potential internship. Frankly, in professional communication fields, you will always need to talk with someone in person, and the rapport you build can mean the difference between getting a great interview or a promotion. Think of it this way, calling someone on the phone and getting to know her/him is far easier than meeting someone in person for the first time.

According to research, there is some clear evidence regarding the difficulty associated with talking on the phone. For example, millennials haven't used the phone as a significant and daily form of verbal communication. Because of this, millennials feel a sense of pressure in having to respond immediately, as you would on the phone, be warm and friendly, and clearly communicate goals (Sugar 2015). Still, if you want to get that internship, you'll need to interact "live" with a person eventually. Why not practice and prepare for that interaction? Today, interviews over the phone and via Skype or some other video/audio technology are common. Below are some suggestions on good phone strategy that could help you land the internship and maybe later a job.

Good Phone Strategy

Email is great for sending out something quickly, like a meeting invitation or answering a simple question. But email isn't good at conveying emotion even if you include the ☺; the reader won't actually *feel* your warm and pleasant nature. Calling someone on the phone is a much better way of conveying your personality, your friendliness, and your excitement about an internship. A phone call represents a sincere effort to build a relationship. Think of it this way: if the majority of your generation aren't using the phone for the reasons mentioned, your choice to actually make a phone call, instead of sending an email, is a potential advantage for you in the job market.

Plan on what you're going to say during a phone call. Having specific goals you'd like to achieve is critical. When it comes to an internship, the goals might be (1) introducing yourself and making sure your resume and materials got to the right person; (2) establishing a rapport with someone inside the company; (3) getting the specific phone number and/or email of the hiring person; and (4) requesting an appointment to meet with the hiring person. Whatever your plan, make sure that after you hang up the phone, you have something from your conversation other than a sick feeling in your stomach.

In terms of good phone strategy, the last thing to remember is that phone calls can and will go badly just like face-to-face conversations. It's important to move on and understand that everyone has a bad day. Learn from the experience, and try to figure out what went wrong so it doesn't happen again.

Phone Techniques to Help Get an Interview

There are a few great phone techniques we wanted to highlight that can help you secure an in-person interview for an internship and handle a phone interview.

As you might have experienced, sometimes phone interviews will happen out of the blue and with more than one person listening on the other line. No one knows the future, so how can you prepare for this possibility? Researching the company in advance and making sure you can talk about the company is a great start. Also, you can practice talking about the company with someone you know, like a professor or classmate who really wants to help you.

While it's best to be able to schedule a phone call, if you're watching Netfilx or you're at work and you get a phone call, go find a quiet place to talk. If you absolutely cannot be interviewed over the phone when the call comes in, politely ask to reschedule the interview. Even if it's an hour later, this delay could be all the time you need to get ready. Take notes during the phone call, just the main ideas, and be sure to have information about the company handy. Last, avoid selfish questions like "how much is the salary" until you're offered the job (DeCarlo n.d.) Are you kidding? You haven't even gotten the interview yet. Besides, it's best to ask about salary only when the interviewer brings it up. That way, you can say, "Well, since we're talking about salary …"

PHONE STRATEGY: ETHICS, AUDIENCE, STORY, SKILLS

As we've discussed, your warmth and authenticity come through best over the phone. There is no form of written communication—certainly not emails—that can replace the sound of the human voice. As in the case of email communication, imagine your phone call with the core principles of the Applied Communication Model in mind.

Phone and Ethics

How can a phone call be unethical? The most obvious answer is lying to the interviewer over the phone. When the moment comes that you're asked a question, and you don't know the answer, pause before you respond. It's perfectly fine to start with, "I'm not really sure about that, can I think about it for a second?" This strategy will give you time to collect your thoughts and come back with an honest and authentic answer. Your voice will also sound more natural and not strained and tight because you're trying to fake it.

Phone and Audience

When you make a call, you're talking to someone from the company. You have no idea who she/he knows or what influence she/he has. Most likely, she/he is someone who can "lose your number," or when all the co-workers are sitting around the lunchroom, the person speaks well or badly about you. Keeping in mind everything you've read about talking on the phone, also remember to put a "smile" in your voice when you make a call, have a script if you need it, and be sure your voice sounds grateful. Listen carefully to how the person on the other end of the line sounds. Do they seem rushed or at ease? If you're not too good at listening, and research shows most people aren't, practice **active listening** techniques like paraphrasing what the other person says. Lastly, start the conversation off with the reason you're calling. This can take the form of saying the words, "Hello Ms._____ (if you don't know the name of the person before you called be sure you listen carefully to her name when she picks up) I'm calling because I'd like to find out if my resume was received."

Phone and Story

Your voice is what gives your story life; that's why emails aren't as good for storytelling. If you sound tired, happy, bored, or afraid, most people can sense these things during a phone call. Remember that often there aren't any other distractions when you call; it's only your voice. Drink some water before you call someone. Take a deep breath, and have all your supporting documents ready. Who knows, maybe you'll sound good enough for the director's assistant to put your call right through to the decision-maker!

Phone and Skills

We've touched on several skills but want to highlight three of them. First, plan and organize your phone calls; this is an important skill. Phone calls can't be treated like you're texting someone. Texting is rarely a substantive conversation. Second, thank the person on the phone, and be grateful. Ingratitude is easy to spot, it just doesn't sound right. Finally, wait for the other person to hang up the phone first. Psychologically this communicates deference and respect for the other person.

Using effective phone and email strategies greatly increases your chance of getting the all-important face-to-face interview. We strongly suggest that during your academic years, you take advantage of your college or university's career services department. Go through practice interviews, have your resumes reviewed and critiqued, and record what you sound and look like when you're interviewing. It's easy to imagine that you sound and look fabulous when you present yourself to a group or an individual. However, the story we tell ourselves is often quite different than what other people see and hear.

Interview with a Professional

Mike Mount was a Senior National Security Producer with CNN in Washington, DC, where he covered the Pentagon and intelligence beats starting in September of 2001. Besides day-to-day coverage of the Department of Defense, the Secretary of Defense, State, and intelligence agencies, he has had multiple overseas postings, covering conflicts in Iraq, Afghanistan, Pakistan, and Gaza, as well as other stories around the Middle East.

Why are good communication skills important in the broadcast journalism field?

There is a long-standing joke among journalists that they are terrible communicators when it comes to getting a message across to one another in a newsroom.

As you try to build your story you want to be able to have the best facts available to you. In order to do that, you have to be clear in the questions that you ask whether on the local police beat or in the White House briefing room. Not asking clear concise questions can get you muddy information or allow somebody with information to hide to work around your questions and give her/him the opportunity to mislead.

Additionally, not communicating a story correctly can get you in trouble. Getting your facts wrong because you were unable to clearly communicate your story or because you were not clear on what you were saying in an interview can damage your reputation as a journalist as well as that of the organization you work for.

What specific skills were the most valuable for you?

The most valuable skills I had were to write for TV and the web quickly as well as being a good communicator. All of these are important for day-to-day life in broadcast journalism. If you can't write, you may want to think of another career. Whether it's print or TV, writing is at the core of this job. If you can't tell a story, you can't keep the audience engaged in the story. If you can't do it fast, you're not going to meet your deadlines. If you don't meet your deadlines, you just wasted the time of your crew, the assignment editors, and maybe even some viewers waiting for that story you were covering.

What skills do you find lacking in people new to the field?

Good communication skills are critical. It's a dynamic and vastly different experience for every story, but there are key elements a journalist should know that will help get the video and facts. I have never seen a person new to the field walk out and nail the job. Listen to the experienced members of the crew. See the big picture around you, look for the best way to get your crew positioned; you are a team and the better you work together, the better your story will be.

How has the knowledge you gained in a college or university been useful to you in terms of your career?

The people I learned from the most were the ones who had real newsroom and field experience, but you have to pay attention in a college or university class-room to how journalism is practiced. Theory gives you just as much experience if you are able to tie it to the real aspects of the business and helps you with a broader understanding of the relationship between journalists, the business side of news, and your place as a journalist in the real world.

Writing classes aren't something you should ignore. A writing class is the one journalism skill that can be realistically simulated in the classroom. There is no significant difference between a deadline for a writing assignment in the classroom and one given to you in the newsroom.

What advice would you give to Communication majors?

Understand where journalism sits in this country. Know the difference between real journalism outlets and blogs or other organizations that consider them-selves journalists. Understand what makes a *real* news organization; it has a code of ethics, guidelines on integrity, and, more often than not, a guidebook on professionalism in journalism. A true news organization will monitor its own performance for inaccuracies, errors in judgment, and other lapses and will admit to the mistakes.

Write, write, and write some more. When you are done with that, keep writ-ing. If you don't use it, you lose it. It's like lifting weights or playing an instrument. Get experience with internships, part-time jobs in the business, and read and watch the news daily. Don't pigeonhole yourself into just journalism experience; follow issues that you are interested in, politics, international affairs, business, diplomacy. If you know how the world works, you will be a better journalist for it.

Thinking back on your career choices, what decision are you most proud of?

I credit friends from school who encouraged me to get involved in a wide variety of communications and news-related activities. Not only did I learn more, I was given opportunities to go from school directly into network news.

Little did I know it, but my interest in the military and world affairs put me in the right spot on September 11, 2001. I was given the opportunity to prove myself in covering the military for CNN. That decision allowed me to see the world, cover wars and conflict, and meet leaders and incredible people from all over the world in some of the most difficult circumstances. I was given a front seat to history and am proud to have been part of teams that broke important stories.

It is a profession like no other, but it comes with an important responsibility that cannot be taken lightly.

Conclusion

Applied Communication and Practice should be used as a tool during your academic career. We've provided suggestions, resources, and real-world interviews to help you decide about the right major for you, great job search and internship strategies, and what professional advice. Most importantly, we hope you can see and understand how some of the most popular communication disciplines connect.

Strong email communication and phone technique are just two elements in a successful internship and job-seeking strategy. Developing a good overall strategy is an individual effort and takes time, it's best to start early and begin developing personal relationships with professors, students, and outside contacts. You may not have much on your resume or talent reel now, but if you develop personal relationships, the opportunities will come. Almost everyone wants to work with a person they can trust and who might contribute something to the field. These needs are satisfied best through personal interactions.

The email you write and the phone call you make are just the beginning.

CLASSROOM ACTIVITY

Using your knowledge about phone strategy, complete the following activity in teams of two.

Activity Specificss

This activity is 30-minutes long. You'll be randomly placed in teams of two. Each person will write down three questions she/he can't stand being asked in an interview situation. Each person then gives her/his questions to the other person.

Next, one person pretends to be an interviewer and *using your partner's mobile phone*, records her/his partner answering questions. The two people then switch roles. At end of the activity, review the recording and constructively critique your partner's interview.

Exercise considerations to make this activity work best:

1   Try to imagine and then act like an interviewer. Adopt some of the characteristics you've seen in interviewers.

2   Observe the body language and how the person looks and sounds during the interview.

3   Help the person. She/he may never have observed a recording of her-/himself like this.

DISCUSSION

1 Determine as a class the value of good email communication, and locate examples of good emails. What characteristics define a good email?

2 Research shows that millennials aren't comfortable and even afraid to talk on the phone. What are some practical strategies for dealing with phone anxiety?

KEY TERMS

Active Listening—occurs when the listener employs specific skills like paraphrasing to enhance and improve one-on-one communication.

DLC—an acronym that stands for *downloadable content* for video games and often takes the form of game maps or expanded game play modules.

Doom—a famous late 1990s game from ID software that was written as a major motion picture and was rereleased in 2016 to gain even wider appeal and popularity.

Indeed—a job search database.

LinkedIn—a business oriented social networking site that makes available job boards and professional contacts to its members.

Naming Convention—every company has a specific way email addresses should be written, sometimes the first letter of a name is matched with the last name and then the @ sign is written. It's best to find out how the company does this to ensure your email makes it to the desired person.

Netiquette—a set of protocols and expectations that establish best practices when sending email communications. For example, CAPITALIZING your email is considered the same as shouting by every professional on the planet.

Pushed—a way of setting up your mobile phone or email server to received emails from a particular company or person.

REFERENCES

Bradford, H. 2015. "5 Reasons The Cover Letter Should Just Die Already." The *Huffington Post*. Retrieved on March 23, 2017, from http://www.huffingtonpost.com/2015/03/10/cover-letter-death_n_6819648.html.

Corrigan, P. T., and C. H. McNabb. 2015. "RE: Your Recent Email to Your Professor—Students who use emojis in their emails and write "heeeeelp!" in the subject line don't necessarily know better." *Inside Higher Education*. Retrieved on March 21, 2017 from https://www.insidehighered.com/views/2015/04/16/advice-students-so-they-dont-sound-silly-emails-essay.

DeCarolo, L. n.d. "12 Smart Phone Interviews Success Tips." *Job-Hunt.org*. Retrieved on March 24, 2017, from https://www.job-hunt.org/job_interviews/telephone-interviews.shtml.

Hofschneider, A. 2013. "Bosses Say 'Pick up the Phone,'" *The Wall Street Journal*. Retrieved on March 19, 2017, from https://www.wsj.com/articles/SB10001424127887323407104579036714155366866.

Patton, Stacey. 2015. "Dear Student: My Name Is Not 'Hey.'" ChronicleVitae.com. Retrieved on March 22, 2017, from https://chroniclevitae.com/news/964-dear-student-my-name-is-not-hey.

Ryan, L. 2016. "Cover Letters Are Dead And Other 2016 Recruiting Trends." *Forbes.com*. Retrieved on March 22, 2017, from https://www.forbes.com/sites/lizryan/2016/02/04/cover-letters-are-dead-and-other-2016-recruiting-trends/#590e98b079c1.

Seppanen, S. 2012. *The Millennial Generation Research Review*. U.S. Chamber of Commerce Foundation. Retrieved on March 21, 2017, from https://www.uschamberfoundation.org/reports/millennial-generation-research-review.

Sugar, R. 2015. "Why millennials are scared of talking on the phone—and how to get over it." *Business Insider*. Retrieved on March 23, 2017, from http://www.businessinsider.com/conquer-your-fear-of-the-phone-2015-5.

Ward, T. 2016. "How Poorly Written Emails Cause Disasters And Cost Lives: 5 Questions for Carolyn Boiarsky." *Huffington Post.com*. Retrieved on March 20, 2017, from http://www.huffingtonpost.com/tim-ward/how-poorly-written-emails_b_12374770.html.

CPSIA information can be obtained
at www.ICGtesting.com
Printed in the USA
BVHW011923310820
587711BV00016B/816